ACOUSTIC JURISPRUDENCE

Acoustic Jurisprudence

Listening to the Trial of Simon Bikindi

JAMES E K PARKER

OXFORD
UNIVERSITY PRESS

OXFORD
UNIVERSITY PRESS

Great Clarendon Street, Oxford, OX2 6DP,
United Kingdom

Oxford University Press is a department of the University of Oxford.
It furthers the University's objective of excellence in research, scholarship,
and education by publishing worldwide. Oxford is a registered trade mark of
Oxford University Press in the UK and in certain other countries

First Edition published in 2015

Published in the United States of America by Oxford University Press
198 Madison Avenue, New York, NY 10016, United States of America

British Library Cataloguing in Publication Data
Data available

Library of Congress Control Number: 2015949664

ISBN 978–0–19–873580–9

For Mum and Dad

Acknowledgements

I am struck by my incredible fortune at having arrived in Melbourne in 2009 to find an institution so immediately welcoming and with such a rich sense of intellectual community. As a student, my time there was generously funded by the Melbourne Law School. I am particularly grateful, however, to my PhD supervisors Andrew Kenyon and Shaun McVeigh. Thanks to Andrew for all the encouragement, advice, and support even when there were so many other demands on your time and energy. To Shaun, thanks for being endlessly generous, for the carefulness and quality of insight and for being an exemplary role model. I could not have hoped for a better supervisor and mentor.

Thanks to all my peers and colleagues at the Law School whose friendship, intellectual engagement, and good humour made my time there so enjoyable and rewarding. For the many conversations at reading groups, conferences, seminars, meetings, Seven Seeds, the Last Jar, and the Corkman, thanks especially to Thomas Andrews, Olivia Barr, Peter Chambers, Madelaine Chiam, Julia Dehm, Sara Dehm, Debolina Dutta, Maria Elander, Luis Eslava, Ann Genovese, Jake Goldenfein, Rebecca Goodbourn, Laura Griffin, Coel Kirkby, Wendy Larcombe, Edward Mussawir, Anne Orford, Yoriko Otomo, Sundhya Pahuja, Rose Parfitt, Connal Parsley, Laura Peterson, Peter Rush, Gerry Simpson, Oishik Sircar, Cait Storr, and Marc Trabsky. I must say a particular thank you, however, to Kevin Heller for having put me on to the *Bikindi* case in the first place.

Thanks to the Institute for International Law and the Humanities (IILAH) and the Asia Pacific Centre for Military Law (APCML), both in their official guises and in the personages of Vesna Stefanovski and Cathy Hutton, and also to Mas Generis, Domingo Cordoba, and Madeline Grey in the Office for Research. For their hospitality and interest during my visit in 2011, thanks to the International Criminal Tribunal for Rwanda (ICTR) and especially to Martha Hunt without whose time and generosity so much of this project would not have been possible. Thanks too to everyone involved with the Institute for Global Law and Policy, both in Boston and Doha, for the collegiality, conversation, and support.

To my PhD examiners, Professors Marianne Constable and Linda Mulcahy, a particular thank you for the generosity of engagement and invaluable advice. For commenting so generously on late drafts of my work, thanks to Huw Hallam and especially to Karen Crawley and Desmond Manderson, both of whom inform my thought in so many ways. For their invaluable last minute editorial efforts, thanks to Cate Read, Anna Sowerbutts, Alex Howard, and Mary Quinn. I must also mention Nicholas Croggon, Joel Stern, Danni Zuvela, and my colleagues at Tiny Mix Tapes because they were so important in the development of my thought about sound and music generally.

Portions of this book are based on pieces originally published elsewhere. Parts of Chapter 3 were originally published as 'The Musicology of Justice: Simon

Bikindi and Incitement to Genocide at the International Criminal Tribunal for Rwanda' in M J Grant and Férdia J Stone-Davis (eds), *The Soundtrack of Conflict* (Olms Verlag, 2013). Parts of Chapter 8 originally appeared as 'The Soundscape of Justice', *Griffith Law Review* 20(4) (2011) 962. Astute readers will notice that I have moved away from the language of 'justice' in this book. What I previously referred to as the 'musicology of justice' I have called the 'musicology of judgment' here. And what I called the 'soundscape of justice' before has now become the 'judicial soundscape'. The alterations are unfortunate in a way but quite deliberate, a consequence of the sharpening of my thought on these matters over time.

Finally, to my family, and especially my brothers, I wish my studies had not taken me so far away for so long. I am so grateful to Mum and Dad, for all their love and support and especially for nurturing and encouraging my interest in music. I am grateful too to Sue and Chris for being so warm and welcoming. But my deepest thanks to Alex, for always listening and for your tremendous, ineffable love and kindness.

Contents

PART 3. SPEECH

PART 4. SOUND

Introduction

> There is always something to see, something to hear. In fact, try as we may to make a silence, we cannot … Until I die there will be sounds. And they will continue following my death.[1]
>
> John Cage, *Silence*

> It came from the radio. At first it was possible to ignore. But the sound would not go away. It only got louder and louder. In the early hours of April 7th 1994, the call to kill got so loud it drowned out everything else. It swept across the country like a storm. For 100 bloody days, Rwanda experienced one of the worst atrocities in human history and the international community stood by.[2]
>
> ICTR, *20 Years Challenging Impunity*

Between September 2006 and December 2008, Simon Bikindi stood trial at the International Criminal Tribunal for Rwanda (ICTR) in Arusha, Tanzania. Though the details of the case against him were complex, its essence was simple. In the early 1990s Bikindi was one of Rwanda's most well-known musicians and popular figures—a politician, but also a celebrity, 'probably the most talented artist of his generation',[3] 'Rwanda's Michael Jackson'[4]—and by the end of 1994 his songs had quite literally soundtracked a genocide. On the back of extensive radio airplay, live performances, and the sale and distribution of audio-cassettes, they were sung even as the genocide's perpetrators 'hacked or beat to death hundreds of Tutsis with government issued machetes and homemade nail-studded clubs' as journalist Donald McNeil provocatively wrote for *The New York Times*.[5] 'Members of the population knew [his songs] by heart', testified one witness at trial, 'and when they perpetrated those crimes, they would sing the songs, they would say that they were furious and that they wanted to avenge the deaths of their relatives'.[6] Although six

[1] John Cage, *Silence: Lectures and Writings* (Marion Boyars, 1968) 8.

[2] '20 Years Challenging Impunity' (video commemorating the twentieth anniversary of the Tribunal's establishment), International Criminal Tribunal for Rwanda, accessed 29 January 2015, <http://www.unictr.org/>.

[3] *Prosecutor v Bikindi* (Transcript) ICTR-01-72-T, T Ch III (Various dates) ('*Bikindi* transcript') 13 February 2007, 11.

[4] Donald G McNeil Jr, 'Killer Songs', *The New York Times*, 17 March 2002, <http://www.nytimes.com/2002/03/17/magazine/killer-songs.html?src=pm>.

[5] McNeil (2002).

[6] *Bikindi* transcript, 2 October 2006, 37.

separate charges were brought against Bikindi in total, at root he stood accused of inciting genocide with his songs.

Bikindi's trial was unprecedented. Never before had an international court or tribunal been called upon to determine a musician's culpability for acts of genocide. This book explores how the ICTR went about that difficult task. In doing so, however, it also attempts something else. To some readers this aspect of the book may at first seem odd. In my view that is exactly why it is so necessary. The *Bikindi* case provides an unusually rich opportunity to examine a dimension of legal thought and practice that is scarcely ever remarked upon, but which is no less real or important as a result. Sound, as American composer John Cage never tired of pointing out, is a fact of life.[7] It is also a condition of the administration of justice. And yet, as a community of jurists we have become deaf to law and to the problem of the acoustic. By means of a close examination of the trial of Simon Bikindi, this book argues therefore for a specifically *acoustic* jurisprudence, an orientation towards law and the practice of judgment attuned to questions of sound and listening.

Law is never without the problem of sound, as we will see. But what makes Bikindi's trial particularly compelling from the perspective of an acoustic jurisprudence is the extent to which it dramatizes that problem. No doubt there is something uncomfortably polemical about invoking genocide and the force of international criminal law as a claim to moral or jurisprudential seriousness. But the gravity of the charges levelled against Bikindi really does matter for the purposes of this book. These charges provide a crucial backdrop for everything that follows. They make it clear that if the idea of an acoustic jurisprudence initially seems either marginal or trivial somehow, a matter of merely 'academic' interest, it shouldn't. At least half a million people were killed in the course of the Rwandan genocide.[8] And here was a major international legal institution alleging a *singer* to have been amongst the ninety-three 'most responsible'.[9]

If the stakes could hardly have been higher, the range of issues raised in the *Bikindi* case was also extremely broad. Although Bikindi's songs were undoubtedly at the case's centre, the Tribunal was also forced to grapple with the nature and significance of radio-broadcasting, the difference between an audio-recording and

[7] Cage (1968) 8.

[8] Estimates of how many people died in the genocide vary considerably. The standard number cited in UN reports is 800,000. However Scott Straus has argued that this number may not be accurate. In this respect he is in agreement with Alison Des Forges, author of probably the most comprehensive historical account of the genocide. Triangulating from three different sets of data, she argues that at least 500,000 Tutsi civilians—approximately three-quarters of the total Rwandan Tutsi population at the time—were probably killed during the genocide. 'Report of the Independent Inquiry into the Actions of the United Nations during the 1994 Genocide in Rwanda' (16 December 1999) UN Doc S/1999/1257; Scott Straus, *The Order of Genocide* (Cornell University Press, 2006) 51; Alison Des Forges, *Leave None to Tell the Story: Genocide in Rwanda* (Human Rights Watch, 1999) 15–16.

[9] 'First Annual Report of the International Criminal Tribunal for the Prosecution of Persons Responsible for Genocide and Other Serious Violations of International Humanitarian Law Committed in the Territory of Rwanda' (24 September 1996) UN Doc A/51/399-S/1996/778, annex ('First Annual Report of the ICTR').

a live performance, the relationship between song and speech, speech and text, and between all of these and the scope and limits of criminal responsibility. These and other related issues were absolutely integral at trial, whether or not they were always acknowledged as such. As a result, the *Bikindi* case presents an ideal opportunity to explore a whole series of questions in relation to what this book calls *law's sonic imagination*: the diverse ways in which legal institutions conceive sound for the purposes of judgment.

Then there are the hearings themselves. As one judge pithily observed midway through proceedings, Bikindi's was a 'musical trial'.[10] Audio and audio-visual recordings of his songs were played regularly throughout. Witnesses including Bikindi himself frequently sang, both of their own accord and at the request of the Tribunal. Remarkably, Bikindi even sang his final 'statement'. And all the while, judges, barristers, and witnesses alike spoke into microphones and listened through headphones: to the swearing of oaths, the delivery of testimony, the rigours of cross-examination, the pronouncing of judgment. The trial was operating in three languages simultaneously—Kinyarwanda, French, and English—and every word uttered was being translated by interpreters in acoustically separate booths and then immediately broadcast to listeners' headsets throughout the courtroom. The *judicial soundscape* in the *Bikindi* case, the ICTR's sonic environment, was particularly rich too.

Acoustic Jurisprudence: Listening to the Trial of Simon Bikindi develops two threads simultaneously: one substantive, the other methodological. Substantively, this is the first detailed study of a trial of considerable legal, historical, and musicological importance, both to Rwandans and to the international community in whose name the ICTR asserted jurisdiction. The book explores what happened at Bikindi's trial, how the Tribunal went about the task of adjudication, what it decided, why, and with what consequences. Inevitably, I devote a lot of attention to the judgment delivered by Judge Inés Mónica Weinberg de Roca on 2 December 2008, but the study also draws on a range of archival materials—including trial transcripts and the available audio and audio-visual records—gathered during a visit to the ICTR in January 2011. I do feel beholden to this archive. There are certain facts, certain passages of text, certain moments or episodes at trial that seem to me to demand inclusion here. A case study is always partial, however, and I will not pretend to an objectivity I cannot deliver. There is clearly a sense in which this book's substantive and methodological ambitions are in tension with each other. Methodologically, because I am interested in sound and listening, because I am asking new questions of legal practice and the administration of justice, and because in doing so I draw on scholarship from a range of disciplines other than international criminal law or jurisprudence—including sound studies, musicology, anthropology, and philosophy—certain matters that other scholars may think important to understanding Bikindi's trial have been left to one side. What is deemed important in law, jurisprudence, or a case like Bikindi's, however, is very

[10] *Bikindi* transcript, 4 November 2007, 35.

much a matter of dispute. And there is so much about this case—indeed much of what was fundamental to its determination—that really does warrant the critical attention to questions of sound I am arguing for here and which a more conventional analysis would certainly leave out.

Bikindi was eventually convicted of incitement to genocide. Crucially, however, it was not his songs that ultimately proved determinative. Instead, the Trial Chamber relied on a number of statements he was found to have made over a loudspeaker by the side of the road one day in June 1994, which is to say right in the middle of the genocide. Bikindi had 'used a public address system', the Chamber said, 'to state that the majority population, the Hutu, should rise up to exterminate the minority, the Tutsi'. And then later on that day he had 'used the same system to ask if people had been killing Tutsi, who he referred to as snakes'.[11] As for the songs, they had clearly been intended to encourage hatred. Moreover, they had actually been *used* by presenters on *Radio Télévision Libre des Mille Collines* (RTLM) and on the government station Radio Rwanda to incite genocidal killings. But it had not been established, the Chamber ruled, that this was also Bikindi's intention.[12]

What I want to suggest is that we cannot possibly begin to assess the quality or justice of this decision without attending to at least some of the following questions. First and perhaps most importantly, how exactly did the ICTR think Bikindi's songs worked? What theory or theories of music manifested themselves in the Tribunal's discourse, why and with what consequences for the Trial Chamber's eventual decision (Chapter 3)? Next, and very much relatedly, how were Bikindi's songs managed at trial? How was his music brought *into* the courtroom and put to work as evidence? And how was it heard and apprehended as a result (Chapter 4)? If Bikindi did not have the requisite genocidal intent where his songs were concerned, how exactly were his statements by the side of the road that day in June 1994 understood to be different? And why did the Tribunal seem to care so much that they were made using a 'public address system' (Chapter 5)? Why were witnesses required to give voice to their testimony at trial? And why, for instance, did so many of them do so from behind a curtain (Chapter 6)? How did media and audio-technologies feature in the Tribunal's thinking? In particular, how did it conceive of radio, which was central both to Bikindi's story and to that of the Rwandan genocide in general (Chapter 7)? Finally, what are we to make of the fact that a case like Bikindi's, indeed the entire apparatus of international criminal justice, now depends fundamentally on audio-technology—microphones, headsets, digital audio files—for its operation (Chapter 8)?

These are not the type of questions that conventional legal analysis is well equipped to ask, let alone answer. But they are important. Moreover, their implications for legal thought and practice are potentially extremely broad. Even though

[11] *Prosecutor v Bikindi* (Judgement) ICTR-01-72-T, T Ch III (2 December 2008) ('*Bikindi* judgment') para 422.

[12] *Bikindi* judgment, para 254.

the gravity of the circumstances in the *Bikindi* case was unusual, the juridical problems it raises are hardly rare. In addition to questions of genocide, the case was concerned with the nature and limits of freedom of expression, the role and responsibilities of artists and the media in promoting hate or inciting violence, the relationship in general between music, violence, and criminality. All these issues are being pursued with vigour in both international and domestic jurisdictions across the world.

The trial of three members of the Russian punk band Pussy Riot, for instance, was one of the biggest global media events of 2012. All three were convicted of 'hooliganism motivated by religious hatred' for an impromptu performance of their 'Punk Prayer' at a Moscow Cathedral. Two served twenty-one months in prison and pre-trial confinement before amnesty was eventually granted in December 2013,[13] just in time for the Sochi Winter Olympics, but not before proceedings against the Russian government could be lodged at the European Court of Human Rights.[14] In China, the popular musician Kalsang Yarphel was imprisoned at the end of 2014 for singing songs encouraging Tibetans to learn to speak, read, and write in their native language.[15] Ten other singers have been jailed under similar circumstances in China since 2012.[16] In 2011, the high profile South African musician and former head of the African National Congress Youth League Julius Malema was found to have breached the Equality Act by a Johannesburg court and ordered to cease performances of the so-called 'struggle song' *Dubul'ibhunu* ('Shoot the Boer') under threat of criminal sanctions should he fail to comply.[17] In June 2012, three well-known Kenyan musicians were charged with inciting ethnic violence by means of their songs.[18] And in March 2013, the Rwandan-born Yvonne Basebya was convicted of incitement to genocide by a domestic court in The Hague, partly on the basis that at a number of public rallies in Kigali in 1994 she had led the crowd in renditions of the Hutu-extremist song 'Tubatsembesembe' (We will kill them all).[19]

Many of the questions this book asks of the *Bikindi* case could equally be asked of these and other similar cases in the future; and I hope they will. But I also hope that the book will speak to scholars and practitioners working in contexts where

[13] 'Pussy Riot: Russia Frees Jailed Punk Band Members', *BBC News*, 23 December 2013, <http://www.bbc.com/news/world-europe-25490067>.

[14] *Mariya Vladimirovna Alekhina and Others v Russia*, Application No 38004/12 (European Court of Human Rights, 19 June 2012).

[15] Agence France-Press, 'China Jails Tibetan Singer Over Political Lyrics', *The Guardian*, 1 December 2014, <http://www.theguardian.com/world/2014/dec/01/china-jails-tibetan-singer-kalsang-yarphel-political-lyrics>.

[16] 'China Sentences Two Tibetan Singers to Prison for Song Content', Voice Project, 2 December 2014, <http://voiceproject.org/post_news/tibetan-singer-sentenced-4-year-prison-term-songs/>.

[17] *Afri-Forum v Malema* 2011 (6) SA 240 (EqC).

[18] 'Kenya Musicians Charged with Hate Speech', *BBC News*, 4 July 2012, <http://www.bbc.co.uk/news/world-africa-18712858>.

[19] *The Prosecutor v Yvonne Basebya* (Summary of the Verdict of the District Court of The Hague, Unofficial Translation) LJN BZ4292 (1 March 2013) <http://www.asser.nl/upload/documents/20130328T104222-Unofficial%20english%20translation%20Decision%20Rechtbank%20den%20Haag%2001-03-2013.pdf>.

music is not so central, where questions of sound and listening do not necessarily foreground themselves. Ultimately, I am claiming that all legal thought and practice *necessarily* takes place in and in relation to sound. This means that an acoustic jurisprudence—the kind of orientation towards the practice of law I am arguing for here—is as relevant to run-of-the-mill domestic procedural hearings and the law of copyright, torts, or contract as it is to high profile international trials and the law of genocide. The stakes may be different, but many of the problems are the same.

This book takes the trial of Simon Bikindi as a kind of provocation then. It offers an account of how this trial was conducted by the ICTR, with a particular emphasis on questions of sound and listening. These questions always matter. In a case which, at its heart, was about whether or not a person had incited genocide with their songs, they are fundamental. In this book, I want to show how thoroughly the outcome of the *Bikindi* case was affected by the ICTR's various approaches to sound, to subject these approaches to critique, and in doing so to begin to fashion some ways in which future institutions in future cases might be able to conduct themselves better. My hope is that the book's most important implications will resonate beyond either the particularities of the *Bikindi* case or the field of international criminal law. I want to demonstrate just how deep the law–sound relation goes: just how many dimensions of legal thought and practice the acoustic touches, and just how important it is, therefore, that those of us who spend our time thinking about and practising law begin to account for it. As a community of legal thinkers and practitioners, we must teach ourselves to *listen to law*, to attend properly to questions of sound in the administration of justice, to 'prick up' our juridical ears.[20] That is the basic impulse or imperative an acoustic jurisprudence both invites and responds to: the demand to listen, or to listen better and more responsibly. Whereas hearing is a physiological phenomenon, listening is a psychological act. For the philosopher Jean-Luc Nancy listening always involves 'strain'.[21] It is an activity. It requires effort, care, work. In law especially, this work matters. By means of a close study of the *Bikindi* case, this book begins to open up some avenues as to how.

Structure

The book is divided into four parts. Part 1, *Acoustic Jurisprudence*, sets the scene for the case study that follows. In Chapter 1, I begin by situating the book relative to historical approaches to the law–sound relation. Unfamiliar as some of the themes explored in this chapter may be to contemporary ears, the relationship between

[20] Costas Douzinas, 'The Metaphysics of Jurisdiction' in Shaun McVeigh (ed), *Jurisprudence of Jurisdiction* (Routledge-Cavendish, 2007) 31.

[21] Jean-Luc Nancy, *Listening*, trans Charlotte Mandell (Fordham University Press, 2007) [trans of: *À L'écoute* (first published 2002)] 6.

law, order, justice, and the acoustic was a central concern in both the Classical and Christian traditions right up to the end of the Renaissance. Having briefly accounted for this history, I then move on to situate the book relative to contemporary legal scholarship. Although this scholarship provides me with many of the analytical tools necessary to an acoustic jurisprudence, it has proven strangely persistent in its deafness. So the chapter then turns to the emerging field of Sound Studies, first in order to account for the recent 'turn to sound' across the academy, second, to introduce some of the critical artillery which I go on to adapt to jurisprudential ends, and third to suggest what an acoustic jurisprudence might have to offer back to Sound Studies in return.

Chapter 2 reintroduces the *Bikindi* case in detail. After providing a brief overview of the Rwandan genocide and the establishment of the ICTR by the UN at the end of 1994, the bulk of the chapter is given to outlining the particulars of the charges against Bikindi along with the case's procedural history and reception both in the media and in the legal literature. I then introduce the main archive on which the book relies and offer a more detailed account of the methods brought to bear on it.

Parts 2, 3, and 4 of the book constitute my primary analysis of Bikindi's trial. This analysis proceeds along two axes. On the one hand, I am interested in the ICTR's *sonic imagination*: the way it thought about acoustics for the purposes of coming to judgment, the diverse techniques by which it made the acoustic amenable to legal analysis, the language it used, its assumptions and blind spots.[22] I am interested, for instance, in how matters of acoustics featured at the level of doctrine, evidence, and rhetoric; what kinds of argumentative strategies were pursued; what politics manifested themselves; when familiar metaphysical attitudes or commitments were engaged; and, in each case, with what consequences. On the other hand, I am interested in the ICTR's *own* acoustics, the nature and workings of what I call the *judicial soundscape*: the Tribunal's 'sonic habitus',[23] how sound operated in the courtroom, what juridical work it did, the techniques by means of which it was used, ignored, co-opted, or otherwise perceived. Each of these two lines of inquiry is further divided into three parts, on the topics of *Song* (Part 2), *Speech* (Part 3), and *Sound* (Part 4) respectively. The book unfolds, therefore, in pairs, each of the three topics being investigated according to each axis in turn: AB, AB, AB. As a result, the book is more episodic than linear, such that to some extent at least each chapter stands alone. Readers interested in the moment, say, when Bikindi sang his final statement to an obviously shocked courtroom or in the ICTR's approach to radio can turn to Chapters 4 and 7 respectively without encountering too much trouble. Nevertheless, definite continuities of argument and critique do emerge.

[22] Mary Douglas, *How Institutions Think* (Syracuse University Press, 1986).

[23] The term 'sonic habitus' is developed in Steve Feld and Donald Brenneis, 'Doing Anthropology in Sound', *American Ethnologist* 31(4) (2004) 462, 468.

I am at my most critical of the Tribunal in Chapter 3 where I consider its approach to Bikindi's songs. Put bluntly, even though these songs were the centrepiece of Bikindi's trial, the Tribunal consistently treated them as if their specifically musical qualities—their sonority, their very existence *as* song—were somehow marginal or irrelevant to its task. Obviously, the lyrics of Bikindi's songs were crucial to any determination of his genocidal intent, but to suggest, as the Tribunal consistently did, that they could somehow be divorced from their sound, setting, or performance involves, in my view, a profound misunderstanding of how songs work, what they do, and why they are socially and normatively important. The reasons for this misunderstanding are complex, but it is clear that doctrine played a major role. The relevant international law facilitated a crude binary between 'idea' and 'expression', form and content, medium and message, and—in the Tribunal's analysis—between music and lyric. And even though a better, more nuanced or musicologically responsible approach would not necessarily have led to Bikindi's conviction in respect of his songs, it is also not possible to rule that out. Needless to say, this is a problem: a failure of law and of the Tribunal's responsibility to hold Bikindi properly to account. Nevertheless, it would be a mistake I think to individualize the blame in this respect. To the extent that the ICTR's account of Bikindi's songs was inadequate, this was partly a symptom of the deafness with which I am suggesting so much of contemporary legal thought and practice is afflicted.

Chapter 4 takes this argument a little further. It is not simply that legal institutions often deal poorly with matters involving songs or music. Insofar as music is an overtly aesthetic enterprise, there is a sense in which it poses a threat to law, in its imagined pursuit of justice according to rule and dispassionate reason. It is clear from the archive that the ICTR always did what it could to domesticate any musical performances throughout Bikindi's trial, and moreover that it was generally successful. Recordings of Bikindi's songs were played and witnesses were invited to sing mainly at the Tribunal's explicit invitation, and invariably with a word or two to frame the way in which they should be heard. The kind of listening thereby encouraged was far from neutral. It both depended on and helped sediment the music/lyric, form/content distinction upon which so much of the Tribunal's thought and practice relied and which left so much to be desired. Bikindi's decision to sing his final 'statement' at the end of his appeals hearing stands out as a rare moment of resistance to this logic. The performance is at once compelling and obviously different to all of the other musical performances at trial, including Bikindi's own. Why? The answer, as we will see, has to do with Bikindi's ability to take charge of the listening situation for once. When Bikindi sang his final statement, he was no longer singing *for* the Tribunal, he was singing *to* it; and to a large extent he was singing *past* it as well, to a projected audience in Rwanda. In this and other respects the performance was undoubtedly transgressive. But it was also the exception that proved the rule.

Speech is much more pervasive a concern for law than song is. Nonetheless, the two are intimately related. The voice is their common denominator. Chapter 5 explores how the voice figured in the ICTR's thinking, first at the level of doctrine, then evidence, then rhetoric. It is in relation to doctrine that the links with other chapters are at their clearest. Throughout Bikindi's trial the voice was consistently depicted as language's instrument, the necessary medium in speech, its acoustic form, and material support. In this respect it performed precisely the same function for the Tribunal as music did in song. When it came to attributing responsibility to Bikindi for the three crucial statements made over a public address system that day in 1994, however, the voice also did something else. In its apparent proximity to the ideality of thought, the voice operated as a kind of surrogate for and material embodiment of Bikindi's intentions. It was Bikindi's voice that guaranteed the expressive chain, as it were, between his intent, words, and the ears of his listeners, and in doing so enabled juridical responsibility to attach.

Chapter 7 sees a similar set of moves play out in relation to radio. The ICTR consistently presented this complex technical and social apparatus as little more than a means of extending and intensifying the speaking voice, like a particularly effective loudspeaker. This sort of instrumentalism is consistent with much of the broader discourse on the role of radio in the Rwandan genocide, but it is also partly the result of specifically juridical concerns, most of all the institutional demand that responsibility be individualized. Both here and in Chapter 5, the Tribunal's approach is of course amenable to critique. My suggestion, however, is that in both cases this critique is at its sharpest when related back to the Tribunal's more profound case of deafness when it came to Bikindi's songs.

The ICTR was not uniformly hard of hearing then. Chapters 6 and 8 in particular provide many examples where the Tribunal showed real sensitivity to questions of sound. In Chapter 6, I consider the diverse ways in which the voice was called upon in court throughout Bikindi's trial. The so-called 'solemn declaration' for instance—the ritual practice of oath swearing which nearly all participants in the judicial soundscape are required to undergo as a condition of their participation—is both highly anomalous from an institutional perspective and, in a sense, foundational: an act of community formation by means of the voice: the submission of one's body to the authority of the institution. With the 'principle of publicity', by contrast, the Tribunal is less concerned with the act of vocalization than the voice's audibility, a fact that is particularly obvious in relation to its treatment of 'protected witnesses', who would testify from behind a curtain, hidden from public view. Having opened up the question of relations between the audible and the visible, Chapter 6 then turns to the role played by text in the soundscape, and in particular to the practices of pronouncing judgment, court reporting, and speaking 'for the record'. In each case I observe a highly ambiguous dynamic whereby the voice is at once privileged in relation to the written word and simultaneously made ancillary to it, transformed into a kind of necessary supplement.

Finally, Chapter 8 zooms out a little to consider the soundscape of the Tribunal itself, beginning with Arusha, the city in which the ICTR is located, and working from there in towards the courtroom. I show how soundproofing has become a condition of international juridical practice and how the international courtroom has become increasingly compartmentalized acoustically such that headphones are now virtually a condition of participation. Today, lawyers, judges, and witnesses alike must learn how to navigate a soundscape that is increasingly wired for sound. In the international context, this wiring can be traced to the introduction of 'simultaneous interpretation', which was first conceived and put into practice at Nuremberg. Since then, its effects on the conduct of legal proceedings have been considerable. In particular, the practice of interpretation radically changes the nature of legal eloquence. It gives courtroom orality a peculiar tempo, rhythm, and accent, and requires practitioners to listen increasingly with their eyes as well as their ears. The chapter ends with a consideration of broadcasting and archival practices at the ICTR and the ways in which these are increasingly expanding the spatial and temporal limits of the courtroom such that the nature of the judicial soundscape is in the process of being significantly redefined.

In general then I am far more critical of the Tribunal's thought about sound than I am its use of it. This is partly just my attempt at an honest response to the archive, but it is also symptomatic, I think, of a much more deeply rooted phenomenon in relation to the practice of law and the administration of justice. Although there are continuities between each limb and each pair of the book, the Tribunal was nothing if not pragmatic in relation to the problems with which it was presented. It was perfectly happy to adopt one approach to music or the voice at the level of rhetoric or doctrine, only to contradict itself at the level of evidence. It was more than capable of being sensitive to sound in one context, only to marginalize it in another. That is why this book does not propose a theory or critique of law, but a jurisprudence. There is no one story here, no single narrative capable of capturing or appraising the Tribunal's thought and practice as a whole, either in relation to the acoustic or otherwise. Nor should this come as a surprise. Legal institutions are necessarily complex entities, comprising people, places, objects, ideas, technologies, conventions, rules, senses, sensibilities, sounds, and listeners. The practice of judgment is unavoidably messy. It always takes place *in media res*, in the midst of things, constantly afflicted by competing or even overtly contradictory demands.

For Cicero, prudence was a 'means for negotiating a dynamic field of expectations and demands, one replete with tensions that could be managed only through skilful attention to the requirements of public performance'.[24] It is the cultivation of precisely this sort of attention to the performance of legal judgment that this book is aiming for. An acoustic jurisprudence must attend to the particular techniques and methods by means of which legal institutions come to judgment in relation to sound. Its task is to test such techniques both against the institution's own internal account and other, external approaches to sound. The necessary attitude in this respect is neither purely internal nor external, neither that of apologist nor critic. An acoustic jurisprudence requires both a knowledge of law and a certain distance from it: a matter of walking alongside, an interested listener. The purpose

[24] Robert Hariman, *Prudence: Classical Virtue, Postmodern Practice* (Pennsylvania State University Press, 2003) viii.

is not to escape law then, but to hold institutions like the ICTR to account, to treat them as if—having asserted jurisdiction in cases like Bikindi's—they were capable of enacting a kind of justice. Life and law are necessarily lived in sound. The wager of an acoustic jurisprudence is that those of us who work and think with law have a responsibility to pay attention.

PART 1
ACOUSTIC JURISPRUDENCE

1

Listening to Law

Harmony

When exactly jurisprudence stopped listening is hard to say. For the Greeks, 'generalized order was distinguished by a musical character, and was typically thought of as harmonic'.[1] This was because of music's intimate relation with number. The mathematics of the octave and tonal harmony were an overt and scientifically measurable manifestation of the divine law in the material world.[2] For Pythagoras there was a fundamental identity between so-called '*musica instrumentalis*, the ordinary music made by plucking the lyre, blowing the pipe, and so forth; *musica humana*, the continuous but unheard music made by each human organism, especially the harmonious resonance between the soul and the body; and *musica mundana*, the music made by the cosmos itself, which would come to be known as the music of the spheres'.[3] Strange as it may seem today, this Pythagorean theme of a musical universe, binding man to natural law through harmony, proved extraordinarily persistent, even 'ubiquitous' throughout the intellectual history of the West.[4] We see it in Cicero's *De Republica*, in Augustine's *De Musica*, Boethius' *De Institutione Musica*, Bodin's *Colloquium Heptaplomeres*, and in Kepler's *De Harmonice Mundi*, to say nothing of Handel's setting to music of the John Dryden poem *Ode for St Cecilia's Day* or, more recently, the German-American composer Paul Hindemith's

[1] Edward A Lippman, *Musical Thought in Ancient Greece* (Columbia University Press, 1964) 1.

[2] This relation between harmony and number was most famously related by the neoplatonist Iamblichus in his *On the Pythagorean Life*. Under the heading 'How Pythagoras discovered the principles of harmony, and handed that science on to his followers', he writes: 'He was once engaged in intense thought about whether he could find some precise scientific instrument to assist the sense of hearing, as compass and rule and the measurement of angles assist the sight and scales and weights and measures assist touch. Providentially, he walked past a smithy, and heard the hammers beating out the iron on the anvil. They gave out a melody of sounds, harmonious except for one pair. He recognised in them the consonance of octave, fifth and fourth, and saw that what lay between the fourth and fifth was in itself discordant, but was essential to fill out the greater of the intervals. Rejoicing in the thought that the gods were helping on his project, he ran into the smithy, and discovered by detailed experiments that the difference of sound was in relation to the weight of the hammers, not the force used by those hammering, the shape of the hammer heads, or any change in the iron as it was beaten out.' Iamblichus, *On the Pythagorean Life*, trans Gillian Clark (Liverpool University Press, 1989) 51.

[3] Jamie James, *The Music of the Spheres: Music, Science, and the Natural Order of the Universe* (Abacus, 1993) 31.

[4] Jonathan Willis, *Church Music and Protestantism in Post-Reformation England* (Ashgate, 2010).

Die Harmonie der Welt.[5] It is no exaggeration to say that the Western tradition understood there to be a fundamental relation between the acoustic, cosmic order and divine law for the best part of the last 2,000 years.[6]

This was largely a result of the immense influence wielded by Plato. Plato was an ardent Pythagorean. It is in his work that Greek conceptions of harmony achieve their 'maximum diffusion and influence'.[7] In the *Republic*, for instance, 'the conceptions of harmony are so numerous and so important that they actually govern the argument and provide a basis for its organization and aesthetic form'.[8]

> The musician creates harmony in the pitch and duration of tone and in gesture; man creates harmony in the conduct of his life; the statesman creates harmony in society; the Demiurge creates harmony in the cosmos; the philosopher creates the harmony of dialectic and the music of discourse.[9]

This is why for Plato the regulation of music was so crucial from a juridical perspective too. A direct line was drawn between harmonious music and a just and orderly society. 'Let us speak of the laws about music', he writes.

> As time went on the poets themselves introduced the reign of vulgar and lawless innovation. They were men of genius, but they had no perception of what is just and lawful in music; raging like Bacchanals and possessed with inordinate delight … And by composing such licentious works, and adding to them words as licentious, they have inspired the multitude with lawlessness and boldness.[10]

Plato was careful to elaborate not only the kinds of music which ought to be proscribed, but also its importance from a pedagogical, ethical, and normative perspective, and particularly as far as the instruction of young statesmen was concerned. Education based on music and gymnastics—one for the soul, the other for the body—was mandatory. The acceptable modes (distant relatives of the

[5] Plato, *The Republic*, trans Richard W Sterling and William C Scott (Norton, 1985); Plato, *Timaeus*, trans Donald J Zeyl (Hackett, 2000); Marcus Tullius Cicero, 'The Dream of Scipio' in *The Republic and the Laws*, trans Niall Rudd (Oxford University Press, 2009); William F Jackson Knight, *St Augustine's De Musica: A Synopsis* (Hyperion Press, 1979); Anicius Manlius Severinus Boethius, *Fundamentals of Music*, ed Claude V Palisca, trans Calvin M Bower (Yale University Press, 1989) [trans of: *De institutione musica* (first published fifteenth century)]; John Bodin, *Colloquium of the Seven about Secrets of the Sublime*, trans Marion Leathers and Daniels Kuntz (Princeton University Press, 1975) [trans of: *Colloquium heptaplomeres de rerum sublimium arcanis abditis* (first published sixteenth century)]; Johannes Kepler, *The Harmony of the World*, trans E J Aiton, Alistair M Duncan, and Judith V Field (American Philosophical Society, 1997) [trans of: *De harmonices mundi* (first published 1619)]; George Frideric Handel, *Ode for St Cecilia's Day* (1739); Paul Hindemith, *Die Harmonie der Welt* (1957).

[6] For further detail see Joscelyn Godwin (ed), *The Harmony of the Spheres: A Sourcebook of the Pythagorean Tradition in Music* (Inner Traditions International, 1993); Joscelyn Godwin, *Harmonies of Heaven and Earth: The Spiritual Dimension of Music from Antiquity to the Avant-Garde* (Thames and Hudson, 1987); Lippman (1964); Paolo Gozza, 'Number to Sound' in Philippe Vendrix (ed), *Music and the Renaissance: Renaissance, Reformation and Counter-Reformation* (Ashgate, 2011) 209; James (1993).

[7] Lippman (1964) 44. [8] Lippman (1964) 41. [9] Lippman (1964) 41.

[10] Plato, *The Laws*, trans Benjamin Jowett (Prometheus, 2000) para 700.

'keys' familiar to Western harmonic theory since the sixteenth century)[11] were the Dorian and the Phrygian, used in songs of peace and war respectively, because they were thought to imitate temperance and courage, the two primary virtues of the ruler. But above all for Plato, instrumental compositions were to be prohibited on account of their tendency to inflame the passions, to address only the senses, without recourse to either language or reason. Music should have lyrics or not be heard at all.[12]

Music in the Church

There is a real continuity between Platonic thought in this respect and the great debates concerning the regulation of sacred music in Europe during the Renaissance. The question of music's place both in and in relation to the Christian church was much more than 'merely' aesthetic. It was theological, political, and juridical too, a recurring theme of doctrinal debate both within and between denominations and jurisdictions. Was music *inventio* or *creatura*, a work of man or God? Did it elevate the soul or appeal to base and bodily desires? Did it enhance the power of the divine message or obscure it? These questions went to the heart of the church's project of instituting God's law on earth and in the faithful. The Dutch humanist and Catholic theologian Erasmus, for instance, lamented that 'modern church music is so constructed that the congregation cannot hear one distinct word … yet according to priests and monks it constitutes the whole of religion'.[13] 'We have introduced an artificial and theatrical music into the church', he complained. 'Horns, trumpets, pipes, vie and sound along constantly with the voices … The people run into the churches as if they were theatres, for the sake of the sensuous charm of the ear.'[14] Sure enough, the point would soon be subjected to papal scrutiny. The following is a famous passage from the proceedings of the Council of Trent, convened by Pope Pius IV between 1545 and 1563 in response to the Protestant Reformation fast sweeping the continent.

Since the sacred mysteries should be celebrated with utmost reverence, with both deepest feeling toward God alone, and with external worship that is truly suitable and becoming, so that others may be filled with devotion and called to religion: … Everything should indeed be regulated so that the Masses, whether they be celebrated with the plain voice or in song,

[11] On the rise of this particular version of harmonic theory along with some of its competitors, see Michael Chanan, *Musica Practica: The Social Practice of Western Music from Gregorian Chant to Postmodernism* (Verso, 1994) 59–69; Max Weber, *The Rational and Social Foundations of Music*, ed and trans Don Martindale, Johannes Riedel, and Gertrude Neuwirth (Southern Illinois University Press, 1977) [trans of: *Die rationalen und soziologischen Grundlagen der Musik* (first published 1921)].

[12] See Lippman (1964) ch 2 ('Theories of Musical Ethics'). For the Plato, see Books II and III of the *Republic* and generally the *Timaeus*.

[13] Cited in Peter le Huray, *Music and the Reformation in England* (Cambridge University Press, 1978) 11. For more on Erasmus' views on music, see Hyun-Ah Kim, 'Erasmus on Sacred Music', *Reformation and Renaissance Review* 8(3) (2006) 277.

[14] Cited in Gustave Reese, *Music in the Renaissance* (rev edn, W W Norton, 1959) 448.

with everything clearly and quickly executed, may reach the ears of the hearers and quietly penetrate their hearts. In those Masses where measured music and organ are customary, nothing profane should be intermingled, but only hymns and divine praises. If something from the divine service is sung with the organ while the service proceeds, let it first be recited in a simple, clear voice, lest the reading of the sacred words be imperceptible …[15]

Whereas for Erasmus and the councillors, music was to be figured primarily in terms of clarity, moderation, and restraint, for Swiss reformer Huldreich Zwingli music should simply be banned in its entirety from the public liturgy.[16] 'The power of music over men's minds was too great to allow it to compete with the word of God.'[17] For Martin Luther, by contrast, music stood alone in its proximity to the divine.[18] As such, his agenda was overtly inclusive. Worship was above all a corporate activity, 'an expression of the unity of the community of faith, a reality that was uniquely demonstrated in the song of the whole congregation'.[19] With Luther, sacred music was no longer a matter of passive receptivity, but of active participation. 'Music and the joy it gave men, Luther claimed, were the foretaste of the much greater joys of Heaven; for music was near theology: it made the words come alive'.[20] Moreover, because music was fundamentally a divine good, Luther was also prepared to allow secular melodies into the fold. Why, after all, should the devil have all the best tunes?[21]

In all these examples, music is being imagined at once as a technique of divine law and its object. But just as it was for Plato, music was crucial to Renaissance pedagogy too. Along with arithmetic, geometry, and astronomy, it was one of the four pillars of the so-called *quadrivium*, which, together with the *trivium* of rhetoric, grammar, and logic, comprised the *ars liberales*, or liberal arts.[22] And

[15] Although this passage is often cited in support of the claim that the Council of Trent legislated a virtual ban on polyphony (a formal device whereby there are two or more independent melodic voices), recent primary research has shown that it was never actually accepted in this form. Nevertheless, bans on polyphony *did* occur under the Catholic Church both prior to Trent and subsequently. Moreover, within a few years of the Council's sitting, the issue of textual intelligibility and the use of polyphony 'had come to be taken for granted as part of its reforms', Craig Monson explains. When the composer Giovanni Animuccia composed five masses in 1677, he did so, in his own words, 'according to the requirements of the Council', such that 'the music may disturb the hearing of the text as little as possible'. For statements of the old orthodoxy on Trent, see Reese (1959) 449; Karl G Fellerer, 'Church Music and the Council of Trent', *The Musical Quarterly* 39(4) (1953) 576; Donald J Grout and Claude V Palisca, *A History of Western Music* (5th edn, Sony Music, 1996). For the more recent revision of this orthodoxy, see Craig A Monson, 'The Council of Trent Revisited', *Journal of the American Musicological Society* 55(1) (2002) 1.

[16] Willis (2010) 47.

[17] Helmut Georg Koenigsberger, 'Music and Religion in Early Modern European History' in Philippe Vendrix (ed), *Music and the Renaissance: Renaissance, Reformation and Counter-Reformation* (Ashgate, 2011) 275, 287.

[18] On Luther's musical education and its influence on his mature theological views on the subject, see Robin A Leaver, *Luther's Liturgical Music: Principles and Implications* (Wm B Eerdmans, 2007) 21–65.

[19] Leaver (2007) 199. [20] Koenigsberger (2011) 286. [21] Koenigsberger (2011) 286.

[22] Bernard F Dick, 'The Artes Liberales as the Basis of the Humanities', *International Journal of the Humanities* 5(8) (2007) 111, 113.

as Quintilian points out in his *Institutio Oratoria*, a key text for the Renaissance humanists, the relationship between music and rhetoric was particularly close.[23]

Rhetoric as Oratory

The rhetorical tradition, Roland Barthes explains, was 'born 2500 years ago in legal cases concerning property'.[24] 'Long before the emergence of any distinct class of lawyers or legal professionals in the west, the manuals of the rhetoricians of classical Greece had set down and taught the art of effective presentation and argumentation in the law courts of Sicily and Greece.'[25] Here is a discipline that has been especially self-conscious in its attention to law's acoustic qualities: those dimensions of legal practice which come closest to song. As rhetoric, juridical discourse was originally figured overtly in terms of oration: the prudential combination of reason *and* resonance, word *and* voice, proof *and* performance.

In Aristotle, even as rhetoric was concerned with 'all the possible means of persuasion in any subject', from the deliberative (political) to the forensic (legal) to the epideictic (panegyric and ceremonial), the whole third book of his famous *Rhetoric* was already devoted specifically to oratorical technique.[26] In Cicero this is expanded into a general theory of *elocutio*, or style. *Elocutio*, Barthes writes, 'defines a field which bears on *all* language: it includes both our grammar … and what is called *diction*, the theatre of the voice. The best translation of *elocutio* is perhaps not *elocution* (too limited) but *enunciation* or even *locution* (locutory activity)'.[27] It comprises a whole artillery of verbal and oratorical techniques located specifically at the level of voice or delivery. Think of alliteration, for instance, the close repetition of consonants for effect, *apophony* (the repetition of timbres), or *anacoluthon* (a syntactical and rhythmic break mid-sentence). Or again, irony, reticence, and suspension, all of which can be conveyed acoustically at the level of vocal tone and rhythm.[28] For Cicero, 'rhetoric was indissociable from rhetorical practice, it was the study of power or res publica as dialogue rather than monologue, it was the politics of the phonocentric rather than the scriptural'.[29] Likewise for Quintilian, 'eloquence cannot be perfect without the knowledge of music'.[30]

[23] On music, see Marcus Fabius Quintilian, *The Institutio Oratoria of Quintilian*, trans H E Butler (Harvard University Press, 1922) 1. X. 9–33. For discussion of the music/rhetoric relation in Quintilian and elsewhere, see Brian Vickers, 'Figures of Rhetoric/Figures of Music?' *Rhetorica* 2(1) (1984) 1.

[24] Roland Barthes, *The Semiotic Challenge*, trans Richard Howard (University of California Press, 1994) [trans of: *L'aventure sémiologique* (first published 1985)] 14.

[25] Peter Goodrich, *Reading the Law: A Critical Introduction to Legal Method and Techniques* (Blackwell, 1986) 169.

[26] Aristotle, *The Art of Rhetoric*, trans H C Lawson-Tancred (Penguin, 1991) Book I.2, para 1355*b*; Book III.

[27] Barthes (1994) 83. [28] Barthes (1994) 87–8.

[29] Peter Goodrich, 'Rhetoric as Jurisprudence: An Introduction to the Politics of Legal Language', *Oxford Journal of Legal Studies* 4(1) (1984) 88, 98.

[30] Quintilian (1922) 1. X. 11. Translation taken from Kim (2006) 281.

Originally rhetoric referred to the arts of juridical and political speech, which in turn were necessarily bound to their oral or phonic form.

This was still very much the case during the formative years of the common law. The very first lay legal experts 'were orators or indeed rhetoricians, the oral pleaders (narrators) before the royal courts'. As a result, 'eloquence and indeed elegance of speech were clearly regarded as virtues by the medieval legal profession'.[31] To some extent they still are today. For many law students the promise of a career in oral advocacy and the apparent glamour of the theatrical and sonorous courtroom will be the very things that attracted them to legal studies in the first place: straight from the screens of *The Good Wife*, *Silk*, *Rake*, and *Kavanagh QC* to the classrooms of the common law. Nevertheless, the recent history of rhetoric is more or less the history of its decline, which is to say its confinement to and then marginalization as the study of 'mere' style: of voice, delivery, and performance over substance.[32] Today the term is most commonly used, particularly outside of the academy, as a term of abuse. Rhetoric is empty, florid, overblown, bombastic: the *misuse* of language through oratory. Even though law schools do still encourage mooting, and practising lawyers do learn the (dark) arts of eloquence (*elocutio*) both in their practical training courses and informally on the job, today the official line of legal education and of the vast majority of jurisprudence is that law lives most of all in reason, not resonance, and in the quality of arguments based on precedent, principle, and policy rather than orality. As the place of legal education in the common law has moved increasingly away from the courtroom, hearings, and the Inns of Court to the domain of the textbook and the University, jurisprudence has become less and less interested in law as a specifically acoustic practice.

It is not the purpose of this book to explain exactly how or when jurisprudence's concern for the acoustic began to wane. My intention thus far has simply been to show that many of the themes we will go on to explore here are far less strange or novel than they might initially seem. Not only do they have a lineage, for a long time they were virtually central to juridical thought in the West. Besides, an adequate genealogy of jurisprudence's recent deafness would be far beyond the scope of this project. In particular, it would need to grapple with the problem of modernity itself. The changing fortunes of acoustics in relation to legal thought must be understood as both symptomatic and productive of a much larger complex of forces—at once historical, sociological, metaphysical, theological, technical, scientific, mediological, and much more besides—all of which are commonly glossed as the Enlightenment. It is the Enlightenment we are told that is responsible both for the modern privileging of sight and script and their apparent alignment with the project of rationality itself. It is the Enlightenment according to a now 'pervasive narrative' that accounts for modernity's move away from a culture of hearing towards the now allegedly predominant culture of seeing.[33] But we will come back to that.

[31] Goodrich (1986) 170. [32] Goodrich, 'Rhetoric as Jurisprudence' (1984) 104.

[33] Jonathan Sterne, *The Audible Past: Cultural Origins of Sound Reproduction* (Duke University Press, 2003) 3.

Law's Institutional Life and the Practice of Judgment

This book is less in conversation with jurisprudential history than it is with certain strands of contemporary legal scholarship. Much of this scholarship has been 'critical' in the sense that it invokes a heritage in the critical tradition of continental European philosophy since Kant.[34] Some of it understands itself as part of a broader field of 'sociolegal' inquiry which emerged in the wake of legal realism and which tends to conceive law as an object for empirical and ethnographic study.[35] In either case, this work is important for an acoustic jurisprudence because in one way or another it has concerned itself with the formal and material dimensions of law's institutional life and the practice of judgment: 'not so much with the subjects and objects of legal knowledge', as Edward Mussawir explains, 'but with law's medium, technology, performance and articulation'.[36] This scholarship proceeds, in other words, from the starting point that law is less a 'system of rules' than it is a complex adjudicatory practice that engages the full range and diversity of human and non-human action.[37] As a result, it has devoted considerable attention to law's unfolding by means of language, architecture, image, and screen, as well as to its tools, technologies, and procedures. It is in this scholarship, therefore, that one would expect to find a sustained engagement with sound. No such engagement exists, however. Where the acoustic is concerned, contemporary jurisprudence has been virtually silent. That is the point of departure for this book. On the one hand, it is addressed to this gap in the literature. It is both an *argument for* the importance of attending to the acoustic in law and an *exemplification* of what it might mean to do so. On the other hand, it builds on the many insights of the literature into which it inserts itself.

[34] For one discussion of this critical tradition, see Costas Douzinas and Adam Gearey, *Critical Jurisprudence: The Political Philosophy of Justice* (Hart, 2005), especially at 36–8. See also, for instance, Shaunnagh Dorsett and Shaun McVeigh, *Jurisdiction* (Routledge, 2012) 20–5.

[35] For a survey of sociolegal perspectives on law, see Mathieu Deflem, *Sociology of Law: Visions of a Scholarly Tradition* (Cambridge University Press, 2008); William M Evan (ed), *The Sociology of Law: A Social-Structural Perspective* (Free Press, 1980); Roger Cotterrell, *The Sociology of Law: An Introduction* (2nd edn, Butterworths, 1992). For more critical engagements with law's relations with sociology, see Marianne Constable, 'Genealogy and Jurisprudence: Nietzsche, Nihilism and the Social Scientification of Law', *Law and Social Inquiry* 19(3) (1994) 551; Austin Sarat (ed), *Law and Society Reconsidered* (Emerald, 2008); Donald R Kelley, *The Human Measure: Social Thought in the Western Legal Tradition* (Harvard University Press, 1990).

[36] Edward Mussawir, *Jurisdiction in Deleuze: The Expression and Representation of Law* (Routledge, 2011) 10.

[37] For orthodox accounts of law as a system of rules, see H L A Hart, *The Concept of Law* (2nd edn, Oxford University Press, 1994); Hans Kelsen, *Pure Theory of Law*, trans Max Knight (University of California Press, 1967) [trans of: *Reine rechtslehre* (first published 1934)]; Joseph Raz, *The Concept of a Legal System: An Introduction to the Theory of Legal System* (Clarendon, 1980). For a reading of this orthodoxy in relation to the heretical realist and critical legal traditions which framed themselves in contrast to it, see Desmond Manderson, 'Apocryphal Jurisprudence', *Australian Journal of Legal Philosophy* 26 (2001) 27.

Language

Language is law's lifeblood. For Peter Goodrich, if law is anything at all it is a linguistic tradition, produced, shaped, and maintained by a variety of historically specific institutional forms.[38] A 'system of communication and of non-communication',[39] law consists in a 'community of speakers' and a range of techniques for the attribution of authority to those speakers, as well as to the texts they author.[40] Law thus is a 'register of language', a distinct 'literary genre', 'a very specialised form of literary pursuit', involving the mastery of a whole range of highly regularized but nevertheless obstinately unscientific hermeneutic procedures and discursive techniques.[41] But if it is a literary pursuit, the practice of law is nevertheless a highly peculiar one because of its intimate and necessary connection with violence and the responsibilities that attach to it as a result.

Judith Butler, Marianne Constable, and others influenced by the work of philosopher J L Austin have emphasized the performative aspects of juridical speech, this sense in which to say something in law is always also to do something: to contract, to swear, to pass judgment, or to deliver a verdict.[42] In doing so, certain affects are inevitably produced (relief, sorrow) and certain institutional arrangements engaged (payment, imprisonment). Legal interpretation, Robert Cover explains, always 'takes place in a field of pain and death'.[43] It is never simply an exercise in semantics. It is always somehow *more* than that, because 'a legal world is built only to the extent that there are commitments that place bodies on the line'.[44] Lawyers, judges, and jurists all are necessarily caught up in a discursive chain that will ultimately claim to both justify and authorize violence. To engage in the project of *legal* interpretation is to assume a very particular form of responsibility.

Moreover, because it takes place in and through language, the practice of law is amenable to the full repertoire of linguistic, literary, and rhetorical analysis. Legal texts are so much more than vessels for the articulation of doctrine. They are metaphysical and political.[45] They have a grammar and are subject to the laws

[38] Peter Goodrich, *Languages of Law: From Logics of Memory to Nomadic Masks* (Weidenfeld and Nicolson, 1990) 2.

[39] Peter Goodrich, 'Law and Language: An Historical and Critical Introduction', *Journal of Law and Society* 11(2) (1984) 173, 174.

[40] Goodrich (1986) 91.

[41] Goodrich, 'Law and Language' (1984) 174; Goodrich (1986) 91.

[42] Marianne Constable, *Our Word is Our Bond: How Legal Speech Acts* (Stanford University Press, 2014); Marianne Constable, *Just Silences: The Limits and Possibilities of Modern Law* (Princeton University Press, 2005), especially ch 7; Judith Butler, *Excitable Speech: A Politics of the Performative* (Routledge, 1997); John L Austin, *How to Do Things with Words* (Harvard University Press, 1962).

[43] Robert Cover, 'Violence and the Word', *The Yale Law Journal* 95(8) (1986) 1601, 1601.

[44] Cover (1986) 1605.

[45] For critical accounts of law's metaphysics, see Costas Douzinas and Ronnie Warrington with Shaun McVeigh, *Postmodern Jurisprudence: The Law of Text in the Texts of Law* (Routledge, 1991); Douzinas and Gearey (2005); Gary Peller, 'The Metaphysics of American Law', *California Law Review* 73(4) (1985) 1151. For diverse engagements with the politics of legal texts, see Mark Kelman, *A Guide to Critical Legal Studies* (Harvard University Press, 1987); Peter Gabel and Duncan Kennedy, 'Roll Over Beethoven', *Stanford Law Review* 36(1) (1984) 1; Roberto Unger, *The Critical Legal Studies Movement* (Harvard University Press, 1986); Peter Fitzpatrick and Alan Hunt (eds), *Critical Legal Studies* (Blackwell, 1987); Catherine MacKinnon, *Towards a Feminist Theory of the State* (Harvard

of genre.[46] They can be read with an eye for structure, narrative, metaphor, and characterization, for their assumptions and strategic silences, for their use of implication and insinuation at least as much as for the quality of their syllogisms.[47] They can be read for their poetry, or indeed for their apparent lack thereof.[48]

To think of law in terms of language, then, is to open up an inquiry into its form. The work of Jacques Derrida has been extremely important to jurisprudence in this respect, and in particular the techniques and practices he variously referred to as 'grammatology' and 'deconstruction'.[49] Here is Goodrich transposing Derrida on philosophy directly into a juridical key. The jurisprudential task, accordingly, is to study:

> the [legal] text in its formal structure, its rhetorical organisation, the specificity and diversity of its textual types, its models of exposition and production—beyond what were once

University Press, 1989); Nicola Lacey, *Unspeakable Subjects: Feminist Essays in Legal and Social Theory* (Hart, 1998); Joanne Conaghan, 'Reassessing the Feminist Theoretical Project in Law', *Journal of Law and Society* 27(3) (2000) 351; Kimberlé Crenshaw, Neil Gotanda, Gary Peller, and Kendall Thomas (eds), *Critical Race Theory: The Key Writings that Formed the Movement* (New Press, 1995); Irene Watson, 'Indigenous Peoples' Law-Ways: Survival against the Colonial State', *Australian Feminist Law Journal* 8 (1997) 39; Leslie J Moran, *The Homosexual(ity) of Law* (Routledge, 1996); Shaunnagh Dorsett and Shaun McVeigh, 'Just So: The Law Which Governs Australia Is Australian Law', *Law and Critique* 13(3) (2002) 289; Valerie Kerruish, *Jurisprudence as Ideology* (Routledge, 1992).

[46] On the juridical power of grammar, see Marianne Constable (2005) 46–8; Alain Supiot, *Homo Juridicus: On the Anthropological Function of Law*, trans Saskia Brown (Verso, 2007) [trans of: *Homo juridicus: Essai sur la fonction anthropologique du droit* (first published 2005)]; Margaret Davies, *Asking the Law Question* (3rd edn, Thomson, 2008) 349–53. On the laws of genre, see Jacques Derrida, 'The Law of Genre', trans Avital Ronnel, *Critical Inquiry* 7(1) (1980) 55; Margaret Davies, 'Pathfinding: The Way of the Law', *Oxford Literary Review* 14(1) (1992) 107; Pierre Schlag, 'The Aesthetics of American Law', *Harvard Law Review* 115(4) (2002) 1047.

[47] For general examples, see James Boyd White, 'Law as Rhetoric, Rhetoric as Law: The Arts of Cultural and Communal Life', *The University of Chicago Law Review* 52(3) (1985) 684; James Boyd White, *Justice as Translation: An Essay in Cultural and Legal Criticism* (University of Chicago Press, 1990); James Boyd White, *The Legal Imagination* (University of Chicago Press, 1973); Jack M Balkin, 'A Night in the Topics: The Reason of Legal Rhetoric and the Rhetoric of Legal Reason' in Peter Brooks and Paul Gewirtz (eds), *Law's Stories: Narrative and Rhetoric in the Law* (Yale University Press, 1996) 211; Constable (2005) ch 1 ('The Rhetoric of Modern Law'); Robin West, 'Jurisprudence as Narrative: An Aesthetic Analysis of Modern Legal Theory', *New York University Law Review* 60(2) (1985) 145; Bernard S Jackson, *Semiotics and Legal Theory* (Routledge & Kegan Paul, 1985); Roberta Kevelson, *The Law as a System of Signs* (Plenum Press, 1988); Goodrich (1990) 173–208 ('Modalities of Legal Annunciation').

[48] James Boyd White, *Heracles' Bow: Essays on the Rhetoric and Poetics of the Law* (University of Wisconsin Press, 1985).

[49] Jacques Derrida, *Of Grammatology*, trans Gayatri Chakravorty Spivak (Johns Hopkins University Press, 1998) [trans of: *De la grammatologie* (first published 1967)]; Jacques Derrida, *Margins of Philosophy*, trans Alan Bass (University of Chicago Press, 1982) [trans of: *Marges de la philosophie* (first published 1972)]; Jacques Derrida, *Dissemination*, trans Barbara Johnson (The Athlone Press, 1981) [trans of: *La dissémination* (first published 1972)]; Jacques Derrida, *Speech and Phenomena and Other Essays on Husserl's Theory of Signs*, trans David B Allison (Northwestern University Press, 1973) [trans of: *La voix et le phénomène* (first published 1967)]. For an overview of Derrida's reception by the legal academy, see Pierre Schlag, 'A Brief Survey of Deconstruction', *Cardozo Law Review* 27(2) (2005) 741. For some key texts in that reception, see Drucilla Cornell, Michel Rosenfeld, and David Gray Carlson (eds), *Deconstruction and the Possibility of Justice* (Routledge, 1992); Clare Dalton, 'An Essay in the Deconstruction of Contract Doctrine', *The Yale Law Journal* 94(5) (1985) 997; Jack M Balkin, 'Deconstructive Practice and Legal Theory', *The Yale Law Journal* 96(4) (1987) 743; Goodrich (1990).

called genres—and, further, the space of its stagings (*mises en scenes*) and its syntax, which is not just the articulation of its signifieds and its references to being or to truth but also the disposition of its procedures and everything invested in them. In short, to consider [law] as 'a particular literary genre', which draws upon the reserves of a linguistic system, organising, forcing, or diverting a set of tropological possibilities that are older than [law] itself.[50]

Thus, Costas Douzinas, Ronnie Warrington, and Shaun McVeigh wonder what the laws of the text might be in the texts of law.[51] Not just judgments, but legislation, court transcripts, textbooks, in fact all of the various scriptural paraphernalia that the practice of law depends upon for its efficacy are amenable to this sort of analysis.[52] Desmond Manderson reads a series of influential US judgments on the death penalty less for the quality of the decisions or for their doctrinal import than for the ways in which they aim to convince, the kinds of appeal they make to the reader, the imagery and metaphors they use, their tone and style.[53] In doing so he shows how law's mythic rationality spectacularly fails to govern the work of judgment even in cases where 'judges claim to be able, by an exercise of reason, to determine who will live and who will die'.[54] Pierre Schlag points out that legal scholarship itself is complicit here too.[55] Traditional legal discourse, he writes, 'routinely conceives and (almost invariably) treats the grammar and elements of its own discourse—the words, the sentences—as if they were weightless inconsequential forms allowing the transmission of any important "*substantive*" rational meaning'.[56] As a genre, traditional legal discourse actively works to produce a reader capable of imagining themselves as a neutral arbiter of facts and master of a coherent body of rules. Such is the judicial archetype, Ronald Dworkin's mythic Hercules.[57]

[50] Goodrich (1990) 114, glossing Derrida (1982) 293.

[51] Douzinas and Warrington with McVeigh (1991).

[52] For examples of transcriptual analysis, see Alison Young, 'The Waste Land of the Law, the Wordless Song of the Rape Victim', *Melbourne University Law Review* 22(2) (1998) 442; Austin Sarat, 'Rhetoric and Remembrance: Trials, Transcription, and the Politics of Critical Reading', *Legal Studies Forum* 23(4) (1999) 355; Emma Cunliffe, '(This is Not a) Story: Using Court Records to Explore Judicial Narratives in *R v Kathleen Folbigg*', *Australian Feminist Law Journal* 27 (2007) 71; Robert Barsky, *Constructing a Productive Other: Discourse Theory and the Convention Refugee Hearing* (John Benjamins, 1990); Susan Berk-Seligson, *The Bilingual Courtroom: Court Interpreters in the Judicial Process* (University of Chicago Press, 1990); John M Conley, William M O'Barr, and E Allan Lind, 'The Power of Language: Presentational Style in the Courtroom', *Duke Law Journal* 1978(6) (1979) 1375. For an account of the 'textbook tradition' in law, see David Sugarman, 'Legal Theory, the Common Law Mind and the Making of the Textbook Tradition' in William Twining (ed), *Legal Theory and the Common Law* (Blackwell, 1986) 26.

[53] Desmond Manderson, *Songs without Music: Aesthetic Dimensions of Law and Justice* (University of California Press, 2000) 128.

[54] Manderson (2000) 95.

[55] Pierre Schlag, '"Le Hors de Texte, C'est Moi": The Politics of Form and the Domestication of Deconstruction', *Cardozo Law Review* 11(4) (1990) 1631; Pierre Schlag, 'Normativity and the Politics of Form', *University of Pennsylvania Law Review* 139(4) (1991) 801; Pierre Schlag, 'Normative and Nowhere to Go', *Stanford Law Review* 43(1) (1990) 167.

[56] Pierre Schlag, 'Le Hors de Texte, C'est Moi', 1634; Gerald B Wetlaufer, 'Rhetoric and Its Denial in Legal Discourse', *Virginia Law Review* 76(8) (1990) 1545; Elizabeth Mertz, *The Language of Law School: Learning to 'Think Like a Lawyer'* (Oxford University Press, 2007).

[57] Ronald Dworkin, *Law's Empire* (Harvard University Press, 1986).

Architecture, image, screen

In spite of their many differences, all the scholars working in this tradition remind us that legal practice 'can never escape the intricacies and imprecisions, as well as the promise and power, of language itself'.[58] But legal institutions do not function on words alone. As Goodrich argues, the question of language should 'be taken to include all the other systems of signs—of architecture, dress, geography, ceremony, aura and technology—that accompany legal tradition'.[59] Think of the courtroom itself: its size and space, the isolation of the dock and 'looming height of the judges' bench',[60] the formality and hierarchies of courtroom speech and costume. All these factors and more combine to instil alienation and disempowerment, to exclude certain illegitimate forms of speech or behaviour and to validate the authority of the sovereign.[61] And purposely so. For Linda Mulcahy, the very legitimacy of the trial derives from the setting in which it takes place. Public buildings can both 'inspire and degrade those within them, calm or oppress'.

> The spatial configurations of the courthouse and courtroom can confer prestige or dignity on those who use them or serve to undermine their credibility. Legal architecture can associate law with tradition and conservatism or can equally well symbolise a commitment to change and innovation. Courthouses can act as memorials to the past as well as reflecting aspirations for the future.[62]

What exactly is being memorialized though? What kind of juridical life or legal imaginary? And how do courtrooms operate in the present from a semiotic perspective? Contrast 'the protean decor, the intricate plasterwork, the beveled mirror, or the gilt-framed full-length portraits' that have been prevalent since the seventeenth century, and the Supreme Court of the State of Israel, for example, with its marble floors, sharp geometry, and extensive use of glass.[63] What do these differences tell us about each institution as a whole? Piyel Haldar argues for an understanding of architecture as a form of non-verbal, 'ornamental' rhetoric which became gradually more important in law as the profession sought to make legal language increasingly formal in the pursuit of an ever elusive reason.[64]

58 Austin Sarat and Thomas R Kearns (eds), *The Rhetoric of Law* (University of Michigan Press, 1994) 2.

59 Goodrich (1990) 4.

60 Manderson (2000) 42.

61 See Goodrich (1990) ch 4 ('Modalities of Legal Annunciation'). There is a growing sociolegal literature on this topic which examines the workings of such dynamics in particular cases, courts, and jurisdictions. For a concise summary, see Cotterrell (1992) 222–5. For specific examples, see John Maxwell Atkinson and Paul Drew, *Order in Court: The Organisation of Verbal Interaction in Judicial Settings* (Macmillan, 1979); John M Conley and William M O'Barr, *Rules versus Relationships: The Ethnography of Legal Discourse* (University of Chicago Press, 1990); Lief Dahlberg, 'Emotional Tropes in the Courtroom: On Representation of Affect and Emotion in Legal Court Proceedings', *Law and Humanities* 3(2) (2009) 175.

62 Linda Mulcahy, *Legal Architecture: Justice, Due Process and the Place of Law* (Routledge, 2011) 1.

63 Piyel Haldar, 'The Function of the Ornament in Quintilian, Alberti, and Court Architecture' in Costas Douzinas and Lynda Nead (eds), *Law and the Image: The Authority of Art and the Aesthetics of Law* (University of Chicago Press, 1999) 130.

64 Haldar, 'The Function of the Ornament in Quintilian, Alberti, and Court Architecture' (1999) 135. See also Piyel Haldar, 'In and Out of Court: On Topographies of Law and the Architecture of

Moreover, the visual life of law extends far beyond its own self-representation and configuration through architecture. Think of the way in which maps, for instance, operate as a technology of jurisdiction.[65] Or, indeed, how they and other images have been deployed in the courtroom. Maps have played a central role in property cases for centuries. Paintings and drawings have been used to describe crime scenes and to depict wounds in criminal cases. Plans, models, and diagrams have been indispensable in patents litigation. Portraits have settled questions of identity.[66] Because these images were all manmade, however, they were not originally understood as having intrinsic evidentiary value of their own. In evidentiary terms, they were 'illustrative' rather than 'independent': helpful for the purposes of elaborating a point in oral testimony, but no more than that. It is only with the advent of photography, therefore, that things begin to change in this respect. Jennifer Mnookin has written on the ever-shifting usage, doctrine, procedure, and perceived legitimacy of photographic evidence since its emergence in the mid-nineteenth century.[67] From the early days in which photography was perceived as primarily a human construction, 'manipulable, fallible, and potentially untrustworthy',[68] it was increasingly seen in the early part of the twentieth century (and by virtue of forces both internal and external to law) to perform an independent documentary function, to operate as 'demonstrative evidence', or simply as proof.[69]

A century later the same problems are being played out again in relation to digital images and film. In response to the onset of what philosopher Régis Debray calls the age of the 'videosphere', the era of the electronic, digital, and moving image, the virtual, the synthetic, and the simulated, a new visually oriented jurisprudence is quickly beginning to emerge. Its rhetoric is increasingly urgent.[70] We live in a 'visual culture', Richard Sherwin explains, and 'in a visual culture law, too, operates visually'.[71] So it is not just architecture, ornamentation, gowns, wigs, paintings, and photographs that matter these days, but also films, television, computers, and the internet.[72] Witnesses

Court Buildings (a Study of the Supreme Court of the State of Israel)', *International Journal for the Semiotics of Law* 7(2) (1994) 185. For discussion of the kinds of paintings hung in courtrooms throughout history, see Desmond Manderson, *Kangaroo Courts and the Rule of Law: The Legacy of Modernism* (Routledge, 2012) 39–40. On legal architecture see also Paul Raffield, 'Bodies of Law: The Divine Architect, Common Law and the Ancient Constitution', *International Journal for the Semiotics of Law* 13(3) (2000) 333; David Evans, 'Theatre of Deferral: The Image of the Law and the Architecture of the Inns of Court', *Law and Critique* 10(1) (1999) 1.

65 Dorsett and McVeigh (2012) 63–6.

66 Tal Golan, 'Visual Images in the Courtroom: A Historical Perspective', *Parallax* 14(4) (2008) 77. On the use of models in patent law, see also Alain Pottage, 'Law Machines: Scale Models, Forensic Materiality and the Making of Modern Patent Law', *Social Studies of Science* 41(5) (2011) 621.

67 Jennifer L Mnookin, 'The Image of Truth: Photographic Evidence and the Power of Analogy', *Yale Journal of Law & the Humanities* 10(1) (1998) 1.

68 Mnookin (1998) 47.

69 Mnookin (1998) 68.

70 Régis Debray, 'The Three Ages of Looking', trans Eric Rauth, *Critical Inquiry* 21(3) (1995) 529.

71 Richard Sherwin, *Visualizing Law in the Age of the Digital Baroque: Arabesques and Entanglements* (Routledge, 2011) 2.

72 See eg, Leslie J Moran, Emma Sandon, Elena Loizidou, and Ian Christie (eds), *Law's Moving Image* (Cavendish, 2004); Richard Sherwin, *When Law Goes Pop: The Vanishing Line between Law and Popular Culture* (University of Chicago Press, 2000); Richard Sherwin and Ann Wagner (eds), *Law, Culture and Visual Studies* (Springer, 2013); Richard Sherwin (ed), *Popular Culture and Law* (Ashgate, 2006);

appear by 'live link' from locations external to the courthouse.[73] Evidence, summation and victim impact testimony proceed by video. And in each case they are subject to their own laws, logics, and techniques of persuasion.[74] 'Law and literature was never enough', Goodrich writes, 'a missed opportunity, too narrow'.[75] 'The law of print, the law of black and white spaces, has collapsed. It is time to move on and consider seriously the spectacular character of the legal enterprise and the mediated character of the transmission of law.'[76]

Materiality

There is one final branch of contemporary jurisprudence I want to consider before returning to the matter of acoustics. Here the focus is less on legal practice's formal qualities than on its materiality, less on its rhetorical regimes or strategies of persuasion than on its tools, technologies, and technical procedures. This is the difference between language and a filing system, or between a courtroom's semiotics and its hardwiring with video cameras and computer monitors. Take the first example. Files, as Cornelia Vismann points out, are not simply read. They are *processed*, 'just like stones and other such matter'.[77] Files are objects and media technologies, and as such they don't just convey or store, they always also contour. They subject law and legal actors to their own systematicity and logic.

Throughout legal history, innovations in filing have had enormous consequences for legal practice, lubricating certain kinds of juridical activity and marginalizing others. Indeed, Vismann calls the invention of the 'vertical file' towards the

Sherwin (2011) 2; Austin Sarat, Lawrence Douglas, and Martha Merrill Umphrey (eds), *Law on the Screen* (Stanford University Press, 2005); Steve Greenfield, Guy Osborn, and Peter Robson (eds), *Film and the Law: The Cinema of Justice* (2nd edn, Hart, 2010); Desmond Manderson, 'Trust Us Justice: *24*, Popular Culture and the Law' in Austin Sarat (ed), *Imagining Legality: Where Law Meets Popular Culture* (University of Alabama Press, 2011); Cornelia Vismann, 'Image and Law: A Troubled Relationship' *Parallax* 14(4) (2008) 1; Cornelia Vismann, 'Flashback and Eyewitness', *Parallax* 14(4) (2008) 90; Edward Mussawir, 'The Cinematics of Jurisprudence: Scenes of Law's Moving Image', *Law and Literature* 17(1) (2005) 131; Peter Goodrich, 'The Visial Line: On the Prehistory of Law and Film', *Parallax* 14(4) (2008) 55.

[73] Mulcahy (2011) ch 8, 162–81 ('The Dematerialisation of the Courthouse').

[74] Jessica Silbey, 'Judges as Film Critics: New Approaches to Filmic Evidence', *University of Michigan Journal of Law Reform* 37(2) (2004) 493; Jessica Silbey, 'Cross-Examining Film', *University of Maryland Law Journal of Race, Religion, Gender and Class* 8 (2008) 101; Natalie Taylor and Jacqueline Joudo, 'The Impact of Pre-Recorded Video and Closed Circuit Television Testimony by Adult Sexual Assault Complainants on Jury Decision-Making: An Experimental Study' (Research and Public Policy Series No 68, Australian Institute of Criminology, 2005); Richard Sherwin, Neal Feigenson, and Christina Spiesel, 'What Is Visual Knowledge, and What Is It Good For?' *Visual Anthropology* 20(2–3) (2007) 143; Regina Austin, 'Documentation, Documentary, and the Law: What Should Be Made of Victim Impact Videos?' *Cardozo Law Review* 31(4) (2010) 979.

[75] Peter Goodrich, 'Screening Law', *Law and Literature* 21(1) (2009) 1, 3.

[76] Peter Goodrich, 'Europe in America: Grammatology, Legal Studies, and the Politics of Transmission', *Columbia Law Review* 101(8) (2001) 2033, 2035.

[77] Cornelia Vismann, *Files: Law and Media Technology*, trans Geoffrey Winthrop-Young (Stanford University Press, 2008) [trans of: *Akten: Medientechnik und Recht* (first published 2000)] ix. For my own reading of the effects of processing in relation to legal files, see James Parker, 'Spirited Away: Asylum Law and the Institutional Violence of Legal Discourse', *Law Text Culture* 11 (2007) 231.

end of the nineteenth century (an early predecessor to the modern 'leaver-arch') a reform 'as consequential to modern bureaucracy as was the plow and stirrup to the Middle Ages'.[78] In short, files are precisely what make law modern. They are its bureaucratic marrow, one of its foremost material conditions, even as they have gone largely unnoticed in legal scholarship. From the perspective of the law, 'files are annoying instruments, incessantly breeding beasts that must be caged and tamed. They are therefore hardly suited to becoming an object of reflection. When subjected to legal criteria, files are nothing. They are a noninstitution, a nondocument, nonlaw, nonproperty, legally nonbinding'.[79] And therein lies their great power and efficacy.

This is an approach that grants law's 'tools' an unusually large degree of autonomy. In this respect, the influence of Bruno Latour has been very pronounced, and particularly since the publication of his own consideration of legal practice *The Making of Law: An Ethnography of the Conseil D'État* in 2002.[80] One of Latour's major innovations from a jurisprudential perspective has been his refusal to privilege human activity over non-human. It is not that objects *have* agency exactly, but that as part of a network of knowledge production, or the long unfolding of a trial, it would be a mistake to discount their effects simply for not having been 'intended' in the conventional humanist sense. Law on this account is imagined as a 'network of people and of things'.[81] As Alain Pottage explains:

> what really matters is not the simple materiality of these things—their mass, density, or spatial definition—but rather 'materiality' as the kind of agency that is afforded by, elicited from, or ascribed to them. Indeed, material agency is not an innate quality of these artefacts. Bruno Latour's notion of hybrid actants makes it clear that agency is not inherently either human or non-human; it is an emergent effect of the composition of humans and non-humans, or of their reciprocal engagement or co-variation as moments in the unfolding of an actor-network.[82]

Even language can be thought of in this way: in terms of its material effects as opposed or in addition to either its aesthetic qualities or ideational content. Annalise Riles invites us to think of legal documents as 'objects with uses distinct

[78] Vismann, *Files: Law and Media Technology* (2008) 131.

[79] Vismann, *Files: Law and Media Technology* (2008) 12.

[80] The English translation followed in 2010. Bruno Latour, *The Making of Law: An Ethnography of the Conseil D'État*, trans Marina Brilman and Alain Pottage (Polity, 2010) [trans of: *La fabrique du droit* (first published 2002)]. For other examples of Latour's work see Bruno Latour and Steve Woolgar, *Laboratory Life: The Social Construction of Scientific Facts* (Princeton University Press, 1986); Bruno Latour, *Pandora's Hope: Essays on the Reality of Science Studies* (Harvard University Press, 1999); Bruno Latour, *We Have Never Been Modern*, trans Cathy Porter (Harvard University Press, 1993) [trans of: *Nous n'avons jamais été modernes: Essai d'anthropologie symétrique* (first published 1991)]; Bruno Latour, 'Where Are the Missing Masses? The Sociology of a Few Mundane Artifacts' in Wiebe E Bijker and John Law (eds), *Shaping Technology/Building Society: Studies in Sociotechnical Change* (MIT Press, 1992).

[81] Ron Levi and Mariana Valverde, 'Studying Law by Association: Bruno Latour Goes to the Conseil d'État', *Law and Social Inquiry* 33(3) (2008) 805, 806.

[82] Alain Pottage, 'The Materiality of What?' *Journal of Law and Society* 39(1) (2012) 167, 168.

from their qualities as "texts"'.[83] She examines the way in which UN documents are produced by a complex and highly peculiar process of negotiation at special conferences. One particular technique that interests Riles is the use of 'bracketing' when there is no agreement on a particular phrase. In such cases, she argues, the brackets can be thought of as actors in their own right: 'actants' in Latour's terminology: a 'little technology for governing people, words, and laws'.[84] 'Bracketed text gathers together every possible alternative formulation into a messy and very lengthy document of its own', and the task then becomes to 'whittle away at the brackets, consolidating these two options, dismissing that one, until they achieve the "cleanest" version possible'.[85] The bracket, in other words, is what allows the whole process to stumble along. It gives it shape, purpose, and structure. And it is crucial, therefore, to any understanding of how this sort of important juridical document is made: a little technology with major juridical consequences.[86]

Deaf to Law

What joins each of these diverse strands of scholarship is a common interest in law's conduct, practice, or expression: the methods, devices, and techniques by means of which legal institutions come to judgment. But where is the acoustic through all of this? It is as if contemporary approaches to law suffer a kind of deafness.

On the rare occasions they do feature in legal scholarship, matters of acoustics are invariably framed narrowly and uncritically as problems of mere rule or *doxa*. Scholars working on the law of freedom of expression, copyright, or noise pollution almost never bring a theoretically sophisticated account of sound to the table.[87] Laws are made *about* sound, but the way in which sound is conceived

[83] Annelise Riles, 'Infinity within the Brackets', *American Ethnologist* 25(3) (1998) 378, 378. See also Dorothy E Smith, *Texts, Facts, and Femininity: Exploring the Relations of Ruling* (Routledge, 1990).

[84] Levi and Valverde (2008) 812.

[85] Annelise Riles, 'Models and Documents: Artefacts of International Legal Knowledge', *International and Comparative Law Quarterly* 48(4) (1999) 805, 813. For a longer treatment see Annelise Riles, *The Network Inside Out* (University of Michigan Press, 2000).

[86] For other representative examples of this approach, see Annelise Riles (ed), *Documents: Artifacts of Modern Knowledge* (University of Michigan Press, 2006); Dorothy E Smith (ed), *Institutional Ethnography as Practice* (Rowman & Littlefield, 2006); Eve Darian-Smith (ed), *Ethnography and Law* (Ashgate, 2007); Mariana Valverde, 'Authorizing the Production of Urban Moral Order: Appellate Courts and their Knowledge Games', *Law and Society Review* 39(2) (2005) 419; Bettyruth Walter, *The Jury Summation as Speech Genre: An Ethnographic Study of What It Means to Those Who Use It* (John Benjamins, 1988); Patricia Tuitt, 'Legal Practice and Modes of Dying: Bruno Latour, Technology and the Critical Legal Instance', *Law and Critique* 16(1) (2005) 113; Howard T Senzel, 'Looseleafing the Flow: An Anecdotal History of One Technology for Updating', *The American Journal of Legal History* 44(2) (2000) 115; Thomas Scheffer, 'Materialities of Legal Proceedings', *International Journal for the Semiotics of Law* 17(4) (2004) 365.

[87] There have been several exceptions to this general rule in the field of copyright law. See Joanne Demers, *Steal This Music: How Intellectual Property Law Affects Musical Creativity* (University of Georgia Press, 2006); Simon Frith and Lee Marshal, *Music and Copyright* (2nd edn, Routledge, 2004); Dennis Kurzon, '*Peters Edition v Batt*: The Intertextuality of Silence', *International Journal for the Semiotics of Law* 20(4) (2007) 285; Anthony Seeger, 'Ethnomusicology and Music Law', *Ethnomusicology* 36(3)

for such purposes is barely reflected on. And for all its considerable attentions to language, contemporary jurisprudence has been far less interested in either voice or orality, except insofar as they relate to questions of metaphysics. It cares about architectural but not acoustic space. It worries about the image and film but never the soundtrack. It is concerned with screens but not microphones, files but not audio-formats.

Take Bently and Flynn's *Law and the Senses: Sensational Jurisprudence*, published in 1996 and generally an excellent collection.[88] Here is a place if ever there was one in which you might expect to find some consideration of law's acoustic life. And indeed you do. But it is symptomatic that Haldar's piece *Acoustic Justice*, a brief but dense consideration of the hearsay rule, voice, and oral testimony, takes up just thirteen pages of the entire collection whereas at least five entire chapters are given to vision and to the examination of imagery at the level of the text.[89]

The special edition of the *Cardozo Law Review* from 1996 dedicated to music and legal theory is similarly disappointing from an acoustic perspective.[90] Again, it is a valuable and genuinely interdisciplinary collection. Again, it would have been the perfect opportunity to address the question of acoustics. Instead, music is considered in virtually every way *except* in terms of its sonority. Both Arthur Jacobson and Carol Weisbrod examine the use of music as a metaphor in legal writing.[91] For Timothy Hall, echoing a similar argument made by Jerome Frank in 1947,[92] music resembles law only in the limited sense that both are collaborative forms of textual interpretation.[93] Even in Jack Balkin and Sanford Levinson's piece, in which law and music are both conceived as species of 'performing art', a discussion of the specifically acoustic nature of the performance is conspicuous in its absence.[94] Adam Gearey considers the songs of Bob Dylan not for their musical qualities, but for their lyrics and the perspective they offer on contemporary legal

(1992) 345; Andrew Weintraub and Bell Yung (eds), *Music and Cultural Rights* (University of Illinois Press, 2009).

[88] Lionel Bently and Leo Flynn (eds), *Law and the Senses: Sensational Jurisprudence* (Pluto, 1996).

[89] Piyel Haldar, 'Acoustic Justice' in Lionel Bently and Leo Flynn (eds), *Law and the Senses: Sensational Jurisprudence* (Pluto, 1996).

[90] See Desmond Manderson and David Caudill, 'Modes of Law: Music and Legal Theory—An Interdisciplinary Workshop Introduction', *Cardozo Law Review* 20(5–6) (1999) 1325.

[91] Arthur J Jacobson, 'Origins of the Game Theory of Law and the Limits of Harmony in Plato's Law', *Cardozo Law Review* 20(5–6) (1999) 1335; Carol Weisbrod, 'Fusion Folk: A Comment on Law and Music', *Cardozo Law Review* 20(5–6) (1999) 1439.

[92] Jerome Frank, 'Words and Music: Some Remarks on Statutory Interpretation', *Columbia Law Review* 47(8) (1947) 1259. See also Jerome Frank, 'Say It with Music', *Harvard Law Review* 61(6) (1948) 921.

[93] Timothy S Hall, 'The Score as Contract: Private Law and the Historically Informed Performance Movement', *Cardozo Law Review* 20(5–6) (1999) 1589.

[94] Jack Balkin and Sanford Levinson, 'Interpreting Law and Music: Performance Notes on "The Banjo Serenader" and "The Lying Crowd of Jews"', *Cardozo Law Review* 20(5–6) (1999) 1513, 1518, 1519. A similar argument has been taken up by Sarah Ramshaw in relation to improvisation as interpretation. See Sara Ramshaw, 'Deconstructin(g) Jazz Improvisation: Derrida and the Law of the Singular Event', *Critical Studies in Improvisation* 2(1) (2006) 1 <http://www.criticalimprov.com/article/view/81/188>. See also Thomas Irvine, 'Musical Performance, Natural Law and Interpretation' in Oren Ben-Dor (ed), *Law and Art: Justice, Ethics and Aesthetics* (Routledge, 2011).

and ethical questions,[95] a direction that has been pursued again more recently by Aaron Lorenz.[96] For both, song is a species of literature. It speaks to and about law, but its most important aspect from a legal perspective is the language it uses, not how it sounds.[97]

Of all the contributions, it is Manderson's piece that offers the most radical relationship between the two fields. Music is adopted both as an 'explanatory tool' and as a form of law in its own right.[98] 'Both art and music serve a normative, and thus a legal function', he writes, 'establishing the conditions of life of which the law is but a particular expression ... Music is both a description and a source of law'.[99] But this is not a claim Manderson ever elaborates in detail.[100] Even though his first major jurisprudential work *Songs without Music* explicitly adopts music as its central *leitmotif*, it is only ever as 'a metaphor, a point of historical comparison, a frame of reference, a case study, and a ... structural device'.[101] As far as the book's engagement with acoustics *as such* is concerned, the clue is in the title.[102]

Only a handful of scholars have approached the kind of analysis I am arguing for here. Sara Ramshaw's *Justice as Improvisation* is partly concerned with how jazz—and in particular the bebop made famous by Charlie Parker, Dizzy Gillespie, and others—was imagined and regulated by New York City's cabaret laws in its supposed 'wildness' and even 'lawlessness'.[103] And to this extent Ramshaw's analysis chimes well with some of my own here in Chapter 3. Nevertheless, Ramshaw is mostly interested in musical improvisation 'as a model for social change with a view to shaping political, cultural, and ethical dialogue and action'.[104] Law and justice are 'fundamentally improvisational', she claims, which is not, however, to say acoustic.[105] In 2012, musicologist Lily Hirsch published a study of music's various relations to

[95] Adam Gearey, 'Outlaw Blues: Law in the Songs of Bob Dylan', *Cardozo Law Review* 20(5–6) (1999) 1401.

[96] Aaron R S Lorenz, *Lyrics and the Law: The Constitution of Law in Music* (Vandeplas, 2007).

[97] The same is generally true of Goodrich's consideration of Rossini's *Semiranis*, though it is worth noting that before embarking on his reading of the opera's engagement with legal questions, Goodrich offers an excellent précis of the law's historical investment in musical and sonorous form: from the Greek nihilistic orator Hegesias through the roaming bards of Renaissance England to the theories of 'harmonical justice' posited by the likes of George Puttenham, William Lambarde, and Jean Bodin at the turn of the seventeenth century. Peter Goodrich, 'Operatic Hermeneutics: Harmony, Euphantasy, and Law in Rossini's *Semiramis*', *Cardozo Law Review* 20(5–6) (1999) 1649.

[98] Desmond Manderson, '*Et Lex Perpetua*: Dying Declarations & Mozart's Requiem', *Cardozo Law Review* 20(5–6) (1999) 1621, 1625.

[99] Manderson (1999) 1628–30.

[100] Elsewhere he has occasionally come close. In one recent piece he is similarly suggestive when he briefly considers Jimi Hendrix's infamous improvisation on *The Star Spangled Banner* at Woodstock. See Desmond Manderson, 'Governor Arthur's Proclamation: Images of the Rule of Law' in Oren Ben-Dor (ed), *Law and Art: Justice, Ethics and Aesthetics* (Routledge, 2011) 300.

[101] Manderson (2000) 49.

[102] For more recent takes on the relations between law and music by Manderson, see Desmond Manderson, 'Towards Law and Music', *Law and Critique* 25(3) (2014) 311; Desmond Manderson, 'Making a Point and Making a Noise: A Punk Prayer', *Law, Culture and the Humanities* (June 2013), doi: 10.1177/1743872113490664, 1.

[103] Sara Ramshaw, *Justice as Improvisation: The Law of the Extempore* (Routledge, 2013).

[104] Ramshaw (2013) 2. [105] Ramshaw (2013) 93.

the American criminal justice system.[106] Here, finally, is a work which takes both the legal system's *conceptualization* of music and its *use* of it seriously. Together, Hirsch's considerations of music in the law of obscenity and incitement, on the one hand, and music's use as a form of evidence, on the other, provide a neat counterpoint to Part 2 of this book.[107] Her concerns are similar, but her methods and conclusions importantly different. In particular, this book is far more sensitive to *how* and *why* legal institutions produce the sorts of outcomes that Hirsch is more interested in identifying and subjecting to musicological critique.

Of all law's acoustic dimensions, it is the voice that has fared best when it comes to recent scholarly attentions. In this respect, Helen Fraser's work on 'forensic transcription' and Lawrence Abu Hamdan's on 'forensic listening' both share aspects of the sensitivity to questions of sound I am arguing for here.[108] But invariably, the terms of this engagement have been both critical and metaphysical, concerned more with a diagnosis and critique of law's phonocentrism than the workings of particular voices or particular vocal practices. Both Goodrich and Haldar have touched on law's more oratorical aspects in their work on rhetoric. Both bring acoustics into the equation only in order to subordinate it to the visual. For Goodrich, acoustics is a 'relatively obvious issue' as far as legal architecture is concerned. 'The strategic organising principle of the courtroom is a didactic one', he writes. 'It is that of the visibility of justice rather than of its audibility'.[109] Or again, and apparently without irony, 'any attempt to depict the nature of a legal hearing does well to begin by examining [its] visibility, the physical structure and architecture of a peculiar auditory space'.[110] For Haldar, oral evidence 'seems to be locked into a visual mode of estimating and examining testimony',[111] such that 'what matters is the visibility of the speaker, that the court can see that this evidence is no illusion simply because its source (the voice) is never visually there'.[112] Maybe so. But in their insistence on the primacy of the visible over the audible, both Goodrich and Haldar overstate their case. The fact that visibility is important in law does not necessarily make audibility any less so.[113] That one's ability to see a witness as they testify matters is

[106] Lily E Hirsch, *Music in American Crime Prevention and Punishment* (University of Michigan Press, 2012).

[107] Hirsch (2012) chs 3, 4.

[108] Helen Fraser, Bruce Stevenson, and Tony Marks, 'Interpretation of a Crisis Call: The Persistence of Primed Perception of Speech', *The International Journal of Speech Language and the Law* 18(2) (2011) 261–92; Lawrence Abu Hamdan, 'Aural Contract: Forensic Listening and the Reorganisation of the Speaking-Subject', *Cesura//Acceso: Journal for Music, Politics and Poetics* 1 (2014) 200–24.

[109] Goodrich (1990) 188, 191. [110] Goodrich (1990) 188. [111] Haldar (1996) 124.

[112] Piyel Haldar, 'The Evidencer's Eye: Representations of Truth in the Laws of Evidence', *Law and Critique* 2(2) (1991) 171, 183. See also Piyel Haldar, 'The Return of the Evidencer's Eye: Rhetoric and the Visual Technologies of Proof', *Griffith Law Review* 8(1) (1999) 86.

[113] The same mistake is made by Bernard Hibbitts who in his brief consideration of the 'sound of law' across an extraordinarily broad range of cultures and periods of history, seems almost surprised when he writes that 'even in the midst of a writing culture, Anglo-American law has retained a significant measure of actual and metaphorical aurality'. For Hibbitts, the acoustic is very much associated with *other* legal regimes and *other* times. Bernard J Hibbitts, '"Coming to Our Senses": Communication and Legal Expression in Performance Cultures', *Emory Law Journal* 41(4) (1992) 873, 895.

not yet to explain how it is that we listen when we do see, or how we speak when we are also visible. The hierarchy is both unnecessary and misleading. To insist that we live in a 'visual culture' as Sherwin does is to miss the fact that even if we do, it is always also an aural one.

Neither modernity, nor the Enlightenment, nor the invention of the printing press, nor the arrival of the 'videosphere' has made the world any quieter. What they have done, however, is affect the kinds of sounds we hear and the ways in which we hear them. Ours is the age of the microphone, after all, at least as much as the screen. It is jurisprudence that turns out to have privileged sight at least as much as law itself. Alan Burdick explains it like this. 'The golden age of the ear never ended', he says. 'It continues occluded by the visual hegemony.'[114] For Jonathan Sterne, 'there has always been a heady audacity to the claim that vision is the social chart of modernity'. 'Even if sight is in some ways the privileged sense in European philosophical discourse since the Enlightenment, it is fallacious to think that sight alone or in its supposed difference from hearing explains modernity.'[115] The same is true of law. As a community of jurists, we must learn to listen to law once more. An acoustic jurisprudence is capable of enriching legal thought, of expanding on the insights of those jurists who have already begun to think legal institutions in terms of their formal and material dimensions. Its purpose is not to supplant any of that literature but to supplement it, to provide a fuller account. And it is crucial that it does. Sound, after all, is a condition of the administration of justice, an inalienable part of the legal world.

The Turn to Sound

Why acoustic jurisprudence now? What is it about the present moment that makes the sort of inquiry pursued in this book possible? Legal scholarship is not alone in having maintained a certain deafness in recent years. Twentieth-century philosophy and cultural studies were famously marked by the so-called 'linguistic turn'.[116] The 'gaze' was a preoccupation of feminism, critical race theory, psychoanalysis, and, indeed, much of poststructuralist thought in general throughout the same period. The image was a central concern to these and many other fields of the humanities: semiotics, film, architecture, media, and communication studies.[117] But just as in law, while sound did occasionally crop up in this scholarship, it is only very recently that it has begun to emerge as a central theme and theoretical

[114] Alan Burdick, 'Now Hear This: Listening Back on a Century of Sound', *Harper's Magazine* 303(1804) (2001) 70, 75.

[115] Sterne (2003) 3.

[116] Judith Surkis, 'When Was the Linguistic Turn? A Genealogy', *The American Historical Review* 117(3) (2012) 700.

[117] Martin Jay, *Downcast Eyes: The Denigration of Vision in Twentieth-Century French Thought* (University of California Press, 1993). Although Jay ultimately argues that the predominant attitude of twentieth-century critical thought was *anti*-visual, the book nevertheless offers one of the most comprehensive accounts of Western visuality available.

problematic in its own right. Though there has been a sizeable literature on the history and philosophy of sound for some time, it has tended to be 'conceptually fragmented' until only the last ten years or so.[118] Today, not only is there a real boom in writings on sound by authors across the humanities and social sciences, for the first time this work also tends to be self-conscious of its place in relation to a broader interdisciplinary discussion of sound.[119] Dedicated journals like *Sound Effects* and *The Journal of Sonic Studies* have appeared, along with numerous conferences, special editions of existing journals, and a number of readers that gather older existing literature on sound under a single heading.[120]

What brought about *this* boom is harder to say. It is tempting to suggest technology: that the rapid audio-technological change we have witnessed in the last century and a half—stethoscopes, phonographs, telegraphy, industrial soundproofing, telephones, mobile telephones, microphones, loudspeakers, radio, sonar, hearing aids, electric guitars, vocoders, synthesizers, audiotape, drum machines, CDs, mp3s, and iPods—has led to an increased sensitivity to the role and importance of sound in both public and private life, resulting in a 'turn to sound' across the academy. But that answer may be exactly the wrong way round, a perfect example of 'technological determinism'.[121] After all, technologies don't just descend from the heavens, or materialize unbidden from the ether. They too have a history, and this history cannot fail to be more than merely technological.[122] In order for a particular technology to emerge, on the one hand, and then to spread and sediment itself, on the other—Edison's phonograph, say, or the Sony Walkman—the scientific, theoretical, social, commercial, and legal conditions must also be right. Technology and culture always exist in a state of mutual constitution. They are co-produced.[123] The Walkman is *evidence* of an increased sensitivity to sound and to the changing nature of our sonic environment at least as much as it is productive of it. So if sound is increasingly on the academic agenda, the reasons why are far more complex and wide ranging than technology alone.

[118] Sterne (2003) 4.

[119] Jonathan Sterne (ed), *The Sound Studies Reader* (Routledge, 2012) 1.

[120] For special editions, see Trevor Pinch and Karin Bijsterveld, 'Sound Studies: New Technologies and Music', *Social Studies of Science* 34(5) (2004) 635; Kara Keeling and Joshua Kun, 'Introduction: Listening to American Studies', *American Quarterly* 63(3) (2011) 445; Gustavus Stadler, 'Introduction: Breaking Sound Barriers', *Social Text* 28(1) (2010) 1; Rey Chow and James A Steintrager, 'In Pursuit of the Object of Sound: An Introduction', *Differences* 22(2–3) (2011) 1; Margaret Schedel and Andrew V Uroskie, 'Writing about Audiovisual Culture', *Journal of Visual Culture* 10(2) (2011) 137; Michele Hilmes, 'In Focus: Sound Studies—Foregrounding Sound: New (and Old) Directions in Sound Studies', *Cinema Journal* 48(1) (2008) 115. For readers, see Michael Bull and Les Back, *The Auditory Culture Reader* (Berg, 2003); Sterne, *The Sound Studies Reader* (2012); Trevor Pinch and Karin Bijsterveld, *The Oxford Handbook of Sound Studies* (Oxford University Press, 2011).

[121] Merritt Roe Smith and Leo Marx (eds), *Does Technology Drive History? The Dilemma of Technological Determinism* (MIT Press, 1994).

[122] See generally Sterne (2003).

[123] On 'co-production' generally, see Sheila Jasanoff (ed), *States of Knowledge: The Co-Production of Science and the Social Order* (Routledge, 2004).

In *The Sound Studies Reader*, Sterne offered the following by way of prospectus for this newly emergent field.

> *Sound Studies* is a name for the interdisciplinary ferment in the human sciences that takes sound as its analytical point of departure or arrival. By analyzing both sonic practices and the discourses and institutions that describe them, it redescribes what sound does in the human world, and what humans do in the sonic world … It reaches across registers, moments and spaces, and it thinks across disciplines and traditions, some that have long considered sound, and some that have not done so until more recently. Sound studies is academic, but it can also move beyond the university. It can begin from obviously sonic phenomena like speech, hearing, sound technologies, architecture, art, or music. But it does not have to. It may *think sonically* as it moves underwater, through the laboratory or into the halls of government; considers religion or nationalisms old and new; explores cities; tarries with the history of philosophy, literature or ideas; or critiques relations of power, property or intersubjectivity.[124]

This book also reaches across registers and thinks across disciplines and traditions. It is both inspired by sound studies and in dialogue with it. To lawyers it is an invitation to *think sonically* in relation to the practice of law and the administration of justice; to those in sound studies, an invitation to *listen jurisprudentially*.

You could call this sort of approach 'interdisciplinary'. And it is. This book is informed by sound studies in the same way in which the scholarship on law and the image, for instance, is influenced by the field of art history. Nevertheless, I want to insist on the language of jurisprudence here. One obvious problem with interdisciplinary thinking is that it implies a core instance of each discipline against which any deviations can thereby be measured. The language of disciplinarity then is a language of marginalization. In the case of law, it inevitably concedes the centre ground to legal positivism and a concern for law involving the privileging of rules, which is already to have lost half the battle. If this book is interdisciplinary, therefore, it is only in the sense that legal thought always interacts with other disciplines and is both constantly and necessarily engaged in a form of profligate borrowing, even when it pretends not to be. Neither law nor jurisprudence is a world unto itself, hermetically sealed. This book is first and foremost a jurisprudence, intended both to address a gap in the extant legal scholarship and to enrich the conversation currently being had there. But it speaks to a gap in the sound studies literature too.

Sometimes those outside of law make the most orthodox lawyers, their 'juridical imaginary' confined to an interest in state-posited rules, which are presumed to operate mechanically, as if that were the extent of legal practice or the juridical world.[125] To date, law has been of interest to sound studies mostly in relation to the substance of anti-noise legislation, patent, and copyright law. Law regulates sound, and when it does, most of the time it is both heavy handed and slow on the uptake. This book shows some of the ways in which the law–sound relation goes much deeper than that. By offering a richer and more sophisticated account of law

124 Sterne, *The Sound Studies Reader* (2012) 2.

125 William P MacNeil, *Novel Judgments: Legal Theory as Fiction* (Routledge, 2012) 9.

and the practices and dilemmas of legal judgment, an acoustic jurisprudence has something to offer back to sound studies too.

If this book is also in conversation with *sound* studies then, why do I prefer this language of acoustics? In part, I admit, 'acoustic jurisprudence' just sounds better to me. That is not unimportant. Language is necessarily poetic. So often we choose the words we do for the way they roll off the tongue at least as much as for their semantics. But more than that, it is a language of 'acoustics' that ties us back to Pythagoras, to Plato, and to ancient Greece. Whereas the English word 'sound' derives from the Latin *sonus* and tends to refer to the sound-object 'itself', to vibration, 'acoustics' comes from the Greek *akoustikos* and relates more to hearing.[126] Moreover, today we tend to think of the 'acoustics' of a building, a concert hall, a church, a courtroom. And when we do, the implications are often scientific, technical, and technological. The language of acoustics therefore seems to have more to do with people, spaces, and technique. These are all connotations that seem particularly appropriate in relation to a book concerned so closely with law as an institutional practice. Having said that, the sound/acoustics distinction is not one I want to insist on too rigorously here. I move between the two terms with relative fluidity. In part this is because often I am bound by the terminology I inherit from the sound studies literature. Take the terms 'sonic imagination' and 'soundscape', for instance, each of which provides one of the book's organizing themes.

The expression 'sonic imagination' comes from Sterne, but it is connected to a broader tradition of work in aesthetics, sociology, and science and technology studies.[127] When he coined the term, Sterne had in mind T S Eliot's 'auditory imagination', C Wright Mills' 'sociological imagination', and Anne Balsamo's 'technological imagination', amongst others.[128] In this tradition, the word imagination refers both to a way of apprehending the world and shaping it, at once a mindset and a creative force, both analytic and normative. Imaginations are of course possessed individually, but they are also, necessarily, intersubjective. An imagination is what 'unites members of a social community in shared perceptions', Sheila Jasanoff writes, 'of futures that should or should not be realized'.[129] Some of these shared perceptions may be very local, but some relate to much larger patterns of historical, legal, and political thought, and even metaphysics. Thus for Sterne,

[126] For an account of some recurring definitional problems, and in particular the problem of sonic anthropocentrism, see Sterne (2003) 10–19. For a well-known representative in the debate on the side of sonic materialism, see Christoph Cox, 'Beyond Representation and Signification: Toward a Sonic Materialism', *Journal of Visual Culture* 10(2) (2011) 145. For an example of the other side of the debate, which argues for the necessary social embeddedness of sound, see Seth Kim-Cohen, *In the Blink of an Ear: Toward a Non-Cochlear Sonic Art* (Continuum, 2009).

[127] Sterne, *The Sound Studies Reader* (2012) 5–7.

[128] Thomas S Eliot, *The Use of Poetry and the Use of Criticism: Studies in the Relation of Criticism to Poetry in England* (Harvard University Press, 1986); C Wright Mills, *The Sociological Imagination* (Oxford University Press, 1959); Anne Balsamo, *Designing Culture: The Technological Imagination at Work* (Duke University Press, 2011).

[129] Sheila Jasanoff, 'Future Imperfect: Science, Technology and the Imaginations of Modernity' in Sheila Jasanoff and Sang-Hyn Kim (eds), *Dreamscapes of Modernity Sociotechnical Imaginaries and the Fabrication of Power* (University of Chicago Press, 2015).

sonic imaginations 'reproduce cultural understandings at every turn'. 'There is no knowledge of sound that comes from outside culture, only knowledge that works from particular limits'.[130] When I refer to *law's sonic imagination* in this book, it is with this tradition of thought in mind. I am interested in how institutions like the ICTR conceive sound for the purposes of judgment, how they think and work with it, and what they understand to be sound's nature and social function in various different contexts. I am interested in how legal institutions' collective beliefs, presumptions, and shortcomings in relation to sound shape legal judgments and in doing so feed them back into the world with renewed salience and force. And I am interested because, like all imaginations, law's sonic imagination needs nurturing, care, and cultivation.

The word 'soundscape' was first coined by R Murray Schafer in a series of booklets and articles published more than forty years ago which were soon followed by his more famous book-length treatment, *The Soundscape: Our Sonic Environment and the Tuning of the World* in 1976.[131] Therein Schafer offered the following definition. The soundscape, he said, was our 'sonic environment', or 'technically, any portion of the sonic environment regarded as a field for study'.[132] While this definition has the advantage of succinctness, following Alain Corbin and Emily Thompson, I use the term slightly differently here. When I talk about the *judicial soundscape* in this book I mean to incorporate not just the Tribunal's sonic environment, the acoustic features of the courtroom, but also the way in which that environment is constructed, understood, and perceived.[133] 'Like a landscape, a soundscape is simultaneously a physical environment and a way of perceiving that environment; it is both a world and a culture constructed to make sense of that world.'[134] It is a combination both of the sounds themselves and the set of listening practices developed to make sense of them, of the acoustic ecology and what Sterne has termed 'audile technique'.[135] As Thompson argues:

> the physical aspects of a soundscape consist not only of the sounds themselves, the waves of acoustical energy permeating the atmosphere in which people live, but also the material objects that create, and sometimes destroy, those sounds. A soundscape's cultural aspects incorporate scientific and aesthetic ways of listening, a listener's relationship to their environment, and the social circumstances that dictate who gets to hear what.[136]

[130] Jasanoff (2015) 6.

[131] R Murray Schafer, *The Book of Noise* (Prize Milburn, 1968); R Murray Schafer, *The New Soundscape* (Berandol Music, 1971); R Murray Schafer, 'The Vancouver Soundscape' in R Murray Schafer (ed), *The Music of the Environment* (Universal Edition, 1973) 2; R Murray Schafer, *The Soundscape: Our Sonic Environment and the Tuning of the World* (Knopf, 1977).

[132] Schafer (1977) 274.

[133] Alain Corbin, *Village Bells: Sound and Meaning in the 19th Century French Countryside*, trans Martin Thom (Columbia University Press, 1998) [trans of: *Le cloches de la terre: Paysage sonore et culture sensible dans les campagnes au XIXe siècle* (first published 1998)] ix; Emily Thompson, *The Soundscape of Modernity: Architectural Acoustics and the Culture of Listening in America, 1900–1933* (MIT Press, 2004) 1.

[134] Thompson (2004) 1.

[135] See Sterne (2003) 92–5.

[136] Thompson (2004) 1–2.

For Thompson, therefore, a soundscape ultimately 'has more to do with civilisation than with nature', and as such it is constantly under construction, always undergoing change.[137] This is no less true of the judicial soundscape than any other.

Acoustic Jurisprudence

Now that I have situated the book relative to certain historical approaches to the law–sound relation, contemporary legal scholarship and the broader academy's recent turn to sound, it is time to flesh out some final key terms. First, jurisprudence. Etymologically, the word comes from the Latin *prudentia*, a contraction of *providentia*, meaning 'foresight'. Its earliest application was to actions which had legal consequences, and it is from here that the specialized term *iuris prudentia* developed along with an association between jurists and the language of *prudentia* more generally.[138] Juris-prudence: the prudence of *ius*, 'law's consciousness and conscience',[139] a concern for law's good conduct. When I say jurisprudence in this book then, I am not talking about legal philosophy, even though this is how the term is sometimes used today.[140] Nor am I referring to the body or system of rules pertaining to a particular field or jurisdiction: as in 'Australian constitutional jurisprudence' or the 'jurisprudence of the ICTR'. Despite the English word's Roman origins, the tradition of prudential thought I draw on began in Greece with Aristotle (as *phronesis*, or practical wisdom), was significantly deepened and extended in the work of Cicero (as *prudentia*), became central to Renaissance thinkers such as Machiavelli (*prudenza*), and is experiencing something of a revival today.[141]

Although of course this tradition is extremely diverse, at its heart prudence is about good judgment, where this judgment takes place in a world that is always already underway, in the context of legal institutions that are unavoidably messy and in relation to structures that are far from perfect. For Robert Hariman, prudence is what is required 'precisely when one is no longer safely within a realm wholly determined by one art, one subject, one group, one objective'.[142] Prudence 'cannot be reduced to an abstract set of principles or goals because it recognises that each situation calls for a different response; a different assessment of the forces that are playing themselves out, of strategic possibilities and limitations'.[143] As a way of knowing and relating to the world, prudence is fundamentally attuned to matters

[137] Thompson (2004).

[138] Robert W Cape Jr, 'Cicero and the Development of Prudential Practice at Rome' in Robert Hariman, *Prudence: Classical Virtue, Postmodern Practice* (Pennsylvania State University Press, 2003) 37.

[139] Douzinas and Gearey (2005) 3.

[140] Roger Cotterrell, 'Why Jurisprudence is not Legal Philosophy', *Jurisprudence* 5(1) (2014) 41.

[141] Robert Hariman and Francis A Beer, 'What Would be Prudent? Forms of Reasoning in World Politics', *Rhetoric & Public Affairs* 1(3) (1998) 299, 301. For a recent discussion of the tradition and the contemporary revival of interest in it, see Robert Hariman (2003).

[142] Hariman and Beer (1998) 303.

[143] Douzinas and Gearey (2005) 40.

of context, practice, performance, and action.[144] If it is a form of reason or rationality, therefore, it is certainly not in the usual sense. Prudence is more a matter of conduct and craft. It 'is distinct from both theoretical knowledge and wisdom', Maurice Charland explains, 'in that it is not conceptual but performed: prudence is manifest in "right action" ... not a form of knowledge but an embodied type of understanding'.[145] Which is to say, amongst other things, that prudence is just as concerned with the technical, material, and affective dimensions of the practice of judgment as it is with the logical or calculative. The prudential tradition cares at least as much about the hows and whys of good decision making as it does what is eventually decided, because it knows that these things are inextricably related.

Prudence is about the cultivation of a specifically *practical* wisdom then. But that does not mean it is disinterested in critical or theoretical speculation.[146] This is most obvious in the work of Cicero and in particular his *De Oratore*, where he insists that the best orator, which is also to say the best jurist, the best thinker and practitioner of law, will be a person with both 'extensive practical experience' and 'wide philosophical learning'.[147] For Cicero, prudence was holistic: the conjoining of Greek philosophy with Roman rhetoric, *ratio* and *oratio, sapientia* and *eloquentia*, thought and action.[148] The same is true here. This book advocates a similar conjunction of theory and practice.

What is jurisprudence then? It is a practice, a craft, and a virtue: a way of attending to and taking responsibility for the full range of techniques by which legal institutions make the world amenable to judgment.[149] Technique will be a key word in this book in fact. Again, a brief look at its etymology is helpful. This time the word derives from the Greek *technē*, the Latin equivalent of which is *ars*. Both words can be translated along the lines of craft, art, or strategy, as well as technique.[150] Both refer simply to the power or capacity to bring something about, to cause or produce it. And it is no coincidence, therefore, that it is also from the Greek *technē* that we get the word technology. Strictly speaking, a technology is simply an object or assemblage to which a particular technique or aspect of technique has been delegated.[151] In this sense, the language of technique cuts a very similar line between the practical and theoretical, as does the language of prudence.[152] To think legal

144 Robert Hariman, 'Prudence/Performance', *Rhetoric Society Quarterly* 21(2) (1991) 26.

145 Maurice Charland, 'Lyotard's Postmodern Prudence' in Robert Hariman (ed), *Prudence: Classical Virtue, Postmodern Practice* (Pennsylvania State University Press, 2003) 263.

146 Cape Jr (2003) 39.

147 Marcus Tullius Cicero, *On the Ideal Orator*, trans James M May and Jakob Wisse (Oxford University Press, 2001) [trans of: *De Oratore* (first published BCE 55)] 1.6-23. Cape Jr (2003) 44.

148 Cape Jr (2003) 39.

149 Shaun McVeigh (ed), *Jurisprudence of Jurisdiction* (Routledge-Cavendish, 2007) 4.

150 McVeigh and Dorsett (2012) 55.

151 For an account of the relations between technique and technology see Jacques Ellul, *The Technological Society*, trans John Wilkinson (Random House, 1964) [trans of: *La technique ou l'enjeu du siècle* (first published 1954)]. On technological delegation see Bruno Latour, 'Mixing Humans and Nonhumans Together: The Sociology of a Door-Closer', *Social Problems* 35(3) (1988) 298.

152 For Cicero's own conception of *ars/technē* see James M May and Jakob Wisse, 'Introduction' in Cicero, *On the Ideal Orator* 23–6.

practice in terms of technique is to adopt an attitude which draws an equivalency between human and non-human activity, actor and actant, between the juridical work done by the doctrine of precedent and a filing system, between the rules of evidence and the design of the courtroom.[153]

Moreover, technique has both a conscious and an unconscious element to it. Technique is a product both of will and what Pierre Bourdieu calls 'habitus', a form of 'socially conditioned subjectivity'.[154] It is something that can be learned—a repeatable set of practices: a particular logic, form, or process—but it finds its ultimate realization when the act of repetition becomes simply habitual, internalized, inscribed into the mind and body in the same way that a concert pianist or a factory worker's technique is written into theirs.[155] It is this sense of replicability or habituation that gives technique its institutional or disciplinary flavour even despite the fact that techniques may also cut across or between fields. We could say that while some techniques of judgment are specifically or originally juridical (the doctrine of incitement to genocide, the practice of oath swearing, the elevation of the judge's bench, or the isolation of the dock), some need to be incorporated into the juridical context (microphone usage, soundproofing, certain familiar rhetorical tropes, whether linguistic, visual, or otherwise). Both forms of technique are potentially equally important, equally likely to bear on juridical outcomes.

The language of technique, then, is capable of holding together all the various dimensions of law's formal and material life considered above. Language, architecture, image, screen, object, and process: all these are comprehensible in technical terms, as crucial elements of juridical practice and the craft of judgment. As far as a specifically *acoustic* jurisprudence is concerned, it is simply a matter of expanding the scope of the inquiry to include the huge variety of technical means by which sound also enters into the equation.

Let me offer the following definition. An *acoustic jurisprudence* is an orientation towards law and the practice of judgment attuned to questions of sound and listening. It is a form of attention, a way of relating to law's institutional life and techniques of adjudication, the purpose of which is to enrich legal practice and enable those of us who think and work with law to better account for the role of the acoustic in it. Its ambition is not, or not exclusively, doctrinal change. More

153 For examples of legal technologies see Dorsett and McVeigh (2012) 54 ('Technologies of Jurisdiction').

154 Pierre Bourdieu, *The Logic of Practice*, trans Richard Nice (Stanford University Press, 1990) [trans of: *Le sens pratique* (first published 1980)].

155 See Marcel Mauss' work on the notion of 'techniques of the body'. Marcel Mauss, *Sociology and Psychology: Essays*, trans Ben Brewster (Routledge and K Paul, 1979) [trans of: Parts III, IV, V, and VI of *Sociologie et anthropologie* (first published 1950)] 95 ('Part IV: Body Techniques'). On technique see also Aristotle, *Nicomachean Ethics*, trans Martin Ostwald (Prentice Hall, 1962); Martin Heidegger, *The Question Concerning Technology and Other Essays*, trans William Lovitt (Garland, 1977) [trans of: *Die technik und die kehre* (first published 1962)]; Ellul (1964); Jacques Derrida, *Of Spirit: Heidegger and the Question*, trans Geoffrey Bennington and Rachel Bowlby (University of Chicago Press, 1989) [trans of: *De l'esprit: Heidegger et la question* (first published 1987)]; Bernard Stiegler, *Technics and Time, 1: The Fault of Epimetheus*, trans Richard Beardsworth and George Collins (Stanford University Press, 1998) [trans of: *La technique et le temps, 1: La faute d'Epiméthée* (first published 1994)].

or better laws will not do the work of improving the world on their own. If it is normative, therefore, an acoustic jurisprudence is about developing a greater *sensitivity* to questions of sound with a view to thinking and practising law better. It is a matter of opening up scholars' and practitioners' ears to the diverse ways in which law and sound are deeply and necessarily co-implicated. An acoustic jurisprudence will be concerned, therefore, as much with law's sonic imagination as the judicial soundscape: both the ways in which legal institutions conceive sound and are themselves soundful. In either case, it is a matter of taking responsibility for a dimension of legal thought and practice which is no less real or important simply because we barely attend to it.

It is this notion of responsibility that gives an acoustic jurisprudence its critical edge. In Aristotle, *phronesis* has its end in 'the good', such that the practice of good judgment is a virtue. This is even clearer with Cicero. But in both cases, and despite the grammar, the idea of 'the good' being articulated is not a singular one. Prudential action requires the negotiation of 'multiple and contradictory objectives'.[156] It is not about the performance of one good but many; not about the realization of some foundational, all-encompassing justice, but the responsible navigation of a whole range of competing, and possibly even incommensurable demands. To do jurisprudence is to recognize, in other words, that we are responsible for law for many different reasons and in many different ways. And moreover, that it is precisely when the demands on us are at their least compatible and their most complex that this responsibility is at its greatest.

An acoustic jurisprudence is thus a species of what Edward Mussawir terms the 'practical critique of law'.[157] It draws on the language and resources of critique but is nevertheless not simply critical. For Mussawir, as for myself, 'jurisprudence is not a purely intellectual or abstract critique of law but a trade-practice, a technical activity and an art of juridical innovation co-extensive with the practice of living'.[158] This aspect of an acoustic jurisprudence is worth insisting on because, as Mussawir points out, recent critical legal scholarship has sometimes been guilty of being 'too metaphysical, too detached from the material and local encounters of law'.[159] 'Legal thought has for some time tended to separate the technical craft from the metaphysics and moral philosophies of judgment', he writes.[160] The same might be said of the critical approaches to voice briefly adverted to above.[161] Because the voice has been such a constant theme in recent critical legal scholarship, the example is helpful I think in locating the distinct critical register at which an acoustic jurisprudence operates.

[156] Robert Hariman and Francis A Beer (1998) 305.
[157] Mussawir, *Jurisdiction in Deleuze* (2011) 159.
[158] Mussawir, *Jurisdiction in Deleuze* (2011) 7.
[159] Nick Piška, 'Review: Edward Mussawir, Jurisdiction in Deleuze, the Expression and Representation of Law', *The Modern Law Review* 76(1) (2013) 184, 184.
[160] Edward Mussawir, 'The Activity of Judgment: Deleuze, Jurisdiction and the Procedural Genre of Jurisprudence', *Law, Culture and the Humanities* 7(3) (2011) 463, 466.
[161] Around footnotes 109–12.

In a representative piece, Costas Douzinas claims the following. 'All legislators repeat the gesture of Moses in Sinai', he says:

> Moses speaks and gives the law as a mouthpiece or a ventriloquist's dummy; in reality, it is God who speaks and dictates his words to Moses. According to theologico-political philosophy, the sovereign is he who declares the exception and metes out the excess and incalculability. The function of jurisdiction is to bring the sovereign to life and give him voice.[162]

The voice on this account is what breathes life into the law: what materializes it, makes it present, gives it reality, shape, force, and effect. On this account, in other words, the voice *is* form. It is the medium or technique of law's expression. God's own voice, however, is at once authoritative, excessive, and incalculable. This is the voice not as medium but as law itself. Before God reveals his Law to the people in the form of the Tablets, so the story goes, he announces himself to them as pure vocal force, independent of and unadulterated by language. 'On the morning of the third day there were peals of thunder and lightning, and a heavy cloud over the mountain, and a very loud trumpet blast, so that all the people in the camp trembled'.[163] This is the voice of God: the sound of 'shofar', conventionally translated as trumpet.[164] In testifying to God's presence for the people, shofar epitomizes the Law in its purest possible form, before demanding anything specific. This is the voice 'that commands total compliance', as philosopher Mladen Dolar puts it, 'although senseless in itself'.[165] As Carl Schmitt knew, we find an identical logic in relation to the charismatic voice of totalitarianism.[166]

These are the twin roles assigned to voice in so much contemporary critical legal scholarship. Voice is either law's medium—as juris-diction it is literally that which 'speaks the law'—or its purest manifestation as will or subjectivity. Such is the language of democracy itself, of citizenship and of participatory politics, in their collective 'phonocentrism'.[167] Each of us a little sovereign, together we manifest the collective 'voice' of the people. When Douzinas claims that 'an acoustics regulates our relationship with the law', he means it primarily in this metaphorical and metaphysical sense.[168] He is not especially interested in *how* that regulation might operate in terms of particular practices of giving voice or particular listening practices.

For an acoustic jurisprudence, the problem with always resolving the question of voice back to metaphysics is that it inevitably misses some of the other registers in which voice operates. There is a difference between *the voice* as a juridical problem and *voices*, plural and particular: this voice rather than that one, in this institutional setting rather than another, speaking or singing, this way or that way, bare or amplified. An acoustic jurisprudence is not disinterested in questions of metaphysics as we will see, but it refuses to leave the question of voice entirely to the critics

[162] Costas Douzinas (2007) 21.
[163] *The Holy Bible* (King James Version) Book II: Exodus, 19:16.
[164] Mladen Dolar, *A Voice and Nothing More* (MIT Press, 2006) 54.
[165] Dolar (2006) 53. [166] Dolar (2006) 117.
[167] Derrida (1998); Derrida (1973). [168] Douzinas (2007) 28.

and metaphysicians. Instead, its orientation is more grounded, institutional, and pragmatic.[169] It insists that the question of voice in law can be made 'the subject of a more material and local encounter',[170] one more intimately concerned with the day-to-day practices and responsibilities of coming to judgment. *This* is the register at which an acoustic jurisprudence engages legal thought and practice. Sometimes, yes, legal institutions adopt positions familiar to the metaphysical tradition in the process of judgment, but never without holding open the possibility of future contradiction. And sometimes their concerns seem altogether more mundane, more grounded, more provisional: less metaphysical, more prudent.

It is partly this willingness to take legal institutions' own internal perspectives at face value that distinguishes the work of an acoustic jurisprudence from critique. Unlike that of the critic, the sense of positionality I adopt here is not external to the institution with which I am interested. It is neither a matter of escaping law, nor of demolishing it in order to rebuild. My concern is how to *live with* institutions such as the ICTR, and especially how to do so better, more responsibly, even in the knowledge that this responsibility is overwhelming, that one can never do enough. Thus, it is not simply an internal perspective I offer either. It is more a matter of walking alongside, as an interested listener, trained in and responsible for law, yet not beholden to it.

169 McVeigh (2007) 4.

170 Mussawir, *Jurisdiction in Deleuze* (2011) xii.

2

Listening to the Trial of Simon Bikindi

An acoustic jurisprudence could in principle begin anywhere. This book could have cast its net wide rather than deep, taken a series of case studies across a variety of fields, jurisdictions, and institutions rather than concentrate on just one. I have elected to focus exclusively on the International Criminal Tribunal for Rwanda (ICTR) and the *Bikindi* case for a number of reasons. As I explained in the introduction, mainly this is because as a case study it is especially fertile, because matters of acoustics were so central and because the stakes were so exceptionally high. Indeed, they could hardly have been much higher. To repeat: here, for the very first time, was a major international institution accusing someone of inciting *genocide* with his songs, accusing a *singer* of being amongst the ninety-two 'most responsible' for the deaths of upwards of five hundred thousand people. The *Bikindi* case makes it strikingly clear that how legal institutions think and work with sound matters; and moreover that they can do so much better, more responsibly. By burrowing down into the particulars of a single case, by choosing to provide a thick as opposed to a thin account,[1] I want to show just how deep the law–sound relation goes, just how rich a field of inquiry this potentially is. And I do so in the hope that further studies, in different areas and different contexts, will follow. This book is envisaged as an opening not an end. It is just one possible exemplification of how one might go about taking responsibility for questions of sound and listening in the practice of law. It is to the details of this exemplification that we now turn.

The Rwandan Genocide

Thirteen weeks. One hundred days between April and July 1994. That's all it took for more than half a million Rwandans to be slaughtered: the end result of the most rapid extermination campaign of the twentieth century. Of those killed, tens of thousands were Hutus, but the vast majority were Tutsi: some estimates suggest as much as three-quarters of the total Tutsi population.[2] The violence was

[1] Clifford Geertz, 'Thick Description: Toward an Interpretive Theory of Culture' in *The Interpretation of Cultures: Selected Essays* (Basic Books, 1973) 3–30.

[2] Alison Des Forges, *Leave None to Tell the Story: Genocide in Rwanda* (Human Rights Watch, 1999) 6.

systematic, low-tech and extremely public. Though it was conceived, and to a large extent coordinated, centrally by a small group within the majority Hutu government (MRND) in the context of a civil war, it was carried out by a combination of the military, a government-backed militia group known as the *Interahamwe* and an apparently willing population. The conflict was not simply the result of 'ancient tribal hatred' as some commentators initially and racistly suggested. It came on the back of nearly a century of colonial upheaval, decades of civil unrest following independence from Belgium in 1962, anti-Tutsi massacres in both the 1960s and 1970s, and another civil war as recently as 1990.[3] Not just that. It was fuelled by a propaganda campaign in the media: in the pages of the state-owned newspaper *Kangura*, on *Radio Télévision Libre des Mille Collines* (RTLM), and on the government station Radio Rwanda. When war did finally break out following the assassination of President Juvenal Habyarimana on 6 April 1994, it quickly became clear that the intention of the small group of government hardliners who had seized power was especially sinister this time round. The idea was not just to repel a predominantly Tutsi rebel group known as the Rwandan Patriotic Front (RPF, sometimes also referred to as *Inkotanyi*) in their attempts to seize power, but to eliminate Rwanda's Tutsis entirely. Hundreds of thousands of Rwandans played their part. Not only was this genocide, it was a genocide in which there were nearly as many perpetrators as there were victims.

As the genocide unfolded, the world looked and listened on, and did nothing. Though the UN had peacekeeping forces in Rwanda at the time, they were denied either the manpower or the mandate to prevent the violence to which they bore witness.[4] Yet, no sooner had the conflict ended than talks began to establish an international body to prosecute it.

The International Criminal Tribunal for Rwanda

The International Criminal Tribunal for Rwanda is a UN body. It was officially born on 8 November 1994 by virtue of UN Security Council Resolution 955 in order to 'prosecute persons responsible for genocide and other serious violations of international humanitarian law' committed during the events of that year.[5] Although the Rwandan government had originally pushed hard for the

[3] Ibid; Scott Straus, *The Order of Genocide* (Cornell University Press, 2006).

[4] On Western complicity in the genocide see Gérard Prunier, *The Rwanda Crisis: History of a Genocide* (Columbia University Press, 1995); Michael Barnett, *Eyewitness to a Genocide: The United Nations and Rwanda* (Cornell University Press, 2002); Linda Melvern, *A People Betrayed: The Role of the West in Rwanda's Genocide* (Zed Books, 2000). Nesam McMillan argues that a tendency to frame the Rwandan genocide in terms of Western shame has deflected attention away from the potential legal issues raised by the international failure to act and the global responsibility of other countries regarding the genocide. See Nesam McMillan, '"Our" Shame: International Responsibility for the Rwandan Genocide', *Australian Feminist Law Journal* 28 (June 2008) 3.

[5] Statute of the International Tribunal for Rwanda, UNSC Res 955 (8 November 1994) UN Doc S/RES/955, annex ('ICTR Statute').

establishment of such a Tribunal,[6] it eventually voted against Resolution 955.[7] The reasons why are complex, but amongst other things it objected to the Tribunal's temporal jurisdiction, which it considered too restrictive, to certain aspects of its composition and structure, to the fact that capital punishment had been ruled out, and to the fact that the Tribunal would not be situated on Rwandan soil.[8] Despite these objections, when Resolution 955 was eventually passed by a vote of thirteen to one, with China abstaining, the Rwandan government did agree in principle to cooperate with the Tribunal's investigations,[9] and by February 1995 it had been determined that the Tribunal would have its 'seat' in Arusha, Tanzania.[10] On 27 November 1995, the ICTR moved in to the Arusha International Conference Centre which has been its home ever since.[11]

Although the make-up of the Tribunal is quite diverse—according to figures from 2011, some seventy-seven different nationalities were then represented on its staff—as an institution the ICTR's origins are very definitely in European legal thought and traditions.[12] It is a direct descendant of the Nuremberg Tribunal convened to prosecute war crimes after World War II, its method is adversarial, and its rules of evidence and procedure along with much of its most important doctrine are explicitly grounded in European Common and Civil law. Structurally, the ICTR was modelled on the Tribunal for the former Yugoslavia (ICTY) which, as the Rwandan genocide was taking place, had just been established to prosecute the atrocities that occurred in the Balkans during the early 1990s.[13] Accordingly, the ICTR comprises three main organs. The judicial organ (the Chambers) consists of three Trial Chambers—expanded in 1998 from the original two—and an Appeals Chamber which is shared with the ICTY.[14] Three judges sit in each Trial Chamber and five in the Appeals Chamber. No two judges may be nationals of the same state, and all are elected by the UN General Assembly from a list submitted by the Security Council, which in turn is derived from nominees suggested by UN member states. The Tribunal's investigative and prosecutorial organ (the Office of the

[6] Statement of Rwanda (6 October 1994) UN Doc A/49/PV.21, 5.

[7] Statement of Rwanda (8 November 1994) UN Doc S/PV.3453.

[8] Statement of Rwanda (8 November 1994).

[9] ICTR Statute, art 28(1) and (2). On Rwanda's varying relations with the Tribunal, see for instance Cedric Ryngaert, 'State Cooperation with the ICTR', *International Criminal Law Review* 13(1) (2013) 125; Yves Beigbeder, *International Criminal Tribunals: Justice and Politics* (Palgrave, 2011) 93–5.

[10] UNSC Res 977 (22 February 1995) UN Doc S/RES/977.

[11] 'First Annual Report of the International Criminal Tribunal for the Prosecution of Persons Responsible for Genocide and Other Serious Violations of International Humanitarian Law Committed in the Territory of Rwanda' (24 September 1996) UN Doc A/51/399-S/1996/778, annex ('First Annual Report of the ICTR') 5.

[12] See International Criminal Tribunal for Rwanda, 'About ICTR', accessed 10 February 2015, <http://41.220.139.198/AboutICTR/GeneralInformation/tabid/101/Default.aspx>. On the history of the ICTR and other major international criminal tribunals, see Virginia Morris and Michael P Scharf, *The International Criminal Tribunal for Rwanda* (Transnational Publishers, 1998) vol 1, chs 1–3; William A Schabas, *The UN International Criminal Tribunals: The Former Yugoslavia, Rwanda and Sierra Leone* (Cambridge University Press, 2006) pt 1.

[13] UNSC Res 808 (22 February 1993) UN Doc S/RES/808.

[14] UNSC Res 1165 (30 April 1998) UN Doc S/RES/1165.

Prosecutor) is responsible for all preliminary investigations, decisions in relation to who to indict and on what grounds, and all prosecutorial functions during the pre-trial phase, trial proceedings, and post-trial. And the Tribunal's administrative organ (the Registry), which is by far the most diverse of the three, is responsible for everything from court management, to archiving, to providing support to victims and witnesses, to diplomacy and liaising with defence counsel. Although, of course, accused have a right to legal representation, and without payment if necessary, defence counsel are required to operate independently. No fourth organ—the equivalent, say, of the Public Defenders Office in the United States—is provided for in the Tribunal's Statute.[15]

Like the Yugoslavia Tribunal, the ICTR's mandate was limited at the time of its inception in a number of ways. First, territorially to acts of genocide and crimes against humanity committed in the state of Rwanda or by Rwandan citizens in the territory of neighbouring states;[16] second, temporally to acts of genocide and crimes against humanity committed during the period between 1 January 1994 and 31 December 1994;[17] and third, strategically. Because of the extraordinary nature of the genocide, and the exceptionally large number of responsible parties, the Tribunal's stated policy was to prosecute only those it regarded as having played a particularly significant role in the events of 1994, with the rest of the significant juridical burden being left to Rwanda's own *Gacaca* courts.[18] Evidently, renowned Rwandan singer and public figure Simon Bikindi fell into this category.

Since the Tribunal's foundation in 1994, a total of ninety-three individuals have been indicted. Of these, sixty-one were sentenced, fourteen acquitted, and ten referred to national jurisdictions for trial. Three of those indicted have died either prior to or during their trial, two indictments were withdrawn before trial, and three accused remain on the run.[19] Amongst these proceedings the Tribunal is able to count a number of important milestones.[20] The trial of Jean-Paul Akayesu, for instance, led to the first ever conviction for genocide by an international tribunal.[21] Jean Kambanda, Prime Minister of Rwanda's interim government during the events of 1994, was both the first accused to plead guilty to charges of genocide and the first former head of state to be convicted before an international

[15] For a detailed account of the organization of the ICTR, see Morris and Scharf (1998) vol 1, ch 9.

[16] ICTR Statute, art 7. [17] ICTR Statute, art 1.

[18] Around 400,000 cases have now passed through Rwanda's *Gacaca* courts. For a comprehensive treatment of this system see Phil Clark, *The Gacaca Courts, Post-Genocide Justice and Reconciliation in Rwanda: Justice without Lawyers* (Cambridge University Press, 2010). For the ICTR's policy in relation to prosecutions, see First Annual Report of the ICTR, 12.

[19] Statistics from International Criminal Tribunal for Rwanda, 'The ICTR in Brief', accessed 10 February 2015, <http://www.unictr.org/en/tribunal>.

[20] For more positive appraisals of the Tribunal, see for instance Djiena Wembou, 'The International Criminal Tribunal for Rwanda: Its Role in the African Context', *International Review of the Red Cross* 37(321) (1997) 685; Erik Møse, 'Main Achievements of the ICTR', *Journal of International Criminal Justice* 3(4) (2005) 920; Payam Akhavan, 'Justice and Reconciliation in the Great Lakes Region of Africa: The Contribution of the International Criminal Tribunal for Rwanda', *Duke Journal of Comparative and International Law* 7(2) (1997) 325.

[21] *Prosecutor v Akayesu* (Judgement) ICTR-96-4-T, T Ch I (2 September 1998) ('*Akayesu* judgment').

tribunal since Nuremberg.[22] And in 2003 the trial of Ferdinand Nahimana, Jean Bosco Barayagwiza, and Hassan Ngeze—the so-called *Media* case—resulted in the first verdict holding members of the media responsible for direct and public incitement to genocide.[23]

Nevertheless, the ICTR has also generated a lot of criticism over the years. In addition to the more general difficulties surrounding the normative foundations of international criminal law per se, there have been criticisms of the Tribunal's development and application of doctrine. On the more administrative or procedural side of things, the ICTR has been accused variously of excessive cost and delays, inadequate infrastructure and personnel, poor standards of investigation and evidence collection, and insensitive treatment of witnesses. And politically, the Tribunal has consistently been charged with being too far removed both geographically and substantively from the daily lives of Rwandan citizens, allegations have been made of both mismanagement and corruption, and there have been accusations of victors' justice on the basis that the ICTR refused to prosecute violations of international humanitarian law committed by high-ranking RPF officers, including Rwanda's incumbent President Paul Kagame.[24]

Despite these criticisms, today the ICTR is nearly at the end of its task. Indeed, it was never intended to exist on an ongoing basis. In December 2010, the Security Council established the so-called Residual Mechanism to 'continue the material, territorial, temporal and personal jurisdiction' of both the ICTR and the ICTY as they are gradually wound down.[25] The ICTR officially began the process of transferring its authority on 1 July 2012. With the Tribunal's final judgment delivered at the end of 2012, the Residual Mechanism will now preside over the small number of cases still on appeal and retains the authority to prosecute those accused

[22] *Prosecutor v Kambanda* (Judgement and Sentence) ICTR-97-23-S, T Ch I (4 September 1998) ('*Kambanda* judgment and sentence).

[23] *Prosecutor v Nahimana* (Judgement and Sentence) ICTR-99-52-T, T Ch I (3 December 2003) ('*Nahimana* judgment and sentence'), also known as the '*Media* case'.

[24] For some representative examples of these criticisms, see Larry May, *Crimes Against Humanity: A Normative Account* (Cambridge University Press, 2005); Payam Akhavan, *Reducing Genocide to Law: Definition, Meaning, and the Ultimate Crime* (Cambridge University Press, 2012); Alison des Forges and Timothy Longman, 'Legal Responses to Genocide in Rwanda' in Eric Stover and Harvey M Weinstein (eds), *My Neighbor, My Enemy: Justice and Community in the Aftermath of Ethnic Cleansing* (Cambridge University Press, 2004) 53–5; Timothy Longman, Phuong Pham, and Harvey M Weinstein, 'Connecting Justice to Human Experience: Attitudes Towards Accountability and Reconciliation in Rwanda' in Eric Stover and Harvey M Weinstein (eds), *My Neighbor, My Enemy: Justice and Community in the Aftermath of Ethnic Cleansing* (Cambridge University Press, 2004); Nancy Combs, *Fact-Finding Without Facts: The Uncertain Evidentiary Foundations of International Criminal Convictions* (Cambridge University Press, 2010); Avitus A Agbor, *Instigation to Crimes against Humanity: The Flawed Jurisprudence of the Trial and Appeal Chambers of the International Criminal Tribunal for Rwanda (ICTR)* (Brill, 2013); Kirsten M F Keith, 'Justice at the International Criminal Tribunal for Rwanda: Are Criticisms Just?', *Law in Context* 27(1) (2009) 78; Todd Howland and William Calathes, 'The UN's International Criminal Tribunal: Is it Justice or Jingoism for Rwanda? A Call for Transformation', *Virginia Journal of International Law* 39(1) (1998) 135; Hanna Morrill, 'Challenging Impunity? The Failure of the International Criminal Tribunal for Rwanda to Prosecute Paul Kagame', *Brooklyn Journal of International Law* 37(2) (2012) 683.

[25] UNSC Res 1966 (22 December 2010) UN Doc S/RES/1966, art 1.

still at large should they ever be located. Importantly, it is also responsible for completing and maintaining the judicial archive, including the audio and audio-visual records of every trial conducted throughout the Tribunal's life.[26] This archive will continue to be located in Arusha. However, the Residual Mechanism has been tasked both with preserving the materials contained there and facilitating 'the widest possible access to them while ensuring the continued protection of confidential information'.[27] This, it says, is 'all aimed at ensuring that the rich legacy of the Tribunal, serving as an example of international commitment towards the fight against impunity, will be disseminated widely and preserved for posterity'.[28]

Prosecutor v Simon Bikindi

The charges

Following Bikindi's indictment on 4 July 2001 by the ICTR's then Prosecutor, Carla Del Ponte, the very next day a warrant was issued for Bikindi's arrest.[29] On 12 July he was apprehended by Dutch authorities at the Centre for Asylum Seekers in Leiderdorp,[30] detained, and after losing both his legal battle against extradition and his application for asylum, finally transferred to the ICTR's detention facility in Arusha on 27 March 2002 to await trial.[31] The charges brought against him were about as serious as they get: conspiracy to commit genocide; genocide or, alternatively, complicity in genocide; direct and public incitement to commit genocide; murder as a crime against humanity; persecution as a crime against humanity.[32] While the detail of each of these charges is complex, the crux of the case against Bikindi was simple. In essence, Bikindi stood accused of inciting genocide with his songs, which he was alleged to have performed live at political rallies on several occasions and which had received extensive radio airplay on Radio Rwanda and RTLM, in addition to their sale and distribution on cassette. Although he was also accused of participating personally in some killings during the later stages of 1994's genocide, these charges were eventually dropped. He was being tried primarily as a singer.

Already in the indictment filed a week before his arrest on 4 July 2001, the Prosecutor had this to say under the heading 'The Accused':

> Simon Bikindi was born on 28 September 1954 in Rwerere *commune*, Gisenyi *prefecture*, Rwanda. During the period material to this indictment, Simon Bikindi was a well-known

[26] UNSC Res 1966 (22 December 2010) art 27.

[27] UNSC Progress Report (18 November 2013) UN Doc S/2013/679, annex I, para 57.

[28] UNSC Progress Report (15 May 2014) UN Doc S/2014/343, para 84.

[29] 'Warrant of Arrest and Orders for Transfer and Detention and for Search and Seizure', *Prosecutor v Bikindi*, ICTR-01-72-0039 (5 July 2001).

[30] 'Request of Whereabouts of 3 Scripts of Mr A Waday', *Prosecutor v Bikindi*, ICTR-01-72-0026 (29 May 2002).

[31] 'Takeover of Mr Simon Bikindi', *Prosecutor v Bikindi*, ICTR-01-72-0016 (27 March 2002).

[32] ICTR Statute, arts 2, 3. See *Prosecutor v Bikindi* (Indictment) ICTR-01-72-I (4 July 2001) ('*Bikindi* indictment').

composer and singer of popular music and director of the performance group *Irindiro Ballet.* Simon Bikindi was also an official in the Ministry of Youth and Sports of the Government of Rwanda and a member of the MRND political party.[33]

A singer first and foremost and an official only after, Bikindi's songs were central to three of the six charges brought against him. Each of these was a variation on the central theme of incitement. Bikindi's indictment puts the basic claim in relation to 'direct and public incitement to commit genocide' like this. 'During the period 1990 to 1994', it reads, Bikindi had 'composed, performed, recorded or disseminated musical compositions extolling Hutu solidarity and characterising Tutsi as enslavers of the Hutu'. These compositions were then subsequently 'deployed in a propaganda campaign to target Tutsi as the enemy, or as enemy accomplices, and to instigate, incite, and encourage the Hutu population to separate themselves from the Tutsi and to kill them'.[34] The conspiracy charges also revolved around his songs. He was said to have consulted with President Habyarimana and other MRND officials on the subject matter of his songs' lyrics before going on to record them at Radio Rwanda's studios and perform them at MRND and *Interahamwe* recruitment drives and military training. Not only that, but as one of the founders of RTLM he was purportedly able to participate directly in the so-called 'campaign to defeat the enemy in the media'.[35] The indictment claimed that 'the intertwining objectives of RTLM's media programming and Simon Bikindi's musical recordings' were 'the same': namely, 'to sensitize and incite the listening public to target and commit violent acts against the Tutsis, particularly the civilian militias, the government armed forces and the masses of Rwanda's Hutu peasantry; and to extol Hutu solidarity and to target the Tutsi as accomplices of the enemy'.[36] As such, his songs were said to have been nothing less than 'a crucial part of the genocidal plan'.[37] Not only had Bikindi's songs incited genocide, it was alleged, he had knowingly and actively conspired with the genocide's major architects in relation to both their composition and dissemination. When it came to the charges in relation to 'persecution as a crime against humanity', the Prosecutor's claim was more modest and open ended. Bikindi had composed, written, performed, recorded, and disseminated his songs, it was claimed, not in order to incite *genocide* but simply the *persecution* of Tutsis and sympathetic Hutus.[38]

[33] *Bikindi* indictment, 1.

[34] *Bikindi* indictment, para 28 (emphasis removed).

[35] *Bikindi* indictment, para 8.

[36] *Bikindi* indictment, para 10.

[37] *Prosecutor v Bikindi* (Second Amended Indictment) ICTR-01-72-I (15 June 2005) ('*Bikindi* second amended indictment') para 16.

[38] *Bikindi* indictment, para 46. What this amounted to, as the Chamber would later point out, was essentially a particularly severe form of discrimination: *Prosecutor v Bikindi* (Judgement) ICTR-01-72-T, T Ch III (2 December 2008) ('*Bikindi* judgment') paras 390–5.

The songs

As far as the songs themselves were concerned, just three were named in the indictment and just three would go on to be in issue at trial. Although the defence did attempt to argue that Bikindi's entire body of work should be considered, including the traditional wedding songs that brought him fame at the start of his career, the Chamber pointed out that this approach would not necessarily work in their favour. If the defence wanted to include the wedding songs, it would also have to include the series of so-called 'war songs' Bikindi had recorded in 1991, along with a number of others which may well not be beneficial to their cause.[39]

Just three songs then: one composed and first recorded in 1987, the other two in 1993. Instrumentally they are quite diverse, but the *inanga* for instance, a stringed instrument on which Bikindi was apparently a 'master player', features prominently, as do electric guitar and bass.[40] All three songs are long, well over ten minutes in the case of two of them, though by how much exactly depends on the recording. And the lyrics—which are full of references to Rwandan history, well-known figures, famous episodes—are 'poetic' and 'sophisticated', rich with 'imagery' and 'allusions', in a 'literary high form of Kinyarwanda' as one witness put it.[41] Some parts are sung just by Bikindi, others by a chorus. Sometimes there are multiple characters, and structurally, therefore, extensive use is made of call and response, question and answer, verse and refrain, though often organized in quite complex ways.

I will say more about what the Chamber made of these songs in a moment and then again in detail in Chapter 3. But first, a quick note on their titles, because the question of how to name them for the purposes of this book is a fraught one. The title of one, *Twasezereye* ('We Said Goodbye'), was not deemed especially controversial at trial.[42] The other two titles, however, were hotly contested. Bikindi and the defence claimed that one should be *Akabyutso* ('The Awakening') and the other *Intabaza* ('The Alert') whereas the prosecution preferred *Nanga Abahutu* ('I Hate the Hutu') and *Bene Sebahinzi* ('The Descendants of Sebahinzi') respectively. The problem is that the question of title was directly bound up with the question of Bikindi's criminal intent. Bikindi argued that the titles preferred by the prosecution had been invented by certain radio broadcasters in Rwanda specifically in order to distort the meaning of his songs in concert with the station's genocidal agenda. In its judgment, the Trial Chamber attempted to sidestep this problem

[39] *Bikindi* judgment, paras 200–205 ('7.1.1.6 Other Songs'). See *Prosecutor v Bikindi* (Transcript) ICTR-01-72-T, T Ch III (Various dates) ('*Bikindi* transcript'): 11 October 2006, 40; 9 October 2007, 36, 55; 17 October 2007, 14; 20 February 2007, 25.

[40] Exhibit No P73(E), 'Prosecution Joint Expert Report of Gamaliel Mbonimana and Jean de Dieu Karangwa: "Thematic Analysis of the Songs"', *Prosecutor v Bikindi*, ICTR-01-72-0152 (13 September 2006) 7.

[41] *Bikindi* judgment, paras 197–8.

[42] Originally the prosecution claimed that this song's title should be *Twasezereye ingoma yo cyami* ('We Said Goodbye to the Monarchy') whereas Bikindi said it should be simply *Twasezereye*. In later iterations of the indictment, however, the prosecution also adopted this shorter version: *Bikindi* judgment, para 188.

entirely. 'For the sake of symmetry with the Indictment', it said, it would 'refer to the three songs by the titles selected by the prosecution', and take those offered by the defence into account when it came to inferring Bikindi's intent with respect to the songs' meanings as a whole.[43] This decision is less neutral than it seems. By giving the prosecution's titles default status simply by virtue of their structural location in the technics of the trial, the Tribunal accorded the indictment a sort of semantic gravitational pull. 'For the sake of symmetry' all roads lead back to it. The Prosecutor was effectively being permitted to set the terms of the debate years before the trial.

The results of this decision, moreover, have been significant. In the majority of the secondary literature on the *Bikindi* case, Bikindi's songs have been referred to by the titles originally given by the prosecution with little or no critical awareness that doing so might be problematic, that it might involve a history or a politics. But the titles we choose nest a whole range of interpretative judgments and symbolic alignments which the Chamber's attempt to sidestep both concealed and entrenched. Thus, in a book centrally concerned with how the ICTR understood Bikindi's songs for the purposes of judgment, it behoves me to point out the politics at work here and leave the question of title as an open one. My approach in this book is as follows. Where it is necessary to refer to the songs by name I use *Twasezereye*, *Nanga Abahutu/Akabyutso*, and *Bene Sebahinzi/Intabaza* respectively. All references included in quotation, however, will be left in their original form.[44]

The judgment

Following Bikindi's initial appearance before the court on 4 April 2002, it took more than four years for the trial itself to commence, which it eventually did on 18 September 2006. During the course of the next two years, and more than sixty days in court, hundreds of hours of witness testimony and oral argument were heard. Charges were read and oaths sworn. Recordings of Bikindi's songs were played to the court on multiple occasions, witnesses hummed his melodies and Bikindi himself sang several times during the provision of his testimony. And all of this into microphones, out of speakers, and mediated by either one or a chain of interpreters. Finally, on 2 December 2008 Judge Inés Mónica Weinberg de Roca, who had presided over the trial, read out a summary of the Chamber's judgment to the twenty or so individuals who were officially present and members of the public and media listening from the gallery.

With respect to *Twasezereye*, the evidence was apparently insufficient to establish Bikindi's intentions. The song had been composed in 1987 for the commemoration of the twenty-fifth anniversary of Rwandan independence, and according to

[43] *Bikindi* judgment, para 190.

[44] For the debate concerning the songs' titles at trial, see *Bikindi* transcript: 14 February 2007; 23 October 2007; 25 October 2007; 2 November 2007; 6 November 2007. For the Chamber's discussion of this issue, see *Bikindi* judgment, paras 188–90.

the defence at least, that was exactly how it should be understood: as a celebration, incapable of inciting hatred, let alone genocide.[45] But for the prosecution, the Chamber explained, *Twasezereye* was a 'rallying call for unity among Hutu by reminding them of a past of subservience to the Tutsi'.[46] Bikindi was not celebrating the end of the colonial regime but the monarchy, which was widely associated with Tutsi domination. Bikindi made reference, for instance, to the historical practice of adorning the dynastic drum Kalinga, an 'emblem of the Tutsi', with the testicles of vanquished enemies, and especially Hutu.[47] For the prosecution expert, Bikindi's implication was obvious: if current conditions prevailed, the monarchy would return and 'therefore the Hutu had to strike first'.[48] The Chamber was not convinced.

Where the other two songs were concerned, however, the 'only reasonable inference', the Chamber said, was that Bikindi had composed them with the 'specific intention to disseminate pro-Hutu ideology and anti-Tutsi propaganda, and thus to encourage ethnic hatred'.[49] *Nanga Abahutu/Akabyutso* listed five categories of Hutu who were said to be friends of the Tutsi, a list which bore striking similarities of language to the so-called 'Bahutu Ten Commandments' published in the inflammatory newspaper *Kangura*: Hutu who had forsaken their Hutu identity by becoming Tutsi for employment or educational advantage; Hutu who despise other Hutu; Hutu who are greedy and live off bribes from other Tutsi; Hutu who are naive and engage in war on the side of the Tutsi without any awareness of what is really at stake; Hutu who, when a Hutu makes a mistake, do not correct him by taking him aside, in order to ensure the unity of the Hutu.[50] According to Bikindi, his intention here was not to advocate hatred, but was 'more akin to smacking a small child to stop him from misbehaving'. He was a patriot, he said, and 'could see the trouble his country was falling into'.[51] For the prosecution expert, however, the song's 'message' was far more sinister. It wasn't just the five categories of hated Hutu that were so incendiary. There were also references to the assassinations of historical Hutu figures, presumed to have been by Tutsi monarchs. And in the political context of the time this could not fail, apparently, to exacerbate hatred, 'pushing people to act'.[52] In his opinion the song 'unambiguously encouraged killings'.[53]

Bene Sebahinzi/Intabaza was probably the most complex of the three songs at issue in Bikindi's trial. It tells the story of a crisis, faced in particular by the 'descendants of the father of farmers', then the cause of the crisis, and finally its cure. And it does so with the help of multiple characters and archetypes from the Rwandan historical and poetic tradition: amongst others, the soothsayer, the spitting snake, and the spy.[54] For Bikindi, as for the defence, the song referred to

[45] *Bikindi* judgment, para 214.
[46] *Bikindi* judgment, para 209.
[47] *Bikindi* judgment, para 211.
[48] *Bikindi* judgment, para 211; Exhibit No P73(E), *Prosecutor v Bikindi* (13 September 2006), 23.
[49] *Bikindi* judgment, para 254.
[50] *Bikindi* judgment, para 218.
[51] *Bikindi* judgment, para 229.
[52] *Bikindi* judgment, para 219.
[53] *Bikindi* judgment, para 221.
[54] *Bikindi* judgment, para 211; Exhibit No P73(E), *Prosecutor v Bikindi* (13 September 2006), 18–9.

all Rwandan farmers, irrespective of ethnicity, and constituted a call to stop the chaos raging between them, and in particular by means of democracy.[55] But again, for the prosecution the song was much less benign. Though the Tutsi were never mentioned explicitly, the song clearly framed them as a common enemy, the solution to which was Hutu unity.[56] Its main 'message', the prosecution expert said, was for Hutu to unite against the RPF, and that the RPF could not win, 'even with weapons'.[57] As with *Nanga Abahutu/Akabyutso*, when understood in context the song was unambiguously an 'invitation not only to hate, but also to kill people'.[58]

Though the Chamber was not prepared to go as far as the prosecution here, it was convinced that both *Nanga Abahutu/Akabyutso* and *Bene Sebahinzi/Intabaza* had at least been intended to encourage hatred. It simply didn't believe 'Bikindi's assertion that the songs preached harmony'.[59] He had actively 'manipulated the history of Rwanda to extol Hutu solidarity', the Chamber said.[60] What's more, the Chamber was also persuaded that all three songs had been *used* by presenters on RTLM and Radio Rwanda to incite genocidal killings, by means of their constant and inflammatory editorializing. 'Please listen to Bikindi's advice to the *Inkotanyi*' one RTLM broadcaster entreated his listeners in May 1994. 'He is warning them that they will all be wiped out … That is what is happening now, and the *Inkotanyi* are on the verge of extinction'.[61] While it was clear that the songs had been deployed, therefore, 'in a propaganda campaign in 1994 in Rwanda to incite people to attack and kill Tutsi', in the final analysis there was 'insufficient evidence to conclude beyond reasonable doubt that Bikindi composed these songs with the specific intention to incite such attacks and killings, even if they were used to that effect in 1994'.[62]

The Chamber's argument comprised three distinct steps then. First, at least two of Bikindi's songs had been intended to encourage hatred. Second, recordings of them had clearly been used by presenters on Radio Rwanda and RTLM to incite genocidal killings. Third, this use of the songs had not however coincided with Bikindi's intentions.[63] Though he might have intended to 'extol Hutu solidarity … against a common foe' this did not necessarily extend as far as 'directly and publicly inciting genocide' for the purposes of the Statute. The same went for the charges in relation to conspiracy and persecution. It wasn't simply that the prosecution had failed to prove that Bikindi had collaborated with MRND officials. Even if he had, that would not have been sufficient to show that he had agreed with them to commit genocide.[64] And although Bikindi had intended his songs to 'encourage ethnic hatred' and to be a vehicle of 'anti-Tutsi propaganda', because he had played no active role in their 'dissemination' or 'deployment' in 1994 during the period

[55] *Bikindi* judgment, para 244.
[56] *Bikindi* judgment, para 233.
[57] *Bikindi* judgment, para 236.
[58] *Bikindi* judgment, para 235.
[59] *Bikindi* judgment, para 252.
[60] *Bikindi* judgment, para 254.
[61] *Bikindi* judgment, para 239.
[62] *Bikindi* judgment, para 255.
[63] See Chapter 7 for further discussion of the issue of the 'deployment' of Bikindi's songs by radio presenters at RTLM and Radio Rwanda.
[64] *Bikindi* judgment, para 406.

under the Tribunal's temporal jurisdiction, the prosecution had also failed to make its case in relation to persecution.[65]

In the end it was not Bikindi's songs that the court relied upon in convicting him, therefore, but a number of statements he was reported to have made over a loudspeaker by the side of the road one day in June 1994. Bikindi had 'used a public address system', the Chamber said, 'to state that the majority population, the Hutu, should rise up to exterminate the minority, the Tutsi'. Later on the same day, 'Bikindi used the same system to ask if people had been killing Tutsi, who he referred to as snakes'.[66] *This* the Chamber said was sufficient to ground a conviction. So although Bikindi was declared innocent of five of the six charges against him, on the basis of these statements the Chamber found him guilty of 'direct and public incitement to genocide' under Articles 2(3)(c) and 6(1) of its Statute and sentenced him to fifteen years' imprisonment, with credit for the seven he had already served since his arrest in 2001.[67]

Two concurrent appeals then followed. Whereas Bikindi appealed both his conviction and, failing that, his sentence, the prosecution argued that this sentence was radically insufficient. Nothing less than life would do.[68] A hearing was held on 30 September 2009 before a panel of five senior judges and on 18 March 2010 the Appeals Chamber's judgment was finally delivered. Both appeals were dismissed and in 2012 Bikindi was transferred from Arusha to a prison in the West African Republic of Benin to serve out the remainder of his sentence.[69] He is due to be released in 2016.

The response to the *Bikindi* case

Though this book is the first time the *Bikindi* case has been looked at in detail, it has not gone unnoticed in legal scholarship, musicology, or the media. Indeed, it is fair to say that Bikindi's trial has proven genuinely provocative. Writing on it is often accompanied by eye-catching headlines and titles which tend to emphasize and occasionally to sensationalize the case's musical dimensions. So we have everything from Gregory Gordon's *Music and Genocide* to Donald McNeil's *Killer Songs*. We have *The Soundtrack to Genocide*, *The Drumbeats of Mass Slaughter*, *Sounds of Violence*, and even a piece which riffs extensively off a lyric from Bob Dylan's *It's Alright, Ma (I'm Only Bleeding)*.[70] Despite all this posturing, however, none of these pieces takes seriously the implications of their title.

[65] *Bikindi* judgment, para 254. [66] *Bikindi* judgment, para 422.

[67] ICTR Statute, arts 2(3)(c) and 6(1).

[68] *Bikindi v The Prosecutor* (Judgment) ICTR-01-72-A, Appeals Chamber (18 March 2010) ('*Bikindi* appeal') 2.

[69] 'More ICTR Convicts Transferred to Mali and Benin to Serve Their Sentences', United Nations International Criminal Tribunal for Rwanda, 3 July 2012, <http://www.unictr.org/en/news/more-ictr-convicts-transferred-mali-and-benin-serve-their-sentences>.

[70] Gregory S Gordon, 'Music and Genocide: Harmonizing Coherence, Freedom and Nonviolence in Incitement Law', *Santa Clara Law Review* 50(3) (2010) 607; Donald G McNeil Jr, 'Killer Songs', *The New York Times*, 17 March 2002, <http://www.nytimes.com/2002/03/17/magazine/killer-songs.html?src=pm>; Justin La Mort, 'The Soundtrack of Genocide: Using Incitement to Genocide in the

In the legal literature, the case has been examined primarily for its doctrinal significance in relation to the laws of incitement and freedom of expression. Most of all, it is read as authority for two propositions. First, that there is a right to freedom of expression under customary international law, even if that right is not absolute.[71] Second, that song is at least capable of constituting direct and public incitement to genocide, even if it did not on the facts of this particular case.[72] At the same time, though, the Chamber's reasoning in the *Bikindi* case has been roundly criticized for its supposed lack of rigour.[73]

In musicology, there is only one study of note. In 2013, Jason McCoy submitted his doctoral dissertation on the three songs at the heart of Bikindi's trial. The thesis is based partly on interviews with Bikindi himself, conducted while Bikindi was still being held at the UN Detention Facility in Arusha, and partly on McCoy's own ethnographic work. In addition to some interesting historical detail and discussion of contemporary perceptions of Bikindi and his music in Rwanda, it includes new English translations of all three songs along with McCoy's own lyrical analysis. But even this study explicitly engages 'in little analysis of the music itself, its social and cultural relevance, and its cognitive and emotional impact on audiences in the early 1990s'.[74] And the account of the trial itself is jurisprudentially thin.

In the media, the focus was not so much on doctrine or the detail of the songs themselves as the decision's political ramifications, the possibility that it could be used to justify limitations on musical and other forms of expression by oppressive regimes. For John Floyd, counsel for Rwandan journalist Hassan Ngeze in the so-called *Media* case, even prosecuting Bikindi was a real problem in this respect.[75] It was tantamount to 'putting Bob Dylan on trial for protest songs'.[76] Whether or

Bikindi Trial to Protect Free Speech and Uphold the Promise of Never Again', *Interdisciplinary Journal of Human Rights Law* 4(1) (2010) 43; Thijs Bouwknegt, 'Rwandan Genocide Singer Sentenced to Jail: The Drumbeats of Mass Slaughter', *Radio Netherlands Worldwide*, 2 December 2008 (copy on file with author); Bill Berkeley, 'Sounds of Violence', *New Republic* 211(8–9) (1994) 18; Robert H Snyder, '"Disillusioned Words like Bullets Bark": Incitement to Genocide, Music, and the Trial of Simon Bikindi', *Georgia Journal of International and Comparative Law* 35(3) (2007) 645.

[71] Katharina Margetts and Nicole Janisiewicz, 'Current Developments at the Ad Hoc International Criminal Tribunals', *Journal of International Criminal Justice* 7(2) (2009) 397, 397.

[72] Margetts and Janisiewicz (2009) 398.

[73] Gordon (2010) 2, 3. See also Gregory S Gordon, '"A War of Media, Words, Newspapers, and Radio Stations": The ICTR Media Trial Verdict and a New Chapter in the International Law of Hate Speech', *Virginia Journal of International Law* 45(1) (2004) 139; Susan Benesch, 'Vile Crime or Inalienable Right: Defining Incitement to Genocide', *Virginia Journal of International Law* 48(3) (2008) 485; Susan Benesch, 'Inciting Genocide, Pleading Free Speech', *World Policy Journal* 21(2) (2004) 62.

[74] Jason McCoy, 'Mbwirabumva ("I Speak to Those Who Understand"): Three Songs by Simon Bikindi and the War and Genocide in Rwanda' (PhD dissertation, Florida State University, 2013).

[75] *Nahimana* judgment and sentence, 3 December 2003.

[76] Dina Temple-Raston, 'Journalism and Genocide', *Columbia Journalism Review* 41(3) (2002) 18. The invocation of Bob Dylan in particular here is not insignificant. Dylan is the archetype of the Western protest singer, whose mythology relates to a very particular history of rock's relation to Anglo-American rebellion, on the one hand, and the canonization of the folk musician as 'artist', on the other. See Simon Reynolds, *The Sex Revolts: Gender, Rebellion and Rock'n'Roll* (Harvard University Press, 1995); Michael Gray, *The Art of Bob Dylan* (Hamlyn, 1981); Greil Marcus, *Mystery Train: Images of America in Rock'n'Roll Music* (5th rev edn, Plume, 2008); Greil Marcus, *Invisible Republic: Bob*

not the comparison bears out is less important for the time being than the anxiety being expressed. Ole Reitov, a spokesman for and founding member of advocacy group and 'world forum on music and censorship' Freemuse, was more forgiving. For him the Trial Chamber's decision in the *Bikindi* case was 'pretty clever', even 'wise'. Although the Chamber had not been prepared to rule out the possibility that song could constitute incitement to genocide, it made it clear that it would not reach such a decision lightly.[77] Bikindi's prosecution was a clear statement from the ICTR about the importance of the role played by music in conflict situations, its relation to certain forms of ethnic and national identity and the severity of its perceived abuse. Even though Bikindi was eventually cleared of the charges in relation to his songs, there is a sense in which they were at the heart of his conviction nevertheless. Had Bikindi not been such a prominent singer, had his songs not featured so extensively on the radio as part of the Rwandan 'soundscape' in the run up to and during the genocide, he would never have been indicted by the Tribunal in the first place. Even if his songs did not result in a finding of criminal responsibility, it is possible to draw a direct line between them and his eventual imprisonment nevertheless.

The critical response to the *Bikindi* case has been intriguingly bipolar. It seems simultaneously to be aware that the case raises some profound questions in relation to the acoustic, and singularly disinterested in exploring them. It knows there is something provocative about attempting to hold a singer responsible for the role of his songs in facilitating genocide, about the role of radio, and the emphasis on acoustics in Rwanda's media ecology, but has neither the tools nor the inclination to work the complexities of these issues through. In that sense, this literature too is symptomatic of the deafness of so much current juridical thought.

Archive and Method

How do I approach the *Bikindi* case? In terms of my archive, I am working from a wide variety of sources, many of which are publicly available. As well as the two published judgments in the *Bikindi* case, both at first instance and on appeal, the book makes extensive use of a complete set of redacted transcripts of the trial, in both English and French, as well as the indictments and certain other documents from Bikindi's case file, all of which are downloadable from the ICTR's online Public Judicial Records Database.[78] But I was also lucky enough to visit the Tribunal for a month in January 2011.[79] Although I did conduct a number

Dylan's Basement Tapes (Picador, 1997); Greil Marcus, *Bob Dylan by Greil Marcus: Writings 1968–2010* (Public Affairs, 2010).

[77] 'Singer Sentenced to 15 Years for Incitement', Freemuse, accessed 11 February 2015, <http://www.freemuse.org/sw31145.asp>.

[78] UN ICTR Judicial Records Database <http://www.unictr.org/en/cases>.

[79] Ethics approval for this fieldwork was granted in advance by the University of Melbourne Human Research Ethics Committee.

of interviews with members of the Tribunal during that period, these have not been directly incorporated into the analysis. Mostly the purpose of that trip was the observation of ongoing trials and to collect archival materials which were not already available online. These included certain pieces of audio-visual evidence that had not been submitted to the Tribunal under seal, along with a number of practice manuals and other internal documents. Of particular importance to the book, however, was a complete copy of the audio-record of proceedings along with as much of the audio-visual record as was publicly available.

It is not so long ago that much of the analysis I undertake in this book would not have been possible. Without an audio-visual of the trial, a systematic consideration of the role played by sound in a trial like Bikindi's would be out of the question. Over the next few years, the Residual Mechanism will make public a complete and redacted audio and audio-visual archive for every case heard at the ICTR.[80] When it does, it will be amongst the first legal institutions in the world to do so. But when I began work on this book it had yet to begin. I was particularly fortunate therefore that the Tribunal's chief archivist Martha Hunt agreed to use the *Bikindi* case in the Judicial Record and Archive Unit's pilot programme as they began to develop their archival systems and procedures at the start of November 2009. Without that generosity, this book would simply not exist.

Methodologically, the approach I bring to these materials is heavily informed by the scholarship outlined in Chapter 1, both jurisprudential and in the field of sound studies. Because I am asking novel questions about the role of sound and listening in legal thought and practice, because I am attempting to develop a specifically acoustic jurisprudence, my approach is necessarily wide ranging and eclectic. Although I always attempt to keep institutional questions and the practice of judgment front and centre, I shift regularly between different registers of thought and forms of engagement from a variety of different disciplines. Nevertheless, the distinction which gives each part of the book its structure and rhythm—between *law's sonic imagination*, on the one hand, and the *judicial soundscape*, on the other—does bring with it a number of important methodological consequences.

In the first chapter in each Part of the book—that is, in Chapters 3, 5, and 7 respectively—I am interested in how the ICTR thought about acoustics, how it imagined song, speech, and sound to work, and the consequences of this imagination for the determination the Trial Chamber would eventually reach. To that end, in these chapters I am working mostly with the documentary archive: the indictments, trial transcripts, expert evidence, judgments, and the like. In each case I undertake a *critical reading* practice with a special attention to matters of acoustics, a kind of *reading for sound* if you like. I am trying to track, understand, and critique the diverse techniques by which the Tribunal made the acoustic amenable to legal analysis. In particular, I am reading for the way in which the ICTR's sonic imagination revealed itself during the course of Bikindi's trial at the level of doctrine, rhetoric, politics, and so on. In this regard I am just as interested

[80] See UNSC Res 1966 (22 December 2010) arts 1, 27.

in the discourse at trial as in the judgments that finally eventuated. My question is not whether the Tribunal's various doctrinal concerns were correctly applied to the Rwandan soundscape, but what kind of account of the soundscape those doctrinal concerns facilitated and produced. How did the various different legal actors involved in the *Bikindi* case present their arguments in relation to acoustics? What can the way in which song, speech, and sound were discussed at trial tell us about this institution in particular and about legal thought in general?

By contrast, in the second chapter of each pair—so in Chapters 4, 6, and 8 respectively—I am less interested in how the Tribunal thought about sound than in how it used it. I am concerned with how the courtroom was *itself* soundful, the huge variety of techniques by means of which sound was put to work in court, how it was deployed, ignored, co-opted, or otherwise perceived. When I consider the judicial soundscape then, I am interested both in how the Tribunal sounded in the *Bikindi* case and what the written materials reveal about how those involved related to the judicial soundscape. On the one hand, I undertake a practice of *critical listening*. Some of this listening took place during my visit to the ICTR in 2011, where most days for a month I sat in the public gallery at ongoing trials, listening over the court-provided headphones. Even though Bikindi's trial was already well concluded by the time I arrived at the Tribunal, the proceedings I was able to attend operated in substantially similar ways, meaning that I was able to bring to my analysis of Bikindi's trial a much richer understanding of its performative context than if I only had the recordings to go on. Nevertheless, much of the analysis here is based on the audio and audio-visual archive. A lot of my listening took place in Melbourne, in the library, at home, and always through good headphones. Because I was listening to mp3s, I was able to play and replay pertinent moments as many times as I chose. Sometimes, I just listened: to a few minutes, an hour, or a whole day of proceedings. But often I had the corresponding transcripts out in front of me, meaning that I was able to direct my listening to any episodes that stood out on the face of the text as potentially interesting: a comment by a judge, witness, or lawyer, for instance, on how to listen or otherwise engage with the soundscape. My critical listening practice was frequently supplemented therefore with a practice of *reading for listening*.

And so to the analysis. My hope is that what follows will provide the practices briefly described above with a little more texture. As I say, this book is intended as an opening not an end. It has been envisioned as a preliminary exploration and exemplification: not just an argument for an acoustic jurisprudence, but an attempt actually to show what it might mean to start taking responsibility for questions of sound in legal thought and practice.

PART 2

SONG

3

The Musicology of Judgment

What happens when songs like Bikindi's become the object of legal thought and practice? How does an institution like the ICTR deal with musicological questions? By means of what adjudicative techniques and procedures? What theories, assumptions, and prejudices circulated in the *Bikindi* case, why and with what juridical results? These are the questions addressed in this chapter. They are important for an acoustic jurisprudence because if institutions like the ICTR are going to assert jurisdiction in relation to songs like Bikindi's, they need to be able to provide an adequate account of how music means, what it does, and the particular ways in which artists can and should be held responsible for it. To the extent that the international community shares a 'sense of solidarity' with the victims of the Rwandan genocide, as members of a 'common humanity', we surely also share 'a collective responsibility to respond to those wrongs by calling the perpetrators to account'.[1] Central to that calling to account is our ability to do so with good reasons. That is the demand to which this chapter responds: the responsibility we all share—lawyers, judges, and scholars alike—to take seriously the *musicology of judgment*.

The chapter begins with the initial presentation of Bikindi and his songs at trial, which I suggest was invariably in one of two ways. As a matter of rhetoric, Bikindi's songs were consistently treated as either seductive or civilizing. Bikindi himself was either a Siren or Orpheus. The chapter then shows how, in spite of this rhetoric, by the time it came to judgment, music had nevertheless become irrelevant as far as the Trial Chamber was concerned. Doctrinally, all that mattered was the songs' 'meaning and interpretation', and this was taken to be discernible entirely at the level of their lyrics, quite apart from their sound, setting, or performance. In the final section of the chapter I argue that both approaches involve a profound misunderstanding of how song works. Both can be traced back to the same source in the texts of the international law of freedom of expression.

[1] Antony Duff, 'Authority and Responsibility in International Criminal Law' in Samantha Besson and John Tasioulas (eds), *The Philosophy of International Law* (Oxford University Press, 2010) 602; Raimond Gaita, *A Common Humanity: Thinking about Love and Truth and Justice* (Routledge, 2002).

Rhetoric: Orpheus or the Sirens?

Bikindi's trial officially commenced just after one o'clock on 18 September 2006.[2] From one forty-five until a little after two the Tribunal's Prosecutor Hassan Jallow delivered his opening statement in which he elaborated on the central points of the indictment.[3] After a brief historical account of the genocide Jallow turned to the music question immediately. He was absolutely clear about what he thinks music is for, and why accordingly he considers Bikindi's songs to have been so particularly heinous:

> The Accused, Bikindi, had a talent in art and music, a talent which normally should be directed to enriching the cultural heritage of any community, directed at strengthening its social cohesion and solidarity, but Bikindi chose a different objective for his acknowledged talent. He consciously and deliberately made his artistic works the vehicle for inciting other Rwandans who [respected] his talent to indulge in the atrocities of 1994.[4]

Bikindi's music had 'infected people's minds with ethnic hatred and persecution', he said, and had 'served to mobilise the youth … to join the *Interahamwe* militia'.[5]

Consider the binary according to which this argument operates. On the one hand we have music in general, as it 'normally should' be: both an object and a technique of 'culture' and a means of strengthening the social bond: 'community', 'cohesion', 'solidarity'. On the other hand we have Bikindi's music: 'infectious', a technology of 'mobilization' and 'indulgence'. From a rhetorical and musicological perspective, the tropes here are utterly familiar, even ancient. On one side, the logic of Orpheus: father of song, master of Apollo's lyre, enchanter of the Gods, and pioneer of civilization itself.[6] On the other, the Sirens, whose song leads not to civilization but to death. Throughout Bikindi's trial his songs would be cast as operating at one or other of these two rhetorical poles.

[2] The first of numerous pre-trial hearings was held on 4 April 2002. *Prosecutor v Bikindi* (Transcript) ICTR-01-72-T, T Ch III (Various dates) ('*Bikindi* transcript') 4 April 2002, 'Initial Appearance'.

[3] The ICTR has had four Prosecutors during its lifetime. The first three, Richard Goldstone, Louise Arbour, and Carla Del Ponte, were also responsible for prosecutions at the ICTY. In 2003 Hassan Jallow took sole responsibility of the ICTR. Although it was Del Ponte who had been responsible for Bikindi's indictment and arrest, it was Jallow who administered the bulk of his prosecution. As far as the *Bikindi* case was concerned, he appeared only twice more during proceedings, at the delivery of the judgments at first instance and on appeal.

[4] *Bikindi* transcript, 18 September 2006, 4. The English transcript actually reads 'Rwandans who *represented* his talent' but, suspecting that this was not correct, I checked the passage against the French version, which reads 'Rwandais qui *respectaient* son talent' and amended the translation above accordingly. See *Prosecutor v Bikindi* (Transcript) (French) ICTR-01-72-T, T Ch III (Various dates) ('*Bikindi* transcript (French)') 18 September 2006, 5.

[5] *Bikindi* transcript, 18 September 2006, 4.

[6] Pindar, *The Complete Odes*, ed Stephen Instone, trans Anthony Verity (Oxford University Press, 2007) 4.4.315 ('The Pythian Odes').

Naturalizing Orpheus

The Orphic myth is one of the oldest and most familiar in the Western tradition, of which—as I noted in Chapter 2—the ICTR is undeniably a part.[7] Following the death of his bride Eurydice, Orpheus travels to the underworld where he sings to the gods and implores them to return her to the land of the living. Finding themselves moved by the beauty and power of Orpheus' song, the gods grant him his wish on the condition that he not look back at Eurydice as he leads her home. Right at the last Orpheus fails to do so, Eurydice slips back into the darkness and he is forced to return home to Thrace alone, his grief now redoubled. 'But still he sings', Vanessa Agnew explains, 'and his new listeners are the ones we remember him for'.[8] At the end of the sixteenth century, English jurist and poet George Puttenham explained the enduring significance of the myth as follows. 'And Orpheus assembled the wilde beasts', he writes, 'to come in heards to harken to his musicke and by that means made them tame, implying thereby, how by his discreete and wholesome lessons uttered in harmonie and with melodious instruments, he brought the rude and savage people to a more civill and orderly life'.[9] For philosopher Vladimir Jankélévitch, writing in the twentieth century, the Orphic tradition presents music as that which through its beauty 'humanises and civilises'.[10] It is a technique of spiritual nourishment and of social harmony.

This is precisely the logic we find in the Prosecutor's opening statement, even if he makes no mention of Orpheus. Music is 'enriching' because it is beautiful. And as such it is to be consumed and collected for the sake of the 'heritage': an art object. Such is the logic of the museum and the concert hall. It is both peculiarly Western and highly contemporary. The long road to the eventual realignment of music with cultural rather than use value—or, to be more precise, the establishment of cultural value *as* a privileged form of use value—began only during the Middle Ages with the *jongleur*, and reached its peak in the eighteenth century with Romanticism and the birth of the composer as 'auteur'.[11] Previously music had been perceived largely as a matter of craft, a 'handmaid' to other practices such as education, worship, dance, and—notably—war.[12] Music was a tool, it was productive. It 'served to enhance the sanctity and dignity of worship, the glamour of

[7] For a couple of well-known iterations of the Orphic myth, see Ovid, *The Metamorphoses*, trans David R Slavitt (Johns Hopkins University Press, 1994); Horace, *The Poetic Art: A Translation of Horace's 'Ars Poetica'*, trans Charles H Sisson (Carcanet Press, 1975).

[8] Vanessa Agnew, *Enlightenment Orpheus: The Power of Music in Other Worlds* (Oxford University Press, 2008) 9.

[9] George Puttenham, *The Arte of English Poesie*, ed Gladys Doidge Willcock and Alice Walker (first published 1589, Cambridge University Press, 1939) 6.

[10] Vladimir Jankélévitch, *Music and the Ineffable*, trans Carolyn Abbate (Princeton University Press, 2003) [trans of: *La Musique et l'ineffable* (first published 1961)] 4.

[11] Jacques Attali, *Noise: The Political Economy of Music*, trans Brian Massumi (University of Minnesota Press, 1985) [trans of: *Bruits: Essai sur l'économie politique de la musique* (first published 1977)] 12–18.

[12] Joscelyn Godwin, *Harmonies of Heaven and Earth: The Spiritual Dimension of Music from Antiquity to the Avant-Garde* (Thames and Hudson, 1987) 99.

the festivities at court, and the overall splendour of ceremony'.[13] If it was beautiful or engaging, all the more so. As an object of 'culture', by contrast, music is far more passive. That is, it is active only insofar as it civilizes and soothes. Music 'pacifies the monsters of instinct in all of us and tames passion's wild animals'. It is Orphic, a 'gentleness that makes gentle'.[14] From a more contemporary perspective, this is the line of reasoning from which the mythic 'Mozart effect'[15] flows and which somehow manages to ignore the fact that high-ranking Nazis were listening to Beethoven, Schubert, and Verdi quite literally as they ordered the Jews and other undesirables to their deaths.[16] Music on this account is medicinal, therapeutic, an analeptic for the soul.

As a technique of 'social cohesion' and 'solidarity', by contrast, music is effective because it is sonorous, which is to say public. Because sound moves inescapably through time and space, because its force is not necessarily limited by linguistic community, and because we do not after all have ear-lids, music is the quintessentially shared art form. This is why, since George Harrison and Ravi Shankar's pioneering 'Concert for Bangladesh' in 1971 and 1985's gargantuan 'Live Aid' which is said to have garnered around two billion listeners worldwide, today the musical 'mega-event' persists unabated. It is also why they tend to address themselves towards issues of international justice. Nelson Mandela's Wembley 'Birthday Party', the 'Human Rights Now' tour for Amnesty International, Bono and Bob Geldof's 'Jubilee 2000' and 'Live 8' campaigns for the relief of Third World debt, 2014's 'Band Aid 30' in response to the Ebola epidemic in West Africa: whatever doubts one might have about the effectiveness of these projects or the motives of those who tune in to them, the singular ability of music to bring together and influence people on this sort of a scale is not in question.[17]

What the Prosecutor does in his opening statement is first to naturalize the Orphic position and then to contrast it with Bikindi's. It is not that music is *capable* of enriching the 'cultural heritage' of a given community. It 'normally should' do so, presumably everywhere, all of the time. Similarly, it is not merely that music is *capable* of strengthening 'social cohesion and solidarity'. That is its proper function, an ethical, musicological, and juridical imperative. The fact that music's peculiar ability to bring people together also accounts for its remarkable effectiveness as a means of propaganda and poisonous nationalism is conveniently elided. These

[13] Jürgen Habermas, *The Structural Transformation of the Public Sphere: An Inquiry into a Category of Bourgeois Society*, trans Thomas Burger with Frederick Lawrence (Polity Press, 1992) [trans of: *Strukturwandel der Öffentlichkeit: Untersuchungen zu einer Kategorie der bürgerlichen Gesellschaft* (first published 1962)] 39.

[14] Jankélévitch (2003) 4.

[15] See Don Campbell, *The Mozart Effect for Children: Awakening Your Child's Mind, Health and Creativity with Music* (Harper Collins, 2000).

[16] See Shirli Gilbert, *Music in the Holocaust: Confronting Life in the Nazi Ghettos and Camps* (Oxford University Press, 2005), especially chs 3 and 4 on Sachsenhausen and Auschwitz.

[17] On this concert tradition, see Reebee Garofolo (ed), *Rockin' the Boat: Mass Music and Mass Movements* (South End Press, 1992); John Street, Seth Hague, and Heather Savigny, 'Playing to the Crowd: The Role of Music and Musicians in Political Participation', *The British Journal of Politics and International Relations* 10(2) (2008) 269.

are presented as corruptions of music's true function and purpose rather than the inevitable potentialities of a medium and an art-form whose structure is essentially pharmacological, or ambivalent.[18]

Bikindi as Siren

If Orphic music is enriching and cohesive, that of the Sirens is insidious and seductive. Overwhelming of the will and the rational mind, it operates on the body and at the level of base desire. In Homer's famous telling, the force of the Sirens' song was so beautiful, so powerful and affective, that it drew anyone within earshot inexorably to ruin on the rocky shores of the island which the Sirens inhabited. Odysseus could prevent himself from the same fate only by having himself bound to his ship's mast while his crew sailed on, their own ears plugged with wax.[19] Sirenic music is bewitching, then. It represents precisely music's abuse, the negation of Orpheus.[20] It has one purpose and one purpose only: 'to reroute, mislead, and delay'.[21] With their song, as Jankélévitch explains, the Sirens 'derail the dialectic, the law of the itinerary that leads our mind toward duty and truth'.[22]

In the Prosecutor's account, this is exactly the effect attributed to Bikindi's songs. 'Bikindi chose a different objective for his acknowledged talent', Jallow says. He 'consciously and deliberately' made music that would encourage his fellow Rwandans to 'indulge in the atrocities of 1994'. His music 'infected' peoples' minds and served to 'mobilize' the youth. The language of 'infection' is revealing. The word brings to mind both memorability and disease. The 'infectious' qualities of music are what account today for the peculiar effectiveness of marketing jingles, branded 'soundmarks',[23] our considerable—and often unwelcome—ability to recall nursery rhymes and pop hooks. This is the phenomenon of the 'ear worm':[24] that 'catchy tune that you cannot get out of your head, the vocal refrain,

[18] The classic example is the Pied Piper of Hamelin, whose enchanting flute would turn out to be 'at once angelic and demonic', just as effective for evil as for good. See Adriana Cavarero, *For More than One Voice: Toward a Philosophy of Vocal Expression*, trans Paul A Kottman (Stanford University Press, 2005) [trans of: *A piu voci: Per una filosofia dell'espressione vocale* (first published 2003)] 74. On the structure of the *pharmakon* see Jacques Derrida, *Dissemination*, trans Barbara Johnson (The Athlone Press, 1981) [trans of: *La dissémination* (first published 1972)] 61–172.

[19] Homer, *The Odyssey*, trans Walter Shewring (Oxford University Press, 1980) XII. For a book-length treatment of the myth of the Sirens, see Linda Phyllis Austern and Inna Naroditskaya (eds), *The Music of the Sirens* (Indiana University Press, 2006).

[20] It would turn out to be Orpheus alone who could vanquish the Sirens when, coming to the aid of Jason's *Argonaut*, he drowned out their song with the power and beauty of his lyre. See Apollonius Rhodius, *The Argonautica*, trans Robert C Seaton (Harvard University Press, 1961); Pincar (2007); and generally Agnew (2008) ch 1 ('Argonaut Orpheus').

[21] Jankélévitch (2003) 3. [22] Jankélévitch (2003) 3.

[23] In its original usage by R Murray Schafer, the term 'soundmark' referred to acoustic features of the soundscape of a given time and place: the sound of a waterfall or birdsong, the town clock or churchbells. Today the term can also be applied to certain features of the increasingly regulated sonic ecology of brand identity. See R Murray Schafer, *The Soundscape: Our Sonic Environment and the Tuning of the World* (Knopf, 1977) 10.

[24] Daniel Levitin, *This Is Your Brain on Music: Understanding a Human Obsession* (Atlantic, 2006) 155.

the infectious rhythm or the addictive riff'.[25] Or again, 'an audio insinuation that seeps into the ears and taps out mnemonics on its drums'.[26] The sense both of invasion and bodiliness is key. For Steve Goodman, music is 'virological': a flow of 'contagious vibrations'.[27] Music as infection 'seeps' in against your will. It is addictive. It works directly on the unwitting and unwilling nervous system: invasive and overwhelming.

This relation between music and the body is deployed in the Prosecutor's opening statement in a second way too. Bikindi's music is said to have 'mobilized' the youth to join the *Interahamwe* militia forces: that is, from the Latin *mobilis/movere*, it moved them to do so. Tellingly, the same sort of language appears throughout the various manifestations of the indictment, penned years earlier.[28] Therein, 'as a result of the mobilizing effect of Simon Bikindi's music, members of the Ballet ... were recruited into the *Interahamwe* militia'.[29] 'Bikindi's musical compositions and live performances ... were elements of the plan to mobilize civilian militias to destroy, in whole or in part, the Tutsi'.[30] Their purpose was to 'sensitize the listening public'[31] and to 'animate' them: from the Latin *animare* meaning 'to instil with life', to 'invigorate'. Bikindi apparently 'regularly performed his musical compositions at animation sessions at *Interahamwe* meetings and at political gatherings'.[32] And these 'animation sessions ... were often a prelude or a motivating factor in anti-Tutsi violence against individuals and property in the vicinity ...'.[33]

What we have here is a lexicon of the body. 'Infect', 'mobilize', 'sensitize', 'animate'. It is no coincidence that the Prosecutor chose to frame the act of genocide itself as one of 'indulgence'. To indulge, after all, is to yield to a desire, to give one's rational mind over to the raw pull of affect and sensation: just like Odysseus, to allow oneself to be seduced. The implication is this. At least part of what made Bikindi's songs so insidious as far as the prosecution was concerned was the possibility that they were irresistible: bewitching, seductive, even magical. Bikindi's songs had 'derailed the dialectic'.

Such rhetoric both persisted and intensified as the trial continued. One of the prosecution's expert witnesses Jean de Dieu Karangwa, for instance, sought to draw out the difference between speech and song. 'When you listen to a speech', he argued, 'you can remember one or two main themes thereof, but a song can

[25] Steve Goodman, *Sonic Warfare: Sound, Affect and the Ecology of Fear* (MIT Press, 2010) 147.

[26] Kodwo Eshun, *More Brilliant than the Sun* (Quartet Books, 1998) 143.

[27] Goodman (2010) 155.

[28] There were three in total: *Prosecutor v Bikindi* (Indictment) ICTR-01-72-I (4 July 2001) ('*Bikindi* indictment'); *Prosecutor v Bikindi* (Amended Indictment) ICTR-01-72-I (22 October 2003) ('*Bikindi* amended indictment'); *Prosecutor v Bikindi* (Second Amended Indictment) ICTR-01-72-I (15 June 2005) ('*Bikindi* second amended indictment').

[29] *Bikindi* second amended indictment, para 16.

[30] *Bikindi* indictment, para 16.

[31] *Bikindi* indictment, para 10.

[32] *Bikindi* indictment, para 29.

[33] *Bikindi* indictment, para 30. The language of 'animation' also featured regularly at trial. Sometimes it was even employed by Bikindi's defence. See *Bikindi* transcript: 20 September 2006, 25; 2 October 2006, 31; 10 October 2006, 11; 25 September 2007, 69; 26 September 2007, 47; 27 September 2007, 52.

be repeated and danced to, day in, day out',[34] 'ingraining' its 'message' all the more completely 'in the memory of [the] people'.[35] In the report Karangwa submitted along with fellow expert Gamaliel Mbonimana, the same idea was put forward more forcefully again. 'A single song', apparently, 'could be more effective than a thousand speeches on a particular subject'. Music's mnemonic power made Bikindi's songs 'formidable weapons for mass persuasion' he said.[36] Citing a book from 1939 tellingly entitled *Rape of the Masses: The Psychology of Totalitarian Political Propaganda*,[37] Karangwa argued at trial that 'in order to subject people, music resorts to songs captivating songs [sic], which are imposed on people, who will repeat them mechanically and actually get some sort of a high. So—in order to master the public and actually blend them into a homogenous mass, making them so malleable that you obtain exactly what you are seeking'.[38]

As a mode of communication and a technique of subjugation, music here is effective to the point of being both physically and psychically overwhelming. Like Ecstasy at a rave,[39] it is capable of transforming thinking individuals into a seething mass of obedient bodies: 'mechanical', 'homogenous', 'malleable', entranced.[40] As Karangwa put it in relation to one song of Bikindi's in particular: 'Before the 1990 October war, people got carried away by the *Twasezereye* rhythm'.[41] When you listen to Bikindi's songs, 'you just feel like dancing'.[42] That is, in spite of yourself. In his closing statement, delivered on 26 May 2008, counsel for the prosecution (so not the Prosecutor himself this time) summarized the point like this. Radio RTLM, apparently, had 'achieved a maximum impact in relation to the slaughter by playing Bikindi's music several times a day, day after day, day after day'.[43] The songs, he said, were 'intoxicating'.[44] They were Sirenic.

[34] *Bikindi* transcript, 14 February 2007, 3.

[35] *Bikindi* transcript, 14 February 2007, 4.

[36] Exhibit No P73(E), 'Prosecution Joint Expert Report of Gamaliel Mbonimana and Jean de Dieu Karangwa: "Thematic Analysis of the Songs"', *Prosecutor v Bikindi*, ICTR-01-72-0152 (13 September 2006) 5.

[37] Cited by Mbonimana and Karangwa as Sergei Tchakhotine, *Mob Rape Prompted by Political Propaganda* (Editions Gallimard, 1952). The book is more commonly known in English by the title given above. Exhibit No P73(E), *Prosecutor v Bikindi* (13 September 2006), 26.

[38] *Bikindi* transcript, 14 February 2007, 4.

[39] Karangwa's comparison between the listening experience and drug taking—this idea that listeners 'actually get some sort of high'—invokes a very common theme both in musicological discourse and many socio-musical practices right back to the earliest Dionysian rights of the pre-democratic ancient Greeks. For a contemporary example, see Simon Reynolds, *Generation Ecstasy: Into the World of Techno and Rave Culture* (Routledge, 1999).

[40] For discussion of the history of music in relation to trance and other forms of possession, see Gilbert Rouget, *Music and Trance: A Theory of the Relations between Music and Possession*, trans Brunhilde Beibuyck (University of Chicago Press, 1985) [trans of: *La musique et la transe: Esquisse d'une théorie générale des relations de la musique et de la posse* (first published 1980)].

[41] *Bikindi* transcript, 15 February 2007, 33.

[42] *Bikindi* transcript, 13 February 2007, 11.

[43] *Bikindi* transcript, 26 May 2008, 15.

[44] *Bikindi* transcript, 26 May 2008, 10–11.

Bikindi as Orpheus

Far from attempting to debunk the prosecution's rhetoric in this respect, Bikindi's defence team simply wanted to do a bit of recasting. On 24 September 2007 at a little after nine in the morning, Andreas O'Shea opened the case for the defence. Bikindi had been totally misrepresented by the prosecution, he said. Far from the 'highly political' man they had painted him as, possessed of a 'deep hatred of Tutsis' and 'determined in fulfilling the mission of genocide' by means of his songs,[45] the true picture was as follows. Bikindi was a musician, an artist. He had been born in 1954 to a 'blacksmith' father and an 'agriculturalist' mother in Rwerere *commune* in the north west of Rwanda.

> Both of his parents were dancers and had a passion for music. His mother had an extraordinary voice and was invited to baptisms and weddings, and his father played the guitar and danced. And that is where Bikindi's real passion, music, was born.
>
> Bikindi himself plays several traditional instruments, the *inanga*, the *iningiri*, the *umuduli*, and the *ikembe*. He has developed, without training, an extraordinary talent for singing, a talent which he began in composition when he was 16 and 17 years of age. His first song of note which began to make him famous was, as a boy, *Icyayi cyo ku Mulindi*, 'The Tea of Mulindi'.[46] From that moment this man began to be noticed.
>
> He was in particular noticed by the minister of sports and youth when he pursued his activities later as a teacher. And he formed a ballet for the school, and the minister came to see the ballet and was so impressed and said, 'Who is this man who can perform such beautiful things?' And that is how he was sent to do studies, further studies, at university, and then brought within the ministry not as a politician, but to direct the cultural aspects and to encourage that ballets throughout the *communes* would be brought into place.[47]

For the purposes of his defence, Bikindi wasn't a Siren, he was Orpheus. An artist and auteur, even a genius of sorts, a child prodigy, his 'extraordinary' musical talent was presented as being at once natural, because untutored, and traditional, because a part both of his family's and the wider Rwandan heritage. Far from being insidious or in any way dangerous or malevolent, his music was strikingly 'beautiful' as the minister's astonishment attests. And Bikindi's deployment of it, both originally as a teacher and later by virtue of his involvement with the ministry, was framed as enriching rather than seductive, both civilizing and gentle, and crucial, moreover, to the propagation of art throughout the community.

Above all, though, what O'Shea wanted to emphasize in the opening words of his case for the defence was precisely Bikindi's status *as* a musician: his one 'real passion'. The remainder of his opening statement was devoted to the reinforcement of this simple claim. Bikindi 'was not interested in politics, he was interested

[45] *Bikindi* transcript, 24 September 2007, 4.

[46] The English transcript reads 'His first song of note which began to make him famous was "As a Boy", *Icyayi cyo ku Mulindi*, "The Tea of Mulindi"'. Suspecting that might not be accurate, I checked this against the French transcript. Sure enough, it does not put 'as a boy' (*comme enfant*) in quotation marks and, I have amended the English above accordingly. See *Bikindi* transcript (French), 24 September 2007, 6.

[47] *Bikindi* transcript, 24 September 2007, 4–5.

in music'. 'By the end of this case', O'Shea argued, 'Your Honours will be sure that Mr. Bikindi was a musician, and not a politician'. Again, just in case it wasn't clear enough already, Bikindi 'was a man passioned about music, not politics'.[48] This was a line of argument upon which defence witnesses continued to insist at trial. One testified, for instance, that 'Bikindi did not make any speech. All that he did was to sing'.[49] According to another, Bikindi's 'songs were different. They had to do with entertainment, simply'.[50] Another still did not think it 'possible for youngsters to be led to join political parties because of songs or by songs'.[51] During his own testimony in November 2007, Bikindi insisted that despite his political office he was nevertheless not 'a politician'.[52] He was a musician, a singer, an artist: Orpheus. This is why his songs were consistently framed by the defence as art rather than argument, as beautiful and civilizing as opposed to seductive. To be a musician, they wanted to suggest, was precisely *not* to be genocidal. 'Simon Bikindi is, arguably, one of the most brilliant musical icons of Rwanda', O'Shea claimed in his closing statement to the Tribunal, 'but he lives in the wrong time'.[53]

Songs without Music

I am not suggesting that either prosecution or defence were necessarily conscious in their deployment of these classic rhetorical tropes. Perhaps they were, perhaps not. Either way, what is so interesting about the way these two poles or figures were allowed to frame the discussion at trial is precisely the extent to which they went *un*-interrogated and *un*-developed. So much of the discourse was allowed to subsist precisely at the level of truism and cliché and, moreover, with such an exorbitant and moralistic tone. No one seriously questioned the rhetoric on either side. No one asked whether music really did have the affective properties that both prosecution and defence wanted to attribute to it, or if it did, to enquire into how this might work in any detail. What's more, they had no incentive whatsoever to do so because in doctrinal terms, this dimension of Bikindi's songs didn't matter anyway. The question of affect was left entirely to the whims of an adversarial system geared towards rhetorical excess.

What I want to suggest in this section of the chapter is that the limitations of the Tribunal's musicological discourse in this respect must be understood in relation to a much larger issue it had in relation to Bikindi's songs. A close reading of the Chamber's judgment at first instance reveals that by this point, music simply wasn't relevant in juridical terms at all. This was because the Tribunal's sole concern as far as Bikindi's songs were concerned was their 'meaning and interpretation' which

48 *Bikindi* transcript, 24 September 2007, 5.
49 *Bikindi* transcript, 25 September 2007, 34.
50 *Bikindi* transcript, 5 October 2007, 31.
51 *Bikindi* transcript, 28 September 2007, 5–6.
52 *Bikindi* transcript, 1 November 2007, 11.
53 *Bikindi* transcript, 26 May 2008, 19.

it sought to address exclusively at the level of lyrics: entirely divorced from their acoustic 'setting', their very existence *as song*.

'Score and background music'

The Chamber devoted some twenty pages of its one hundred and sixteen page long judgment directly to the matter of Bikindi's songs. Of those twenty pages, eighteen were given over to the question of the songs' 'meaning and interpretation' and another couple to what the Chamber considered to be the separate question of their 'deployment'.[54] In total, however, the specifically musical qualities of the songs were given just two paragraphs, so that the Chamber could then go on to treat the three songs in question as if they had been nothing but texts all along: as if the particularity of their form—their sonority—was completely irrelevant. The pertinent section of the judgment reads like this. The heading is already highly revealing:

> **7.1.1.4 Score and Background Music**
>
> The Chamber notes that several witnesses highlighted the background music of the songs, for example, the accompanying sitar, the mixed Rwandan-Congolese rhythm and the accompanying traditional dance. Many witnesses spoke positively of his music, describing it as captivating, catchy, having good rhythm and melody, and making listeners want to dance.
>
> While the Chamber does not doubt Bikindi is a talented and popular musician, the Chamber is less interested in the score than the lyrics of his compositions. While the Defence argued that the principal purpose of a song is usually entertainment based on melody and rhythm, and need not even have a message, the Chamber finds that, if anything, emphasising the popularity of the songs may have the effect of assisting the Prosecution's case regarding their impact.[55]

The Chamber begins by separating Bikindi's songs into parts, a distinction which it would sustain for the remainder of the judgment. The 'lyrics', which are foregrounded and primary, and the 'music', which is backgrounded and secondary: 'several witnesses highlighted the background music of the songs, for example the accompanying sitar … '.[56] Music here is mere 'accompaniment', embellishment. It might be 'captivating', 'catchy', 'rhythmic', 'melodic' and eminently danceable, but we understand immediately that these factors are not significant juridically. Music may well contribute to a song's 'popularity', but when it comes to its 'meaning and interpretation' it is simply not relevant. Where meaning is concerned, the Chamber professes to be more 'interested' in the lyrics. As if the act of interpretation were simply a matter of stating a preference between the two and moving on.

From a musicological perspective, such an approach is problematic to say the least. An example will be helpful. Consider Bruce Springsteen's well-known hit

[54] *Prosecutor v Bikindi* (Judgement) ICTR-01-72-T, T Ch III (2 December 2008) ('*Bikindi* judgment') paras 186–264.

[55] *Bikindi* judgment, paras 195–6.

[56] *Bikindi* judgment, para 195.

Born in the USA, for instance. Lyrically, it is clearly a 'protest' song. It's about growing up as a downtrodden working class American:

Born down in a dead man's town,
The first kick I took was when I hit the ground
You end up like a dog that's been beat too much
'Til you spend half your life just covering up.

And then being sent over to fight in Vietnam 'to go and kill the yellow man' only to return to a country with very little sympathy.

Down in the shadow of the penitentiary,
Out by the gas fires of the refinery
I'm ten years down the road
Nowhere to run, ain't got nowhere to go.[57]

Lyrically, *Born in the USA* is relatively transparent. You would think, therefore, that the famous central refrain around which the song is organised—'Born in the USA!'—ought to sound ironic, sour or acerbic. But it doesn't. From a musical perspective, things are far more complex. Musically, the chorus is positively triumphant, anthemic. The apparent irony of the chorus' lyrics is subverted in their setting and performance: their sound. What comes across to the listener, rather, is pride, affirmation, patriotism.

And so it was that Ronald Reagan requested the song for use in his presidential campaign in 1984, leading to a very public debate concerning the song's 'correct' interpretation in both the news media and the press.[58] Commentators on the left ridiculed Reagan and his team for having completely 'misunderstood' the song and its politics. Springsteen was a radical they said, a champion of the working man, and the chorus was a sneer at a country which was systematically betraying its people. But where they had the song's lyrics on their side, the right had its sound. As conservative columnist George Will explained in a review of a Springsteen concert at the time, 'I have not got a clue about Springsteen's politics, if any, but flags get waved at his concerts while he sings songs about hard times. He is no whiner, and the recitation of closed factories and other problems always seems punctuated by a grand, cheerful, affirmation; "Born in the USA!"'[59] He wasn't wrong. As Cowie and Boehm explain, 'for partisan critics looking for an anthem or a protest in 1984, "Born in the USA" had the right "words" in the wrong "setting" or vice versa'. But the artistic decision to juxtapose the song's two contrasting dimensions is not simply a mistake, and it cannot simply be dismissed by means of a mere 'preference' one way or the other. What both sides of the debate missed was that the heart

[57] Bruce Springsteen, *Born in the USA* (Columbia Records, 1984).

[58] See Jefferson R Cowie and Lauren Boehm, 'Dead Man's Town: "Born in the USA", Social History and Working-Class Identity', *American Quarterly* 58(2) (2006) 353, 360.

[59] Quoted in Jim Cullen, *Born in the USA: Bruce Springsteen and the American Tradition* (Wesleyan University Press, 1997) 7.

of the song 'rests at the conjuncture not the selection of its internal oppositions'.[60] Music *and* lyric. Patriotism *and* critique.

Bikindi's songs are no different. What the Chamber failed to realise, and what neither side had attempted to argue at trial, is that the issue in lyrical analysis is never just words but words *in performance*: acoustic, resonant, sonorous. Lyrics, as socio-musicologist Simon Frith argues, are a form of rhetoric or oratory. 'We have to treat them in terms of the persuasive relationship set up between singer and listener. From this perspective', he writes, 'you might say that a song doesn't exist to convey the meaning of the words. The words exist to convey the meaning of the song'.[61] The meaning of a song, then, is always a product of both sound and semantics. The foreground/background distinction invoked by the Chamber as if it were somehow inevitable or obvious was simply a fallacy.[62] Its failure to consider even for a moment that music might bear some relation to the songs' 'meaning and interpretation', rather than simply maximize their entertainment value and popularity, must be understood as involving a profound misunderstanding of how songs work, what they do and how they mean.[63]

In this regard, the Chamber's use of the words 'score' and 'composition' as synonyms for music is also highly revealing. At the level of the score, the separation between 'music' and 'lyrics' is virtually complete.[64] Once both have been rendered graphically as script, the notion that music is nothing more than an embellishment of a central and privileged lyrical content or 'message' is not necessarily so difficult to arrive at. But a score is, first and foremost, an *aide-memoire*: a technology for the subsequent production of sounds, and a necessarily incomplete one at that. 'Think of all the things a singer or instrumentalist can do', Michael Chanan writes, 'for which a conventional score rarely contains even the vaguest suggestion, such as *vibrato*, *portamento* and *rubato*: the wobbles, the scoops and slides, and the subtle alterations in tempo, not to mention variations in tone colour, which are nevertheless regarded as necessary parts of creative interpretation'.[65] Music and score were never equivalent. The Chamber's elision between the two as if they were

[60] See Cowie and Boehm (2006) 360.

[61] Simon Frith, *Performing Rites: Evaluating Popular Music* (Oxford University Press, 1996) 166.

[62] Sometimes a song *can* seem to foreground its lyrics. It can make them particularly clear or easy to discern. But even then the lyric needs to be *voiced*, given melodic shape and emotional weight. And there are plenty of counter-examples where the lyrics are not foregrounded at all. My Bloody Valentine, for instance, were one of the most popular and acclaimed 'alternative rock' or 'shoegaze' acts of the late 1980s and early 1990s, but fans who know any more than a handful of the lyrics to their seminal 1991 album 'Loveless' must be few and far between. The guitars are so constant, so thick and distorted on the album's opening track 'Only Shallow', for example, that Bilinda Butcher's vocals can only barely be made out underneath. So far away from being an error in the production process, this quality of the song is precisely one of the things that marks the band's sound as distinctive and important. For a detailed account of My Bloody Valentine's aesthetic, see David Fisher, *My Bloody Valentine's Loveless: The Epitome of a Genre* (VDM Verlag, 2008).

[63] For discussion of the relations between music and lyric, see Frith (1996) 158–202.

[64] I say 'virtually' because, even in writing, a language always has a certain 'music' to it, the 'sound' of the words in one's head, which it is precisely a part of the poet's craft to exploit. See Chapter 5.

[65] Michael Chanan, *Musica Practica: The Social Practice of Western Music from Gregorian Chant to Postmodernism* (Verso, 1994) 77.

interchangeable expresses a dematerialization, a willingness to treat music as if its sonority were somehow marginal or irrelevant, a preference for the visual and composorial over the acoustic or performative, a form of juridical deafness.

Evidence: experts and expertise

The Chamber did not just pluck this approach to Bikindi's songs from the ether. Although it was never quite made explicit, the approach we find in distilled form in the *Bikindi* judgment was already clearly operative at trial, working alongside the sort of rhetoric we traced in the previous section of this chapter. Numerous witnesses were called upon during the course of the trial to give evidence, both to explain how Bikindi's songs were received at the time of the genocide and to venture their opinion as to what his intentions might have been as their author. None, however, was posed these questions either for as long or in quite as direct terms as the three expert witnesses called to testify: two for the prosecution and one for the defence. In addition to the hundred and eighteen pages of 'expert report' filed between them, together they spent a total of eight full days in the witness stand. During the whole course of the trial, no one testified for longer than lead expert for the prosecution Jean de Dieu Karangwa, including Bikindi himself.

It is safe to say, then, that the experts occupied a privileged position in relation to the overall technics of the trial, and particularly where Bikindi's songs were concerned. In juridical terms, their influence was considerable. And yet this was not simply a matter of one institution reaching out to another—the ICTR to the Academy—in order to 'bring in' knowledge from the 'outside'. The expertise which manifested itself at trial was clearly the function of a pre-existing hermeneutic disposition at the level of the institution as a whole. The production of expertise was managed and coordinated by the Tribunal in at least two senses. First, by the kinds of expert it had sought out to begin with. Second, by the limited capacity in which they were called.

The first point is a simple one. All three experts were sought out by the Tribunal because they were, in one way or another, linguists. Two appeared for the prosecution, having authored their expert report together. One was a professor at *L'Ecole des Langues Orientales* in Paris named Jean de Dieu Karangwa who was tendered as an 'expert on the linguistics of Kinyarwanda, with qualifications sufficient to provide opinions based on the fields of social linguistics, textual and discourse analysis, semantics and expression theory, both written and oral'. The second was a professor at the National University of Rwanda at Butare named Gamaliel Mbonimana, called for his expertise in Rwandan history, literature, and poetics. The defence's expert was Eugène Shimamungu who, having obtained his '*doctorat en sciences du langage*' from the University Paris-Sorbonne in 1990, testified as an expert in 'the science of language', 'linguistics' and specifically 'the grammar of the Kinyarwanda language'. Having received his '*diplôme d'études supérieures spécialisées en lexicographie et terminographie*' a decade later, he also claimed expertise in the 'science of the dictionary', which he explained meant in the 'cataloguing', 'compiling', and 'analysis' of words.[66] The kind of experts chosen to give evidence in the *Bikindi* case was as significant as anything they actually testified. Or to put the same point another way, the evidence they did give was in some respects already a foregone conclusion. From its selection of experts, we can already infer a lot about what the Tribunal thought was important about Bikindi's songs. Foreshadowing precisely the kind of logic which would eventually be applied in the Chamber's judgment, where their 'meaning and interpretation' was concerned, music—sound—simply didn't register as juristically relevant data.

No-one put this point more succinctly than Eugène Shimamungu in the opening lines of the report he tendered as expert for the defence.[67] Evidently, the adoption of such an approach was actually a condition of his employment by the Tribunal. 'According to the contract', he wrote, 'the work should not extend to questions of musicology (a field in which I am not competent) but rather to the texts of the so-called "political" songs which should be analysed relative to the historical, socio-political, national and international context in which they were created'.[68] It is not simply that the Tribunal regarded linguistics as the appropriate disciplinary lens through which to view Bikindi's songs: musicology was both actively and overtly proscribed.

Nevertheless, it is Shimamungu's report that includes the most nuanced musicological account offered at any point during Bikindi's trial. Across the first three or four of the seventy-six pages otherwise given over to '*l'anaylse textuelle*' of Bikindi's songs, Shimamungu makes reference to Adorno and Beethoven as well as to texts like Jean Baptiste Nkulikiyinka's *Introduction à la Danse Rwandaise Tradtionnelle*.[69] He is upfront about the fact that songs present certain difficulties to the interpreter which are simply not an issue in relation to texts. And he offers a brief and general discussion of the *Imbyino*, for instance, the specific genre of song and dance for which Bikindi was particularly well known, and which he writes 'can be analysed from several different angles (textual, musical and rhythmic) as a means of communication'. Moreover, Shimamungu is also sensitive to the role genre plays in relation to the question of interpretation. He makes a distinction between the hermeneutic lens that should be applied to a '*chanson de danse*' such as the *Imbyino* and a '*chanson à texte*' such as the *Indirimbo*. '*Les chansons à texte*', he writes, 'aim to transmit their verbal message over a rhythm which invites listening rather than dancing'.[70] And it was precisely because the three songs in question at trial were *Imbyino*, he argued, because they were intended to be danced to, that the expert witnesses for the prosecution were unable to furnish a single accurate transcription in their report. For Shimamungu, Bikinidi's songs did not necessarily 'foreground'

[66] See *Bikindi* transcript: 12 February 2007, 27; 23 October 2007, 5.

[67] Exhibit No D117(F), 'Defence Expert Report of Dr Eugène Shimamungu', *Prosecutor v Bikindi*, ICTR-01-72-0265 (3 October 2007).

[68] Exhibit No D117(F), *Prosecutor v Bikindi* (3 October 2007) 4 (translation my own).

[69] Jean Baptiste Nkulikiyinka, *Introduction à la Danse Rwandaise Tradtionnelle* (Musée Royal d'Afrique Centrale, 2002).

[70] Nkulikiyinka (2002) 4–8; 25–6 (translations my own).

their lyrics at all. Quite the contrary. It was frequently difficult to make out the words being sung, even on close and repeated listens.[71]

Limited as it may be, this is precisely the sort of musicological detail so conspicuously missing both at trial and in the Chamber's judgment. Shimamungu's refusal to abide strictly by the terms of his contract throws the partiality of the Tribunal's approach into bold relief. Although I have been unable to find evidence of a similar contract in relation to the prosecution's experts, it is reasonable to suppose there was one. Counsel for the prosecution, at least, was adamant that his experts' 'topical analysis' of Bikindi's songs was 'about the meaning of the words, nothing else'. 'Go through the report', he pleaded to the Chamber at one point, and they would 'see for themselves'.[72] Clearly, as far as the Tribunal was concerned, this sort of approach was perceived as a virtue.

This is particularly obvious in relation to the Tribunal's treatment of prosecution expert Gabriel Mbonimana. As well as being a professor of history, Mbonimana was, as Bikindi himself put it at one point during the trial, 'a great Rwandan musician'.[73] He had regularly served on and presided over juries in music competitions throughout Rwanda since 1984, including one in which *Twasezereye* was selected to be performed by Bikindi at a celebration to mark the 25th anniversary of Rwanda's independence from colonial rule. He had lectured on and published extensively in Rwandan musicology for even longer.[74] Out of every witness called before the Tribunal, Mbonimana was the only one who could claim actually to have studied and judged songs for a living. He was not just a linguist and historian, but a musicologist too. You would hardly know it from his testimony though. In part this was because it was so exceptionally brief when compared with that of Shimamungu and Karangwa. Where they were each given three and four days respectively, Mbonimana got three hours.

No explicit justification for the differential treatment is given anywhere in the archive. But what is clear is that the prosecution had not wanted Mbonimana to testify at all. On 9 February 2007, just seven days before he would eventually appear before the Tribunal, the defence had filed a 'very urgent' motion objecting to the 'presentation' of the co-authored expert report by Karangwa alone. 'The presentation of the report by only one witness', it argued, would 'prejudice the Accused's right to challenge the evidence of both witnesses as provided under Article 20 of the Statute'.[75] Perhaps because of the late notice—though because the discussion in this respect did not take place during 'official' proceedings, the rationale was not recorded in the transcript—it was apparently 'not possible' to get him to Arusha in person.[76] Mbonimana was forced to testify at great expense to

[71] *Bikindi* transcript, 23 October 2007, 73.

[72] *Bikindi* transcript, 12 February 2007, 7.

[73] *Bikindi* transcript, 16 February 2007, 19.

[74] 'Disclosure of Curriculum Vitae's [sic] of Expert Witnesses', *Prosecutor v Bikindi*, ICTR-01-72-0149 (11 July 2006) 8–10.

[75] 'Very Urgent Defence Motion Objecting to the Presentation of Experts Report by Jean de Dieu Karangwa Alone and Requesting the Compulsion of Gamaliel Mbonimana to Give Evidence', *Prosecutor v Bikindi*, ICTR-01-72-0208/1 (9 February 2007) 4.

[76] *Prosecutor v Bikindi* (Case Minutes) ICTR-01-72-T, T Ch III (13 February 2007).

the Tribunal via video-link from Kigali, a factor which undoubtedly contributed in part to the brevity of his testimony.[77] The prosecution declined to examine the witness at all, electing simply to have him confirm that he 'adopted' the joint report as his own.[78] During his limited cross-examination by the defence, Mbonimana was never asked to comment explicitly on the musical aspects of Bikindi's songs. As far as the Tribunal was concerned, and quite possibly as a matter of contract too, Mbonimana was not an expert on music at all. Or more precisely, if he was, that was not the capacity in which he featured at trial. As counsel for the prosecution put it, for the purposes of the *Bikindi* case he was 'a linguistic expert with a history background'.[79] With Karangwa having testified at length already, the prosecution was unclear as to what another linguist could possibly add, and the defence was simply hoping for another opportunity to undermine the prosecution's interpretation of Bikindi's 'texts'. In both discursive and procedural terms, any explicitly musicological expertise on offer had already been rendered irrelevant.

Doctrine: The Musicology of International Justice

So far in this chapter I have traced what seem to be two very different approaches to Bikindi's songs. One paid attention to their specifically musical qualities which it then immediately resolved into a crude affective binary. Bikindi was either Orpheus or a Siren, his songs either civilizing or seductive. In this respect the discussion was always both brief and pitched in extremely general terms. When a song was considered in any detail it was always for its lyrics rather than its sound. This brings us to the second and by far the predominant approach to song in the *Bikindi* case. More than anything else, the Tribunal was interested in the *meaning* of Bikindi's songs: not what they *did* but what they *said*. And what they said was taken to be discernible entirely apart from their sound, setting, and performance. This approach was pervasive, evidenced everywhere from the kinds of experts selected by both prosecution and defence, to the contracts they signed, the kinds of arguments that got traction and the way they were questioned, right on up to the judgment eventually delivered by the Chamber at first instance.

I want to end this chapter by suggesting that these two approaches are not necessarily so different after all, that they may in fact be flipsides to the same coin, and attributable moreover to the same cause. That cause, I argue, can be found at the level of doctrine. Even though the relevant international legal instruments had nothing to say about music *as such* they did offer a mediology nevertheless, and this in turn was responsible for the twin approaches to song in the *Bikindi* case.

[77] *Bikindi* transcript, 16 February 2007, 2.
[78] *Bikindi* transcript, 16 February 2007, 5.
[79] *Bikindi* transcript, 16 February 2007, 15.

Freedom of expression and the form/content distinction

In its discussion of the relevant doctrine relating to 'freedom of expression', in the final pages of its judgment, the Chamber explained that 'the international definitions of expression and speech are broad enough to include artistic expression such as songs'. 'Expression', it said, 'has been defined as the freedom to "impart information and ideas", "either orally, in writing or in print, in the form of art, or through any other media..."; or alternatively, to '"express and disseminate ... opinions"',[80] citing the *Universal Declaration of Human Rights* (article 19), the *International Covenant on Civil and Political Rights* (article 19), the *European Convention for the Protection of Human Rights and Fundamental Freedoms* (article 10), the *American Convention on Human Rights* (article 13), the *African Charter on Human and Peoples' Rights* (article 9), and the *UN Declaration on the Elimination of all Forms of Racial Discrimination* (article 9) by way of authority.[81] On this basis, the Chamber was happy to consider 'the words accompanying a score of music' (here is that revealing use of the word 'score' again) as 'comparable from a legal perspective to the words used in a speech'. They were both limited and protected by international criminal law in a similar way.[82] More specifically, 'depending on the nature of the message conveyed and the circumstances', the Chamber could not exclude 'the possibility that songs may constitute direct and public incitement to commit genocide'.[83] The same went for persecution as a crime against humanity.[84]

Although the authority cited by the Chamber for this position is silent on the question of music per se, its mediology comes through loud and clear. Expression, for the purposes of the relevant international law, is about 'information', 'opinions' and 'ideas', or in the predominating language of the Tribunal in the *Bikindi* case: 'messages'.[85] In other words, *content*. As far as *form* is concerned, the relevant statutes and treaties are ambivalent. Any medium will do. An idea may be conveyed, 'orally, in writing or in print, in the form of art, or through any other media'. A song is as good as a speech is as good as a newspaper article. The consequences of this mediology in the *Bikindi* case were twofold, a double excision of music if you like, a double institutional deafness.

[80] *Bikindi* judgment, para 384.

[81] The language in each case is so similar that they are virtually in unison in this respect. Universal Declaration of Human Rights (adopted 10 December 1948) UNGA Res 217A (III) art 19; International Covenant on Civil and Political Rights (adopted 16 December 1966, entered into force 23 March 1976) 999 UNTS 171, art 19; European Convention for the Protection of Human Rights and Fundamental Freedoms (opened for signature 4 November 1950, entered into force 3 September 1953) 213 UNTS 222, art 10; American Convention on Human Rights (entered into force 18 July 1978) 1144 UNTS 123, art 13; African Charter on Human and Peoples' Rights (entered into force 21 October 1986) 1520 UNTS 217, art 9; Declaration on the Elimination of All Forms of Racial Discrimination (20 November 1963) UNGA Res 1904, art 9.

[82] *Bikindi* judgment, para 384.

[83] *Bikindi* judgment, para 389.

[84] *Bikindi* judgment, para 392.

[85] *Bikindi* judgment, paras 192, 196, 199, 204, 207, 211, 213, 215, 217, 221, 226, 236, 242, 246, 247, 253, 260, 261, 387, 389, 395, 423, 424.

First, by reducing 'expression' to the register of content, the doctrine brought to bear on Bikindi's songs ensured that the only relevant questions for the Tribunal from a doctrinal perspective were hermeneutic. What did they mean? What opinions, what ideas were being expressed? What 'message' or 'messages' had Bikindi intended to convey? Doctrinally speaking, any other qualities of his songs—what they did, how they worked, their force, intensity and effect—simply weren't relevant, and could happily be left therefore to be dealt with at the level of rhetoric. This crude opposition between Orpheus and the Sirens, endorsed equally by both prosecution and defence, was sufficient as far as both sides were concerned because it was not being asked to do any of the real heavy lifting.

Second, the Tribunal's mediological ambivalence, consistent with a number of major international legal instruments, seems to have led to the mistaken idea that form, and therefore sound, was irrelevant as far as the task of interpretation is concerned. As counsel for the prosecution said during the trial: 'the fact that it's a song is not the point… They were openly talking about killing the Tutsi. And when I say "openly talking" about it, they sang about it too. And it's simply a means of communicating that direction. Whether it is a song or a speech or a written pamphlet…'[86] Music on this account is an empty vessel, a delivery system, just one amongst many possible means of getting some discrete nugget of thought—'Hutu solidarity', for instance, or the idea 'to attack and kill Tutsi'[87]—from A to B, the equivalent of posting a letter or sending an email. In practice, the effect of framing music as 'simply a means of communication' was to make it irrelevant at the level of hermeneutics. Once it had been rendered as a mere method of delivering linguistic content, the Tribunal was free to get on with the 'proper' legal work of verbal analysis.[88] So it employed linguists as expert witnesses and contracted music out of the problem.

From a musicological perspective, the problem is as follows. If songs play a significant role in peoples' lives, if they are capable of influencing thought, sentiment or behaviour, it is surely not, or not only, because of the 'messages' they convey. Songs matter to people because of what they do and how they make us feel, at least as much as what they mean. It is hard to believe, moreover, that things are any different where genocide is concerned. In fact, to suggest that a song *ever* merely expresses an 'idea' or 'opinion' is surely to miss the point entirely. A song is not a container truck, suitable for the conveyance or 'expression' of this idea or that. It is *itself* an expression, which is to say something much more complex.

Simon Frith puts it like this. Songs, he says, never simply transmit or convey language, they 'work with and on' it.[89] This is because to sing words is always 'to elevate them in some way, to make them special, to give them a new form of

[86] *Bikindi* transcript, 17 October 2006, 11. [87] *Bikindi* judgment, para 217.

[88] Such an approach is not without precedent in the musicological literature. For a survey of academic approaches to lyrics in relation to popular song in the twentieth century West, including so-called 'content analysis', see Simon Frith, *Music for Pleasure: Essays in the Sociology of Pop* (Routledge, 1988) 105–28 ('Why Do Songs Have Words?').

[89] Frith (1996) 166.

intensity'.[90] To breathe life into them, to give them resonance, a certain kind of material existence, cultural weight, and affective force. Clearly, on one level, the Tribunal was cognisant of this fact, because it was precisely this dimension of Bikindi's songs to which so much of its rhetorical energies were addressed. Nevertheless, the doctrinal privileging of content over form seems to have disabled the Tribunal from addressing this issue as a matter of *law*, with the result that the very quality that distinguished Bikindi's songs *as songs* was rendered nonjusticiable, out of juridical reach.

Law's deafness

To be sure, the ICTR foundered here at precisely the point at which musicological discourse always does. This is nothing less than the problem of the 'ineffable', after all; the difficulty—even the impossibility—of putting into words a piece of music's force, intensity or significance, which of course is a requisite of judgment. For philosopher of music Vladimir Jankélévitch, ineffability is that which 'provokes bewilderment'.[91] Clearly, Bikindi's songs bewildered the Tribunal. But crucially for Jankélévitch, music is ineffable not because it is somehow meaningless. Music is bewildering, it can often seem to resist description not because it expresses nothing, but 'because it does not express this or that privileged landscape'.[92] If it cannot be explained it is because 'there are infinite and interminable things to be said of it', not zero.[93] The same is true of song. A song, for Jankélévitch, is musical precisely 'to the degree that it is never an unequivocal, unambiguous expression of meaning'.[94] It always says somehow more and otherwise than its lyrics seem to. It is precisely the musical in song which both resists its reduction to hermeneutics and which ensures that the hermeneutic task is never limited to a consideration of lyrics. 'Always signifying in general and never in particular', music is 'the domain where ambiguity holds sway' even if we can and must do our best to pin down and alleviate that ambiguity.[95] And this is the really crucial point. For Jankélévitch, music's ineffability is not a reason to stop trying to explain it, as the Tribunal did. It is only in the 'imagining and dismissing, and doing it again, and again' of a piece of music's meaning, power, and import, that 'one asymptotically approaches an intimation of something that will elude any and all searchlights'.[96]

This was the imperative, the responsibility that the ICTR failed to take up in the *Bikindi* case. Not only did the Tribunal's approach render certain crucial elements of Bikindi's songs out of juridical reach, it came up short *even on its own terms*. The ICTR's failure to consider Bikindi's music even when it came to the 'meaning and interpretation' of his songs misses the crucial fact that, although it may not express 'ideas' exactly, or 'opinions', music does nevertheless express.[97] Music itself is a

[90] Frith (1996) 172. [91] Jankélévitch (2003) 72. [92] Jankélévitch (2003) 74.
[93] Jankélévitch (2003) 72. [94] Jankélévitch (2003) 62. [95] Jankélévitch (2003) 58.
[96] Carolyn Abbate, 'Introduction' in Vladimir Jankélévitch, *Music and the Ineffable*, trans. Carolyn Abbate (Princeton University Press, 2003) [trans of: *La musique et l'ineffable* (first published 1961)] xiii.
[97] Music is neither a 'language' nor an instrumental means of conveying 'concepts', as some authors have occasionally maintained. See Fred Lerdahl and Ray Jackendoff, *A Generative Theory of Tonal Music* (MIT University Press, 1983); Nicolas Ruwet, 'Musicology and Linguistics', *International Social*

kind of expression. This is true whether or not there are lyrics involved. But where there are, music can bear on the meaning of those lyrics in all sorts of different ways, and vice versa. Sometimes music will emphasize one aspect of the lyrical 'content' over another.[98] Sometimes it will colour, enrich or embody the sense of the lyrics as a whole.[99] Sometimes it will overshadow the lyrics altogether, making them inaudible or peripheral to the total listening experience.[100] Sometimes music will completely undermine, or at least vastly complicate the lyrical 'message' as we saw in the case of Springsteen above. In all these examples, contra counsel for the prosecution, 'the fact that it's a song' is *precisely* the point. The medium is a crucial part of the message.[101] Form and content, music and lyric, were never truly separable in the first place.

The Tribunal's double deafness in the *Bikindi* case was no mere aberration or anomaly. It was a deafness of the law itself: the result of an institution attempting to think song juridically in a situation where the relevant doctrine seemed to privilege content over form and, by extension, lyrics over music. It was by means of this juridical deafness that Bikindi's alleged crimes were defined, prosecuted,

Science Journal 19(1) (1967) 79. Music is, however, capable of possessing what Umberto Eco calls 'explicit denotative value'. Eco gives the example of trumpet signals in the army, but we could think also of the peal of church bells. See Umberto Eco, *A Theory of Semiotics* (Macmillan, 1977) 11; Alain Corbin, *Village Bells: Sound and Meaning in the 19th Century French Countryside*, trans. Martin Thom (Columbia University Press, 1998) [trans of: *Les cloches de la terre: Paysage sonore et culture sensible dans les campagnes au XIXe siècle* (first published 1998)]. It is also worth noting the many West African traditions in which drums have been used to convey messages, not by means of a code but by imitating the rhythmic and prosodic qualities of speech. See John F Carrington, *Talking Drums of Africa* (Carey Kingsgate Press, 1949); James Gleick, *Information: A History, a Theory, a Flood* (Pantheon Books, 2011); George Herzog, 'Drum Signalling in a West African Tribe' in Margin Clayton (ed), *Music, Words and Voice: A Reader* (Manchester University Press, 2008); Walter J Ong, 'African Talking Drums and Oral Noetics', *New Literary History* 8(3) (1977) 411.

[98] Consider 'She Loves You', the classic Beatles song. This is a particularly clear case of a song in which musical form is directly and irretrievably bound up with lyrical content. As text, the meaning of the classic line is undecidable without more information. Its meaning shifts according to whether the emphasis is placed on 'she' (rather than someone else), 'loves' (rather than hates), or 'you' (rather than me, him or her). Musically, however, the meaning is absolutely clear and even before we know the rest of the song's lyrics. The stress is decisively on the middle term. 'She loves you.' And in terms of key (major), tempo (an upbeat 4/4), rhythm (the word 'love' falls on the downbeat), melody (its pitch raises to the tonic), and delivery (emphatic) we already 'know that can't be bad'. This example expands on an analysis originally made by Frith (1996) 181.

[99] To take an example from the classical idiom, Marie-Agnes Dittrich explains that 'in contrast to the keyboard treatment in most eighteenth-century Lieder, Schubert's piano parts typically are no longer structured as simple, subordinated supplement to a more important vocal line; the piano has at least becomes its equal and sometimes more than that, for frequently it sets the tone for an entire Lied. This could encompass the rapid motion of the trout in the brook in *Die Forelle*; the rocking of the boat in *Gondelfahrer* or *Des Fischers Leibesglück*; the rattling chains of the dogs in *Im Dorfe* (*Winterreise*, No. 17).' Elsewhere, 'when the piano part closely matches the vocal line, the result seems to be that the text is bolstered by a kind of empathetic unanimity.' In both cases, the point is not that you need to 'get' the reference in order to fully 'appreciate' the musical work, but that Schubert's ingenious setting actually affects the way in which the lyrics are heard, felt, and understood. Marie-Agnes Dittrich, 'The Lieder of Schubert', trans. Sven Hansell in James Parsons (ed), *The Cambridge Companion to the Lied* (Cambridge University Press, 2004) 86, 88.

[100] See the My Bloody Valentine example at n 62.

[101] Marshal McLuhan, *Understanding Media: The Extensions of Man* (2nd edn, New American Library, 1964) 23–35.

and eventually judged. That is not to say, however, that if the Tribunal had been more open to musicological concerns, the outcome of the case would have been different, or even necessarily better or more just. To argue that the musicology of judgment deserves more attention is not to suggest that musicology as a discipline has all the answers. This is not a case of one field intervening to somehow redeem another. For one thing, 'musicology' is hardly a stable or uncontested term to begin with. Like any discipline, it has its fair share of internal disputes: methodological, theoretical, political, ethical, and otherwise.[102] More importantly, the very particular problems of judgment posed by law—its particular 'urgency', for instance, and its pairing with institutionalized and apparently 'legitimate' violence—surely exacerbate problems of this sort rather than diminish them.[103] Justice, as Derrida puts it, 'is that which must not wait'.[104] And in that sense the demands of legal judgment are inherently in tension with Jankélévitch's insistence that we approach music like Bikindi's 'again and again', on to infinity. In law, after all, judgment *must* be finite. But this tension, the demand to speak about and judge songs like Bikindi's even in the face of the ineffable, is surely a problem for legal institutions to confront, not circumvent or sidestep.

For my own part, as tempting as it is to conclude by offering a more nuanced or responsible analysis of Bikindi's songs than the one proposed by the ICTR, I will refrain from doing so. That is a job for another book, another trial, or another institution.[105] Precisely because of the Tribunal's deafness where Bikindi's songs were concerned, too many important questions remain unasked. In spite of all the time and energy invested by the ICTR, in spite of all the witnesses heard and reports filed, too much about these songs remains uncertain. There is too little to go on. In this sense, Bikindi's trial represents more than just a failure of law and of the ICTR properly to account for the songs in relation to which it had asserted jurisdiction. It is also a missed opportunity from a musicological perspective and for anyone interested in the role of music in conflict, whether in the Rwandan context or otherwise. As things currently stand, the literature both on Bikindi's songs in particular and on contemporary Rwandan music in general is exceptionally thin on the ground.[106] Recently in fact, law has tended to be the lens through

[102] Joseph Kerman, *Contemplating Music: Challenges to Musicology* (Harvard University Press, 1985); Giles Hooper, *The Discourse of Musicology* (Ashgate, 2006); Alastair Williams, *Constructing Musicology* (Ashgate, 2001).

[103] Robert Cover, 'Violence and the Word', *The Yale Law Journal* 95(8) (1986) 1601; Jacques Derrida, 'Force of Law: The "Mystical Foundations of Authority"', trans. Mary Quaintance [trans of: 'Force de loi: Le "fondement mystique de l'autorité"'] *Cardozo Law Review* 11(5-6) (1990) 920, 973 ('Part Two').

[104] Derrida (1990) 967.

[105] For one such attempt, see Jason McCoy, 'Mbwirabumva ("I Speak to Those Who Understand"): Three Songs by Simon Bikindi and the War and Genocide in Rwanda' (PhD dissertation, Florida State University, 2013).

[106] Jos Gansemans, *Les instruments de musique du Rwanda: Étude ethnomusicologique* (Leuven University Press, 1988); Gamaaliel Mbonimana, *La musique Rwandaise traditionelle* (Unpublished, 1971); Nkulikiyinka, (2002); McCoy (2013).

which both have been discussed, leaving the consequences of the ICTR's deafness to proliferate, amplify, and entrench themselves.[107] The musicology of judgment is not just a problem for an acoustic jurisprudence, in other words. It is a problem for anyone interested in Bikindi, his songs, and their role in the Rwandan genocide too.

[107] Bill Berkeley, 'Sounds of Violence', *New Republic* 211(8–9) (1994) 18; Dylan Craig and Nomalanga Mkhize, 'Vocal Killers, Silent Killers: Popular Media, Genocide, and the Call for Benevolent Censorship in Rwanda' in Michael Drewett and Martin Cloonan (eds), *Popular Music Censorship in Africa* (Ashgate, 2006); Gregory S Gordon, 'Music and Genocide: Harmonizing Coherence, Freedom and Nonviolence in Incitement Law', *Santa Clara Law Review* 50(3) (2010) 607; Justin La Mort, 'The Soundtrack of Genocide: Using Incitement to Genocide in the Bikindi Trial to Protect Free Speech and Uphold the Promise of Never Again', *Interdisciplinary Journal of Human Rights Law* 4(1) (2010) 43; Robert H Snyder, '"Disillusioned Words like Bullets Bark": Incitement to Genocide, Music, and the Trial of Simon Bikindi', *Georgia Journal of International and Comparative Law* 35(3) (2007) 645; Jason McCoy, 'Making Violence Ordinary: Radio, Music and the Rwandan Genocide', *African Music Journal* 8(3) (2009) 85.

4

A Musical Trial

The meaning and power of a song does not simply inhere in the lyrics, notes, rhythms, voices, timbres, and harmonies which it comprises. Nor is it just a matter of the listener's fluency with a particular music culture or 'scheme of interpretation',[1] the peculiar sound-grammar of rock or the madrigal, dubstep, or the Rwandan *imbyino*. Musical meaning is always also a function of context, the way in which the listening experience is framed. Theorist of music education Lucy Green puts it like this: 'Music can never be played or heard outside a situation', she says, 'and every situation will affect the music's meaning.'[2] Thus, when piped through the tinny, treble-rich speakers of a shopping centre, the very same piece of Mozart that in concert approaches the sublime,[3] becomes both a highly effective marketing device and a form of 'sonic architecture'.[4] In a train station, by contrast, it is a mode of what Steve Goodman calls 'sonic warfare',[5] quite literally a weapon

[1] Simon Frith, *Performing Rites: Evaluating Popular Music* (Oxford University Press, 1996) 249.

[2] Lucy Green, *Music on Deaf Ears: Musical Meaning, Ideology, Education* (Manchester University Press, 1988) 384.

[3] On the concert hall as listening situation see Ola Stockfelt, 'Adequate Modes of Listening' in Christoph Cox and Daniel Warner (eds), *Audio Culture: Readings in Modern Music* (Continuum, 2004) 90; Michael Chanan, *Musica Practica: The Social Practice of Western Music from Gregorian Chant to Postmodernism* (Verso, 1994) chs 5 and 6. R Murray Schafer, *The Soundscape. Our Sonic Environment and the Tuning of the World* (Knopf, 1977) 103; Emily Thompson, *The Soundscape of Modernity: Architectural Acoustics and the Culture of Listening in America, 1900–1933* (MIT Press, 2004); Christopher Small, *Musicking: The Meanings of Performing and Listening* (University Press of New England, 1988).

[4] Jonathan Sterne, 'Sounds like the Mall of America: Programmed Music and the Architectonics of Commercial Space', *Ethnomusicology* 41(1) (1997) 22. See also Gordon C Bruner II, 'Music, Mood, and Marketing', *Journal of Marketing* 54(4) (1990) 94; Simon C Jones and Thomas G Schumacher, 'Muzak: On Functional Music and Power', *Critical Studies in Mass Communication* 9(2) (1992) 156; Judy McDermott, 'If It's to Be Heard But Not Listened to, Then It Must Be Muzak', *Smithsonian* 20(10) (1990) 70; Ronald M Radano, 'Interpreting Muzak: Speculations on the Musical Experience in Everyday Life', *American Music* 7(4) (1989) 448.

[5] Steve Goodman, *Sonic Warfare: Sound, Affect and the Ecology of Fear* (MIT Press, 2010). See also Martin Cloonan and Bruce Johnson, 'Killing Me Softly with His Song: An Initial Investigation into the Use of Popular Music as a Tool of Oppression', *Popular Music* 21(1) (2002) 27; Suzanne G Cusick, 'Music as Torture/Music as Weapon', *Transcultural Music Review* 10 (2006) <http://www.sibetrans.com/trans/a152/music-as-torture-music-as-weapon>; Suzanne G Cusick, '"You Are in a Place That Is Out of the World …": Music in the Detention Camps of the "Global War on Terror"', *Journal of the Society for American Music* 2(1) (2008) 1; Jonathan Pieslak, *Sound Targets: American Soldiers and Music in the Iraq War* (Indiana University Press, 2009).

for warding off 'youths' and 'hoodlums'.[6] In Auschwitz, for some it was a defence mechanism, a crucial salve, 'a kind of escape or "asylum"' from the horrors of the camp.[7] And in the car, far more banal: something to unwind to after a hard day at the office.[8]

That Bikindi's was a 'musical trial', as Judge Arrey joked towards the end of proceedings, is clear.[9] Recordings of his songs were played throughout on CD, DVD, and tape. Witnesses regularly hummed and sang. Clearly, though, the fact that they did so in a courtroom rather than a concert hall or a shopping centre was significant. No listening situation is neutral. The circumstances in which music is encountered necessarily condition one's perception of the music itself.[10] Every soundscape has its norms, conventions, rules, and politics. In the judicial context, it is up to an acoustic jurisprudence to illuminate them. As far as the *Bikindi* case is concerned, the questions are as follows. In what ways did the judicial soundscape frame the performance of Bikindi's songs at trial? How did it influence the way or ways in which they were heard and with what results? Finally, to what extent was there room through all of this for either manoeuvre or resistance?

This chapter is about the courtroom as a soundscape and a 'listening situation', a very particular kind of musical setting or context.[11] It begins with a general sketch of the trial as acoustic scene. Each and every appearance of song during the *Bikindi* case, I argue, must be understood in light of the fact that the judicial soundscape is fundamentally oral and discursive, not musical, that it works mainly with speech, not song. From this general starting point, the chapter goes on to explore the primary way in which Bikindi's songs featured at trial. The Tribunal's approach may not have been legislated anywhere or even put explicitly into words, but it was nevertheless highly consistent. Bikindi's songs were played and witnesses sang predominantly at the explicit invitation of the Tribunal and invariably with a word or two to frame the way in which they should be heard. The kind of listening thereby encouraged was almost entirely non-analytical. In this respect, the approach to the performance of Bikindi's songs at trial was consistent with the logic we have just tracked in Chapter 3. The chapter ends with a detailed consideration of the one moment during Bikindi's trial where a musical performance may have succeeded in resisting the Tribunal's otherwise successful efforts at containment. This moment came at the very end of official proceedings when, having been offered

[6] Lily E Hirsch, *Music in American Crime Prevention and Punishment* (University of Michigan Press, 2012) 12–28 ('Classical Music in Crime Prevention').

[7] Shirli Gilbert, *Music in the Holocaust: Confronting Life in the Nazi Ghettos and Camps* (Oxford University Press, 2005) 188.

[8] Karin Bijsterveld, 'Acoustic Cocooning: How the Car Became a Place to Unwind', *The Senses and Society* 5(2) (2010) 189. For another perspective on the socio-material aspects of musical consumption in and in relation to motor vehicles see Brandon LaBelle, 'Pump Up the Bass: Rhythm, Cars, and Auditory Scaffolding', *The Senses and Society* 3(2) (2008) 187.

[9] *Prosecutor v Bikindi* (Transcript) ICTR-01-72-T, T Ch III (Various dates) ('*Bikindi* transcript') 5 November 2007, 35.

[10] Stockfelt (2004) 89.

[11] Stockfelt (2004) 88–93.

the opportunity to make a 'final statement' at the close of his appeals hearing, for five-and-a-half minutes, Bikindi sang.

Song in the Judicial Soundscape

Imagine a legal hearing. You don't expect to hear just anything. Certain sounds spring immediately to mind: the swearing of oaths, an aggressive cross-examination, formulaic and technical expressions, Latinisms, the portentous eloquence of a barrister in closing, the pronouncing of judgment, or the delivery of sentence. In a word, words. Speech, discourse, and dialogue. This may not be controversial but as far as an acoustic jurisprudence is concerned, clearly it is important. In Chapter 6 we will address in detail many of the ways in which the speaking voice was deployed in the *Bikindi* case. For the time being, however, it is sufficient to point out that the courtroom is simply not a place in which song features very often, and that this fact provided the common framework according to which Bikindi's songs were necessarily heard at trial. Judge Arrey was able to qualify Bikindi's as a specifically 'musical' trial only because its presence there was so obviously a deviation from the norm.

Music isn't simply rare in judicial contexts. Everything about the design and technical infrastructure of the contemporary courtroom suggests a space intended more for speech than song. The courtroom's primary purpose is legible—both audible and visible—at the level of its architecture. Because proceedings are required to be public at the ICTR, there is a gallery for observers to sit and listen, but the majority of the space is given over to the participants themselves who are all situated at close quarters, within earshot of one another.[12] Only the judges' dais is raised slightly.[13] The prosecution and defence teams are both seated so that they face inwards, at once towards each other, the witness stand, the registry, and the bench, all of which are positioned at the centre of the space. Although this centre provides a focal point to proceedings, the organizing principle is one of mutual audibility and visibility. Unlike a concert hall, this is not a space which insists on the strict demarcation between performer and listener. Most participants will be both. And as such the courtroom's soundscape is multi- rather than uni-directional. It is designed to facilitate a certain kind of highly regimented conversation rather than provide a neutral stage for performance (see Figure 4.1)[14].

Consider too the courtroom's technical set up, the way in which it is wired for sound.[15] Audio-technicians commonly distinguish between two models of sound representation.[16] In the so-called 'phonographic model', which first emerged at the

[12] On the publicity of proceedings at the ICTR, see Chapter 6.

[13] Modern courts tend to be flatter than their nineteenth-century counterparts. In this way and others, the ICTR's design is in keeping with contemporary trends in courtroom design. Linda Mulcahy, *Legal Architecture: Justice, Due Process and the Place of Law* (Routledge, 2011) 143.

[14] See above n 3.

[15] For more detail on this see Chapter 8.

[16] James Lastra, 'Fidelity versus Intelligibility' in Jonathan Sterne (ed), *The Sound Studies Reader* (Routledge, 2012).

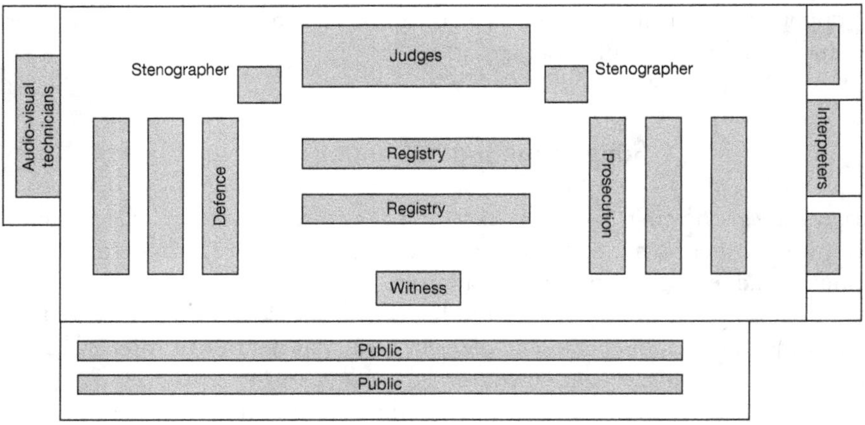

Figure 4.1 Courtroom at the ICTR
© James E K Parker.

end of the nineteenth century in relation to musical recordings, the aim is 'perceptual fidelity', as faithful a rendering of the 'original' sonic event as possible.[17] In the 'telephonic' model, by contrast, the aim is not fidelity but intelligibility. Despite early experiments with the broadcasting of musical performances, telephony quickly settled into the point-to-point conversational model we are familiar with today.[18] As such, clarity of speech soon established itself as the main priority from both a technical and economic perspective on the basis that the less data being transmitted, the more calls could be crammed onto a single wire.[19] Signal quality could be sacrificed at the altar of efficiency so long as the speech transmitted was still rendered clearly. This is precisely the logic we find in the courtrooms at the ICTR. Intelligibility is clearly prioritized over fidelity there. This is both immediately palpable aurally in the patina of crackle and fuzz which accompanies every moment of the heavily mediated listening experience at trial and, by contemporary standards, a technical fact.[20]

Whereas the standard frequency response for contemporary 'high-fidelity' audio is 20 to 20,000 Hz, the headphones supplied by the Tribunal have a range of between 35 and 15,000, approximately that of an FM radio transmission. Once these are plugged into the infrared receivers, however, the means by which everyone present was required to tune in to proceedings, including to the majority of musical performances,[21] the top end of that frequency range is reduced to just

[17] Jonathan Sterne, *The Audible Past: Cultural Origins of Sound Reproduction* (Duke University Press, 2003) 215.

[18] Sterne (2003) 192–4.

[19] On the history of bandwidth maximization in telephony see Jonathan Sterne, *MP3: The Meaning of a Format* (Duke University Press, 2012) 61–91 ('Nature Builds No Telephones').

[20] Such technical standards are both constantly changing and highly political. See generally Sterne (2003); Sterne, *MP3* (2012).

[21] *Bikindi* transcript, 19 September 2006, 2.

10,000 Hz.[22] Similarly, whereas a Total Harmonic Distortion of less than 1 per cent is generally regarded as the standard for high-fidelity sound today and, moreover, frequently approaches zero, the headphones provided by the ICTR offer something closer to 1.5 per cent. Danish Interpretation Systems, the company that supplies the ICTR with its equipment puts it like this: 'The DH9001H offers excellent listening quality with development emphasis put on speech intelligibility'.[23] The audio-equipment employed at the ICTR was selected with durability and dialogue in mind, not absolute acoustic precision.[24] Even if music would occasionally feature at trial, the Tribunal's priority was to render speech clearly and with a degree of fidelity appropriate to the tonal and expressive range of the speaking voice, which it did. From an institutional perspective, to have invested in anything more would have been a waste.

A soundscape is more than just the sum of its spatial features and audio-technological parts however. It is also an attitude, a sensibility, a way of framing, interacting with, and listening to sound in a given context. Music is not just unfamiliar to the judicial soundscape, it feels odd, out of place, even potentially transgressive. When invited to sing a portion of Bikindi's *Nanga Abahutu/ Akabyutso* on one occasion early on in proceedings, witness AJY responded as follows; 'Of course, there are songs of Bikindi that I know but I would not dare burst into song'.[25] For an acoustic jurisprudence, such reticence is highly revealing. Even if the Tribunal was in general encouraging as far as the performance of Bikindi's songs was concerned, it was never quite able to eradicate this aura of impropriety entirely. It always loomed somehow in the background, ready to rear its head again when Bikindi eventually sang his final statement, the one occasion at trial when a musical performance escaped the Tribunal's control. There are plenty of examples we could offer by way of confirmation that witness AJY was wise to tread carefully in this respect.

Consider the infamous 1969 trial of the so-called 'Chicago Seven' for charges in relation to anti-war protests held at the Democratic National Convention the previous year. Witnesses attempted to sing to the court on several occasions, and every time they were immediately shut down. Here is a characteristic episode from the testimony of the well-known American folk singer Phil Ochs:

MR KUNSTLER: What is your occupation?
THE WITNESS: I am a singer, a folksinger.
...

[22] The hardware is manufactured by a company called Danish Interpretation Systems. Product specifications for the IR 15 Infrared Receivers in use at the ICTR are available at Danish Interpretation Systems, 'Infrared Digital Daylight Receivers' (Data Sheet No 4.05f, DIS), accessed 18 February 2015, <http://www.dis.su/pdf/IR15-xx_EN.pdf>.

[23] Danish Interpretation Systems, 'Conference Headphones' (Datasheet No 2.06c, DIS), accessed 18 February 2015, <http://www.prase.it/files/PDF/DH%209001+DH%20800x+DH%206005-2.06c.pdf>.

[24] The product specifications refer to the headphones' 'extreme rigid construction': Danish Interpretation Systems, 'Conference Headphones', 1.

[25] *Bikindi* transcript, 28 September 2006, 30.

MR KUNSTLER: Now, would you stand and sing that song so the jury can hear the song that the audience heard that day?

MR SCHULTZ: If the Court please, this is a trial in the Federal District Court. It is not a theater. We don't have to sit and listen to the witness sing a song. Let's get on with the trial. I object.

MR KUNSTLER: Your Honor, this is definitely an issue in the case. Jerry Rubin has asked for a particular song to be sung. What the witness sang to the audience reflects both on Jerry Rubin's intent and on the mood of the crowd.

THE COURT: I sustain the objection.

MR KUNSTLER: Your Honor, he is prepared to sing it exactly as he sang it on that day,

THE COURT: I am not prepared to listen, Mr Kunstler.[26]

When Arlo Guthrie, son of Woody, took the stand, the Court would put it even more emphatically. 'Oh, no, no. No. I am sorry', it said. 'No singing. No singing. No singing.'[27]

Even where courts have been more willing to allow musical performances at trial, that does not necessarily mean they are listening. Peter Goodrich has addressed this issue in his discussion of the case of *Western Forest Products Ltd v Richardson*, heard by the Supreme Court of British Columbia on 6 November 1985.[28] The proceedings arose because the government of British Columbia had granted a logging licence in relation to the traditional lands of the Haida people, a group indigenous to the pacific north-west of Canada. By a variety of non-violent means the Haida had set about preventing the logging, and in response the logging company issued a writ for an injunction against further interference, which the Haida duly contested. For Goodrich, what is so interesting about the case is less the substance of the testimony presented to the court than its *form*, or more precisely the fact that the two are indissociable. The testimony, he writes, 'took the form of symbolic dress, mythologies, masks and totem poles as well as the legends, stories, poems, songs and other forms of interpretation that such art and mythology implied'.

Of the other anecdotes and histories presented the most striking occurs towards the end of the evidence, when one of the women elders sang traditional songs to the court for a full

[26] 'Testimony of Philip David Ochs', University of Missouri Kansas City (The Chicago Seven Trial: Excerpts from the Trial Transcript), accessed 18 February 2015, <http://law2.umkc.edu/faculty/projects/ftrials/Chicago7/ochs.html>.

[27] The *Chicago Seven* case was highly charged politically, and song was not the only mode of disruption attempted by the defendants and their lawyers. In total, 159 citations were issued for contempt. Michael P Scharf, 'Chaos in the Courtroom: Controlling Disruptive Defendants and Contumacious Counsel in War Crimes Trials', *Case Western Reserve Journal of International Law* 39(1–2) (2006–7) 155, 159. For a detailed general account of the trial, see Pnina Lahav, 'Theater in the Courtroom: The Chicago Conspiracy Trial', *Law and Literature* 16(3) (2004) 381. 'Testimony of Arlo Guthrie', University of Missouri Kansas City (The Chicago Seven Trial: Excerpts from the Trial Transcript), accessed 18 February 2015, <http://law2.umkc.edu/faculty/projects/ftrials/Chicago7/Guthrie.html>.

[28] Peter Goodrich, *Languages of Law: From Logics of Memory to Nomadic Masks* (Weidenfeld and Nicolson, 1990) 179–208. See also Moira Johnston and Dewitt Jones, 'Queen Charlotte Islands, Homeland of the Haida', *National Geographic* 172(1) (1987) 102; Norbert Ruebsaat, 'Speaking with Diane Brown: An Investigation of Testimony Presented Before His Honour, Mr Justice Harry McKay in the Supreme Court of BC, November 6th 1985, in the Matter of *Western Forest Products Ltd v Richardson and Others*' (MA thesis, Simon Fraser University, 1987).

afternoon. The songs repeated ancestral legends and evidenced again that in Haida custom and art, inhabitant and nature were one; that as occupiers of the islands the Haida do not differentiate themselves from their environment but rather see their culture and community as being inextricably and intrinsically bound up in the land. She ends her songs weeping.[29]

The judge who presided over the case delivered an unreserved and extremely brief judgment the day immediately after argument ended. Despite its dramatic presentation, the evidence was simply not relevant to the issue before the court which concerned only the formal validity of the logging licence in question. As such, he had no alternative at law but to decide in favour of the logging company and grant the injunction. In doctrinal terms at least, the songs, like the tears, were completely ignored.

Sometimes it is only from the edge that the centre becomes clearly discernible. For Goodrich, the *Western Forest* case is not strange but symptomatic. The Haida's argument, he writes, the way in which it addressed the court, 'was both lyrical and visual, narrative and aesthetic', which is to say that it 'extended far beyond the contours of contemporary Western languages of law' as they are conventionally understood.[30] It was precisely this going beyond, the excess and unfamiliarity of song as a mode of testimony and juridical argumentation which both provoked and justified the Supreme Court's 'legal deafness' in this instance.[31] In so doing it exemplified for Goodrich 'an habitual logic of law, one which throughout its history has systematically obliterated difference in all its manifestations, in all its discourses'.[32]

Here is the key to understanding song's place in the judicial soundscape then. Song is not just unusual in a judicial context, it is everything that law in the West is not supposed to be.[33] 'The law, both as an institution and as a profession, represents itself as an arcane and elite pursuit; its image of a language is that of a peculiarly legal reason, that of the logic of rules'.[34] In acoustic terms, this self-representation, the well-worn myth of legal rationality, makes itself felt at trial in the difference between speech and song. Whereas the former stands for sober reason and the promise of dispassionate judgment, and helps moreover to produce phenomenologically the 'aura of rationality and of specialism that surrounds legal hearings',[35] the latter becomes a sign of passion, illogic, and the ineffable and as such must be either shut down, ignored, or contained. That this logic is inscribed directly into the law's material structures as much as its social practices is evidence of the extent to which it is entrenched. To participate acoustically in a trial thus is presumptively always to speak rather than sing, precisely as witness AJY had sensed. This is what Goodrich's 'habitual logic' amounts to as far as an acoustic jurisprudence is concerned. In the contemporary Western courtroom—the ICTR included—speech actually *sounds* legal, whereas song unequivocally does not.

29 Goodrich (1990) 182. 30 Goodrich (1990) 183.
31 Goodrich (1990) 184. 32 Goodrich (1990).
33 Richard Sherwin makes a similar argument in relation to images. Richard Sherwin, *Visualizing Law in the Age of the Digital Baroque: Arabesques and Entanglements* (Routledge, 2011) 38.
34 Goodrich (1990) 184. 35 Goodrich (1990) 185.

Song in the *Bikindi* Case

How did song come to feature in the *Bikindi* case? If this was indeed a 'musical trial', and if song is not a permissible legal idiom in the Western courtroom, how was it that performances of Bikindi's songs were managed, domesticated, or otherwise made amenable to the project of judgment and to the orderly conduct of proceedings? As we will now see, the Tribunal was always very careful in this respect. Songs were permitted only for certain very specific purposes, and listeners were always encouraged to listen in very particular ways.

The first time music featured at trial was just a few minutes into the second day of proceedings. A witness was running late so counsel for the prosecution decided to take the opportunity to play the Chamber each of the three songs in issue. Perhaps 'whilst we're waiting', he wondered, 'Your Honours might like to hear the songs?'[36] Because the idea was simply to get the 'flavour' of the songs at this early stage, only a short excerpt of each song would be played.[37] Where the recording of *Bene Sebahinzi/Intabaza* was some twenty minutes long, for instance, the Tribunal heard only four. Where the recordings of *Nanga Abahutu/Akabyutso* and *Twasezereye* came in at thirteen and seven minutes respectively, again the Tribunal heard only four minutes in each case.[38] The Chamber was encouraged to attend to the songs' 'rhythm' as well as what counsel referred to as 'the quality, frankly, of the music'.[39] And because the correct translations of the lyrics were 'hotly contested', no lyrics were provided at this point at all.[40] In other words, on this the very first occasion Bikindi's songs were heard by the Chamber, it was being asked to listen purely for their aesthetic qualities, but without any criteria for doing so other than whatever experience with music they happened to bring with them to the bench. The purpose at this point was not understanding, but a heavily attenuated form of appreciation: the focus was not meaning but 'flavour', the showcasing of a kind of bare artistry. Very little would change as proceedings continued.

This moment can be read as part of a more general tendency towards the exoticization of Bikindi's songs at trial. At one point about six months into proceedings, for instance, Presiding Judge Weinberg de Roca agreed to listen to all seventeen minutes of a recording of *Nanga Abahutu/Akabyutso*, in spite of the fact that no corresponding transcript was available and the Tribunal would therefore not 'understand what is in the song', simply on the basis that it was 'nice music'. 'Just play it', she said. 'We'll listen.'[41] Bikindi's songs were constantly framed this way, as pleasant interludes, a brief moment of acoustic respite in relation to the otherwise mundane soundscape of the trial. They were often heard, in other words, at least

[36] *Bikindi* transcript, 19 September 2006, 2.
[37] *Bikindi* transcript, 19 September 2006, 2.
[38] *Bikindi* transcript, 19 September 2006, 3.
[39] *Bikindi* transcript, 19 September 2006, 2.
[40] *Bikindi* transcript, 19 September 2006, 2.
[41] *Bikindi* transcript, 13 February 2007, 26–7.

as much for their bare aesthetic qualities as for their probative value, a fact which played into the hands of the defence inasmuch as it tended to emphasize their status precisely *as* art, the alignment between Bikindi and the figure of Orpheus. Counsel for the prosecution claimed at one point to be 'looking forward' to hearing one recording.[42] Following their performance of Bikindi's *Twasezereye*, one witness was described as an 'absolutely lovely singer'.[43] For counsel for the defence, similarly, another witness's performance of the same song was 'very beautiful'. The 'quality of the singing' had significantly improved since the end of the prosecution's case, he joked.[44] Indeed, the Chamber hardly ever missed an opportunity to hear a witness sing, especially where Bikindi himself was concerned. 'Yes, I agree with Judge Arrey', said the presiding judge to Bikindi at one point, 'we would like to hear you sing'.[45] When on another occasion she asked if there would be more singing following an upcoming recess, counsel for the defence quipped 'I'm sure I can find a way'.[46] And sure enough, he did.[47]

While the Tribunal clearly appreciated listening to Bikindi's songs, it was simply not interested in exploring their aesthetic qualities in any detail. In juridical terms, this mode of listening always amounted to a kind of marginalization, *even as* the songs were apparently being incorporated into the legal sphere. From an evidentiary perspective, the Tribunal had other priorities in mind. Songs were generally played for one of three reasons: so that their lyrics could be recorded for the benefit of the transcripts, in order to verify the identity of the singer or to confirm a witness's familiarity with the song under consideration.

Occasionally, Bikindi's songs featured at trial for primarily *transcriptual* purposes. Bikindi would be asked to sing largely as a way of getting his lyrics onto the formal record of proceedings, 'for the transcripts' as the presiding judge put it at one point.[48] This method was adopted only when no other record yet existed, in relation to the songs Bikindi recorded after the genocide for instance: *Les Mendiants de la Paix* ('Beggars of Peace'), *Merci* ('Thankyou'), *Les Enfants de la Guerre* ('Children of War'), *Isuku* ('Cleanliness') and 'A Better World'.[49] While the majority of participants listened on appreciatively, the important juridical work was being done by the Tribunal's interpreters and stenographers, first rendering the song as lyrics in French and English and then finally as texts, in both cases by means of a complex listening practice which we will consider in detail in Chapters 6 and 8.

Other times, witnesses would be asked to verify that Bikindi's was the voice heard on a recording. This is an example of what Michel Chion calls *causal listening*: 'listening to a sound in order to gather information about its cause

42 *Bikindi* transcript, 9 October 2006, 19.
43 *Bikindi* transcript, 11 October 2006, 39.
44 *Bikindi* transcript, 26 September 2007, 42.
45 *Bikindi* transcript, 31 October 2007, 52.
46 *Bikindi* transcript, 31 October 2007, 52.
47 *Bikindi* transcript, 31 October 2007, 54.
48 See *Bikindi* transcript, 1 November 2007, 35–6.
49 *Bikindi* transcript, 1 November 2007, 34.

(or source)', in this case the identity of the singer.[50] Here is counsel for the prosecution to one of his expert witnesses, for instance: 'Professor Karangwa, you've listened to the song *Bene sebahinzi*. My first question to you is, do you recognise the voice of Mr Bikindi in that song?'[51] Or again, 'Now, we have just played *Nanga abahutu*. Is it your position—is it still your position that you recognise the voice of Bikindi in this song?'[52] On both occasions, once Karangwa had answered in the affirmative and the 'rhythm' had been quickly 'defined',[53] the discussion moved on to the more serious business of establishing the songs' 'principal message',[54] which evidently required neither that they be played again nor that their acoustic aspects be discussed in detail. Instead, the Tribunal was happy to work directly from the transcripts included in the joint expert report, which it went on to do at length.[55] 'Is there any language in the lyrics of this song that incites ethnic violence?'[56] 'Could you kindly read that passage, please?'[57] 'Yes, I am reading from document 6. I am talking—I am reading from the French text'.[58] 'Passage', 'lines', 'document', 'text': from a hermeneutic perspective, the Tribunal need hardly have listened to the songs at all. As we saw in Chapter 3, it was the lyrics that mattered in doctrinal terms. The purpose of the *listening* itself was simply a formal prerequisite to their consideration as texts. And it comes as no surprise therefore to find that at no point during the defence expert's three days of testimony did the Tribunal deem it necessary to hear a single song again.[59] Having already heard them once, the analysis could proceed immediately to the transcripts. 'Now, if you could turn to the song *Twasezereye* in your binder, yesterday we were discussing the paragraphs from 20 to 29 in that song … Now, if we could go on to lines 30 to 33 … Could you please explain that paragraph?'[60]

A very similar way of framing Bikindi's songs was at work when it came to non-expert witnesses, except that this time the mode of listening encouraged was not so much 'causal' as what we might call *indexical*. The purpose was not to confirm the identity of the singer but rather that the witness did in fact recognize the song under consideration. There were two common methods in this respect. In the first case, a witness would be asked to name the song in question immediately after hearing it. The following example, taken from the eleventh day of proceedings, is typical:

[50] Michel Chion, *Audio-Vision: Sound on Screen*, ed and trans Claudio Gorbman (Columbia University Press, 1994) [trans of: *L'audio-vision: Son et image au cinema* (first published 1990)] 25.

[51] *Bikindi* transcript, 13 February 2007, 41.

[52] *Bikindi* transcript, 13 February 2007, 28.

[53] *Bikindi* transcript, 13 February 2007, 43.

[54] *Bikindi* transcript, 13 February 2007, 43.

[55] Exhibit No P73(E), 'Prosecution Joint Expert Report of Gamaliel Mbonimana and Jean de Dieu Karangwa: "Thematic Analysis of the Songs"', *Prosecutor v Bikindi*, ICTR-01-72-0152 (13 September 2006) 5.

[56] *Bikindi* transcript, 13 February 2007, 44.

[57] *Bikindi* transcript, 13 February 2007, 44.

[58] *Bikindi* transcript, 13 February 2007, 47.

[59] *Bikindi* transcript: 23 October 2007; 24 October 2007; 25 October 2007.

[60] *Bikindi* transcript, 24 October 2007, 2.

MR MORLEY (assistant counsel for the prosecution): With Your Honours' leave, this is *Nanga abahutu*, from P.34, the first three minutes. I hope it works.
(Audio CD played)
Thank you, that's the first three minutes.
...
MS WRIGHT (assistant counsel for the prosecution): Mr Witness, were you able to listen to the song we just played?
WITNESS AJS: I heard it, Madam President.
MS WRIGHT: Was that the song you referred to here as '*Nanga abahutu*'?
WITNESS AJS: Yes, that was the song.[61]

Ms Wright moves immediately on to ask the witness about the 'message' it 'carried'.[62]

In the second case, the Tribunal would simply request that a witness sing a few lines of the song in question as evidence that they were acquainted with it. When counsel for the defence asked one witness if they could give 'the titles or describe any of the songs' performed at a celebration to mark the twenty-fifth anniversary of Rwanda's independence from Belgium, the presiding judge remarked: 'singing them is what we used during the Prosecution case'.[63] And the witness duly did. Here is one of the occasions being referred to. Again, the purpose was not to help anyone understand or appreciate the songs. The point was simply to produce a certain kind of juridical effect: to satisfy the Chamber that the witness really was familiar with the song that they claimed to be.

MR GABAAKE (assistant counsel for the prosecution): Do you know a song called *Twasezereye*?
WITNESS BHI: Yes, I know a part of that song.
MR GABAAKE: If you remember any part of it, could you sing it for us?
WITNESS BHI: Yes, I will do so. 'We have said goodbye to the monarchy. The monarchy and the colonial regime left together. We support independence. We are going to get independence. We have said goodbye to the monarchy. The monarchy and the colonial regime have left together. We support independence. We are going to get independence.' There you are; that is the part which has remained in my memory, because that was a long time ago.[64]

In each case, whether Bikindi's songs were heard for 'transcriptual', 'causal', or 'indexical' purposes, the listening situation was very carefully managed by the Tribunal. The kinds of 'audile technique' put to work by the Tribunal were always for very specific institutional purposes and had equally specific institutional effects.[65] Most of all, they were bound up directly with the analytical distinction between music and lyric which we tracked in detail in Chapter 3. As far as the Tribunal was concerned, Bikindi's songs were worth listening to either as a kind

[61] *Bikindi* transcript, 2 October 2006, 17.

[62] For some other examples of this approach see *Bikindi* transcript, 10 October 2006, 3; 31 October 2007, 54.

[63] *Bikindi* transcript, 26 September 2007, 41.

[64] *Bikindi* transcript, 13 October 2006, 4.

[65] Sterne (2003) 92–5.

of pleasant distraction or for highly specific and predetermined evidentiary purposes. The act of listening was not where the important interpretative work would be done.

Bikindi Sings his Final Statement

At about a quarter to four in the afternoon on 30 September 2009, after six hours of oral submissions, the appeals hearing in the *Bikindi* case was about to draw to a close without incident. More than eight years had now passed since Bikindi was originally indicted on 4 July 2001. More than sixty days in court had been and gone and judgment had been pronounced. Counsel for the defence had just finished summarizing his argument. 'Can it really be just?' he asked in his plummy English accent, 'Can it really be a deserving punishment for this man to spend most, if not all of the rest of his life in prison? The divergence between the facts of this case and the facts of other cases is, in my submission, vast. And that is why the documents that we have brought to the attention of your honours, both my analysis of the Rwandan law and the national provisions, are, in my submission, of a persuasive nature'.[66] At this point a few amiable formalities were exchanged between the respective counsels and the bench to the effect that no one had any further submissions. And then finally, at four o'clock exactly according to the daily case minutes, Presiding Judge Patrick Robinson offered the floor to Bikindi himself one last time before the hearing came to an end.[67] 'Well in that case', said the judge, 'I have to inform Mr. Bikindi—Mr. Bikindi?—that you have an opportunity now to make a statement. If you wish to, you may make a statement'.[68] Bikindi, it seems, had come prepared. '*Ma declaration est simple*', he explained: 'my statement is simple'. And for the next five-and-a-half minutes, he sang.[69]

In dramatic terms, the performance is compelling. It helps, no doubt, that the audio-visual technician on duty that day seems to have been of an artistic persuasion.[70] In the archival footage, the shot pans across from the bench and zooms immediately in on Bikindi as he takes to his feet with a broad and knowing smile, staring directly into the camera. That he was fully aware of the provocative nature of his performance is not in doubt. And, as if to confirm it, a security guard remains in shot at all times, reminding the viewer that we are not after all at a concert.

Otherwise, it would be easy to forget. This has many of the hallmarks of a recital. Bikindi is in traditional costume, all in white, as he has been throughout the trial.[71] His *a cappella* is met with perfect quiet. As he sings, his body sways gently,

[66] *Bikindi v The Prosecutor* (Audio-Visual Record of the Appeals Hearing) ICTR-01-72-A, Appeals Chamber (30 September 2009) 7:25:42–7:26:17 ('*Bikindi* appeal audio-visual record').

[67] *Bikindi v The Prosecutor* (Case Minutes) ICTR-01-72-A, Appeals Chamber (30 September 2009).

[68] *Bikindi* appeal audio-visual record, 7:27:03–7:27:23.

[69] *Bikindi* appeal audio-visual record, 7:27:30–7:33:10.

[70] On the incorporation of visual rhetoric into legal practice, see generally Sherwin (2011).

[71] As one witness testified: 'Yes Bikindi is present. He is sitting to my left. He is wearing a white piece of cloth. The kind of clothing he is wearing are clothes that Rwandan men would wear in those

he closes his eyes sometimes, gestures constantly to emphasize his key points, taps out a rhythm with his hands. His voice is full and resonant, calm and controlled, perfectly pitched. There is a slight vibrato but no obvious sign of nerves. Above all one hears confidence and composure. Then, towards the end of the performance, there is a silence which lasts for seconds. Bikindi's head is bowed, his hands clasped together; a sombre look. The volume raises, his tone more insistent now, and with a shake of his hands and a long held note brought to a sudden end, he finishes.

There is no applause, though you half expect to hear it. With a bow of apparent deference to the bench, Bikindi thanks the court and the camera pans out and cuts back to the bench where at least four of the five judges are still wearing their headphones. The rest remain out of shot. A few moments elapse before the presiding judge eventually speaks again. He has been listening, it seems, to the 'simultaneous interpretation' of Bikindi's lyrics and this break in the rhythm of proceedings is a result of what is called *décalage*.[72] 'Thank you Mr Bikindi', he says. Where he had been positively jovial prior to the performance, the smile is now definitely gone from his voice. And then louder, more authoritatively: 'That ends the hearing. We are adjourned'.[73] There is no engagement at all, order immediately restored by means of a formulaic speech act which is palpably, even comfortingly legal in terms of its sound, content, and illocutionary force.[74] Judge Robinson switches off his microphone, removes his headphones and starts shuffling the papers on the desk in front of him as the great blue and white UN logo looms behind. After one final glance in Bikindi's direction he does not look across again. Clearly, when he invited Bikindi to make his final statement, this was not the sort of thing he'd had in mind.

What are we to make of this extraordinary episode? That is the question to which this chapter now turns. One thing is clear. Bikindi's final statement would have been experienced as transgressive to some extent by everyone present. Indeed, it still feels transgressive years after the fact on recording, as if some unspoken norm of judicial decorum was in the process of being breached. How is it that this moment feels so different to all of the other musical performances at trial, including Bikindi's own? The answer has to do with Bikindi's ability to take charge of the listening situation for once, to wrest it away from the Tribunal. When Bikindi sang his final statement, he was no longer singing *for* the Tribunal, he was singing *to* it. And to a large extent he was singing *past* it as well, to the people of Rwanda. The most obvious thing about Bikindi's final statement is also the most radical, the very fact that it is so difficult to know what to make of it, so hard to interpret, get a precise handle on, or pin down. Precisely because it feels so out of context, deprived of the comfort of a stable and familiar interpretative frame, as an acoustic event Bikindi's final statement is rich, multivalent, ambiguous, and conflicted. Its

days. These are clothing or attire which is attributable to the Rwandan tradition'. *Bikindi* transcript, 3 October 2006, 32.

[72] For a detailed consideration of simultaneous interpretation, see Chapter 8.

[73] *Bikindi* appeal audio-visual record, 7:33:25–7:33:30.

[74] See Chapter 6 for more detail on speech acts.

meaning refuses to fix itself, to submit to the ordinary rigours of the listening situation. In the judicial context, that is undeniably a transgressive gesture.

Singing to the Tribunal

Insofar as Bikindi's song is addressed to the ICTR itself, there are at least two ways of interpreting it. On the one hand, we could understand the resort to song at this crucial moment as an appeal to conscience, an attempt by Bikindi to *move* the court, to insist on his status as an artist and to play on this link we sometimes make between artistry and the ethical; one last effort, in other words, to present himself as Orphic, a gentle civilizer of men. One of the central functions of the final statement, as Cornelia Vismann points out, is to 'set the right mood for verdict-giving'. 'Judges are supposed to come to their decisions with the defendant's voice still ringing in their ears'.[75] And here was a particularly effective method of ensuring that they did.

But if so, Bikindi must surely have known that he ran a serious risk of being misconstrued. Even though at first instance the Tribunal had cleared him of all charges in respect of his songs, it went out of its way to declare them at least unsavoury. He had composed two songs with 'the specific intention to disseminate pro-Hutu ideology and anti-Tutsi propaganda, and thus to encourage ethnic hatred'.[76] '*Nanga Abahutu* and *Bene Sebahinzi* characterised the Tutsi as Hutu enslavers, enemies or enemy accomplices, blamed the enemy for the problems in Rwanda, encouraged Hutu solidarity against a common foe, the Tutsi, and finally supported the spirit of the Bahutu Ten Commandments published in *Kangura*'.[77] Moreover, 'if the songs were as innocent as portrayed by the Defence', the Chamber argued, 'they could not have been used in the manner they were'.[78] Whatever Bikindi's intentions may have been as his songs' author, even if it was not their 'composition' but their 'deployment' by Radio Rwanda and RTLM that had been particularly insidious,[79] the fact remains that they were sung literally as the perpetrators of Rwanda's genocide hacked and beat people to death. 'Witness BGH testified that she heard inhabitants of Gikongoro singing *Bene Sebahinzi* while they bore machetes and held their radio handsets', wrote the Trial Chamber. 'Members of the population

[75] Cornelia Vismann, 'Three Versions of a Defendant's Final Statement to the Court', *Law and Literature* 23(3) (2011) 297, 300.

[76] *Prosecutor v Bikindi* (Judgement) ICTR-01-72-T, T Ch III (2 December 2008) para 254 ('*Bikindi* judgment').

[77] The Bahutu Ten Commandments were published in a Rwandan magazine called *Kangura* in 1990. They consisted of a series of anti-Tutsi propositions: any Hutu who married a Tutsi woman, for instance, would be considered a 'traitor'; or 'Hutus must cease having any pity for the Tutsi'. The prosecution had argued that Bikindi's song *Nanga Abahutu/Akabyutso* expressed a very similar set of sentiments. The Ten Commandments were central in the *Media* case in which the editor of *Kangura* was convicted of genocide, conspiracy to commit genocide, direct and public incitement to genocide, and two counts of crimes against humanity. *Bikindi* judgment, paras 187, 220, 228–30, 254. *Prosecutor v Nahimana* (Judgement and Sentence) ICTR-99-52-T, T Ch I (3 December 2003) para 2.2.1 ('*Nahimana* judgment and sentence'). Also known as the '*Media* case'.

[78] *Bikindi* judgment, para 250.

[79] *Bikindi* judgment, para 263.

knew the song by heart, and when they perpetrated those crimes, they would sing his songs, and say that they were furious and wanted to avenge the deaths of their relatives'.[80]

Bikindi must surely have realized that his resort to song at this crucial moment ran the risk of being heard by the Tribunal, particularly insofar as it stood for the victims of 1994's atrocities, as in the worst possible taste. Bikindi's performance was not just an appeal to conscience, therefore, or at least not unproblematically so. There is an element here of straightforward defiance or dissent. His transgression of the ordinary principles of courtroom orality, his decision to adopt *precisely* the form which had landed him in court in the first place, can be understood as a refusal right at the very last to submit to the authority of the Tribunal which had already imprisoned him for eight years and which would in all likelihood keep him locked up for at least seven more.

Singing for yourself

Whatever the case, clearly there was an extent to which this was also an intensely personal gesture. Bikindi sang *to* the Court, but he also sang *for* himself. Song was his profession, even his calling. He had inherited his passion for music, he said, from his parents. His mother was 'what we commonly call a *griot*, which is somebody within a village who is well known for her singing capacity. She is also well known for—this person is well known for dancing, and also for story telling'.[81] Both his talent and his love of music were 'borne out of my childhood where my mother, taking part in the various festivities that I mentioned, always took me with her … She would practically always invite me along, invite me to sing, to dance, and to recite poetry that I had had the occasion to memorise'. Indeed his mother was his inspiration 'to become a proper artist and I really owe her very much for that'.[82] Although Bikindi's father was a farmer and a blacksmith by trade, 'at his time of rest, even at home, without it necessarily taking part—or, without necessarily taking part in festivities, he would play the sitar to us. The instrument is one of the instruments that I can play very well'.[83] Having been raised in such a musical environment, Bikindi went on to study music and theatre throughout his time at school, both in Rwanda[84] and at the Pan African Development Institute in Douala, Cameroon,[85] before being 'discovered' while still a teenager by a government minister and recruited directly into the 'Ministry of Youth and Association Movement' in 1976.[86] Although he was originally employed in the so-called 'division for folklore' to conduct rehearsals of the national ballet, in 1985 he was promoted and continued to be employed as 'head of the division for the supervision of social-cultural activities' until June 1994 when he fled Rwanda. Furthermore, since its foundation in 1987 he had served variously as a member and leader of the

[80] *Bikindi* judgment, para 253.
[81] *Bikindi* transcript, 31 October 2007, 4–5.
[82] *Bikindi* transcript, 31 October 2007, 5.
[83] *Bikindi* transcript, 31 October 2007, 5.
[84] *Bikindi* transcript, 31 October 2007, 7.
[85] *Bikindi* transcript, 31 October 2007, 3.
[86] *Bikindi* transcript, 31 October 2007, 14.

private and extremely well-known *Irindiro* ballet company.[87] As for his recording career, at trial Bikindi testified to having authored a total of between forty and sixty songs during his lifetime.[88] A list compiled by the expert witness for the defence presents fifty-five recordings in total ranging from 1983 to 2007. Most of these Bikindi had both authored and performed.[89] An entire life in music then, both a calling and a vocation. For Bikindi, song was not just a means of dissent or transgression. It was his favoured means of expression, quite simply what he did best.

But if Bikindi was deeply invested personally in song as a communicative and expressive form, it is worth adding that there is also something intensely personal about it per se. Song, after all, foregrounds the voice, and in doing so reverses what we tend to think of as the ordinary hierarchy. Rather than a mere leftover, a mediological by-product of verbal communication, in song the voice's sound, materiality, and resonance are precisely the point. In song, as Italian philosopher Adriana Cavarero explains, it is the vocal that 'commands the semantic'.[90] What does it mean to foreground the voice in this way? In a wonderful short story entitled *A King Listens*, Italo Calvino puts it like this: above all 'a voice means this: there is a living person, chest, feelings, who sends into the air this voice, different from all other voices'.[91] Taking her lead from Hannah Arendt, Cavarero insists, too, on what she calls a 'vocal ontology of uniqueness'.[92] Thereby before it conveys a content, the human voice always communicates first and foremost itself, its uniqueness: the singularity of this person, and no other.

From a personal and professional as well as a metaphysical standpoint, therefore, we can understand Bikindi's decision to sing his final statement both as an expression of and an insistence on selfhood. Not just a commitment to a mode of expression in which he was heavily invested, to a way of living and an entire life lived, but a refusal finally to be reduced to law's categories (genocidaire, artist, Rwandan): to be framed as anything other than his unique self.

Singing to Rwandans

This was an intensely personal gesture then, but also one which inevitably invoked a tradition and by extension a community. No music is absent a lineage, a relationship to genre. Indeed genre is a key part of what gives a piece of music its meaning, what makes it comprehensible, prevents it from being just so much noise.[93] We cannot understand this song as an expression of selfhood alone. When Bikindi sang his final statement he inevitably summoned both a musical and interpretative

[87] *Bikindi* judgment, para 41.

[88] *Bikindi* transcript, 31 October 2007, 14.

[89] Annex 1 of Exhibit No D117(F), 'Defence Expert Report of Dr Eugène Shimamungu', *Prosecutor v Bikindi*, ICTR-01-72-0265 (3 October 2007).

[90] Adriana Cavarero, *For More than One Voice: Toward a Philosophy of Vocal Expression*, trans Paul A Kottman (Stanford University Press, 2005) [trans of: *A piu voci: Per una filosofia dell'espressione vocale* (first published 2003)] 80.

[91] Ital Calvino, *Under the Jaguar Sun*, trans William Weaver (Yarcourt Brace, 1988) 33–64 ('A King Listens').

[92] Cavarero (2005) particularly ch 3.

[93] Stockfelt (2004).

heritage. If some of the meaning of this performance is lost both on the Tribunal and other non-Rwandan listeners, that should come as no particular surprise. Overcoming the problem of understanding is not simply a matter of listeners tuning in to an interpretation in their language of choice on their headsets. As outsiders to the Rwandan musical tradition, its particular 'scheme of interpretation', there is much about this performance which they simply cannot help but miss. Part of the meaning and force of Bikindi's final address consists precisely in his refusal to speak directly to the court, or only to it, in his decision to adopt a mode of expression which a non-expert or non-Rwandan audience would never fully be able to understand. We can think of Bikindi's chosen mode of expression as an index of culture, as both a dramatic reminder of the postcolonial context in which he found himself and an exemplification of some of the difficulties which such a context elicits.

If Bikindi is clearly singing past the Appeals Court to some extent, therefore, if his audience is seemingly the Rwandan people too, and if that is already evident at the level of sound, it is just as clear where the song's lyrics are concerned. They begin as follows: 'The tragic events that occurred in Rwanda constitute an unspeakable tragedy', he sings, 'tragic events that will leave you stunned, a real tragedy. Let us pray that never again will they happen, never again will they occur. Oh my people. Never again. Never never never ever again'.[94] An acceptance, then, of the facticity, even the 'tragedy' of the genocide—although he never names it as such—but nothing approaching responsibility. Compassion but not remorse. And notice the language here. It will be immediately familiar to both Western and Rwandan listeners. 'Never again'. The common refrain of international justice mechanisms since the Holocaust, it was precisely this injunction that the Rwandan genocide so spectacularly breached.[95] Bikindi takes this refrain and turns it into his chorus, not only echoing the language of international justice directly back at it, but placing it front and centre. These few lines will turn out to be the song's thematic anchor, both the lyrical and melodic bookends between which a much longer, discursive middle section is elaborated. Bikindi continues:

> Were I again to have the opportunity to sing, to sing for Rwandans, I would go to the country of a thousand hills so that all Rwandans can hear me. I would climb right up to the highest peaks and once at the pinnacle I would lodge my appeal: I would invite the Rwandans, Hutu, Twa and Tutsi alike, I would remind them that the tragic events that occurred in Rwanda have injured the hearts of all of us. I would invite them to sing in unison:
>
> The tragic events that occurred in Rwanda constitute an unspeakable tragedy: tragic events that will leave you stunned, a real tragedy. Let us pray that never again will they happen, never again will they occur. Oh my people, never again. Never ever ever ever again.[96]

[94] *Bikindi* appeal audio-visual record, 7:27:45–7:28:15.

[95] See eg, Philip Gourevitch, *We Wish to Inform You That Tomorrow We Will Be Killed with Our Families: Stories from Rwanda* (Picador, 1998) 170; Martin Gilbert, *Never Again: A History of the Holocaust* (Universe, 2000).

[96] *Bikindi* appeal audio-visual record, 7:28:15–7:29:39.

'Were I again to have the opportunity to sing, to sing for Rwandans'. The conditional is strictly unnecessary. Bikindi is well aware of the mediascape in which his performance operates. He knows on the one hand that both Rwandan journalists and members of the Rwandan public are actually present in the public gallery, and that his performance is being recorded by the Tribunal for posterity and eventually distribution.[97] The courtroom is deployed here as both a stage and a media-technology. It actually becomes Bikindi's 'highest peak', a broadcasting device for addressing the Rwandan people, and moreover in an idiom which only they will fully understand.

As for the precise form of address, it is both a call to prayer and an 'appeal', the invocation of a higher authority and, finally, a socio-political one, as the song goes on to elaborate:

> Then will come the political leaders and the ordinary citizens, sages, experienced and honest men will also be invited there. To come too will be specialists of Rwandan history so they can do a thorough analysis. Present also at the appointed hour will be our experts in the socio-economic fields. They will come together to identify the real causes of our misfortunes and make proposals for a final solution to the endemic tragedies among Rwandans. All this with a single objective for everyone: the reconstruction of Rwanda. So that she becomes a nation spared of wars, killings and tears, a nation in which Tutsis, Twa and Hutu will together live in peace like brothers, without tearing each other apart.[98]

Bikindi's 'appeal' to Rwandans consists not just of the imperative 'never again' therefore, but also and crucially a call for reconstruction via historicization. Whether or not this amounts to a critique of the efforts of incumbent President Paul Kagame's ministry since 1994 is an open question.[99] But it must surely be read as an indictment of the Tribunal before which he was singing. The appeal here is clearly for an internal rather than an external mechanism.

If Bikindi has already staged a rejection of the ICTR's authority at the level of form, here it is asserted at the level of substance. Rwanda's experts and specialists, he sings, along with the 'political leaders', 'ordinary citizens, sages, experienced and honest men', will come together to conduct a '*thorough* analysis', to identify the '*real* causes' of Rwanda's misfortunes and 'make proposals for a *final* solution' to the country's 'endemic tragedies'. The contrast we are being invited to make with the international community's own efforts is only barely implicit. He goes on:

> I will seize the opportunity to remind Rwandans that Rwanda is the home of three ethnic groups, Hutu, Twa and Tutsis and no-one chooses to be born Hutu, Tutsi or Twa. No-one pays to be born Rwandan. The Twa is a Rwandan Twa. The Hutu is a Rwandan Hutu. The Tutsi is a Rwandan Tutsi. No-one can change that. We must all understand and always

[97] For more detail on the ICTR's broadcasting and archival practices, see Chapter 8.

[98] *Bikindi* appeal audio-visual record, 7:29:39–7:30:58.

[99] For an overview of the criticisms levelled at President Kagame, see Filip Reyntjens, 'Rwanda, Ten Years On: From Genocide to Dictatorship', *African Affairs* 103(411) (2004) 177; Filip Reyntjens, 'Constructing the Truth, Dealing with Dissent, Domesticating the World: Governance in Post-genocide Rwanda', *African Affairs* 110(438) (2011) 1.

bear in mind that no-one should be a victim of his ethnicity or have to live as an outcast because of it. Above all, the most important thing is the acceptance of the other person and the respect of his individual integrity, respect for their rights and freedoms throughout the national territory.[100]

Where in the previous section Bikindi had outlined an instrumental vision for Rwanda's reconstruction, here the account is overtly normative. The grammar is different now. 'We must ...' he sings. 'The most important thing is ...' And if the sermon being preached here—formal racial equality, individual integrity, respect for rights and freedoms—bears an uncanny resemblance to that of the very institution whose authority he had been calling into question only moments ago, we are left to wonder whether this is intentional on Bikindi's part or simply the product of a system of interpretation incapable of doing anything other than echoing the institution's own language back at itself. In any case, Bikindi is clear enough in what follows that it is Rwanda's *own* norms, Rwanda's *own* culture, that he regards as being ultimately authoritative:

Dear fellow citizens, be careful! Division is only of benefit to others. It is forbidden dear fellow citizens, it is against our culture to remind someone of painful events. To the contrary, Rwandan culture teaches us that victims of the same misfortune try to support and console one another. Faced with the same misfortune, they provisionally set aside their quarrels. They close ranks without bitterness so they can better understand the truth and make it see the light of day. The innocent are proved innocent, pardon is at last given and the guilty are punished. Thus these exchanges based on truth, mutual respect and understanding firmly cement reconciliation.[101]

If the language had already begun to take on a normative tone before, here the juridical claims come thick and fast. 'It is forbidden dear fellow citizens', Bikindi insists, 'it is against our culture...' And he sings of guilt and innocence, pardon and punishment, all in the name, he suggests, of truth, mutual respect, and reconciliation. This finally is Bikindi as jurist, singing his law back to a rival juridical order.

Singing the law

This is the most difficult and potentially contentious register of Bikindi's final statement. If law in the West defines itself partly in terms of its difference from song—if music registers there as precisely the limit or opposite of legal expression conventionally understood—the same cannot necessarily be said of other juridical traditions,[102] and particularly not when it comes to Africa. For Ugandan poet,

[100] *Bikindi* appeal audio-visual record, 7:30:58–7:31:38.

[101] *Bikindi* appeal audio-visual record, 7:31:38–7:32:35.

[102] For a jurisprudential reading of indigenous Australian songlines, eg, see Christine F Black, *The Land is the Source of the Law: A Dialogic Encounter with Indigenous Jurisprudence* (Routledge, 2011) 15, 17. See also Allan Marett, *Songs, Dreamings, and Ghosts: The Wangga of North Australia* (Wesleyan University Press, 2005). For discussion specifically on the role of song and ceremony in Australian native title claims, see Grace Koch, *We Have the Song, So We Have the Land: Song and Ceremony as Proof of Ownership in Aboriginal and Torres Strait Islander Land Claims*, AIATSIS Discussion Paper 33 (July 2013).

writer, lawyer, and jurist Okot p'Bitek, 'in any society, anywhere, in any age, there are two types of rulers'. First the artist, 'who provides and sustains the fundamental ideas, the foundation of society'. Second, 'the political chieftain' who 'merely puts these ideas into practice in ruling or misruling society'.[103] In this respect he claims the West is in denial.[104] In what he refers to as the 'Africa of tradition', by contrast, the artist's legal function is at once 'fully acknowledged, admired' and, he adds, 'feared'.[105] In what sense is the artist's function a legal one?

> The artist proclaims the laws but expresses them in the most indirect language: through metaphor and symbol, in image and fable. He sings and dances his laws. It is taught, not in the school of law, not at the Inns of Court, but around the evening fire, where elephants and hares act as men. The body movement, the painting, the sculptures are his law books. The drums, the flutes, the horns, the strumming and plucking on the strings of the musical instruments, are the proclamations of his decrees.[106]

It is clear both from the historical literature and a good deal of the testimony in the *Bikindi* case that the claim could equally be made of historical Rwanda.[107] One particularly obvious example of this is the central juridical role played for so long by the royal drum Kalinga.[108] As Jan Vansina explains, 'in the ideology of the Great Lakes region a kingdom only exists when it has a dynastic drum'.[109] It was the discovery of Kalinga by Ruganzu Ndori which was said to have both signalled and authorized the arrival of the Nyiginya kingdom in the mid-seventeenth century.[110] And it was according to the rhythms of Kalinga along with its battery of smaller siblings[111] that

[103] Okot p'Bitek, *Artist, the Ruler: Essays on Art, Culture and Values* (Heinemann, 1986) 39. For a commentary on Okot p'Bitek's works *Song of Lawino and Song of Ocol* (Heinemann, 1984), see Peter Leman, 'Singing the Law: Okot p'Bitek's Legal Imagination and the Poetics of Traditional Justice', *Research in African Literatures* 40(3) (2009) 109.

[104] This view is consistent with that of legal pluralists, who have long argued against the state-centric account of law in the West. Instead, they prefer an approach that would acknowledge the active role played by all citizens—artists, musicians, and singers included—in the creation of and engagement with normative order. See John Griffiths, 'What is Legal Pluralism?' *Journal of Legal Pluralism and Unofficial Law* 24(1) (1986) 1; Sally Engle Merry, 'Legal Pluralism', *Law and Society Review* 22(5) (1988) 869; Robert Cover, 'The Supreme Court, 1982 Term—Foreword: Nomos and Narrative', *Harvard Law Review* 97(1) (1983) 4; Roderick A Macdonald and David Sandomierski, 'Against Nomopolies', *Northern Ireland Legal Quarterly* 57(4) (2006) 610; Roderick Macdonald, 'Here, There ... and Everywhere: Theorizing Legal Pluralism; Theorizing Jacques Vanderlinden' in Nicholas Kasirer (ed), *Étudier et enseigner le droit: Hier, aujourd'hui et demain—Études offertes à Jacques Vanderlinden* (Éditions Yvon Blais, 2006); Roderick A Macdonald, 'Custom Made: For a Non-Chirographic Critical Legal Pluralism', *Canadian Journal of Law and Society* 26(2) (2011) 301.

[105] p'Bitek (1986) 39.

[106] p'Bitek (1986) 39.

[107] See Jan Vansina, *Antecedents to Modern Rwanda: The Nyiginya Kingdom* (University of Wisconsin Press, 2004).

[108] Historian Jan Vansina uses the alternate spelling 'Karinga'. Because the subject of this thesis is the ICTR, however, I have preferred their spelling here. See Vansina (2004) xiii.

[109] Vansina (2004) 48. For Alexis Kagame, the drum was a symbol of monarchy in the region at least as early as the fifteenth century. Alexis Kagame, *La poésie dynastique au Rwanda* (IRSAC, 1951) 30–50.

[110] Vansina (2004) 44.

[111] Vansina (2004) 55, 59; Exhibit No P73(E), *Prosecutor v Bikindi* (13 September 2006), 19, 23; *Bikindi* transcript, 14 February 2007, 35.

the region was governed all the way up until Rwanda's independence from Belgium and the unseating of the colonially endorsed Tutsi monarchy in 1962.[112] For defence expert Eugene Shimamungu, Kalinga was a 'symbol of divine power'.[113] Not only did it reside permanently by the side of the king at the centre of the capital, together they were 'the concrete manifestation of the very existence of the kingdom and its unity'.[114] As such, the drum played a central role in relation to both the everyday business and institutional structure of government. On the one hand, 'the daily schedule that regulated the life of the whole court was marked by the rhythm of [the king's] drum of summons',[115] and other drums, moreover, could be used as a means of ordering a person's arrest, or even their execution.[116] On the other hand, Kalinga and the so-called 'ritualists of the drums' were at the centre of a whole complex of offices—dynastic poets,[117] historians, musicians (string and wind instrumentalists), artisans, magicians, diviners, and many more—all regarded as essential to the running of the court and the maintenance and development of its traditions, norms, customs, and history. They were essential, in other words, to both the provision and sustenance of the 'fundamental ideas of society':[118] at once its lore and, in the absence of a codified body of rules or formal tribunal system, we might also say with Okot p'Bitek, its law.[119]

Much as Rwanda's political and legal structures had changed by the time of the genocide in 1994, all this was by no means ancient history. Indeed, one of Bikindi's most controversial lyrics, from the song *Bene Sebahinzi/Intabaza*, was regarded as inflammatory precisely *because* of the way in which it invoked this tradition. The lyric made reference to the practice, infamous throughout Rwanda, of adorning the dynastic drum with the testicles of vanquished enemies, particularly Hutus.[120] As one witness would testify at trial, Kalinga 'was the emblematic drum of the monarchy' and therefore, historically, the Tutsi. And it was 'decorated with the genitals of the Hutus'. Bikindi's song warned, the witness said, that 'the drum was, once again, going to be beaten in Rwanda'.[121] It warned of a return of the old monarchy, the old law, and was taken by many to have sounded a call to arms, 'an

[112] For an account of the historical evolution of the terms Hutu and Tutsi and their changing roles in the governance of the Nyiginya kingdom, see Vansina (2004) 134–9.

[113] Exhibit No D117(F), *Prosecutor v Bikindi* (3 October 2007) 17 (translation mine).

[114] Vansina (2004) 82. [115] Vansina (2004) 84.

[116] Vansina (2004) 90. This practice is also referred to in Rose Brandel, *The Music of Central Africa: An Ethnomusicological Study—Former French Equatorial Africa, the Former Belgian Congo, Ruanda-Urundi, Uganda, Tanganyika* (Martinus Nijhoff, 1973) 39; René Bourgeois, *Banyarwanda et Burundi* (Institut Royal Colonial Belge, 1954) 41.

[117] The distinction between oral poetry and song is a fine one, but it is clear that in Rwanda the poet was often also a singer in the sense that they often worked specifically with melody. Jan Vansina, *Oral Tradition as History* (University of Wisconsin Press, 1985) 46, 80, 114. Stephen Belcher, *Epic Traditions of Africa* (Indiana University Press, 1999) 17.

[118] p'Bitek (1986) 39. [119] Vansina (2004) 89.

[120] Vansina makes reference to one episode of this sort that occurred during the reign of Gahindiro in the early ninteenth century. Throughout the *Bikindi* case, however, witnesses were much less specific. Vansina (2004) 159, 212. *Bikindi* transcript: 12 October 2006, 30; 4 October 2006, 6; 10 October 2006, 16; 16 February 2007, 26; Exhibit No P73(E), *Prosecutor v Bikindi* (13 September 2006) 5, 18, 19; Exhibit No D117(F), *Prosecutor v Bikindi* (3 October 2007) 17.

[121] *Bikindi* transcript, 2 October 2006, 34.

invitation not only to hate, but also to kill people, especially given the surrounding context of war and genocide', whatever Bikindi's intentions may have been.[122]

Bikindi would deny that as a singer he exercised any overtly juridical function. Indeed, his strategy at trial was to insist on a strict demarcation between artistry and authority, as we saw in Chapter 3. Nor was the ICTR interested in thinking song as a specifically legal form. Nevertheless, some appreciation of the Rwandan musico-legal tradition must surely inform our understanding of Bikindi's final statement. For an acoustic jurisprudence the fact that throughout the region's history music was so intimately bound up with the juridical imagination cannot help but colour the way we hear the performance. What I am suggesting is that in Bikindi's very decision to sing we can detect a juridical resonance that would not exist in many other contexts. If Bikindi's final statement did not necessarily stage a contest between two rival laws and juridico-expressive traditions in quite the same way the Haida's performance did in the *Western Forest* case, it surely contained at least the echo of one. We can understand Bikindi's decision to sing, finally, as an affirmation at the level of form at least as much as content of a certain brand of traditional Rwandan values; and an assertion of both political and juridical sovereignty in the face of an institution which has not always been free of charges of imperialism.[123]

The final statement as listening situation

I do not want to exaggerate the importance of this moment. Even though it was clearly transgressive, even if it constituted an extremely interesting and complex juridical moment, in the end Bikindi's final statement was no great challenge to the Tribunal's authority. A descendant perhaps of the pleas for mercy of the early modern era, Cornelia Vismann argues that the final statement exists totally outside of the ordinary rules of procedure.[124] 'How a defendant fills up the discursive frame allotted to him', Vismann writes, 'is his decision alone. Above all, he is allowed to pull out all the stops in an effort to make the judge more favourably disposed toward him. Heartrending tales of woe, irrelevancies, untruths are all permitted; there is not even a limit specified for the amount of time the last word may take up. Here, everything must be allowed to be said'.[125] Or, for that matter, sung. The final statement is the one moment at trial in which the ordinary listening situation is suspended. It is this fact which both enabled Bikindi's transgression in this respect and, in the end, ensured its containment. For Vismann, the final statement isn't just a procedural oddity. Because it comes only after the hearing of evidence and

[122] *Bikindi* judgment, para 235.

[123] Jose Alvarez has argued that the structure of the ICTR serves to obscure Western complicity in the genocide. Jose E Alvarez, 'Crimes of State/Crimes of Hate: Lessons from Rwanda', *Yale Journal of International Law* 24(2) (1999) 365. On the question of international law and imperialism generally, see Anthony Anghie, *Imperialism, Sovereignty and the Making of International Law* (Cambridge University Press, 2005).

[124] Vismann (2011) 298–300.

[125] Vismann (2011) 298.

cannot therefore have any bearing on the finding of facts, there is a sense in which it is simply not counted as an element of the trial itself.[126] And sure enough, it is not even mentioned in the ICTR's *Rules of Procedure and Evidence*.[127] We can think of the final statement as a kind of purposeful anomaly, therefore, a 'luxury' as Vismann puts it, both for the defendant and, most of all, the court itself.[128] If it seems like a gift to the accused, it is the kind of gift that only an institution in a position of absolute authority could ever give.

Bikindi ends his song as follows. 'Thus Rwandans, I invite you to observe a brief moment of silence so that all together we can honour the memory of all those innocent victims so savagely killed'. And after that pause has been duly observed, one last iteration of the chorus. 'And we shall finish by singing in unison: The tragic events that occurred in Rwanda constitute an unspeakable tragedy: tragic events that will leave you stunned, a real tragedy. Let us pray that never again will they happen, never again will they occur. Oh my people. Never again. Never ever ever ever again'. And as if to confirm, finally, the limits of his transgression, Bikindi says with his hands held in apparent sincerity to his chest: '*Merci beaucoup, Monsieur Le President. Merci beaucoup Honorables Juges . . .*' 'Thank you very much your Honours for having given me this opportunity'.[129]

[126] Vismann (2011) 298.

[127] International Criminal Tribunal for Rwanda, 'Rules of Procedure and Evidence' (29 June 1995) UN Doc ITR/3/REV.1.

[128] Vismann (2011) 298.

[129] *Bikindi* appeal audio-visual record, 7:32:33–7:33:30.

PART 3

SPEECH

5
Voices of Law

It may have been Bikindi's songs that landed him in court, but it was speech that would eventually found his conviction: three statements he was said to have made over a loudspeaker one day in June 1994.[1] This chapter tracks how these and other utterances were understood by the Tribunal on the way to judgment. In doing so, it always sticks closely to the particulars of Bikindi's trial, but because the theme is speech now rather than song much of the discussion here necessarily resonates more widely than before. The speaking voice is an ongoing concern for law in a way that music obviously is not, even if the ICTR's response to Bikindi's songs was often symptomatic of certain broader problems legal institutions have with form, affect, and the ineffable, as we have already begun to see. One important consequence is that this chapter addresses questions of philosophy and metaphysics more directly than any other in the book. In some ways, this is inevitable. The ties between legal thought and the metaphysical are strong, and the voice is fundamental to the question of metaphysics, as Derrida in particular has shown.[2] An acoustic jurisprudence must be sensitive to the role of metaphysics in shaping legal outcomes. In doing so, however, it must equally be attentive to the work of legal form and technique, the precise ways in which the metaphysical comes in and out of focus throughout the project of adjudication. And it must also be conscious that there are other registers, oriented towards more local and institutional concerns, at which questions of voice and the juridical engage each other. At the ICTR at least, there were many *voices of law*, not just one.

The chapter begins by establishing the Tribunal's general approach. Throughout Bikindi's trial, the voice was consistently depicted as language's instrument: the necessary medium in speech, its acoustic form and material support. In this respect it performed the same function for the Tribunal as music was imagined to in song. It was a way of delivering 'messages', a container truck for thoughts. When it came to securing Bikindi's conviction, however, the voice also appears to have done something else important. In the apparent proximity of the spoken word to the ideality of thought itself, the voice seems to have operated at a key moment in the

[1] *Prosecutor v Bikindi* (Judgement) ICTR-01-72-T, T Ch III (2 December 2008) ('*Bikindi* judgment') paras 268–9.

[2] Adriana Cavarero, *For More than One Voice: Toward a Philosophy of Vocal Expression*, trans Paul A Kottman (Stanford University Press, 2005) [trans of: *A piu voci: Per una filosofia dell'espressione vocale* (first published 2003)] 213.

Trial Chamber's judgment as a kind of surrogate for and material embodiment of Bikindi's intention. In the end, it was Bikindi's voice that guaranteed the expressive chain, as it were, between his intent, words, and the ears of his listeners, and in doing so enabled juridical responsibility to attach. If this was the approach to the speaking voice that proved decisive, however, it was not the only one. There were moments at trial where the ICTR does seem to have been sensitive to other dimensions of speech: to the bodiliness and audibility of the act of vocalization, to ways of apprehending the voice that do not reduce it to thought's instrument. It is with such moments that a critique of the Tribunal's approach to voice might begin. In this respect, the work of Shoshana Felman, Judith Butler, and Julia Kristeva amongst others shows how the necessary corporeality of the speech act can function as a kind of limit to intentionality as opposed to its guarantor. Even though this sort of critique has a lot to offer an acoustic jurisprudence in general, my suggestion is that in the particular circumstances of the *Bikindi* case it doesn't necessarily get us very far because it misses the specifically institutional character of the problems the Tribunal was required to address. For an acoustic jurisprudence, the ICTR's account of voice was at its most troubling when it came to Bikindi's songs.

The Linguistic Voice

The voice was everywhere and nowhere in the *Bikindi* case. So much of the discussion at trial related to speech in one way or another, and yet exceptionally little attention seems to have been paid to either the fact or the possible significance of its existence as sound. This was true right from the earliest drafts of the indictment, through years of trial, all the way up to the judgments delivered by the trial and appeals chambers respectively. The examples are far too many to enumerate, but to take just one characteristic illustration of the Tribunal's general approach, in its description of a rally held at a football field in 1993, the Trial Chamber wrote the following:

> Bikindi was accompanied by the former *bourgmestre* of Nyamyumba *commune*, Faustin Bagango, and Wellars Banzi, all three of whom spoke at the rally … According to Witness AKJ, Bikindi addressed the crowd saying '[y]ou know this well: you must exterminate or get rid of those serpents which are among you.' He explained that 'serpents' was a reference to the Tutsi who must be killed. Witness AKJ testified that Bikindi was very clear about who the enemy of the Hutu was. He said: 'You must not be mistaken, [y]our enemies are the Tutsis; your enemies are the Tutsis.'[3]

Three speakers then. In each case we know that the speech was heard. And yet this audibility seems not to matter compared with the obvious and overriding significance of *what* was said.

[3] *Bikindi* judgment, para 135.

Both in legal practice and elsewhere, this approach to speech is so deeply entrenched that it can seem almost natural, totally unsurprising, a matter of simple 'common sense'. For Mladen Dolar the strange reticence of the voice, the way in which it can sometimes seem to resist its very existence as sound, is a result of its 'inner relationship with meaning'.[4] It is this relationship, most of all, which 'singles the voice out against the vast ocean of sounds and noises', which 'defines the voice as special among the infinite array of acoustic phenomena'.[5] It is not that other sounds are necessarily meaningless. In Chapter 7 we will consider how noise often operates as an acoustic sign of social unrest. In Chapter 8 we will attend briefly to the signifying function of the gavel. But even these sounds seem to be deprived of meaning 'in themselves'.[6] Sometimes the sound of wood coming into contact with wood is just that: it *means* nothing. The voice is different. The voice 'is a sound which appears to be endowed in itself with the will to "say something," with an inner intentionality'.[7] It has a teleology, a purpose. 'It is as if there is an arrow in it which raises the expectation of meaning'.[8] So when we listen to a person speak, even though we may initially be aware of their accent, tone, and other vocal characteristics, soon enough we accommodate to them and the voice begins to recede from our attention. Sooner or later we start to focus exclusively on the meaning, on *what* is being said as opposed to *how*. This is why the voice can often seem to 'disappear' in the utterance, to 'go up in smoke in the meaning being produced'.[9]

Though its reach is extremely broad, and its history extends back 'at least as far as Plato's *Cratylus*', we could think of this as the 'linguistic' approach to voice.[10] In addition to being so prevalent at the ICTR, it is foundational, for instance, to the contemporary discipline of phonetics. Phonetics is concerned with the voice in its physicality, its resonance, in how we make and control vocal sounds, in breath, the larynx, the tongue, jaw, lips, lungs, and palate.[11] It is the study of the physiological production and acoustic properties of the voice as the bearer of language, specifically as a medium, quite literally an instrument. But this approach is equally characteristic of phonology too. Unlike phonetics, phonology is concerned with the voice's role in cognition, in its implication in the project of language itself. It is phonology therefore that lays claim to the discovery of the *phoneme*. Like its typographical sibling the *grapheme*, the phoneme is a purely contrastive or differential unit. Its value consists simply in one's ability to distinguish it aurally from any other such unit.[12] Phonemes are the senseless 'sound-atoms' that in combination and in their difference from one another, enable speech to 'make sense'.[13] Phonemes, in other words, are what enable us to distinguish aurally between bat

[4] Mladen Dolar, *A Voice and Nothing More* (MIT Press, 2006) 14.

[5] Dolar (2006) 14. [6] Dolar (2006) 14. [7] Dolar (2006) 14.

[8] Dolar (2006) 14. [9] Dolar (2006) 15. [10] Cavarero (2005) 9.

[11] See Jody Kreiman and Diana Sidtis, *Foundations of Voice Studies: An Interdisciplinary Approach to Voice Production and Perception* (Wiley-Blackwell, 2011) 25–71 (ch 2, 'Producing a Voice and Controlling Its Sound').

[12] Ferdinand de Saussure, *Course in General Linguistics*, trans. Roy Harris (first published 1986, Open Court Classics, 2006) [trans of: *Cours de linguistique générale* (first published 1916)] 116–17.

[13] Dolar (2006) 18.

and cat and kite, but not between sight and site without more by way of context. It is phonemes that constitute the acoustic matter of language, that together comprise its sonorous content and structure.[14]

And yet, at exactly the same moment as the phoneme seems to turn our attention towards the audible in speech, it enacts a kind of dematerialization, a silencing. By dissolving sounds into a system of pure differences, a structure, a schema, phonology 'stabs the voice with the signifying dagger; it does away with its living presence, with its flesh and blood', its materiality and resonance.[15] 'The essence of language', as Ferdinand de Saussure claimed, 'has nothing to do with the phonic nature of the linguistic sign'.[16] Even as phonology seems to foreground the voice, therefore, it sublimates it and in doing so reinforces the conventional hierarchy between sense and sound, meaning and medium. In legal thought as elsewhere—and in this respect the *Bikindi* case was absolutely typical—the materiality of voice frequently evaporates into the ideality of the language it seems to convey. Voice becomes the 'instrument, the vehicle, the medium', and signification the goal.[17]

The Voice of Doctrine

Just three utterances proved determinative in the *Bikindi* case. Two witnesses testified to having seen and, crucially, heard Bikindi one day in June 1994 on the road between Kivumu and Kayove, two *communes* (districts) to the west of Rwanda's capital Kigali. Bikindi had been riding in a vehicle, they said, as part of a convoy comprising mostly *Interahamwe* militia. And this vehicle, which was 'outfitted with a loudspeaker', was broadcasting recordings of his songs as well as 'intermittent statements' by Bikindi himself. The most important passage of the Trial Chamber's judgment in this respect is as follows:

> Witness AKK heard Bikindi say 'You sons of *Sebahinzi*, who are the majority, I am speaking to you, you know that the Tutsi are minority. Rise up and look everywhere possible and do not spare anybody.' Witness AKK interpreted this to mean that although some Tutsi had already been killed, others were hiding and Bikindi was calling on people to do all that was necessary to eliminate the Tutsi. The witness also testified that on the way back from Kayove, Bikindi stopped at a roadblock and met with leaders of the local *Interahamwe* where he insisted, 'you see, when you hide a snake in your house, you can expect to face the consequences.' After Bikindi left the roadblock, members of the surrounding population and the *Interahamwe* intensified their search for Tutsi, using the assistance of dogs and going into homes to flush out those still hiding. Witness AKK stated that a number of people were subsequently killed …[18]

Later on the same day, another witness, AKJ, 'heard Bikindi ask over a loudspeaker, "Have you killed the Tutsi?" and whether they had killed the "snakes"'.[19]

[14] Dolar (2006) 19.
[15] Dolar (2006) 19.
[16] Saussure (2006) 7.
[17] Dolar (2006) 15.
[18] *Bikindi* judgment, para 268.
[19] *Bikindi* judgment, para 269.

Factually speaking, this much the Chamber ruled had been proven beyond reasonable doubt.[20]

As for its 'legal findings',[21] the Chamber was again concerned with the shape and limits of the law of freedom of expression that we considered at the end of Chapter 3. Again, the relevant definitions referred to 'information', 'ideas', and 'opinions'.[22] This time, however, the Tribunal was on more familiar ground. Speech was its expressive archetype, the paradigm against which song and other forms of expression would be measured. 'The Chamber therefore considers that the words accompanying a score of music are comparable from a legal perspective to the words used in a speech'.[23] There was a 'discernible hierarchy' of expression, the Chamber said. 'Whereas most forms of expression clearly remain within the limits of the legality, others are unequivocally of a criminal nature and should be sanctioned as such'.[24] Incitement to genocide was just such an example. As a species of exception to the general right to freedom of expression, the Chamber explained the doctrine of incitement as follows.[25] 'A person commits the crime of direct and public incitement to commit genocide', it wrote, 'if he directly and publicly incites the commission of genocide with the intent to directly and publicly incite others to commit genocide, which presupposes a genocidal intent. As an inchoate crime, public and direct incitement to commit genocide is punishable even if no act of genocide has resulted therefrom'.[26]

If that comes perilously close to tautology, Gregory Gordon has usefully clarified, relying on the Tribunal's decision in the *Akayesu* case by way of authority.[27] Accordingly, the crime of 'direct and public incitement to genocide' comprises three parts:

> (1) its mens rea element (consisting of the dual intent to provoke another to commit genocide and to commit the underlying genocide itself); (2) its 'direct' element (viewing the speech 'in the light of its cultural and linguistic content' to determine if the persons for whom the message was intended immediately grasped the implication thereof); and (3) its 'public' element ('a call for criminal action to a number of individuals in a public place,' or to 'members of the general public at large by such means as the mass media, for example, radio or television').[28]

[20] *Bikindi* judgment, para 285. [21] *Bikindi* judgment, ch IV ('Legal Findings').

[22] Universal Declaration of Human Rights (adopted 10 December 1948) UNGA Res 217A (III) art 19; International Covenant on Civil and Political Rights (adopted 16 December 1966, entered into force 23 March 1976) 999 UNTS 171, art 19 (ICCPR); European Convention for the Protection of Human Rights and Fundamental Freedoms (opened for signature 4 November 1950, entered into force 3 September 1953) 213 UNTS 222, art 10 (ECHR); American Convention on Human Rights (entered into force 18 July 1978) 1144 UNTS 123, art 13; African Charter on Human and Peoples' Rights (entered into force 21 October 1986) 1520 UNTS 217, art 9; Declaration on the Elimination of All Forms of Racial Discrimination (20 November 1963) UNGA Res 1904, art 9 ('UN Declaration on Racial Discrimination').

[23] *Bikindi* judgment, para 384. [24] *Bikindi* judgment, para 383.

[25] *Bikindi* judgment, ch IV ('Legal Findings').

[26] *Bikindi* judgment, para 419. *Prosecutor v Nahimana* (Judgment and Sentence) ICTR-99-52-T, T Ch I (3 December 2003) ('*Nahimana* judgment and sentence' or '*Media* case') paras 677, 678, 720.

[27] *Prosecutor v Akayesu* (Judgement) ICTR-96-4-T, T Ch I (2 September 1998) ('*Akayesu* judgment') paras 556–60.

[28] Gregory S Gordon, 'Music and Genocide: Harmonizing Coherence, Freedom and Nonviolence in Incitement Law', *Santa Clara Law Review* 50(3) (2010) 607, 611.

The second and third elements, which together constitute the *actus reus* of the crime, correspond perfectly with the linguistic model of speech outlined above. The former is concerned with the 'message', the 'cultural and linguistic content' of the statement, whereas the latter is concerned with the medium, the vocal in speech, its resonance and audibility. Voice is to content or message here as music was to lyric in Chapter 3. The one contains the other and is a technique for its dissemination.

In this respect, the Chamber's constant pairing of Bikindi's speaking voice with the loudspeaker is at once symptomatic and highly revealing. 'Witness AKJ heard Bikindi ask over a loudspeaker'.[29] 'Witness AKK testified that Bikindi made statements through speakers on the drive to Kayove'.[30] Or again, in a later reformulation: 'Bikindi used the public address system to state the majority population, the Hutu, should rise up to exterminate the minority, the Tutsi. On his way back, Bikindi used the same system to ask if people had been killing Tutsi, who he referred to as snakes'.[31] Notice that the Chamber comes very close to a form of metonymic substitution here. Bikindi's voice is entirely subsumed by the logic of the loudspeaker. It is a media technology, an instrument of amplification, a way of delivering a statement directly from Bikindi to his listening public, 'those standing by the side of the road'. In doctrinal terms, Bikindi's use of the loudspeaker goes directly to the element of 'publicness', indeed evidences or proves it without the need for more. This is because to amplify is necessarily to assert oneself in an acoustic space, to stretch out into the soundscape. Amplification always has a certain authoritarian quality to it, a wilfulness, which is why it is so often subject to restriction or regulation in anti-noise legislation. To 'use a loudspeaker', as the Chamber put it, like the village bell in Christianity or the muezzin's call to prayer in Islam, is necessarily to invoke a community of listeners, to institute a public and to distinguish one's voice from the noisy surrounds.[32] To amplify one's voice is to insist that *what* you say is heard, and in doing so to prove that your message is neither personal nor confidential, public not private.

Once the Chamber had determined that 'both statements, broadcast over loudspeaker, were made publicly', and likewise that both were also sufficiently 'direct' for the purposes of the Statute—it was 'inconceivable', apparently, that 'the audience to whom the message was directed, namely those standing on the road, could not have immediately understood' Bikindi's 'meaning and implication', and particularly in the context of a genocide—it continued as follows.[33] 'Based on the words he proffered and the manner he disseminated his message, the Chamber finds that Bikindi deliberately, directly and publicly incited the commission of

[29] *Bikindi* judgment, para 269. [30] *Bikindi* judgment, para 275.

[31] *Bikindi* judgment, para 422.

[32] Alain Corbin, *Village Bells: Sound and Meaning in the 19th Century French Countryside*, trans Martin Thom (Columbia University Press, 1998) [trans of: *Les cloches de la terre: Paysage sonore et culture sensible dans les campagnes au XIXe siècle* (first published 1998)]; Naveeda Khan, 'The Acoustics of Muslim Striving: Loudspeaker Use in Ritual Practice in Pakistan', *Comparative Studies in Society and History* 53(3) (2011) 571.

[33] *Bikindi* judgment, para 423.

genocide with the specific intent to destroy the Tutsi ethnic group'.[34] 'Bikindi's direct and public address on the Kivumu-Kayove road' left the Chamber in 'no doubt as to his genocidal intent'.[35]

So now, finally, we have a finding as to *mens rea*, Bikindi's intention. But notice that at no point does the Chamber actually justify itself in this respect. It simply derives Bikindi's state of mind from the utterances themselves. What enabled it to do so? What enables this sort of inference to pass as an argument? On the one hand, I want to suggest, the structure of the doctrine of incitement. On the other, a metaphysical tradition which this doctrine both echoed and drew upon in order to make a technical legal decision meaningful, to give it a certain kind of plausibility and weight.

The linguistic account of voice in which the ICTR was so obviously and deeply invested, both when it came to the application of the relevant doctrine and elsewhere, has always been guilty of a certain kind of prejudice. In the linguistic account, even as the voice seems to disappear in the utterance, it is nevertheless understood as language's 'natural embodiment', 'consubstantial with it', its most 'basic element'.[36] In this respect the speaking voice is traditionally positioned in contrast to writing, which 'presents its derivative, auxiliary, and parasitic supplement (it merely fixes the spoken word)'.[37] This hierarchical opposition between speech and writing is what Jacques Derrida refers to as 'phonocentrism'. It is exemplary of what he famously calls the 'metaphysics of presence', which in turn is both constitutive and symptomatic, he says, of the majority of the metaphysical tradition in the West, including in its juridical manifestations at institutions like the ICTR.[38]

In Derrida's account, the logic of phonocentrism is founded on an illusion which is as pervasive as it has been widely naturalized. This illusion takes root in the impression that 'when I speak, it belongs to the phenomenological essence of this operation that *I hear myself [je m'entende] at the same time* that I speak. The signifier, animated by my breath and by the meaning-intention … is in absolute proximity to me'.[39] The voice offers 'the illusion that one could get immediate access to an unalloyed presence, an origin not tarnished by externality, a firm rock against the elusive interplay of signs'.[40] As such, it is constitutive of interiority and ultimately of consciousness itself, this sense we have of the autonomy and so also the capacity for responsibility of the discrete and unitary subject.[41]

[34] *Bikindi* judgment, para 424. [35] *Bikindi* judgment, para 425.
[36] Dolar (2006) 37. [37] Dolar (2006) 37.
[38] Jacques Derrida, *Of Grammatology*, trans Gayatri Chakravorty Spivak (John Hopkins University Press, 1976) [trans of: *De la grammatologie* (first published 1967)]; Jacques Derrida, *Speech and Phenomena and Other Essays on Husserl's Theory of Signs*, trans David B Allison (Northwestern University Press, 1973) [trans of: *La voix et le phénomène* (first published 1967)]; Jacques Derrida, *Margins of Philosophy*, trans Alan Bass (University of Chicago Press, 1982) [trans of: *Marges de la philosophie* (first published 1972)]; Jacques Derrida, *Limited Inc*, trans Samuel Weber, Jeffrey Mehlman, and Alan Bass (Northwestern University Press, 1988).
[39] Derrida (1973) 77. [40] Dolar (2006) 37. [41] Dolar (2006) 38.

Perversely, therefore, phonocentrism involves a profound inattention to the acoustic at precisely the moment of the voice's privileging. The double sense of the French *entendre* captures the point perfectly. Meaning both 'to hear' and 'to understand', a direct line is drawn between the speaking voice and ideality per se. Derrida writes: 'the voice is *heard* (understood)—that undoubtedly is what is called consciousness—closest to the self as the absolute effacement of the signifier: pure auto-affection … It is the unique experience of the signified producing itself spontaneously from within the self'.[42] This is the logic which allows us to substitute the language of voice for that of subjectivity, both in legal discourse and elsewhere: the individual's voice, the narrative voice, the voice of the people, the voice of the law, whether or not anyone is actually speaking. But it is an illusion. Language is fundamentally afflicted by an absence which not even the voice can sure up or secure. Its essence is precisely to be without origin, always already conditioned by the subtle work of the 'trace' and a system of endless self-differentiation and deferral, '*différance*' in Derrida's language, which proves finally to be inevitable.[43] Nevertheless, this illusion—the illusion of 'auto-affection' Derrida terms it—is one which has not only been fundamental to the history of Western metaphysics but also turns out to be deeply bound up with how institutions like the ICTR, in cases like Bikindi's, go about attributing juridical responsibility in relation to speech.

What I am suggesting then is that, in the Trial Chamber's mapping of the doctrine of 'direct and public incitement to genocide' onto Bikindi's three crucial utterances by the side of the road that day in 1994, it was the apparent proximity between the act of vocalization and thought itself that secured the connection—the *expressive chain*, as it were—between Bikindi's intent, his words, and the ears of his listeners. For the Chamber, to speak, to oralize, was *self-evidently* an act of expression, the exteriorization of one's 'ideas' and 'opinions'.[44] It was to give substance to one's thoughts, to breathe life into them, to issue them forth into the world, literally to publicize them or make them real: the fusion of *actus reus* and *mens rea*. In other words, the account of speech which finally secured Bikindi's conviction rendered voice in absolute proximity to intention. It did so because this is what the doctrine of 'direct and public incitement to genocide' facilitated. Here is the key moment again: 'Bikindi's direct and public address on the Kivumu-Kayove road leaves no doubt as to his genocidal intent'.[45] No more justification necessary. Voice was imagined by the Trial Chamber at once as the medium in speech and its ground or guarantor, a mechanism both for fastening juridical responsibility, on the one hand, and presenting this fastening as at once inexorable and natural, on the other. Discreet as the voice generally was in the Chamber's account, it was nevertheless doing crucial juridical work.

[42] Derrida (1976) 20. [43] Derrida (1982) 3 ('Différance').

[44] Universal Declaration of Human Rights, art 19; ICCPR, art 19; ECHR, art 10; American Convention on Human Rights, art 13; African Charter on Human and Peoples' Rights, art 9; UN Declaration on Racial Discrimination, art 9.

[45] *Bikindi* judgment, para 425.

The Voice of Evidence

This was the approach to speech which turned out to be decisive in the *Bikindi* case, but it was not the only one. There were a number of moments, in fact, in which the ICTR was more sensitive to the specifically vocal in speech. As a matter of evidence, for instance, as far as the Tribunal was concerned the voice was certainly capable of proving a speaker's identity. For instance, when counsel for the defence asked one witness how he knew that the songs under consideration were sung by Bikindi, the witness responded as follows: 'We saw him enter and he danced, and we heard his voice, so we recognised him. Even today, if Bikindi were to start speaking, I would be able to easily recognise his voice'.[46] On another occasion, counsel for the prosecution elicited a very similar response:

Q. How did you know it was Bikindi speaking?
A. That young man told me that it was, indeed, Bikindi, and as a matter of fact it is Bikindi's voice that I heard.
Q. What was Bikindi saying?[47]

In both examples, the *who* precedes the *what*. It is not just that each witness offers Bikindi's voice as evidence of his identity, but that the question asked of them seems designed to produce exactly this sort of response. In both cases counsel moves immediately on afterwards. Clearly they got the answer they were hoping for.

The sort of evidentiary logic exhibited both here and elsewhere throughout the *Bikindi* case does more than simply tell us something about Bikindi's apparent fame and popularity in Rwanda in the period in question, his familiarity as one of the most well-known voices in the Rwandan soundscape.[48] It also suggests the juridical recognition and acceptance of what Adriana Cavarero calls the 'phenomenon of vocalic uniqueness', which we considered briefly at the end of Chapter 4. The uniqueness of the voice, Cavarero explains, 'is an incontrovertible given of experience, technologically proven by digital machines that can trace it'.[49] Analytically separate from and phenomenologically prior to the communication of any linguistic content, a voice always also conveys 'the embodied uniqueness of the one who emits it'.[50] Its precise accent, pitch, timbre, and rhythm is a form of acoustic signature or fingerprint, each one subtly different from every other. And this is true, moreover, even if without the aid of technology we often find it

[46] *Prosecutor v Bikindi* (Transcript) ICTR-01-72-T, T Ch III (Various dates) ('*Bikindi* transcript') 13 October 2006, 5.

[47] *Bikindi* transcript, 5 October 2006, 34–5.

[48] For other examples, see *Bikindi* transcript: 18 October 2006, 14; 13 February 2007, 9.

[49] Cavarero (2005) 8.

[50] Paul A Kottman, 'Introduction' in Adriana Cavarero, *For More than One Voice: Toward a Philosophy of Vocal Expression*, trans Paul A Kottman (Stanford University Press, 2005) [trans of: *A piu voci: Per una filosofia dell'espressione vocale* (first published 2003)] vii, xv.

difficult to distinguish between them, as some of the recent controversy around voice identification in forensic contexts suggests.[51]

Whereas Cavarero would construct an entire 'antimetaphysical ontology' from this phenomenological starting point, however, in the ICTR's hands the uniqueness of the voice becomes a thoroughly routine and uncontroversial matter of evidentiary technique.[52] Where Cavarero finds in the uniqueness of the voice a challenge to the metaphysical project discerned by Derrida—one 'founded not on the activity of thinking, or on abstract entities like Man or Individual or Justice, but rather irremediably rooted in a radically embodied, contextual, relational ontology that takes seriously Arendt's notion of the human condition as a "plurality" of unique existents'[53]—in the ICTR's account it does just the opposite. It is precisely that project's verification or proof. In the *Bikindi* case, the uniqueness of the voice, its ability to evidence the identity of the speaker, in no way troubled either the juridical attribution of responsibility addressed in the previous section or the metaphysics on which it depended. The voice functioned simply as a kind of sonorous marker of the autonomous juridical self. It was an acoustic barcode to the soul.

The Voice of Rhetoric

The possibility that tone of voice, intonation, or prosody—what is commonly referred to as 'paralinguistics'—might matter juridically was never overtly considered in the *Bikindi* case. But it is clear that as an institution the Tribunal was at least open to this kind of thinking. Tone of voice, for instance, was cited as a relevant factor on more than one occasion in the *Media* case.[54] In its discussion of one particularly inflammatory radio broadcast, a recording of which was played at trial, the Trial Chamber there made a point of noting the broadcaster's 'sarcastic tone' in relation to the Tutsi, which it thought communicated his disdain for them.[55] Later, it would be even more explicit: 'in the Chamber's view, the accuracy of the statement is only one factor to be considered in the determination of whether a statement is intended to provoke rather than to educate those who receive it. The tone of the statement is as relevant to this determination as is its content'.[56]

Clearly, the ICTR is not entirely deaf to the paralinguistic qualities of speech then. Moreover, just because matters of paralinguistics were never *explicitly* at issue in the *Bikindi* case doesn't mean they were entirely absent from the Tribunal's

[51] See Kreiman and Sidtis (2011) 156–88 (ch 5, 'Recognizing Speaker Identity from Voice: Theoretical and Ethological Perspectives and a Psychological Model'), 237–59 (ch 7, 'Identifying Unfamiliar Voices in Forensic Contexts'). See also Lawrence M Solan and Peter M Tiersma, 'Hearing Voices: Speaker Identification in Court', *Hastings Law Journal* 54(2) (2003) 373. For a major recent study of the law in relation to 'voice comparison evidence' in the Australian context, see Gary Edmond, Kristy Martire, and Mehera San Roque, 'Unsound Law: Issues with ("Expert") Voice Comparison Evidence', *Melbourne University Law Review* 35(1) (2011) 52.

[52] Kottman (2005) xxi.

[53] Kottman (2005) xxi.

[54] *Media* case.

[55] *Media* case, para 355.

[56] *Media* case, para 1022.

thinking. Look again at some of the passages cited above. Bikindi 'addressed', 'said', 'asked', 'explained', and 'insisted'. Elsewhere in the judgment he and others 'spoke', 'stated', 'talked', 'told', 'announced', 'called', 'read out', 'discussed', 'urged', 'praised', 'boasted', 'insisted', and 'ordered'. This is the language the Tribunal used to describe speech in the *Bikindi* case; or, more precisely, to give voice to it. Even though, as a general rule, the Tribunal may not have been overtly interested in the sound of speech, even if the voice was mostly extremely discreet, this sort of language does convey something about it nevertheless. In conventional grammatical terms, these kinds of words are known as 'reporting verbs' because they describe the 'action of speaking'.[57] They are the *how* as opposed to the *what* or the *who* of speech: its modality or manner.

Consider the difference between the following two examples. On the one hand, Bikindi '*asked*' 'if people had been killing Tutsi, who were referred to as snakes'.[58] On the other, he '*ordered*' 'that Gasasira be killed' before Gasasira was then allegedly 'finished off' in Bikindi's presence (an allegation which would eventually be dismissed by the Tribunal as unsupported by the evidence).[59] In both cases, the reporting verb implies something in relation to vocal delivery. Far from being merely incidental, moreover, this dimension of the speech act cannot help but matter juridically because it goes directly to the questions both of meaning and, especially, of effectiveness: what J L Austin famously termed 'felicity'.[60]

Austin was interested in what he called 'speech acts': utterances, that is, in which to *say* something is also to *do* something, or in which *by* saying or *in* saying something a person *does* something too: swearing an oath, for instance, or pronouncing judgment, to take a couple of prototypically legal examples which we will consider in detail in Chapter 6.[61] We could think equally of the ways in which we often use speech to ask, advise, warn, order, promise, apologize, deny, explain, thank, or tell.[62] Even though Austin's analysis focuses almost exclusively on the spoken word, and even though it depends significantly on the association of voice with the material and active in contrast to the text's supposed alliance with the passive and ideal, Austin was nevertheless 'lamentably silent on the role of the voice'.[63] 'Tone of voice', 'cadence', and 'emphasis' *are* briefly alluded to in Austin's sixth lecture, but they are never taken up again in detail.[64] In his well-known discussion of the 'felicity' of the utterance, for instance, Austin misses the fact that the voice is necessarily bound up in the achievement of linguistic effect. As we will

[57] **reporting,** ***n.*** in *Oxford English Dictionary* (3rd edn, Oxford University Press, December 2009) <http://www.oed.com>.

[58] *Bikindi* judgment, para 281.

[59] *Bikindi* judgment, para 305.

[60] J L Austin, *How to Do Things with Words* (Harvard University Press, 1962).

[61] The indebtedness of Austin's theory to juridical notions of performance, on the one hand, and his friendship with colleague and well-known English jurist H L A Hart has been widely noted. See Austin (1962) 7 n 1. For a recent consideration of specifically legal speech acts, see generally Marianne Constable, *Our Word is Our Bond: How Legal Speech Acts* (Stanford University Press, 2014).

[62] For Austin's overview and typology of speech acts, see Austin (1962) 148–64 ('Lecture XII').

[63] Michelle Duncan, 'The Operatic Scandal of the Singing Body: Voice, Presence, Performativity', *Cambridge Opera Journal* 16(3) (2004) 283, 289.

[64] See Austin (1962) 74.

see in our consideration of the solemn declaration in Chapter 6, the manner in which an utterance is spoken, the precise way in which it is 'given voice'—whether spoken, whispered, shouted, or sung—necessarily enters into any consideration of its effect.[65] If a question doesn't *sound* a certain way—in English, if the questioner doesn't raise their intonation towards the end of the sentence and their pitch slightly overall (Kinyarwanda would have its own equivalent conventions in this respect)—it is liable to 'misfire', or simply fail to be understood as a question.[66] If an order doesn't *sound* authoritative, if it seems ironic, sarcastic, or too jovial, if it doesn't come off as sufficiently 'serious' in one way or another, it may not function as an order at all.

The way in which speech is reported necessarily entails something about its sonority. That much is simply unavoidable, a grammatical and rhetorical inevitability. To write that Bikindi 'asked' rather than 'ordered' is already to imply a certain amount about his vocal delivery and therefore its doctrinal significance. For an acoustic jurisprudence, it is significant therefore that the *Bikindi* case has subsequently been read as authority for the position that even questions can be a form of incitement.[67] It tells us something important not just about the kinds of words that will be sufficient for the purposes of international legal doctrine, but also about the way in which they may be delivered.

Having said that, not even the most precise reporting verbs could ever do more than hint at the infinity of possible vocal nuance. There are a million different ways of asking something, and as many again of ordering, insisting, or urging it, or whatever the case may be. The way Bikindi asked his audience 'if they had killed the Tutsi' will be totally different to the way in which a journalist or a judge might ask the very same question. Clearly, if we think we can discern a trace of the vocal in speech at the level of grammar, it is a minimal one. Moreover, the evidentiary chain could hardly have been any less reliable in this respect. What sort of precision could the Tribunal ever realistically have hoped for when the majority of speech reported was being remembered more than a decade after the fact and in almost every case by means of a chain of interpretation, from Kinyarwanda to French and then from French to English?[68]

On some level at least, the Tribunal seems to have been cognizant of these problems. We can see this most clearly of all in relation to the choices it made in terms of narration. The reporting verbs which predominated in the *Bikindi* case were those which conveyed the least of all—'said', 'told', 'stated', etc—those which were the most neutral vocally. We don't have to think of this as the result of a simple ambivalence for the acoustic qualities of speech on the Tribunal's part. Instead we could understand it, more generously, as evidence of a certain kind of care or attention to the voice in the narration of speech, a relatively sophisticated rhetorical, grammatalogical, and, moreover, specifically jurisprudential technique for leaving

[65] Duncan (2004) 291. [66] Austin (1962) 16. [67] Gordon (2010) 624.
[68] For a detailed consideration of simultaneous interpretation at the ICTR, see Chapter 8.

those acoustic qualities purposely *unsaid*. We could say that precisely in the process of 'giving voice' to speech, the Tribunal did as much as it could to quieten it.

This would also be one reason why reporting verbs almost never came with a modifying adverb in the *Bikindi* case. Where in a novel or a news report you might expect to find people speaking 'forcefully', insisting 'angrily', interjecting 'hurriedly' or 'menacingly', saying 'with disdain' or 'love' or 'hate' or 'pride', in the *Bikindi* case we find none of these things. Instead, the Tribunal flattens out and diminishes the voice as much as possible. Even as the *what* undeniably mattered more for the ICTR's purposes than the *how*, we could equally say that at the level of grammar and narrative technique the Tribunal was highly sensitive to the problem of voice and the paralinguistic qualities of speech. Paradoxically, we know that voice mattered on some level precisely by virtue of its quietness, its relative absence.

We could push this point even further, because the strange quietness of the voice in legal discourse—this sort of rhetorical technique is not limited to the *Bikindi* case—carries with it certain other associations too. It is surely bound up, for instance, with the legal institution's self-image as neutral arbiter of facts and purveyor of sober legal judgment. To quieten the voice *in* law is also to quieten the voice *of* law. Just as in a courtroom speech actually *sounds* legal where song so manifestly does not, as we saw in Chapter 4, the 'neutrality' conveyed by this kind of narration *sounds* legal too.[69]

Neutrality is not just about the presence or absence of bias. It is also, crucially, a genre-effect, the adoption of a suitably 'professional' or judicial voice.[70] Legal discourse is not meant to be too 'evocative'. Etymologically, the word derives from the Latin *evocare* meaning 'to call out' or 'forth': either way, to vocalize.[71] In more contemporary usage, to evoke is to elicit, rouse, or summon, possibly 'by use of magic charms', but certainly not by means of reason, and certainly not with the degree of aesthetic distance we traditionally expect of legal judgment.[72] To evoke is to bring into being through voice, but the voice in question here is not so much authoritative as suggestive, more literary or poetic than juridical. To evoke is to manifest the voice of the author, but precisely *as* author. Where in literature people might 'exclaim', 'retort', 'sob', or 'whine', in legal discourse they invariably 'explain', 'say', 'state', or 'claim'. The choice of words communicates something to the reader about the author's own sense of positionality in the text: the degree of objectivity they hope to project, the extent of their involvement in the process of narration. For Pierre Schlag, the formal and discursive appearance of 'neutrality' is a key factor in the production of the sense of detachment which has come to characterize contemporary legal discourse.[73] The way the voice is narrated in law

[69] See Chapter 4.

[70] On the 'professional voice' in legal discourse and the way in which it tends to minimize expressions of empathy and 'humanity' see Julius G Getman, 'Colloquy: Human Voice in Legal Discourse', *Texas Law Review* 66(3) (1988) 577.

[71] **evocative,** ***adj.*** in *Oxford English Dictionary* (2nd edn, Oxford University Press, 1989).

[72] **evoke,** ***v.*** in *Oxford English Dictionary* (1989).

[73] Pierre Schlag, 'The Aesthetics of American Law', *Harvard Law Review* 115(4) (2002) 1047, 1060.

is not separate from this. It was partly by means of this rhetorical quietening of the voice that the Chamber was able to generate the sense of aesthetic distance and judicial propriety expected of it when it came to judgment. We could say, finally, that to foreground the voice, to give it centre stage, is in some respects also to move beyond the domain of the properly legal, to move into the realm of the literary and aesthetic, even perhaps the musical, to allow the voice of the legal institution itself too much room to resonate.

The Voice of Critique

So far in this chapter, we have seen that the account of speech produced in the *Bikindi* case operated according to a kind of double movement. On the one hand, the voice was discreet, quiet, withdrawn. It invariably deferred to the semantic, to the specifically linguistic in speech. At the same time as it did so, however, the voice operated as a crucial link in what I have termed the 'expressive chain'. It provided the necessary connection between meaning and intention for the purposes of the law of incitement to genocide, a connection which was discernible too in the Tribunal's approach to the voice as evidence of a speaker's identity and intent. Even as the voice tended to disappear in the *Bikindi* case, therefore, it never did so entirely. It never quite resolved itself into pure mediality. In particular, it always left a trace at the level of grammar. This was both inevitable, a product at once of the phenomenology of the speech act and the very process of narration itself, and something to which the Tribunal seems to have been highly sensitive at the level of rhetorical technique. The kind of language used to report speech in the *Bikindi* case was always as neutral as possible. And although this was partly an evidentiary issue, a grammatalogical by-product of very real jurisprudential concerns, it was also partly, and just as significantly, a matter of genre. The formal conventions of legal writing and legal discourse in general require a certain kind of aesthetic and critical distance which would be very obviously jeopardized if the Tribunal started adopting too literary a voice of its own. I now turn to consider some of the consequences of thinking voice this way.

One response to the Tribunal's account would be to fasten in on its phonocentrism, to mount a critique of it based on Derrida's observations about the metaphysics of presence and the illusion of 'auto-affection'. Such a critique would identify the limits of an account of speech oriented around the idea of 'expression',[74] the antimetaphysical valence of writing and the 'trace', the way in which *différance* always works to undermine the sort of unalloyed presence which the Tribunal's account sought to secure, and on which both the law of freedom of expression and the doctrine of incitement to genocide seem to have invoked.

I want to approach from another direction, however, by means of another tradition of critical scholarship. While this tradition is admittedly indebted to Derrida

[74] Derrida (1973) 31.

for having opened up the 'philosophically disturbing theme of the voice', it pursues an importantly different line of inquiry, one more directly attuned to the specifically vocal in speech, to the overtly acoustic.[75] This tradition has sought to show how the voice *already* carries with it the antimetaphysical and therefore juridically disturbing potential that Derrida attributes to writing. This potential takes the form of a kind of unavoidable excess or remainder in the act of vocalization, an ineradicable trace of the unthinking body, which necessarily prevents the utterance from ever truly resolving itself into ideality. It is possible, in other words, to imagine a different account of the metaphysics of voice where, far from being the safeguard of presence or the link between speech and intention for the purposes of the relevant doctrine, the voice is 'dangerous, threatening, and possibly ruinous'.[76] It is only by pursuing this avenue, I want to suggest, that the most important implications of the Tribunal's approach to voice begin to reveal themselves. Nevertheless, for an acoustic jurisprudence, even this tradition of critique has its limits. Having addressed some of those limits, the chapter ends by opening up the relationship between speech and song, which, it seems to me, is where an attention to the excessive and the ineffable in voice would have mattered most in the *Bikindi* case.

Speech is always a bodily activity, an 'encounter … between act and language'.[77] This is a simple point, but its implications—both in law and elsewhere—are potentially very significant. For Shoshana Felman, for instance, the necessary corporeality of the act of speaking—the way it engages the throat, vocal cords, and lungs in the process of making itself audible—inevitably 'reveals something other than what is revealed intentionally by the ego through language'.[78] Because the speech act emanates from the body, it 'destroys from its inception the metaphysical dichotomy between the domain of the "mental" and the domain of the "physical", breaks down the opposition between body and spirit, between matter and language'.[79] Far from providing a natural link to the intentionality of the speaker, therefore, the act of vocalization can be understood as both excessive and subversive in its relation to language, meaning, subjectivity and, so, for our purposes, also responsibility. What this means is that it is not just by virtue of language's iterability, as in Derrida's account, that the speech act is always to some extent 'out of our control'.[80] The voice, and particularly the way in which it engages what Judith Butler calls the 'unknowing body', marks a kind of limit to intentionality itself.[81] The speech act, the spoken word, the word as embodied sound, 'always says more, or says differently, than it means to say'.[82] By definition, it cannot know what it is doing. And for Felman, this is what makes it 'scandalous'.[83]

[75] Cavarero (2005) 215. [76] Dolar (2006) 42–3.

[77] Shoshana Felman, *The Scandal of the Speaking Body: Don Juan with J L Austin, or Seduction in Two Languages* (Stanford University Press, 1983) 66.

[78] Duncan (2004) 292. [79] Felman (1983) 65.

[80] Derrida (1988) 1 ('Signature Event Context'); Duncan (2004) 15.

[81] Judith Butler, *Excitable Speech: A Politics of the Performative* (Routledge, 1997) 10.

[82] Butler (1997) 10.

[83] Felman (1983) 67. What is scandalous about the speech act is the way in which it engages the unconscious. As Duncan points out, Felman's understanding of performativity comes as much from psychoanalysis as it does from the philosophy of language. Duncan (2004) 292.

Moreover, this scandalous dimension of the voice is not even limited to orality. The acoustic pleasure of the specifically vocal makes itself present in writing too. In *Contre Sainte-Beuve*, Marcel Proust gives an example that is neatly illustrative. 'As soon as I would read a writer', he explains,

> I would discern almost immediately under the words the air of a song, which is always different in each one; and, as I would read, without realizing it, I would sing. I would raise the notes or slow them down or interrupt them, as one does when one sings—keeping time, following the rhythm, before saying the end of a word.[84]

Perhaps you're doing the same as you read this, feeling the way in which the text 'sings' itself, allowing yourself to be led by the ear. The vocal *always* haunts the semantic, Proust is saying, even at the level of writing.[85] Likewise for Julia Kristeva, the pure semantic simply doesn't exist. It is always already afflicted by the phonic, the acoustic, or the vocal, and often unconsciously so. This is clearest perhaps in relation to the overtly poetic text but it is not limited to it. What Kristeva calls the 'semiotic *chora*'—the 'preverbal and unconscious sphere, not yet inhabited by the law of the sign, where rhythmic and vocalic drives reign'[86]—permeates the whole of language, is there right at its very root. Sound both 'organises the text' and at the same time 'disorganises language's claim to control the entire process of signification'.[87] In Kristeva's work, 'rather than stand in opposition to writing as happens in the studies focused on orality, the voice stands in opposition to language—that is, to the disciplining codes of language, to grammar and syntax'.[88]

What each of these different approaches to the voice does is undermine or challenge 'the absolute sovereignty of language and thus the absolute intentionality of the speaking subject' which is so important to the law of freedom of expression, as we have seen.[89] In each case the act of vocalization works to 'untether' the utterance to some extent from the speaker's will.[90] The 'scandalous' nature of the speech act identified by Felman, the way in which for Butler the 'unknowability' of vocalization renders speech in some ways always 'out of our control', Kristeva's insistence that a certain kind of poetics, music, or unconscious phonics pervades language in its entirety: all these dimensions of the voice are metaphysically and therefore juridically disturbing. In one way or another they all work to trouble the account of voice entailed in the doctrine of 'direct and public incitement to genocide' considered above. They suggest the need for a richer, more complex, more acoustically sensitive account.

For Butler, the debunking of what she terms the 'conceit' of sovereignty necessitates that we also rethink the way in which we conceive agency and, therefore, responsibility in law.[91] It requires us to imagine a model of speech and of

[84] Marcel Proust, *Contre Sainte-Beuve*, quoted and translated in Cavarero (2005) 131.

[85] Julia Kristeva, *Revolutions in Poetic Language*, trans Margaret Waller (Columbia University Press, 1984) [trans of: *La révolution du langage poétique* (first published 1974)]; Walter J Ong, *Orality and Literacy: The Technologizing of the World* (Routledge, 2002).

[86] Cavarero (2005) 133. [87] Cavarero (2005) 130. [88] Cavarero (2005) 131–2.

[89] Duncan (2004) 291. [90] Butler (1997) 15. [91] Butler (1997) 15.

subjectivity 'afflicted' with the impurity of the unknowing body from the start.[92] Crucially, however, this sort of critique is not an attempt to undermine the concepts of agency per se, nor to limit the possibilities of holding people to account for their speech. Quite the reverse. 'Agency begins where sovereignty wanes', Butler claims.[93] And to the extent that it does, the fact that Bikindi's speech, for instance, was not completely within his sovereign control would work to 'enhance and intensify' his responsibility not diminish it.[94] Because speech *always* goes beyond intention, it ought to be possible to be held accountable to that extent too.

What difference, if any, would such an approach have made in the *Bikindi* case? What is the significance of this sort of critique for an acoustic jurisprudence? As far as the utterances for which Bikindi was eventually convicted are concerned, made 'over a loudspeaker' on the road to Kayove that day in June 1994, it is unclear that the outcome would have been any different at all. Although a model of the speaking subject revised along the lines suggested by Butler might have yielded a more just or responsible outcome to the extent that it would not have been founded on either the 'illusion' of 'auto-affection' or the 'conceit' of sovereignty, it would almost certainly not have meant a different result in substantive terms. The Tribunal didn't *need* to enhance or intensify Bikindi's responsibility, after all. Whether or not the utterances in question were fully within his sovereign control, he would surely still have been found culpable.

This is the point at which the concerns of critique and jurisprudence diverge. The critical accounts of voice developed by the likes of Butler, Felman, and Kristeva get very little juridical purchase in situations such as we have been considering here. From the perspective of the metaphysician or the critic, the question of voice can appear to be foundational. Everything turns on it. And yet for prudential purposes, on the facts of the *Bikindi* case and from a perspective more attuned to institutional questions and the particular concerns of the practice of judgment, the issue seems much less pressing. It is not just that Bikindi would have been found culpable either way. The problem of properly accounting for the work of the 'unknowing body' in vocalization is surely exacerbated by the practical limits both of evidence and of language itself. It is much easier, after all, to recount *what* a person said than the disruptive or excessive qualities of the *way* in which they said it, and especially if we are interested in something more complex and ineffable than a mere 'sarcastic tone'. The critique of voice outlined above is crucial for an acoustic jurisprudence because it turns our attention towards certain aspects of the act of vocalization for which legal institutions must ultimately be able to account. But the critical project simply isn't interested in the institutional character of these problems, as they are brought into the domain of law and made amenable to the project of adjudication. This is the task of an acoustic jurisprudence. And in this respect, the kind of approach advocated by Butler—one attentive to the bodily, the excessive, or the unintended in vocalization—may have been precisely what was needed when it came to Bikindi's songs. From an institutional and prudential

[92] Butler (1997) 28. [93] Butler (1997) 16. [94] Butler (1997) 27.

perspective, *this* was where the question of voice turns out to have resonated loudest. In the final section of the chapter, therefore, I return briefly to some of the themes of Chapter 3. In doing so, we will see that the questions of speech and song, music and voice, are much closer than they originally appeared, and that the Tribunal appears to have invested a lot, in fact, in keeping them apart.

The Singing Voice

Speech and song are coextensive, separated more by degree than by type. It is the voice which presents their common denominator, the means by which the one always approaches the other. Indeed, we could say that the voice is precisely the musical in speech. Not only does it necessarily enter into the hermeneutic equation, into any determination of the meaning or significance of the utterance as we saw in our consideration of paralinguistics above, it also and inevitably exceeds that register. Like music, the voice is always 'ineffable' to some extent. It too resists description and is irreducible either to semantics or the will of the subject. The voice is also potentially dangerous, sensual, affective, effeminate, perfidious, decadent, and intoxicating.[95] It perpetually threatens to undermine, complicate, or exceed the meaning of the word as language, lyric, or text.

Like Felman, Butler, and Kristeva above, in his famous 1972 essay *The Grain of the Voice*, Roland Barthes was interested in the voice–language relation as an 'encounter' which yields something other than and in excess of meaning or intention.[96] In Barthes' case, however, the concern for voice, and especially the musical voice, is even more overt.[97] What interests Barthes specifically is the fact that certain voices seem possessed of a weight that is simply not comprehensible in terms of either intention, signification or the usual range of expressive conventions, anger, sadness, joy, and so on. Barthes refers to this dimension of the voice as its 'grain': the 'body in the voice as it sings';[98] 'something … manifest and stubborn … beyond (or before) the meaning of the words, their form … the melisma, and even the style of execution: something which is directly the cantor's body';[99] 'the cavities, the muscles, the membranes, the cartilages';[100] 'the materiality of the body that springs from the throat, there where the phonic metal is forged'.[101] Not, or not merely, timbre: the 'grain'

[95] On the gender politics of the voice throughout the philosophical tradition, see Cavarero (2005) 95–161 ('Part II: Women Who Sing').

[96] Barthes, *Image, Music, Text*, trans Stephen Heath (Fontana, 1977) 179–89 ('The Grain of the Voice'). It is worth noting, however, that Barthes is rather more interested in particular encounters—in this case between the voice of favourite singer Panzéra and the particularities of the French language *as* sound, with its rolled r's and peculiar vowels: 'the opposition of é and è', the 'purity' of the ü—as opposed to the encounter in general: 180–1.

[97] Barthes (1977) 188.

[98] Barthes (1977) 188.

[99] Barthes (1977) 181.

[100] Barthes (1977) 181.

[101] Roland Barthes, *The Responsibility of Forms: Critical Essays on Music, Art, and Representation*, trans Richard Howard (Hill and Wang, 1985) [trans of: *L'obvie et l'obtus: Essais critiques III* (first published 1982)] 245–60, 255 ('Listening').

of a voice 'forms a signifying play having nothing to do with communication, representation (of feelings), expression'.[102] Instead, it opens up a new 'scheme of evaluation', a new way of listening in fact, concerned with manifestations of and relations between resonant bodies as opposed to subjectivities.[103] Barthes heard 'grain' in the voice of Swiss baritone Charles Panzéra and in the burly depths of the Russian 'church bass'.[104] Music critic and sociologist of rock Simon Frith heard it in Elvis. 'In the end', Frith claims, 'this is the only way to explain his appeal: not in terms of what he "stood for," socially or personally, but by reference to the *grain* of the voice'. Elvis celebrated 'more sensuously, more voluptuously than any other rock 'n' roll singer—the act of symbol creation itself'.[105] Hélène Cixous makes a very similar point when she writes that 'what is musical and phonic in language, which could also appear as an accompaniment, is in effect inseparable from a *significance*'.[106] For Cixous, music and meaning are 'absolutely indissociable'.[107] Whenever we speak, whenever we write, she claims, we always also sing. And when we do, the vocalic always intervenes to reach out beyond the codes of language, beyond signification, intention, and our conscious control.

On one level the jurisprudential tradition has always known this. The fact that singing supposedly 'blurs the word and makes it difficult to understand' has long served as the basis for a 'philosophical distrust for this flourishing of the voice at the expense of the text'.[108] The core danger is 'the voice that sets itself loose from the word', 'the voice beyond logos', the voice, Dolar says, that is 'lawless'.[109] The results in this respect have frequently taken juridical form. We could remember Plato's famous condemnation of the Homeric epic tradition, for instance, and his corresponding injunction in the *Republic* that in song the music should always follow the lyrics, that everything possible should be done to subdue the voice, to return it to its proper place as handmaid to the semantic.[110] Or again, we could think of the constant attempts by the Christian church centuries later to regulate sacred music, and particularly the performance of the liturgy, in order to 'secure an anchorage' in the word of God.[111]

For an acoustic jurisprudence it is telling, therefore, that in the pertinent section of the judgment in the *Bikindi* case, where the distinction and hierarchy between music and lyrics was at its most prominent and distilled, the voice was nowhere

[102] Barthes (1977) 182. [103] Barthes (1977) 188.

[104] This in contrast to the 'operatic bass'. Opera, Barthes provocatively claims, 'is a genre in which the voice has gone over in its entirety to dramatic expressivity, a voice with a grain which little signifies': Barthes (1977) 181.

[105] Simon Frith, *Sound Effects: Youth, Leisure, and the Politics of Rock 'n' Roll* (Pantheon Books, 1981) 165.

[106] Cavarero (2005) 141, citing Cixous in an interview that appears in the appendix to a thesis written by Monica Fiorini, 'Scrittura e dicibilità dell'esperienza: Sulla poetica di Hélène Cixous' (PhD dissertation, University of Bologna, 1995–96) 175.

[107] Hélène Cixous and Mireille Calle-Gruber, *Rootprints: Memory and Life Writing*, trans Eric Prenowitz (Routledge, 1997) [trans of: *Photos de racine* (first published 1994)] 46.

[108] Dolar (2006) 30. [109] Dolar (2006) 45.

[110] Plato, *The Republic*, trans Richard W Sterling and William C Scott (Norton, 1985).

[111] Dolar (2006) 30.

to be seen. Whereas in Plato and in Christianity the threat posed by the voice was recognized and subjected to extreme regulatory measures as a result, at the ICTR it was simply ignored, silenced, made irrelevant as a juridical concern.

Remember the Tribunal's account of Bikindi's songs from Chapter 3. In its description of the so-called 'background music', the Chamber referred to the 'accompanying sitar' and the songs' 'melody' and 'rhythm', which it said 'made listeners want to dance'. Bikindi's voice, however, was simply not mentioned at all.[112] This is significant because it is precisely in the voice that music and lyric come together, where the distinctions between form and content, medium and message, idea and expression, which were so central to the Tribunal's account at the level of doctrine, most obviously breaks down. It is the musical voice, therefore, which renders the foreground/background distinction insisted on by the Chamber—and which, as we saw in Chapter 3, did so much important juridical work—at its least tenable.

If anything, the Tribunal had things exactly the wrong way round. Song, after all, is precisely that which 'takes the distraction of the voice seriously', and in doing so 'turns the tables on the signifier', reverses the normal hierarchy.[113] It is in song that the sonorous, the bodily, the unconscious and unintended are at last allowed the 'upper hand' to some extent.[114] It is in song that the voice is finally given permission to luxuriate in itself, precisely *not* to defer to the semantic, to take the leading role for once and to be the bearer of that which 'cannot be expressed by words'.[115] In that sense, the musical voice has something important in common with the sitar, drum, or any other musical instrument. In each case, the 'pleasure of the ear is at play'. 'Not the ears as the vehicles of a signified that goes straight to the mind, or as tubes of transmission from one intellect to another', Cavarero writes, 'but rather as acoustic chambers that enjoy the vibrations and resonances, just as the palate enjoys the sweet and the salty'.[116]

This is no less true of Bikindi's songs than anyone else's. Yet this was clearly not a register that the ICTR was interested in exploring. Nor was it required to by the relevant doctrine, as we have seen. The Tribunal's approach to speech was intimately bound up with its approach to song. It was only in song, however, that the implications of its failure to recognize the work of the voice in complicating or exceeding the registers of language, meaning, and intention became particularly apparent.

I ended Chapter 3 by resisting the temptation to offer my own account of Bikindi's songs. It was not just that I had so little data to go on, nor that the relative poverty of literature in this respect was partly the result of a deafness on the Tribunal's part in any case. Once one begins to open up the question of the musicology of judgment, I said, a whole new set of problems present themselves. Musicology is an extremely diverse field and it is far from clear either what would

[112] *Bikindi* judgment, para 195. See Chapter 1. [113] Dolar (2006) 30.
[114] Dolar (2006).
[115] Vladimir Jankélévitch, *Music and the Ineffable*, trans Carolyn Abbate (Princeton University Press, 2003) [trans of: *La Musique et l'ineffable* (first published 1961)] 72.
[116] Cavarero (2005) 127.

constitute an appropriate musicological lens where Bikindi is concerned, or how well suited the discipline of musicology is to the peculiar urgency of legal judgment. The question of how best to hold a person such as Bikindi responsible in relation to his songs, therefore, is still very much an open one. What this chapter has suggested is that, at the very least, any such model of responsibility would need to have some account of the singing voice which allowed that it was more than simply the bearer of language. It would need to recognize that by virtue of its sensuousness and its 'grain', the way in which it engages the 'unknowing body', the voice interrupts or complicates what Butler terms the 'sovereign conceit' in certain respects, and that this in turn implies a certain kind of openness to other associated questions: not just the relation or relations between song and speech, but also between voice and instrumentation, and between music and song.

Neither music, nor voice, nor the acoustic ought to be thought of as barriers to responsibility in law, problems to be circumvented or sidestepped at trial. They are issues to be confronted. If institutions such as the ICTR are going to attempt to judge songs and speech like Bikindi's, they surely owe it both to Bikindi and to the international community in whose name they claim to speak, to take seriously their existence as and in relation to sound.

6

Giving Voice

The most prominent feature of the judicial soundscape is the human voice. Or, to be more precise, the 'reciprocal communication' of voices plural: the ritual, public, and heavily codified dialogue of lawyers, judges, and court reporters, security guards, witnesses, and interpreters.[1] These are the sounds which populate our courtrooms and which we tend to think of as being characteristically or even properly legal. In Chapter 4 we saw how this fact was crucial to the way in which Bikindi's songs were heard at trial. This chapter considers some of the practices of courtroom orality in more detail. I am particularly interested here in the different ways in which the voice was called upon in the *Bikindi* case, why, and what seems to have been at stake for the Tribunal in each of the specific practices of *giving voice* it either facilitated or required. These issues are extremely important for an acoustic jurisprudence because they are so intimately bound up with the question of the hearing itself, with the very audibility of legal practice, its existence precisely *as* an acoustic enterprise. The resonant voice is so fundamental to the practice of law that it can be easy to miss the nature and extent of the work it does. This chapter suggests that a close attention to the role of the voice in court is crucial to any responsible account of law's institutional life and the practice of judgment.

The chapter begins with a consideration of the 'solemn declaration', the ritual practice of oath swearing which nearly every participant in the *Bikindi* case was required to undergo as a condition of their participation and which, I argue, is both highly anomalous from an institutional perspective and, it seems, foundational. From there I move on to consider the relationship between oralization and the 'principle of publicity', the requirement that all judicial proceedings at the ICTR be 'held in public, unless otherwise provided'. Here I am especially interested in the treatment of so-called 'protected witnesses', who were required to testify from behind a curtain, hidden from public view.[2] The third part of the chapter turns to the relation between speech and text, voice and letter, and in doing so begins to complicate the very idea of the hearing. When participants speak at trial, I suggest, they do not necessarily do so in order to be heard. In fact the chapter ends by

[1] Adriana Cavarero, *For More than One Voice: Toward a Philosophy of Vocal Expression*, trans Paul A Kottman (Stanford University Press, 2005) [trans of: *A piu voci: Per una filosofia dell'espressione vocale* (first published 2003)] 197.

[2] International Criminal Tribunal for Rwanda, 'Rules of Procedure and Evidence' (29 June 1995) UN Doc ITR/3/REV.1 ('Rules of Procedure and Evidence') r 78.

suggesting—counterintuitive as it may seem—that an acoustic jurisprudence must be careful not to overemphasize the significance of audibility to the project of judgment. There is a sense in which the very language of the hearing, with its implications of publicity, accessibility, and even democracy, is importantly misleading. Silence and inaudibility are crucial to the institutional practice of judgment too.

Viva Voce: The Solemn Declaration

The voice is not just a material condition of participation in the acoustic life of the courtroom. It is a procedural one too. It is legislated, regulated, required: overtly called upon by the Tribunal at certain key moments in the judicial process to do certain very particular things. The 'solemn declaration' is both a particularly clear example in this respect and, in a sense, foundational. For a majority of participants in the judicial soundscape it is the 'speech act' which both necessarily precedes and, moreover, authorizes the rest. And it must be rendered *viva voce*, out loud, by means of the living voice.

In the *Bikindi* case, this was most obvious in relation to the fifty-seven witnesses heard at trial, each and every one of whom was required to perform their declaration in open court immediately prior to testifying.[3] They did so by virtue of Rule 90(B) of the Tribunal's *Rules of Procedure and Evidence*, which states that every witness who takes the stand at the ICTR must, 'before giving evidence, make the following solemn declaration: "I solemnly declare that I will speak the truth, the whole truth and nothing but the truth."'[4] The declaration is so common in practice that it generally takes place quickly, without incident or comment. Once the witness has been ushered into the courtroom, a member of the Registry will be instructed to 'swear them in', the witness will be asked to stand, to raise their right hand and to repeat each part of the formula in turn before being invited to take their seat again so that their testimony can begin. The whole process generally lasts little more than a minute. If the declaration can sometimes seem like an unremarkable or even a marginal instance of courtroom orality, however, it is worth pausing to reflect on just how anomalous and important it actually is.

The strangeness of the solemn declaration is immediately intelligible at a number of levels of institutional practice. Unlike virtually every other word uttered at trial, it is neither interpreted nor transcribed. After the formula has been recited in English it will normally be rendered directly into either French or Kinyarwanda by an interpreter so that the witness can then echo it in their preferred language:

REGISTRAR: I solemnly declare that.
INTERPRETER: Je déclare solennellement que.
WITNESS: Je déclare solennellement que.

[3] *Prosecutor v Bikindi* (Judgement) ICTR-01-72-T, T Ch III (2 December 2008) annex A, paras 17, 29 ('Procedural History') ('*Bikindi* judgment').
[4] 'Rules of Procedure and Evidence', r 90(B).

REGISTRAR: I will speak the truth.
INTERPRETER: Je dirai la vérité.
WITNESS: Je dirai la vérité.[5]

And so on. With the solemn declaration alone, the interpretation precedes the witness's utterance rather than following it. The actual *performance* of the declaration remains un-interpreted.

Whenever a declaration is made in court, moreover, it is annotated like this: '*(Declaration made by Witness BHB in Kinyarwanda)*', or '*(Declaration made by Simon Bikindi in French)*'.[6] The pertinent section of the *Manual for English Court Reporting*, the formatting bible developed for use by the Tribunal's English court reporters, reads: 'At that place in the transcript where the solemn declaration is made by a witness ... it is not necessary to include either the verbatim declaration in the transcript or the introduction by the registry assistant asking the witness to raise his or her right hand, et cetera. Rather, a simple parenthetical remark indicating the person so declared is sufficient'.[7] The similarity with certain other parts of the transcript is striking. When an exhibit is admitted into evidence, or a witness enters or exits the courtroom, the format is identical: '*(Exhibit No P 1 admitted)*', '*(Witness entered courtroom)*', '*(Witness excused)*'.[8] For an acoustic jurisprudence, the parallel with the annotation used when a CD is played or, in some cases, when a witness sings is even more conspicuous: '*(Audio CD played)*', '*(Verse sung by witness)*', '*(The Accused sings)*'.[9] Both the typography and the disruption of the ordinary flow of the verbatim transcript is the same. Why? Because in each case what is being recorded is not words, but an action. The declaration operates according to a totally different audio-logic to the rest of the discourse at trial. Although the particular formulation of words recited is undoubtedly important, it is the act of giving voice to these words that matters most.

The solemn declaration is heard by the Tribunal as what Austin would have called either a 'performative utterance' or a 'speech act'.[10] This performative or active dimension of the declaration is what justifies the Tribunal treating it in the same way it does a witness leaving the courtroom and hearing it in the same way as it does a song or musical performance. From a juridical perspective, it is not the meaning of the declaration that matters, but how it sounds and what it does. In this sense, it isn't simply that the Tribunal chooses not to transcribe the solemn declaration. As a vocal act, a unique sonorous event, the solemn declaration is not strictly transcribable. It can be reported or recorded, but what is juridically

[5] Transcription mine.

[6] *Prosecutor v Bikindi* (Transcript) ICTR-01-72-T, T Ch III (Various Dates) ('*Bikindi* transcript'): 20 September 2006, 20; 31 October 2007, 2.

[7] International Criminal Tribunal for Rwanda, *Manual for English Court Reporting* (as at January 2011), 10.

[8] See, eg, *Bikindi* transcript: 18 September 2006, 10; 19 September 2006, 4; 22 September 2006, 25.

[9] See, eg, *Bikindi* transcript: 2 October 2006, 17; 28 September 2006, 31; 31 October 2007, 35. These are referred to as 'interruptions' in the *Manual for English Court Reporting*, 17.

[10] J L Austin, *How to Do Things with Words* (Harvard University Press, 1962) 12.

essential to it—its audibility and performance—can never be rendered as script. Moreover, because the declaration's effectiveness or 'felicity' is crucially dependent on its oralization by this particular legal subject, in all their 'vocalic uniqueness', and at this particular moment, it is not strictly interpretable either.[11] The act of vocalization itself is simply not amenable to the logic of interpretation. It can be heard, experienced, or witnessed, but never translated or reconfigured. It is, in the truest sense of the word, ineffable. Moreover, this very ineffability—precisely the dimension of the voice which the Tribunal failed to explore when it came to Bikindi's songs—is the key to the declaration's procedural force.

This point about the uniqueness and irreducibility of the voice goes some way to explaining the significance of the declaration for the ICTR. The voice, as Dolar explains, is 'intimately linked with the dimension of the sacred and ritual'.[12] Although the Tribunal does not require that the declaration be made on a Bible or other religious artefact, a theology haunts the process nevertheless. As Jonathan Sterne points out, according to the conventional somatics of traditional Christian spiritualism, 'the sonic dimension of experience is closest to divinity', and closer certainly than the visual which 'suggests distance and disengagement'.[13] For media theorist and Jesuit priest Walter Ong, for instance, 'religion has to do somehow with the invisible'. It has more in common with the 'earlier oral-aural world', with its concentration on voice and sound than with the more 'markedly visual world incident to script and print' which, he argues, characterizes modernity.[14] Indeed, for Ong, in the revealingly titled *Presence of the Word*: 'sound is more real or existential than other sense objects, despite the fact that it also more evanescent',[15] and 'voice is not inhabited by presence as something added: it simply conveys presence as nothing else does'.[16] Sound is a 'special sensory key to interiority'.[17] 'In all human cultures, the spoken word appears as the closest sensory equivalent of fully developed interior thought.'[18]

This is the sensory logic which haunts the solemn declaration at the ICTR. Nowhere on the record is it ever made explicit, but it is palpable nevertheless as a phantom residue of the overtly Christian legal traditions out of which contemporary international law has emerged.[19] The Bible may be absent from the international courtroom as a material object, but its impact, its metaphysical weight, still resonates. Thus, the requirement that witnesses vocalize their commitment to speak the truth is intended to render that commitment both 'present' and

[11] On the 'felicity' of the utterance see Austin (1962) 12–24 ('Lecture II'). Cavarero (2005) ch 3.2.

[12] Mladen Dolar, *A Voice and Nothing More* (MIT Press, 2006) 107.

[13] Jonathan Sterne, *The Audible Past: Cultural Origins of Sound Reproduction* (Duke University Press, 2003) 17.

[14] Walter J Ong, *Presence of the Word: Some Prolegomena for Cultural and Religious History* (Yale University Press, 1967) 10.

[15] Ong (1967) 111.

[16] Ong (1967) 114.

[17] Ong (1967) 117.

[18] Ong (1967) 138.

[19] For a detailed account of the role of oaths in the early Modern English tradition, for instance, albeit one that is not overtly attentive to questions of sound and voice, see Conal Condren, *Argument and Authority in Early Modern England: The Presupposition of Oaths and Office* (Cambridge University Press, 2006).

(therefore) 'real' to them, to ensure that it comes right from their interior, that it represents as pure a manifestation of their thought as possible, without mediation. It is meant to engage them deeply, to conjure something not unlike the presence of God: the full weight and secular virtue of international criminal law.

For Derrida, as we saw in Chapter 5, the kinds of 'theological prejudice'[20] put to work here by the Tribunal—the association of speech with subjectivity, consciousness, and ideality, and the positioning of voice as the privileged point of access to the divine—would be absolutely prototypical of the metaphysics of presence.[21] 'They are essential', he writes, 'to the history of the West', and therefore to 'metaphysics in its entirety, even when it professes to be atheist',[22] which international law generally does. Derrida wanted to critique such a metaphysics. The alleged unity of voice and ideality, he argued, was radically contradicted by the *différantial* work of the trace, which is also to say of 'time itself'.[23] But the solemn declaration as it features at the ICTR is neither reducible to metaphysics nor, indeed, to its critique.

What Derrida criticizes, writes Michelle Duncan, 'is the founding of *metaphysics* on the illusion of presence—that is, what Leonard Lawlor calls the "valorization of presence" or "presence as a foundation"'.[24] The ability of the act of vocalization to conjure the *experience* of presence is a different matter entirely. It is important to differentiate between a *metaphysics* of presence and the juridical deployment of vocalization as a material and psychosomatic event, 'even as we acknowledge that there is no experience of material events in a present time that is fundamentally absolute'.[25] The sensory logic entailed in the ICTR's 'solemn declaration' may be metaphysically suspect, indeed it may also involve a theory of sound which is very far from being either philosophically, biologically, or psychologically inevitable, but that does not mean it is incapable of being either experientially or juridically effective.[26] This is the key point for an acoustic jurisprudence. Sometimes 'theological prejudices' such as those deployed by the Tribunal do actually work. That is what the Tribunal is banking on when it continues to require that the declaration be oralized. In this respect, it clearly engages the register of the metaphysical, but its motivations are nevertheless firmly prudential. For some witnesses, the act of ritually declaring their commitment to 'speak the truth, the whole truth and nothing but the truth'—out loud and publicly—really will render that commitment more 'real' or 'present' to them than any other form of expression would have.

[20] Jacques Derrida, *Of Grammatology*, trans Gayatri Chakravorty Spivak (John Hopkins University Press, 1976) [trans of: *De la grammatologie* (first published 1967)] 323 n 3.

[21] See Chapter 3. [22] Derrida (1976).

[23] Jacques Derrida, *Speech and Phenomena and Other Essays on Husserl's Theory of Signs*, trans David B Allison (Northwestern University Press, 1973) [trans of: *La voix et le phénomène* (first published 1967)] 86.

[24] Michelle Duncan, 'The Operatic Scandal of the Singing Body: Voice, Presence, Performativity', *Cambridge Opera Journal* 16(3) (2004) 283, 295, quoting Leonard Lawlor, *Derrida and Husserl: The Basic Problem of Phenomenology* (Indiana University Press, 2002) 2–3.

[25] Duncan (2004) 295–6. [26] Sterne (2003) 14–19.

Having said that, it hardly ever sounded like it. For an acoustic jurisprudence, the irony is that compared with the rest of the speech heard at trial, the solemn declaration invariably sounded the *most* detached from the speaker's intentionality, the *least* sincere or authentic of all. In practice, this seems to be a function of the declaration's citationality, its scriptedness, the fact that when a person makes the declaration they are always, and necessarily, giving voice to someone else's words. It doesn't help that the phrase is broken down into parts for the purposes of repetition. Registrar: 'I solemnly declare that', Witness: 'I solemnly declare that', Registrar: 'I will speak the truth', Witness: 'I will speak the truth'. The rhythm of the declaration, thus, is thoroughly *un*-natural. It involves the suspension of the ordinary patterns of 'normal' or authentic speech. As a result, at the ICTR the declaration can tend to sound expressively empty, lacking in either sincerity or the fullness of the speaker's intent.

This is not inevitable. There are many contexts in which it is precisely the fact that you are speaking words you did *not* author, which you have heard before, and possibly many times over, that lends the moment its special gravitas or force. If a person's vows sound particularly sincere at a wedding, for example—'Do you take this woman to be your lawfully wedded wife?' 'I do'—that is partly *because* of the phrase's citationality, not in spite of it. Much of its force derives from the fact that it *does* have a history, that it seems to bind you to those who have spoken these words before. At the ICTR, by contrast, the declaration tends to sound lacklustre, neutral, half-hearted. What's more, as far as the Tribunal is concerned this doesn't even appear to be a problem. For juridical purposes, this turns out to be precisely the *sound of 'solemnity'*.

In Chapter 5, we saw how the sound of a given speech act was crucial to achieving linguistic effect, even despite Austin's own silence in this regard. 'As a condition of enunciation, the manner in which an utterance is spoken—whether whispered, snarled, screamed, murmured, hissed, or mumbled—must surely enter into the equation of its variability', Michelle Duncan writes, 'for manner is ultimately part and parcel of what makes an utterance felicitous or infelicitous'.[27] This is no less true at the ICTR. It is not enough for a witness simply to speak the words of the declaration. They must be spoken with an appropriate tone. This does not mean that every time a witness makes their declaration the Tribunal must engage in a minute tonal analysis as to their sincerity or otherwise. Sincerity is precisely *not* a relevant factor. But it is surely the case that if a witness tried to whisper or shout or sing their declaration, or if their delivery seemed overtly ironic or sarcastic, doing so would render it ineffective. It would not be merely incomprehensible, terrifying, or beautiful, but 'infelicitous' too. As a speech act, the declaration would fail. In all likelihood, the Tribunal would require that the witness have another go and possibly also hold them in contempt.[28] The fact that the list of possible acoustic

[27] Duncan (2004) 291.

[28] 'Rules of Procedure and Evidence', r 77A, states that the Tribunal may hold in contempt anyone who 'knowingly and wilfully interferes with the administration of justice'.

infelicities is neither closed nor even known by participants in advance does not make it any less real in this respect. That the delivery of the solemn declaration is almost never a problem for the Tribunal—certainly it wasn't in the *Bikindi* case—is evidence of the extent to which these norms are embedded, rather than proof of their absence. We could understand the 'solemn' in 'solemn declaration' as a kind of stage direction then, an institutional direction as to vocal style. But what this solemnity turns out to entail in practice is not so much sincerity as a kind of bland seriousness, above all the sober and manifestly un-ironic vocalization of the Tribunal's formula, regardless of one's state of mind.

According to the conventional account, the ICTR's 'solemn declaration' would be what Austin called a 'commissive', that particular subset of performative utterance intended to commit its speaker to a particular course of action, on the one hand—to 'speak the truth, the whole truth and nothing but the truth' in the course of their future testimony[29]—and, on the other hand, to endow that commitment with a set of juridically actionable consequences in the event of its proven breach.[30] The penalty for 'false testimony under solemn declaration', is a fine of up to US$10,000, a term of imprisonment of up to five years, or some combination of the two.[31] But what the strange 'solemnity' of the declaration suggests from an acoustic perspective is that it also involves a kind of bodily subjugation, perhaps this most of all. As far as the solemn declaration is concerned, and in spite of its Christian heritage, the witness's intentions are juridically irrelevant. Far from actually *being* sincere, it is not even necessary to *sound* sincere. It is 'solemnity' that counts as far as the institutional and juridical efficacy of the declaration is concerned. And 'solemnity' in these circumstances turns out to mean the sound of a kind of sober passivity. Desmond Manderson writes that 'the purpose of ritual is not to convey information; it is not about thinking but about feeling, not about the mind but about the body'.[32] At the ICTR, the activity of giving solemn voice is about surrendering one's (speaking) body to the authority of the institution, *whether or not* the soul is in tow. It is this founding act of vocal submission which matters most juridically. Indeed, its ritual repetition does vital work in terms of the constitution of the institution as a whole.

It is not just witnesses who are required to make the declaration. They were simply the most common and obvious example in the *Bikindi* case. The solemn declaration was a necessary prerequisite to participation for judges, interpreters, translators, the Registrar, and every last member of the Registry too: which is to say, almost everyone employed by the Tribunal (we will come to the exceptions in a moment). There are a number of important differences in each case. Where for judges and the Registry the declaration takes place outside of a trial context,

[29] The Chamber often reminds witnesses they are 'still under oath'. See, eg, *Bikindi* transcript: 18 September 2006, 50; 19 September 2006, 4; 20 September 2006, 4, 51.

[30] On 'commissives' generally see Austin (1962) 157–60.

[31] 'Rules of Procedure and Evidence', r 91(G).

[32] Desmond Manderson, '*Et Lex Perpetua*: Dying Declarations & Mozart's Requiem', *Cardozo Law Review* 20(5–6) (1999) 1621, 1642.

interpreters are required to make their oath actually *in* court like witnesses.[33] The particular formula that each office is required to recite varies according to the particular exigencies of the role. Where with witnesses truth-telling is paramount, for judges the emphasis is on the 'honourable', 'faithful', 'impartial', and 'conscientious' performance of one's 'duties', on the one hand, and exercise of one's 'power', on the other.[34] Similarly, for interpreters there is a special focus on 'confidentiality',[35] whereas for the Registry 'loyalty', 'discretion', and 'good conscience' seem to be particularly important.[36]

Although there is a correlation between the particular formulation of words recited and the nature of the juridical 'commitment' which follows in each instance, except in the case of witnesses, it is neither especially direct nor complete.[37] It is the act of oralization itself which matters most from an institutional perspective. Even for Judges, who are additionally required to sign 'the text of the declaration' in the presence of either the 'Secretary-General of the United Nations or his representative', to be kept on file by the Tribunal, this extra layer of formality merely records, bolsters, and archives the oral declaration itself. In no sense does it supersede it. The declaration is still the crucial rite of passage. For almost everyone involved in the institution, the solemn declaration is a necessary precursor to participation. It is a vocal act which constitutes the institution as a community of speakers. In this respect, the exceptions to the rule make perfect sense. The only institutional actors not subjected to the declaration are those employed by the Office for the Prosecutor and those employed by the Defence, including counsel in both instances. In the former case, although the Prosecution is, strictly speaking, one of the three main organs of the Tribunal, along with the Chambers and the Registry, it is nevertheless meant to act as independently from the rest as possible.[38] According to Article 15 of the *Statute*, for instance, 'the Prosecutor shall act independently as a separate organ of the International Tribunal for Rwanda. He or she shall not seek or receive instructions from any government or from any other source'.[39] The Defence, by contrast, operates independently from the Tribunal altogether.[40] Insofar as either

[33] Although this rule is not enumerated anywhere in the rules explicitly, it does appear to be customary practice. At a pre-trial hearing in the *Bikindi* case, two interpreters were sworn in immediately after proceedings had commenced: *Bikindi* transcript, 8 March 2004, 1.

[34] 'Rules of Procedure and Evidence', r 14(A).

[35] 'Rules of Procedure and Evidence', r 76.

[36] 'Rules of Procedure and Evidence', r 32.

[37] For witnesses the obligation to tell the truth corresponds to a penalty for 'false testimony' under r 91(G). For Judges, according to r 15, disqualification may follow if they fail to withdraw from a case in which they have a 'personal interest' or 'any association' which might affect their 'impartiality'. In the case of both Interpreters and the Registry, however, there are no specific penalties for breach of the responsibilities relating to office enumerated in the Rules. However, the ordinary provisions in relation to contempt would apply. Rule 77(A)(ii), for instance, covers the disclosure of confidential information and rr 77(A)(iv) and 77(A)(v) cover matters which might be understood as relating to 'conscience': 'Rules of Procedure and Evidence', rr 15, 77A.

[38] Statute of the International Tribunal for Rwanda, UNSC Res 955 (8 November 1994) UN Doc S/RES/955, annex, art 10 ('ICTR Statute').

[39] ICTR Statute, art 15.

[40] In practice, both Prosecution and Defence are housed at the Arusha Conference Centre. The Defence does not, however, have access to identical resources, a fact which is very significant as far

Prosecution or Defence counsel are required to swear an oath or make any sort of public declaration, it is not to the ICTR.[41]

The solemn declaration is both inaugural of the institution as a community and definitional of its limits. The performance of the declaration, as regulated by the Tribunal's *Rules of Evidence and Procedure*, is an act of community formation, an institutional rite through which all members of the institution must pass in order to engage themselves in the judicial process. As Manderson explains, rites such as oath swearing 'mark the transition of the subject from the external world to the internal order of legal process'.[42] This is why, despite the declaration's theological heritage, the sincerity of the speaker is ultimately unimportant in juridical terms, and why an emphasis on metaphysics ultimately misses the mark from a jurisprudential perspective. It is also why it is sufficient not even to sound sincere so long as you do sound sufficiently 'solemn', and why there isn't necessarily a close connection between the words declared and the nature of the obligations attached to them. It is the ritual activity of submission to the institution and its authority that matters most. An act of submission which is performed by means of one's speaking body: resonant and audible. Just like everyone else.

The Principle of Publicity

The ICTR operates according to a 'principle of publicity'. Though the phrase itself recalls Kant's famous iteration of the categorical imperative in *Perpetual Peace*, its focus at the ICTR is very different.[43] For Kant, the principle of publicity was about a law's moral rationality. Specifically, whether or not it is logically acceptable for a state to publicize a law where that publication would in all likelihood defeat the law's very purpose.[44] At the ICTR, the principle relates to the *material*

as access to justice is concerned. The principle of 'equality of arms' is laid out at art 20 of the Statute of the International Tribunal for Rwanda. However, in *Prosecutor v Kayishema* the Trial Chamber held that the principle did not necessarily entail an equality of resources. On the way in which the system works at the ICTR and its relation to the other international tribunals, see Stefania Negri, 'The Principle of "Equality of Arms" and the Evolving Law of International Criminal Procedure', *International Criminal Law Review* 5(4) (2005) 513, especially 552–60. *Prosecutor v Kayishema* (Judgement) ICTR-95-1-T, T Ch II (21 May 1999) ('*Kayishema* judgment') paras 20, 55–60.

41 This does not mean that Prosecution and Defence counsel are immune to the Tribunal's authority. Rule 46 of the Rules allows a Chamber, after a warning, to either impose sanctions on counsel 'if, in its opinion, his conduct remains offensive or abusive, obstructs the proceedings, or is otherwise contrary to the interests of justice' or to refer the matter to the relevant professional body. In 1998 the Registry at the ICTR drew up the *Code of Professional Conduct for Defence Counsel* (entry into force 4 June 1998). Part II of this code outlines the 'general obligations of counsel to clients'. These obligations do not need to be assented to by declaration: 'Rules of Procedure and Evidence', r 46.

42 Manderson (1999) 1642–3.

43 Immanuel Kant, *On History*, ed Lewis White Beck, trans Lewis White Beck, Robert E Anchor, and Emil L Fackenheim (Bobbs-Merrill, 1963) 381 ('Perpetual Peace: A Philosophical Sketch').

44 Kant's answer is no. Importantly, for Kant the issue is not whether the law actually *is* proclaimed. See Kevin R Davis, 'Kantian "Publicity" and Political Justice', *History of Philosophy Quarterly* 8(4) (1991) 409, 414–15; Kant (1963).

accessibility of judicial proceedings to the accused, the press, and the public. It is concerned with whether or not people can see or hear them.

The principle's founding provision at the Tribunal is Article 20 of its Statute which, in accordance with Article 14(1) of the International Covenant on Civil and Political Rights,[45] enshrines an accused's right to a 'fair and public hearing',[46] subject to such measures as may be necessary for the 'protection of victims and witnesses'.[47] In procedural terms this right manifests itself at Rules 78 to 80 of the Tribunal's Rules of Procedure and Evidence. Rule 78 provides that 'all proceedings before a Trial Chamber, other than deliberations of the Chamber, shall be held in public, unless otherwise provided'.[48] Rule 79 states that the Trial Chamber may order a 'closed session'—which is to say one where the press and the public (but not the accused) are temporarily excluded—only for reasons of: (i) public order or morality; (ii) safety, security, or non-disclosure of the identity of a victim or witness;[49] and (iii) the protection of the interests of justice.[50] Even these exceptions to the principle do involve a certain amount of deference to it, however. Whenever the Tribunal does order a 'closed session', the *reasons* for such an order must at least be publicized.[51] Rule 80 involves a similar logic. On the one hand, it governs the very limited circumstances in which a member of the public may be excluded from ongoing proceedings. On the other, one of the principal reasons it gives for doing so is specifically in order to '*protect* the right of the accused to a fair and public trial'.[52] The exception flows directly from the rule, a commitment to the principle itself.

The Office for the United Nations High Commissioner for Human Rights has called the principle of publicity 'an important safeguard for the interest of the individual and of society at large', presumably in the sense that publicity is a pre-requisite to critique.[53] As Judge Arrey explained at one point during the *Bikindi* case, the Tribunal 'wants to have as much public proceedings as possible'.[54] 'The hearing', she said, 'in principle, should be in public unless there's a compelling reason'.[55] In this section of the chapter I consider how this mandate was put into practice. I argue that a careful analysis of the principle's application in the *Bikindi* case reveals audibility to be both its necessary and, in many cases, its sufficient

[45] International Covenant on Civil and Political Rights (adopted 16 December 1966, entered into force 23 March 1976) 999 UNTS 171 (ICCPR) art 14(1).

[46] ICCPR, art 20.

[47] ICCPR, art 21. The provisions regarding such protection appear at 'Rules of Procedure and Evidence', r 75.

[48] 'Rules of Procedure and Evidence', r 78.

[49] As provided in 'Rules of Procedure and Evidence', r 75.

[50] 'Rules of Procedure and Evidence', r 79(A).

[51] 'Rules of Procedure and Evidence', r 79(B).

[52] 'Rules of Procedure and Evidence', r 80(A) (emphasis added).

[53] UNHCR, 'General Comment No 32: Article 14—Right to Equality before Courts and Tribunals and to a Fair Trial' (23 August 2007) UN Doc CCPR/C/GC/32, para 28. See also UNHCR, 'General Comment No 13: Article 14 (Administration of Justice) (1984)' (27 May 2008) UN Doc HRI/GEN/1/Rev.9 (Vol. I) 184.

[54] *Bikindi* transcript, 26 September 2006, 20.

[55] *Bikindi* transcript, 19 September 2006, 9.

condition. When the Tribunal purports to guarantee the right to a 'public hearing', it thinks of the two words as being virtually synonymous. Judicial proceedings will be public at the ICTR so long as voices can be heard. Nowhere was this truer in the *Bikindi* case than in relation to the testimony of so-called 'protected witnesses'.

Of the fifty-seven witnesses to testify in the *Bikindi* case, only fifteen were not 'protected' in the sense imagined by the Statute.[56] Of those fifteen, one was Bikindi himself, one was a UN investigator,[57] and three were expert witnesses,[58] and the option was never open to them anyway. As a result, an overwhelming majority of testimony in the *Bikindi* case was heard in circumstances where it was open to the Tribunal to exclude the public 'from all or part of the proceedings' if it so wished.[59] Protected witnesses provide an intriguing opportunity, therefore, to investigate the principle of publicity at its limit. With protected witnesses at the ICTR, the limit becomes the centre, the exception actually is the rule.

The Tribunal went into closed session on only nine occasions in the *Bikindi* case and even then it was mostly only very briefly, primarily in order to record a witness's name, address, and any other private details for the purposes of the record.[60] For the most part, protected witnesses were dealt with in accordance with Rule 75(A) and (B) which allow for 'appropriate measures' to be taken by the Tribunal in order to 'safeguard the privacy and security of witnesses' in ways which do *not* involve the complete exclusion of the public. Rule 75(B), for instance, permits the assignment of a pseudonym to a witness,[61] and the 'giving of testimony through image- or voice-altering devices or closed circuit television'.[62] But the standard practice at the ICTR is not specifically delineated anywhere in the Rules.

Every time a protected witness testified during the *Bikindi* case, a curtain was drawn to the public gallery and the video-monitors there were switched off. What this meant was that the witness's testimony could be heard by the public on their headsets, but not seen. Counsel for the Prosecution explained the rationale to one witness like this: 'You are a protected witness', he said, 'which means that your identity is protected from the public. The public can hear what you say, but they will not see your face, nor learn your name'.[63] Their testimony would be 'acousmatic'.

The word 'acousmatic' was introduced to the contemporary lexicon by the French poet and essayist Jérôme Peignot, and then theorized by composer and early pioneer of *musique concrète* Pierre Schaeffer[64] soon after. This was in 1966, in

[56] ICTR Statute, art 21.

[57] Aaron Musonda. See *Bikindi* transcript: 18 September 2006; 22 September 2006; 25 September 2006.

[58] *Bikindi* transcript: 12 February 2007; 13 February 2007; 14 February 2007; 15 February 2007; 16 February 2007; 23 October 2007; 24 October 2007; 25 October 2007.

[59] 'Rules of Procedure and Evidence', r 79(A)(ii).

[60] *Bikindi* transcript: 20 September 2006, 5; 27 September 2006, 12; 28 September 2006, 33; 19 February 2007, 3; 24 September 2007, 9, 45, 73; 25 September 2007, 7; 26 September 2007, 6.

[61] 'Rules of Procedure and Evidence', r 75(B)(i)(d).

[62] 'Rules of Procedure and Evidence', r 75(B)(i)(c).

[63] *Bikindi* transcript, 5 October 2006, 29.

[64] Not to be confused with R Murray Schafer, who coined the term 'soundscape'.

his influential *Traité des objets musicaux*.[65] In Schaeffer's hands the word refers to any 'sounds one hears without seeing their originating cause'.[66] Primarily, he had audio recordings in mind. But the term was borrowed from Pythagoras and the fabled *akousmatikoi*: those of the great philosopher's students who were required to remain silent for the first several years of their apprenticeship and who, in certain ceremonial and instructional contexts, were permitted to hear their master's voice only from behind a veil or curtain.[67]

Despite the curtain, the precise form of acousmatics practised at the ICTR could hardly be more different from that of Pythagoras and his disciples. For the *akousmatikoi* the method worked to confine their attention to the voice of their master, to prevent them from being 'distracted by his looks or quirks of behaviour, by visual forms, the spectacle of presentation', to protect them, in other words, against the tyranny of the visual.[68] Not only was the identity of the speaker never in question, it was precisely what gave Pythagoras's orations their gravitas. His invisibility simply added to the sense of import and mystery. At the ICTR the logic is just the opposite. The curtain works as a mask, and a rather mundane or juridico-bureaucratic one at that: decisively non-mystical. Moreover the tyranny being protected against here is precisely the facility of the visual to *reveal* truth, not to compromise or distract from it. Specifically, a line is being drawn between identity and the face.

How to square this practice with the fact that, elsewhere in the *Bikindi* case, the Tribunal was willing to draw a similar line with the *voice*? That it actively relied on the voice in discerning the identity of a speaker, as we saw in Chapter 5? Contradiction is not the only option. It is equally possible to understand the ICTR's practice in this respect as a form of compromise, an exercise in prudence. On the one hand, because many listeners will be listening to the speaker's testimony in interpretation, which amounts to a kind of acoustic masking anyway. On the other, because such a practice enables the Tribunal to filter out as much data as possible without either falling foul of some of the problems associated with other methods of de-identification or, more importantly, giving up on the publicity of proceedings entirely. The ICTY, for instance, has experimented with distorting the voices of protected witnesses directly as they testify, but this method poses a number of problems. First, even distorting the timbre or pitch of a person's voice is not necessarily enough to de-identify them to a listener who knows them really well. The human ear is sufficiently discerning to be able to recognize the metre

[65] Pierre Schaeffer, *Traité des objets musicaux* (Seuil, 1967).

[66] Schaeffer (1967) 91. The English translation here is taken from Michel Chion, *Audio-Vision: Sound on Screen*, ed and trans Claudia Gorbman (Columbia University Press, 1994) [trans of: *L'audio-vision: Son et image au cinéma* (first published 1990)] 71. As far as I am aware, this treatise has never been translated into English.

[67] Edwin L Minar Jr, 'Pythagorean Communism', *Transactions and Proceedings of the American Philological Association* 75 (1944) 34, 39. George Boas, 'Ancient Testimony to Secret Doctrines', *The Philosophical Review* 62(1) (1953) 79, 89–90. For a critical reading of the aesthetic and psychoanalytical dimensions of this key moment in the history of philosophy, see Dolar (2006) 60–70.

[68] Dolar (2006) 61.

and rhythm of a person's speech even if the 'voice itself' is completely unrecognizable. Second, the process of distortion itself produces a kind of acoustic injustice whereby the testimony is liable to sound literally lifeless or robotic, crucially lacking in what Barthes called 'grain'—that essential connection between voice and the human body—and sometimes in jarring contrast, moreover, to what may well be a particularly affecting piece of testimony in substantive terms.[69] Third, the techniques used to create this form of instantaneous distortion—normally a simple pitch-shift—are relatively easy to reverse for someone with even a relatively small amount of technical knowledge. For the purposes of the archive, therefore, it seems that the Residual Mechanism may end up having to do further work on the audio-archive 'post production' as it were in order to render the identity of its protected witnesses private once and for all, probably using a digital 'vocoder'.[70]

What the Tribunal's treatment of protected witnesses suggests is that proceedings will be 'public' at the ICTR so long as they can be heard. As far as the principle of publicity is concerned, audibility turns out to be both its necessary and sufficient condition. This equation between sound and publicity, and conversely between sight and privacy, is by no means unfamiliar. Indeed, they are essential to what Sterne calls the 'audio-visual litany', a series of apparently natural and extremely persistent assumptions about the biological, psychological, and physical nature of these two senses which are treated as having direct metaphysical, political, and juridical consequences: hearing is spherical, whereas vision is directional; hearing immerses its subject, whereas vision offers a perspective; sounds come to us, but vision travels to its object; hearing is concerned with interiors, vision with surfaces; hearing is about affect, vision about intellect; hearing is a sense that immerses us in the world, vision is a sense that removes us from it; and so on.[71] Thus for Walter Ong, sound and voice are not simply keys to the interiority of the subject, as we saw at the outset of the chapter. They are both necessary to and inaugural of human sociality as well. He writes: 'It would appear that precisely because sound is so interiorizing and thus exploitable by man at depths unknown to less interiorized creatures, it implements socialization or even forces it as nothing else can.'[72] True interiority, for Ong, 'makes it possible to address others' because only insofar as a person has interior resources, only insofar as he experiences his full self, can he also relate to others, who, of course, are interior beings themselves.[73] Voice thus is the privileged medium of authentic human interaction. A very similar dynamic is at work when the language of voice appears so commonly in discourse on democracy, citizenship, and participatory politics. In the aftermath of the French Revolution, the voice was figured as one of the most essential mediums in what Dolar calls the

[69] Roland Barthes, *Image, Music, Text*, trans Stephen Heath (Fontana, 1977) 179–89 'The Grain of the Voice'.

[70] For more information on the vocoder, see Dave Tompkins, *How to Wreck a Nice Beach: The Vocoder from World War II to Hip-Hop* (Melville House, 2010) 19.

[71] Sterne (2003) 15. Michel Chion has argued similarly we need to 'disengage sound thinking … from its naturalistic rut': Chion (1994) 94.

[72] Ong (1967) 124. [73] Ong (1967).

'democratisation of justice'.[74] The ideal democracy thus would be one where 'everybody could hear everybody else's voice'.[75]

The emphasis on hearing in this latter example suggests the importance of physics in the equation too. The conventional relation between voice and publicity is also partly to do with its existence as sound. Above all, the voice is resonant, and as such has both a very particular temporality and a tendency to spread through space. Whereas vision, for Ong, is a 'one-way operation' and thus necessarily individualistic, the voice by contrast is inherently shared.[76] 'Unlike the gaze', as Adriana Cavarero puts it, 'the voice is always, irremediably relational. It does not allow a detached focus on the object because, properly speaking, it has no object. The voice vibrates in the air, striking the ear of the other, even when it does not mean to'.[77] Sound thus becomes not simply the privileged sense of subjectivity, but of sociality too. The sonorous voice is figured as the very condition of public discourse and, therefore, also of justice.

The Voice and the Letter

If the ICTR's is a predominantly oral soundscape, the solemn declaration and the principle of publicity are its two primary conditions. With the declaration, the act of giving voice is directly associated with the very act of institution making, both with bringing it into being and determining its shape and limits. It is above all a vocalization which both precedes and authorizes the rest of the discourse at trial, irrespective of the precise substance of the declaration or indeed the intentionality 'behind' it, so long as the body is adequately engaged. The solemn declaration is thus a rite of passage and an act of community formation. With the principle of publicity, by contrast, the significance of the voice is reconfigured in terms of its audibility. Now it is the voice which ensures the material accessibility of proceedings and which is deeply bound up, moreover, with the legitimacy of the institution as a whole, its very claim to serve the interests of justice. In both cases we could observe that, contra Goodrich, for whom the 'strategic organising principle of the courtroom … is that of the visibility of justice rather than of its audibility', voice and the audible enjoy a particularly privileged position as far as the overall mediascape of the trial is concerned.[78]

We could venture plenty of other examples. Consider the requirement at Rule 62(A), for instance, that the indictment be 'read to the accused in a language he understands', and that the accused reciprocate by 'entering' a plea of guilty or not guilty on each count, both out loud and in the presence of the Trial Chamber, which is also to say the public.[79] 'The purpose of this initial appearance', as Judge

74 Dolar (2006) 109.
75 Dolar (2006).
76 Ong (1967) 167.
77 Cavarero (2005) 177–8.
78 Peter Goodrich, *Languages of Law: From Logics of Memory to Nomadic Masks* (Weidenfeld and Nicolson, 1990) 191.
79 'Rules of Procedure and Evidence', rr 62(A), 62(A)(ii), 62(A)(iii). In the *Bikindi* case this occurred on three occasions. First on Bikindi's 'initial appearance' on 4 April 2002, when he was read

Pavel Dolenc explained to Bikindi, 'is that after you listen to the indictment you may plead about the charges'.[80] Consider too the logical counterpart in this respect, the requirement that both judgment and sentence be 'pronounced in public', and in the accused's presence.[81] Or look at Rule 92 *bis* which provides that 'there is an overriding public interest' that the presentation of evidence be made orally rather than in writing, before going on to provide the limited exceptions to that rule.[82] In each case, it seems that the voice is again being put to work by the Tribunal as a means of activating the text, on the one hand, of breathing life into it, of engaging the speaking body, and as a way of ensuring its publicity, on the other, of making it audible. In each case, it is not until the written word, the 'dead letter', has been 'bathed in the stream of orality', as Isabel Hofmeyr elegantly puts it, that it will achieve its full force and juridical effect.[83] The voice thus appears as an essential gateway through which the text must pass as a condition of its efficacy.

Yet from another perspective we could equally read each of these examples in precisely the opposite way, not as instances of the voice's priority over the written word, but rather of its servitude to it. Dolar argues that above all it is the 'unchangeable nature' of the letter, 'which makes the law possible, as opposed to the fleeting nature of voices'.[84] Law aspires to solidity and permanence, he claims, in a way that the voice, in its evanescent sonority, seems to defeat. So for Dolar, when the voice is needed from a juridical perspective, it is always a voice that has been 'properly circumscribed, tamed, pacified'.[85] The division of labour is strict. The voice is only to be called upon 'in specific and well-defined places and times'.[86] It merely 'completes' and 'accomplishes' the letter, and is thereby secondary to it, even if the act of completion or accomplishment is nevertheless absolutely essential. The voice, thus, is rendered as a kind of necessary supplement.[87]

For an acoustic jurisprudence, the sense of hierarchy in both alternatives is a distraction. It misses the mutability of the relationship between institutions and across time, as well as the specificity of particular practices. As this chapter turns now to three examples where such a dynamic seems to have been at work at the ICTR, it follows each of them through closely and in detail, without attempting to

the original version of the indictment by a representative of the Registrar and plead not guilty to all counts. Second, some two years later, when Bikindi was read an amended version of the indictment and again plead not guilty. Third, in August 2005, when he was read the 'operative sections' of a further amendment and plead similarly: *Bikindi* transcript: 4 April 2002; 8 March 2004; 11 August 2005.

[80] *Bikindi* transcript, 4 April 2002, 6.

[81] 'Rules of Procedure and Evidence', rr 88, 100. This the Trial Chamber did on 2 December 2008.

[82] See also 'Rules of Procedure and Evidence', r 94 *bis* in relation to the testimony of expert witnesses (as introduced by amendments dated 8 June 1998).

[83] Isabel Hofmeyr, 'The Letter and the Law: The Politics of Orality and Literacy in the Chiefdoms of the Northern Transvaal' in Graham Furniss and Liz Gunner (eds), *Power, Marginality and African Oral Literature* (Cambridge University Press, 2008) 38, 44.

[84] Dolar (2006) 113. [85] Dolar (2006). [86] Dolar (2006).

[87] Derrida's well-known discussion of the logic of the supplement begins from exactly the opposite starting point. He takes issue with Rousseau's claim that 'languages are made to be spoken' and that writing, therefore, served 'only as a supplement to speech'. At the ICTR it is frequently the reverse. It is the voice, not writing, that is figured as supplementary: Rousseau quoted in Derrida (1976) 144. On supplementary in general, see Derrida (1976) 141–64.

impose a homogeneity of approach if it isn't there. In the practices of pronouncing judgment, court reporting, and speaking 'for the record' we can observe a more complex and ambiguous role for the voice than the roles identified for it in the first two parts of this chapter, whereby vocalization is re-configured as a formal technique in the juridical production of the written word.

Pronouncing judgment

Even though judgment must be pronounced at the ICTR, everything about this pronouncement seems designed to underline its servility to the text which both preceded it and would immediately dwarf it in importance as far as the broader media ecology of international law was concerned. When the time came in the *Bikindi* case, on 2 December 2008, Presiding Judge Weinberg de Roca began as follows: 'Trial Chamber III will now render its judgment in the case of *The Prosecutor v Simon Bikindi*. The Chamber will read out a summary of the Judgment'.[88] And for the next three-quarters of an hour she did exactly that. Not only was she reading from a pre-prepared script, it sounded like it too. She read slowly and carefully. Her delivery was both sober and serious, dry and deliberate even to the point of being dull.

Acoustically this was no great feat of oratory then. But neither was that the result of any mere lapse or failure on Weinberg de Roca's part. What is proper to the pulpit or the lecture theatre may not be so to the courtroom. The difference here is between two competing forms of authority and the contrasting ways in which the voice is encoded in relation to them. One places the emphasis on vocal drama and tends towards the charismatic voice of dictatorship (from the Latin *dictare*, to 'say' or 'speak'), and in particular that of totalitarianism. Max Horkheimer and Theodor Adorno had the voice in mind, for instance, when they wrote of the *Führer's* 'metaphysical charisma'.[89] According to this way of imagining the voice, its function is not of the order of the formal or ritual. It exists entirely outside of the bounds of procedure and the institution. If it is authoritative, this is not by virtue of its conventionality, but because voice and law are absolutely proximate. The jurisprudential register here is that of natural law. The voice being manifested is God's:

> The Führer may well be Chancellor of the Third Reich, commander in chief of the army, and occupy many political functions, yet he is not the Führer by virtue of the political functions he happens to be charged with, not by election and also not on the basis of his abilities. It is the relationship of the voice which makes him the Führer, and the tie that links the subjects to him is enacted as a vocal tie; its other part is the answer to the voice by mass acclamation which is an essential feature of the speech. It is the voice that makes

[88] *Prosecutor v Bikindi* (Summary of Judgment and Sentence) ICTR-01-72 (2 December 2008) ('*Bikindi* summary') para 1.

[89] Max Horkheimer and Theodor W Adorno, *Dialectic of Enlightenment: Philosophical Fragments*, ed Gunzelin Schmid Noerr, trans Edmund Jephcott (Stanford University Press, 2002) [trans of: *Gesammelte Schriften: Dialektik der Aufklärung and Schriften 1940-1950* (first published 1987)] 129.

the law—*Führerworte haben Gesetzkraft*, as Eichmann will say in Jerusalem; his words supported by the mere voice make the law, the voice immediately turns them into law, that is, the voice suspends the law. This is what Carl Schmitt proclaimed in 1935: the 'Führer's will and plan' are manifested in oral guidelines (*Leitsätze)*, which are 'in immediate and most intense way positive law'.[90]

The voice that pronounces judgment, by contrast, is an overtly formal one. It also has a certain sacred quality to it, but this is a result of its rituality, not its ability to suspend or exceed the ritual. Its authority and effectiveness in implementing the chain of violence that will, in this instance, ultimately result in Bikindi's continued imprisonment depends on its proper and timely institutional deployment rather than its ability to appear as either naturally or spontaneously commanding.[91] It will succeed juridically precisely to the extent that it refuses to operate on the level of charisma, precisely to the extent that it showcases its own beholdenness to a prior law and to the rigours of procedure; even if this attitude of beholdenness always and necessarily bears the echo of the institution's founding act of violence.[92] This is why there is no attempt to downplay the role of the text in the delivery of judgment at the ICTR. The very scriptedness of the judge's pronouncement speaks immediately of the real mental and material labour involved in a specifically textual practice of judgment. And this is undoubtedly one of the very sources of its legitimacy.

As if to confirm it, no sooner has the judge's pronouncement finished resounding than it ceases to matter juridically. 'The written judgment is the authoritative version and will be distributed after the hearing', Weinberg de Roca explained up front.[93] So it is not just that the act of pronouncement is scripted, and overtly so, its authority is immediately relinquished to the text which had always been its *telos* to begin with. Moreover, this text is no mere record of the pronouncement, as with the solemn declaration. Nor is it simply a verbatim transcript. Not only is it much longer, so long in fact as to make it effectively unpronounceable or undeliverable in practice, it depends on a whole range of specifically textual devices both for its legibility and its juridical efficacy. Headings and sub-headings, the table of contents, the subtle and constant interaction of text and footnotes, the hypertextuality that has always been so characteristic of legal writing with its intricate relations to a whole range of other juridical documents and prior judgments: these are all

[90] Dolar (2006) 117.

[91] Even 'oral decisions' often work in this way. They exist previously as writing and need to be read onto the record in order to be actualized. 'In the meantime, I will read an oral decision on the motion of the Defence challenging the Prosecutor's preliminary pre-trial brief.' And in the case of other instances of the authoritative judicial voice—the practice of adjourning proceedings, for instance, or of qualifying an expert witness—even though a specific formula is not strictly necessary, the language used is nevertheless highly conventional: a kind of *arche-writing*, to adapt Derrida's term: *Bikindi* transcript: 18 September 2006; 18 October 2006, 38; 13 February 2007, 6; Derrida (1976) 92.

[92] Jacques Derrida, 'Force of Law: The "Mystical Foundations of Authority"', trans Mary Quaintance [trans of: 'Force de loi: Le "fondement mystique de l'autorité"'] *Cardozo Law Review* 11(5–6) (1990) 920, 975. Robert Cover, 'Violence and the Word', *The Yale Law Journal* 95(8) (1986) 1601.

[93] *Bikindi* summary, para 1.

crucial material–technical devices, essential to the judgment's use by future judges and practitioners, members of the academy, and the public. None of them has anything to do with the activity of pronouncement.

Court reporting

The voice doesn't simply actualize the letter at the ICTR. It doesn't simply 'complete' or 'accomplish' it. It produces it too. The practice of court reporting is an essential but little remarked upon feature of contemporary juridical practice. Its Western roots are in ancient Rome and the method of shorthand (the *notae tironianae*) developed by Cicero's clerk Marcus Tullius Tiro.[94] The system practised at the ICTR is much more sophisticated. Nearly every word uttered in either French or English at trial is taken down by the two court reporters stationed on either side of the judges' bench. No transcription of the Kinyarwanda audio-channel is produced, either in 'real time' at trial or for archival purposes. On one level this policy is not at all surprising given that French and English are the two official languages of the UN, but there is clearly also a sense in which it undermines the Tribunal's claims that it is conducting these trials with the people of Rwanda in mind. In any case, the court transcripts produced by the reporters at the ICTR are a complex function of at least three technical registers. First, the technological: the theoretico-technical assemblage of the court reporter's shorthand machine and a proprietary software program called Case CATalyst, which claims to be the 'industry leader' in so-called 'computer aided transcription'.[95] Second, the skill of the reporter: both a highly developed form of audile technique—which depends on their ability to listen phonetically rather than semantically, like witnesses, lawyers, judges, and everyone else involved in the judicial soundscape—and an impressive manual dexterity. Third, a whole series of judgments in relation to both *what* should be transcribed and *how* this should then be represented on paper. Many of these were arrived at by the Tribunal's own internal Court Reporters Unit, a subdivision of the Court Managements Section under the authority of the Registry, and are contained in the *Manual for English Court Reporting* and *Manuel de Procédure à L'intention des Sténotypistes Officiel(le)s*, both of which are subject to regular and ongoing refinement.[96] Many are simply standard practice, the product of years of sedimentation by professional and educational institutes like America's *National Court Reporters Association*.[97] Nevertheless, they are far from neutral. All involve

[94] Isaac Pitman, *A History of Shorthand* (I Pitman & Sons, 1891) 1–2; Anthony Di Renzo, 'His Master's Voice: Tiro and the Rise of the Roman Secretarial Class', *Journal of Technical Writing and Communication* 30(2) (2000) 155; Lee Honeycutt, 'Literacy and the Writing Voice: The Intersection of Culture and Technology in Dictation', *Journal of Business and Technical Communication* 18(3) (2004) 294.

[95] 'Case CATalyst', Stenograph, accessed 28 February 2015, <http://www.stenograph.com/V3MiniSplash.aspx?id=V3Soft>.

[96] 'The Court Management Section', International Criminal Tribunal for Rwanda, accessed 28 February 2015, <http://207.150.203.251/tabid/108/default.aspx>.

[97] NCRA: Setting the Standard for Capturing the Record, accessed 28 February 2015, <http://www.ncra.org/>.

a certain theory of what sights and sounds are worthy of 'enscription'.[98] Not only is this always a 'deeply political' question, as Charles Briggs claims.[99] As we saw at the outset of the chapter in relation to the Tribunal's method of representing the solemn declaration, it is a highly juridical one too. What court reporters transcribe reveals a lot about what aspects of a hearing are thought to be important in a judicial context.

In combination, the system of court reporting practised at the ICTR has two major implications as far as its soundscape is concerned. First, it has meant that since 2005 all speech at the Tribunal has effectively come with subtitles. Where Tiro would have had to laboriously decode his shorthand after the event in order for anyone else to read it, today the reporter's key-strokes can be converted instantaneously into text. Because the system is so quick, that stream of text is then able to be transmitted wirelessly via Bluetooth and be picked up immediately by anyone with a receiver plugged into their laptop. Evidently practitioners take advantage of the so-called 'real time', 'live', or 'online' transcript on a regular basis and for a variety of different reasons. Sometimes to contradict a witness:

> You testified today orally that when you got to the point where Ancilla was killed—as a matter of fact, let me quote you: 'When we arrived there, we noticed that someone was being killed.' That is in the transcript at page 21, line 34. Is it your testimony now that you were present when Ancilla was being killed?[100]

Sometimes they use it simply because they have lost the flow of the dialogue, the thread of their questioning, or found themselves unable to recollect the start of a witness's long answer. The ability to consult a transcript in close to real time allows them to reorient themselves, to regain their bearings. Thus, 'I beg your pardon, Your Honour. I just need to retrace the last bits … online …' becomes a reasonably typical refrain.[101] The system was a clear 'assistance', as counsel for the prosecution put it at one point, when 'listening to the evidence'.[102]

Second, even when the transcript is not being read in 'real time', it means that the orality of the trial is permanently underscored by a kind of latent textuality, the knowledge that whatever is said will soon appear in writing, and be made amenable to the specific logics and codes of law's documentary life.[103] Even though, as we will see in Chapter 8, the Tribunal has been doing pioneering work as far as the creation of a publicly accessible audio and audio-video archive is concerned,

[98] For a critical approach to the politics and practice of transcription, see the special issue of *Text & Talk*: Joseph Sung-Yul Park and Mary Bucholtz, 'Public Transcripts: Entextualization and Linguistic Representation in Institutional Contexts', *Text and Talk* 29(5) (2009) 481. See also Ruth Finnegan, *The Oral and Beyond: Doing Things with Words in Africa* (University of Chicago Press, 2007) 158–78 ('Creating Texts: Transformation and Enscription').

[99] Charles L Briggs, 'Metadiscursive Practices and Scholarly Authority in Folkloristics', *Journal of American Folklore* 106(422) (1993) 387, 390.

[100] *Bikindi* transcript, 25 September 2007, 60.

[101] *Bikindi* transcript, 19 September 2006, 23.

[102] *Bikindi* transcript, 20 September 2006, 4.

[103] Cornelia Vismann, *Files: Law and Media Technology*, trans Geoffrey Winthrop-Young (Stanford University Press, 2008) [trans of: *Akten: Medientechnik und recht* (first published 2000)] ix.

it is these transcripts which undoubtedly matter most in juridical terms.[104] It was the transcripts which the Chamber used to reference proceedings when it came to judgment, and it was the transcripts which participants were able to consult as the trial unfolded.[105] Despite the incursion of the microphone and the camera into the ICTR's courtrooms, the record there is still primarily textual.

'For the record'

The Tribunal's may be an oral soundscape, therefore, but it is also one which is constantly in the process of being 'entextualized'.[106] The practices both of speaking and listening at the ICTR are profoundly and moreover *self-consciously* bound up with the ongoing institutional production of text. Participants frequently spoke in the *Bikindi* case *not* in order to be heard but specifically so that what they said could be transcribed. They were speaking, in other words, 'for the record'. We could say that the Tribunal's logic in this respect is not so much one of orality as *dictation*.

The twin practices of 'reading the case' and the recitation of 'appearances' at the start of each day of proceedings were just two particularly overt examples of such a logic:

MADAM PRESIDENT: Good afternoon. Ms Kouo, could you please read the case?
MS KOUO (representative of the Registry): Yes, Madam President, thank you. Trial Chamber III of the International Tribunal for Rwanda, composed of Judge Inés Weinberg de Roca, presiding, Judge Florence Arrey and Judge Robert Fremr, is now sitting in open session today, Tuesday, 26th of September 2006, for the continuation of the trial in the matter of Prosecutor v Simon Bikindi, case No. ICTR-01-72-T.[107]

And then the appearances for each side:

MADAM PRESIDENT: The appearances for the Prosecution, please.
MR EGBE: Thank You, Your Honours. For the Prosecution, I appear in person, and with me,[108] are attorneys Veronica Wright, Iain Morley, Patrick Gabaake; legal advisor, Suleiman Khan; and the case manager, Amina Abrahim.
MADAM PRESIDENT: Thank you very much. Appearances for the Defence, please.
MR NDERITU: Thank you, Your Honour. Wilfred Nderitu, counsel for Mr Bikindi, assisted by my co-counsel, Mr Jean de Dieu Momo. Thank you.[109]

[104] The Registrar is required to 'make and preserve' a 'full and accurate record of all proceedings, including audio recordings, transcripts and, when deemed necessary by the Trial Chamber, video records': 'Rules of Procedure and Evidence', r 81.

[105] Draft transcripts were required to be completed by court reporters within hours of adjournment at the end of each day. On the rare occasions when a hearing went past the usual 17:30 finish time, the transcript was to be submitted by 10:00 the next morning: *Manual for English Court Reporting*, 22.

[106] Park and Bucholtz (2009). [107] *Bikindi* transcript, 26 September 2006, 1.

[108] On another occasion Mr Egbe was required by the presiding judge to specify who 'me' was for the purposes of the record: *Bikindi* transcript, 28 September 2006, 1.

[109] *Bikindi* transcript, 21 September 2006, 1.

Both practices have a familiar ritual quality to them. In their habitual repetition they form a key part of the rhythm of proceedings. But in neither case is the act of oralization doing the same kind of work it does when it comes to pronouncing judgment. The point is neither to give effect to anything, to engage either the soul or the body, nor, in any immediate sense, to publicize it. Rather the purpose is mainly to establish a usable archive of proceedings, one which both anticipates and appreciates the material labour involved in managing the 'Babylonian stacks of files' upon which contemporary legal practice depends.[110] Both practices have the record specifically in mind.

MR EGBE: I was wondering if it is okay if I just place on the record that the appearances today are the same as before.

MADAM PRESIDENT: No—no, that is not enough, because then the record would mean going back to the previous days, and after 30 days of trial, and it would be quite cumbersome.

MR EGBE: I am obliged, Your Honours. The appearance for the Prosecution is as follows … [111]

There were many other instances in the *Bikindi* case where a similar logic was at work, even if the precise motivations were subtly different each time. Often one or other counsel would note something immediately apparent to everyone present, simply for the purposes of the transcripts. 'For the record … the witness has identified the accused'.[112] Or, 'just for the record that Mr Bikindi is back in court'.[113] On other occasions counsel would 'place' their objection 'formally on record,' with all the implications of solidity and permanence such a turn of phrase entails, and in implicit contrast to the transience of the voice.[114]

Finally, if a text ever needed to be read either by or to a witness, which was often, this was out loud. 'Just a clarification, Madam President. Should I read this out loud, so it is on the record or not?' 'Yes please, that is why it is useful to have you there, so it is on the record'.[115] Here is counsel for the prosecution to Professor Karangwa, one of the three expert witnesses to testify at trial. 'Now, I want to deal with the issue of the impact of the message in Bikindi's songs, and I'm going to refer to the part of your expert report that deals with the impact of Bikindi's music. I want you to look at page 5 of your expert report … I want you to read the first four lines … Please read that part for the record'.[116] Or again, this time a few days previously.

MR EGBE: Now Professor Karangwa, you have excerpts of that book in front of you, and could you, please, refer to the footnote wherein your contribution to the production

[110] Vismann, *Files: Law and Media Technology* (2008) 1.

[111] *Bikindi* transcript, 20 September 2006, 1. The Trial Chamber sometimes reneged on its conviction in this respect. See *Bikindi* transcript, 20 October 2006, 1.

[112] *Bikindi* transcript, 19 February 2007, 8.

[113] *Bikindi* transcript, 22 September 2006, 19.

[114] *Bikindi* transcript, 18 September 2006, 16.

[115] *Bikindi* transcript, 22 September 2006, 14.

[116] *Bikindi* transcript, 14 February 2007, 3.

of that book is acknowledged, and be kind enough to read it out to the Court, for the record?

MR KARANGWA: You want me to do that?

MR EGBE: Yes. Just to direct you, it's footnote No. 88.

MR KARANGWA: Though, you see, it's not my nature to talk about myself too much. But let me go ahead. 'Here we would like to extend our gratitude to Jean de Dieu Karangwa, who place his talents as linguistics and his knowledge of Rwandan culture for this indispensable work.' [sic] Is that what you want me to do?

MR EGBE: Yes, that is what I want you to do, and thank you for doing that.[117]

This last example is particularly revealing as far as the peculiar dynamics of the voice–letter relation at the ICTR are concerned. Counsel is in possession of a text. In order for that text to become the subject of judicial discourse, it must first be oralized by the witness. One important result in that respect is its publicity as we have seen, its audibility to everyone present, both in the courtroom and the gallery. But that is not presented as the chief purpose of doing so. The excerpt must be read aloud, Mr Egbe says, 'for the record', which as we know is primarily textual. The role assigned to the voice here is totally instrumental. It is being used by the Tribunal simply as a means of incorporating one text into another. And yet everything seems to depend on this instrumentality. The voice is *both* totally auxiliary to the text then *and* crucial to its proper incorporation *as* text. The eccentricity of such a practice is not lost on the witness. 'You want me to do that?' he asks. 'You see, it's not my nature to talk about myself too much'. 'Is that what you want me to do?'

'The Hearing'

This chapter began with a detailed consideration of two essential features of the judicial soundscape. We observed how together the solemn declaration and the principle of publicity were virtually constitutive of the hearing *as such*. In the case of the declaration we saw how, quite apart from either its substance or its ability to engage the full and present intentionality of the speaker, it was the very fact of oralization that mattered most. This ritual oralization, moreover, was crucial to the establishment of a community of speakers. In the case of the principle of publicity we saw how, especially in relation to the treatment of protected witnesses, audibility became both the necessary and sufficient condition of publicness at the ICTR. A significant majority of proceedings there, we observed, were *acousmatic*.

We have also noted a number of examples where neither orality nor audibility appear as ends in themselves. When it comes to the pronouncement of judgment, although the act of pronouncement is clearly essential in procedural terms, it is nevertheless ancillary in a way to the text of the judgment which both precedes and outlasts it. Moreover, with the practice of court reporting we saw how virtually

117 *Bikindi* transcript, 12 February 2007, 20.

every word uttered at trial was spoken in the knowledge that it would be transcribed and that this fact was frequently seized upon by the Tribunal for the purposes of establishing a juridically useful written record. The result is that the question of the hearing turns out to be far more complex and, indeed, more conflicted than it initially seemed. When people speak at trial, they do *not* necessarily do so primarily in order to be heard.

Let me end the chapter with two more observations by way of conclusion. Both have to do with what we might provocatively term the 'myth' of the hearing. An acoustic jurisprudence must be careful not to overemphasize the significance of the audibility of the trial. First, because even though I have been fortunate enough both to attend proceedings at the Tribunal in person in Arusha and access the audio-visual record, these options are not available to everybody. For a huge majority of people interested in trials like Bikindi's, whether they are practitioners, academics, or members of the public, their predominant means of access will be either the Tribunal's written judgment or a brief summary of it in the newspaper or on the internet. Even if they are sufficiently interested to attempt to access the record of proceedings, it is the transcripts which, freely available to download from the Tribunal's 'Public Judicial Records Database' online, are by far the most accessible.[118] In spite of the Tribunal's apparent equation between audibility and publicity, in other words, it is in textual form—and specifically in the form of .pdf and .doc files—that the *Bikindi* case's significance continues to reverberate. And it is crucial to note that the material, financial, and technical barriers in this respect are very real, and moreover hardly politically neutral. Not everyone has ready access to a laptop and a Wi-Fi connection.

Second, there is a sense in which the language of the hearing, with its implications of publicity, accessibility, and even democracy as we have seen, has *always* been misleading to some extent, incomplete, not the whole story. There is a black hole right at the centre of the project of judgment, an extent to which what is most essential to it has simply *never* been audible, *never* public. Its most obvious locus is the privacy of the judge's chambers, in the judge's thoughts and in her conversations with her fellow judges, colleagues, and interns. But we could think equally of it as taking place in the institution's canteens and corridors,[119] and elsewhere besides: including, in the *Bikindi* case, on a 'site visit' that took place between 14 and 18 April 2008.[120] At the ICTR the practice of deliberation is given formal shape at Rule 87 of the Rules of Procedure and Evidence. 'After presentation of closing arguments, the Presiding Judge shall declare the hearing closed, and the

[118] 'Basic Search', UN-ICTR Judicial Database <http://trim.unictr.org/>.

[119] On the significance and sociality of eating to juridical practice, see Peter Goodrich, *Law in the Courts of Love: Literature and Other Minor Jurisprudences* (Routledge, 1996) 75–94 ('Eating Law: Commons, Common Land, Common Law').

[120] This was by virtue of r 4, which allows that 'a Chamber or a judge may exercise their functions away from the Seat of the Tribunal, if so authorized by the President in the interests of justice': 'Rules of Procedure and Evidence', r 4. This rule was engaged at *Prosecutor v Bikindi* (Decision Authorizing the Site Visit in Rwanda) ICTR-01-72-R4 (12 March 2008). See *Bikindi* judgment, annex A, para 32 ('Procedural History').

Trial Chamber shall deliberate in private. A finding of guilty may be reached only when a majority of the Trial Chamber is satisfied that guilt has been proved beyond reasonable doubt.'[121] But it is clearly an ongoing process. Thus, 'we will make our decisions, we will deliberate during the break' as Weinberg de Roca put it at one point during the *Bikindi* case.[122] To be sure, deliberation is not silent. It is not an exclusively internal or mental practice. But to the extent that it *is* audible, it is not publicly so. This inaudibility moreover is precisely its proper condition. Deliberation turns out to be the name legal institutions give to the quiet heart of the practice of judgment.

[121] 'Rules of Procedure and Evidence', r 87.
[122] *Bikindi* transcript, 25 September 2006, 24.

PART 4
SOUND

7
Judging the Rwandan Soundscape

Songs and speech are always heard somewhere, somehow. They always take place in a particular sonic environment, by means of particular technologies, particular media, and particular ways of listening. This chapter is concerned with how the ICTR went about *judging the Rwandan soundscape*. How did the Tribunal situate Bikindi's songs and speech relative to the sonic world in which they were heard? What function did it envisage for the technologies and media apparatuses which it insisted were so important in this respect? What was their role when it came to contextualizing, shaping, or otherwise framing the listening experience for Rwandan listeners? Such questions were never explicitly asked in the *Bikindi* case, but that does not mean they are unimportant, that the ways in which the Tribunal unwittingly responded to them did not do crucial juridical work. Just like in Chapters 3 and 5, we will see that many of the features, assumptions, and blind-spots of the Tribunal's account are familiar both to sound studies and the critical tradition. And as before, what I try to do here is track how these were given juridical form, why, and with what consequences for the outcome of Bikindi's trial.

In the first section of the chapter, I show how the Trial Chamber's depiction of Bikindi's songs and speech as emerging from a noisy backdrop engages a long tradition of thought about sound's relation to the social and juridical. Rather than being something for which we *must* take responsibility, as in certain other legal contexts, noise appeared in the Tribunal's account as precisely that part of the soundscape to which its jurisdiction did not extend. Noise was the name given to the lawless in sound, that which is both ungoverned and also, in this context, ungovernable. In the second section of the chapter I consider the Tribunal's account of radio and this time I am more critical. The Tribunal's approach, I suggest, was consistent with a very common narrative in relation to the Rwandan genocide which presents radio as a 'symbol' of the genocide itself. And it was important, therefore, that it was also on the radio that Bikindi's songs had achieved their maximum diffusion. But the account of radio offered by the Tribunal was extremely thin. It rendered a complex technical and social apparatus as little more than a means of extending and intensifying the speaking voice. This sort of instrumental thinking is quite common both in relation to radio, in particular, and broadcast media in general. And the Tribunal's approach was clearly symptomatic to some extent of this broader impoverishment of imagination. In the particular circumstances of the *Bikindi* case, however, it was clearly also bound up with the doctrinal imperative to individualize responsibility: the institutional requirement to hold Bikindi and only Bikindi to account. In the final section of the chapter, I turn to the Tribunal's approach to the related matters of audio-recording and reproduction. Insofar as Bikindi's songs were heard throughout Rwanda, it was primarily by means of the recordings he had made prior to the genocide, which featured regularly on radio stations like RTLM and Radio Rwanda. This was a problem for the Tribunal because the nature of audio-recording vastly complicated the hermeneutic task and therefore also the task of judgment. By rupturing the link between the presence of the singer and the listening public, the meaning of Bikindi's songs was displaced onto the radio announcers who framed them for their listeners. It was these radio announcers whose intent was truly genocidal, the Chamber said, not Bikindi. The chapter ends by suggesting that the Chamber failed to take the consequences of its own arguments as far as it might have. When read alongside the analysis in Chapters 3 and 5, moreover, this failure can be understood as symptomatic of a general reluctance on the Chamber's part to hold Bikindi responsible in relation to his songs.

Noise

The following passage is taken from the Trial Chamber's judgment just as it is elaborating the 'factual findings' which would ultimately found Bikindi's conviction. It is both symptomatic and exemplary of an approach which, though presented here in particularly clear and distilled form, was in evidence elsewhere in the *Bikindi* case as well as in other proceedings before the Tribunal. 'Witness AKK testified that he saw Bikindi in June 1994', the Chamber wrote, 'in a vehicle, as part of a convoy heading towards Kayove'.

> AKK lived close to the road and saw buses full of *Interahamwe*, blowing whistles and making lots of noise with clubs and firearms. Bikindi was in a vehicle outfitted with a loudspeaker, over which songs were being broadcast with intermittent statements made by Bikindi. Witness AKK stated that Bikindi was not singing that day, as cassettes of his songs were being used. Witness AKK heard Bikindi say 'You sons of *Sebahinzi*, who are the majority, I am speaking to you, you know that the Tutsi are minority. Rise up and look everywhere possible and do not spare anybody.'[1]

What we have here is a soundscape divided, split in two. On the one hand, the noisy backdrop: hails of gunfire, piercing whistles, clubs on metal, the acoustic terrain of genocide's 'invisible battlefield'.[2] On the other hand, Bikindi's songs and speech: foregrounded, amplified, distinct, and amenable therefore to the Tribunal's jurisdiction. 'Based on the words he proffered and the manner he disseminated his message', the Chamber found that Bikindi had 'deliberately, directly and publicly incited the commission of genocide'.[3]

[1] *Prosecutor v Bikindi* (Judgement) ICTR-01-72-T, T Ch III (2 December 2008) ('*Bikindi* judgment') para 268.

[2] Steve Goodman, *Sonic Warfare: Sound, Affect and the Ecology of Fear* (MIT Press, 2010) xvii.

[3] *Bikindi* judgment, para 424.

Noise is often depicted like this. It is constantly in the process of being defined and redefined by its opposite. In information theory, noise is 'that which a signal has to overcome through reduction or redundancy in order to get across'.[4] This is why composer and sound-theorist Michel Chion calls noise 'segregationist'.[5] For Jacques Attali, noise is 'a resonance that interferes with the audition of a message in the process of emission'. It does not, therefore, 'exist in itself, but only in relation to the system within which it is inscribed'.[6] More than that, though, noise is often the name given to the specifically disorderly and ungovernable in the system in question. For Steve Goodman, it is 'intrinsically radical'.[7] For Chion, that which 'bothers', 'disturbs', or 'pollutes'.[8] And in Hillel Schwartz's gargantuan audio-cultural history *Making Noise: From Babel to the Big Bang & Beyond*, noise by definition is 'what breaks through', a confounding of order.[9] It is no coincidence that the word has its etymological roots in the Latin *nausea*.[10] Well beyond the particular circumstances of Bikindi, Rwanda, or the ICTR, noise is frequently the name we give to the element of disruption or dissonance in both sound and the social: a failure properly to harmonize, the breach of the peace, a kind of sickness.

Throughout human history, noise has invariably figured at once as a technique and a sign of war, conflict and, more generally, social dysfunction. For Onasander, the ancient Greek philosopher most well-known today for his martial writings composed as long ago as CE 49, one should always 'send the army into battle shouting, and sometimes on the run, because their appearance and shouts and the clash of arms confound the hearts of the enemy'.[11] For Roman historian, senator, and early ethnographer Tacitus, an acoustics was central to Germanian military technique too:

> By the rendering of this [chant] they not only kindle their courage, but, merely by listening to the sound, they can forecast the issue of an approaching engagement. For they either terrify their foes or themselves become frightened, according to the character of the noise they make upon the battlefield; and they regard it not merely as so many voices chanting together but as a unison of valour. What they particularly aim at is a harshly intermittent roar; and they hold their shields in front of their mouths, so that the sound is amplified into a deeper crescendo by the reverberation.[12]

[4] James A Steintrager, 'Speaking of Noise: From Murderous Loudness to the Crackle of Silk', *Differences* 22(2–3) (2011) 249.

[5] Michel Chion, 'Let's Have Done with the Notion of "Noise"', trans James A Steintrager, *Differences* 22(2–3) (2011) 240, 242, 245.

[6] Jacques Attali, *Noise: The Political Economy of Music*, trans Brian Massumi (University of Minnesota Press, 1985) [trans of: *Bruits: Essai sur l'économie politique de la musique* (first published 1977)] 26.

[7] Goodman (2010) 7.

[8] Chion (2011) 241, 245.

[9] Hillel Schwartz, *Making Noise: From Babel to the Big Bang & Beyond* (Zone Books, 2011) 28.

[10] Saeed Hydaralli, 'What Is Noise? An Inquiry Into Its Formal Properties' in Michael Goddar, Benjamin Halligan, and Paul Hegarty (eds), *Reverberations: The Philosophy, Aesthetics and Politics of Noise* (Continuum, 2012) 226; Michel Serres, *Genesis*, trans Geneviève James and James Nielson (University of Michigan Press, 1995) [trans of: *Genèse* (first published 1982)] 13, 20.

[11] *Aeneas Tacticus, Asclepiodotus, Onasander*, trans William A Oldfather et al (W Heinemann, 1923) 471 (Onasander, *The General*, ch XXIX), quoted in R Murray Schafer, *The Soundscape: Our Sonic Environment and the Tuning of the World* (Knopf, 1977) 50.

[12] Tacitus, *The Agricola and the Germania*, trans H Mattingly and S A Handford (rev edn, Penguin, 1970) 103, quoted in Schafer (1977) 50.

And this is Ferdowsi, the tenth-century Persian epic poet, in the course of his 60,000 verse-long history of Iran. 'At the shouts of the Divs and the noise made by the black dust rising', he claimed, 'the thunder of drums and the neighing of war-horses, the mountains were rent and the earth cleft asunder. So fierce a combat had been seen by no man before. Loud was the clash of the battle-axes and the clatter of swords and of arrows'.[13]

The noise of war amplified significantly with the advent of gunpowder and its more hi-tech contemporary descendants such as cordite: the whizz and thud of gun, shell, grenade, mortar, and rocket fire.[14] During World War I, 'mechanical Death', as ambulance driver John Hargrave called it, 'whistled and screamed and crashed' over Gallipoli.[15] 'The noise, especially during the two hours before the attack, was appalling. It was unceasing, heartrending, brain-rending. It was noise gone mad, out of all bounds, uncontrolled'.[16] And frequently it was literally deafening too. Deafness was such an utterly normal physiological symptom of time at the front, in fact, that doctors after the outbreak of war in 1914 struggled to develop an entire typology to differentiate between its various species and forms. 'It is very difficult or impossible to draw a line between cases of "noise" deafness and those of "shell" or "explosion" deafness', claimed two English physicians remembered by Schwartz.[17] 'Concussions from shells bursting or detonations of nearby land mines could rupture ear drums and crush the outer hair cells of the organ of Corti',[18] Schwartz writes.

> With proper diet and cleansing, blown-out ear drums would heal after a month of buzzing; on the Front, healing was chancier. Special otological centres had to be opened to deal with the sounds of shattered eardrums and infected ears. 'If you were now to bring from France all the men with chronic middle-ear suppuration,' said an English doctor in 1916, 'you would have battalions of them all over the country.'[19]

So close was the perceived link between noise and conflict during World War I that for many they were virtually inseparable, even synonymous. 'Soldiers knew within

[13] Ferdowsi, *The Epic of the Kings: Shāh-Nāma—The National Epic of Persia*, trans Reuben Levy (Routledge & Kegan Paul, 1967) 57, quoted in Schafer (1977) 50.

[14] Schwartz (2011) 581–2. Gunpowder seems to have been invented in ninth-century China. Its spread to the Middle East, Europe, and India is better documented and can be dated with some specificity to the thirteenth century. The smokeless propellant cordite, which found its most widespread usage in World War I, was first developed in the late 1880s and 1890s. See generally Jack Kelly, *Gunpowder: Alchemy, Bombards, and Pyrotechnics: The History of the Explosive That Changed the World* (Basic Books, 2005).

[15] Schwartz (2011) 583.

[16] Hillel Schwartz quoting a letter from the front to Dan McKenzie—a Scottish laryngologist at the Central London Throat and Ear Hospital, editor of the *Journal of Laryngology, Rhinology, and Otology* throughout the war years and author of *The City of Din: A Tirade against Noise* (1916)—which sparked his anti-noise campaign during World War I. Schwartz (2011) 584.

[17] Schwartz (2011) 581.

[18] The organ of Corti is the main organ of the inner ear. On its discovery by the Italian scientist Alfonso Corti in 1851 and its importance to the history of the science of audition and resonance, see Veit Erlmann, *Reason and Resonance: A History of Modern Aurality* (Zone Books, 2010) 227–34.

[19] Schwartz (2011) 582.

hours on the Front', Schwartz claims, 'that the Great War *was* noise, that the noise was dangerous, and if noise of itself was not fatal then it was advance notice, and emblem, of mortality'.[20] We could say the same about *all* war, in fact. Cacophony and conflict have long gone hand in hand.

As a *technique* of conflict, noise is both a material bodily threat and crucial to the production of the affective experience of dread or terror, what Steve Goodman calls the 'sonic dimension of the ecology of fear'.[21] So, on the one hand, we have the sheer sonic force of World War I, the literally deafening power of shell and mortar fire, along with more recent technologies like the Long Range Acoustic Device (LRAD) used by the US military in Iraq and by the police on the streets of Pittsburgh, London, New York, and Ferguson,[22] or the 'sonic booms' reportedly unleashed over Nicaragua in the early 1980s and over Palestine in 2005.[23] On the other hand, we have the horror instilled by the battle chant, the terrific impact of the Greeks' shouts and screams on the 'hearts of the enemy', the 'heart-rending, brain-rending' hell of 'noise gone mad', so closely linked in World War I with the psychosomatic condition commonly known as 'shellshock'.[24] As philosopher Edmund Burke put it in his 1757 treatise on aesthetics, 'excessive loudness alone is sufficient to overpower the soul, to suspend its action, and to fill it with terror'.[25] In either case, noise is a weapon, a technique of war; its targets both bodies and souls.

As an acoustic *sign* of conflict, by contrast, noise is both a symptom and a warning. It both evidences and heralds. And in this respect the Rwandan situation provides some particularly clear examples. Many witnesses, both in the *Bikindi* case and otherwise, identified noise with genocide itself. In the *Media* case, for instance, the Trial Chamber reported that, 'Witness ABC, a Hutu man

[20] Schwartz (2011) 587.

[21] The term 'ecology of fear' is borrowed from critical urban theorist Mike Davis in Mike Davis, *The Ecology of Fear: Los Angeles and the Imagination of Disaster* (Metropolitan Books, 1998). Its use in a specifically acoustic context comes from Goodman (2010).

[22] For recent news coverage of the LRAD, see Quaoar, '"Voice of God" Weapon Being Used in Iraq', Daily Kos blog, 23 December 2007, <http://www.dailykos.com/story/2007/12/23/425814/--Voice-of-God-weapon-being-used-in-Iraq>; Gavin Thomas, 'Sonic Device Deployed in London during Olympics', *BBC News*, 12 May 2012, <http://www.bbc.com/news/uk-england-london-18042528>; Lily Hay Newman, 'This is the Sound Cannon Used Against Protestors in Ferguson', *Slate*, 14 August 2014, <http://www.slate.com/blogs/future_tense/2014/08/14/lrad_long_range_acoustic_device_sound_cannons_were_used_for_crowd_control.html>; Colin Moynihan, 'Concerns Raised Over Shrill Device New York Police Used During Garner Protests', *The New York Times*, 12 December 2014, <http://www.nytimes.com/2014/12/13/nyregion/lawyers-raise-concerns-over-shrill-device-used-by-police-during-garner-protests.html?_r=0>; 'City of Pittsburgh Settles G-20 Lawsuits', American Civil Liberties Union (ACLU), 14 November 2012, <http://www.aclupa.org/news/2012/11/14/city-pittsburgh-settles-g-20-lawsuits>.

[23] *Military and Paramilitary Activities in and against Nicaragua (Nicaragua v United States of America)* (Jurisdiction and Admissibility) [1984] ICJ Rep 392. See Chris McGreal, 'Palestinians Hit by Sonic Boom Air Raids', *The Guardian*, 3 November 2005, <http://www.theguardian.com/world/2005/nov/03/israel>.

[24] Schwartz (2011) 570–83.

[25] Edmund Burke, *A Philosophical Enquiry into the Origins of Our Ideas of the Sublime and Beautiful*, ed Adam Philips (first published 1757, Oxford University Press, 1990) 36.

from Kigali, testified that he was in Rugunga when RTLM radio announced at around 8.00 p.m. that President Habyarimana's plane had been shot at. After the announcement, the witness heard gunfire and grenade explosions which continued all night. The next morning, RTLM stated that some people who were opposed to the regime had been killed'.[26] Here, gunfire and grenade explosions are the very first evidence—acoustic or otherwise—that everything is no longer as it was, that the fragility of the social order has been breached and that turmoil looms.

The example is hardly an isolated one. At Bikindi's trial, witnesses would often testify to even more specific examples of noise's alertive function. 'Just as the Daihatsu passed', witness AHP explained, 'I also heard a lot of people making noise from where the Daihatsu had come from, and I went there to find out what had happened. When I arrived at where the people were making noise, I learnt from the people who were there that the *conseiller*, Sibomana, had taken some Tutsis who had been hiding in a certain house'.[27] This is witness Antoine Nyetera responding to a question from counsel for the defence. 'Q. Mr. Nyetera, to whom would you attribute those attacks? Or better still, did you hear about those attacks over the radio, for instance? A. If people heard grenade explosions at night, the next morning I would pass by a house blown out—a house blown up'.[28] And here is some testimony from Rwanda's own *Gacaca* courts read 'onto the record' at one point in the *Bikindi* case: 'We heard whistles being blown', the witness remembered, and immediately 'we sought refuge in a—in the bamboo bush'.[29]

Noise often arrives before visual confirmation: a sign, or even a 'signal'[30] of imminent danger. That is both a fact of the phenomenology of conflict and a consequence of sound's peculiar disrespect for architectural and visual space. One witness put it particularly unambiguously in *Prosecutor v Karera*. 'I knew that Tutsi could not be making such noise', he testified, 'only *Interahamwe* could make such noise. So I escaped after hearing that noise'.[31] And in the *Bikindi* case we find an interesting inversion of this example in the transcript of an RTLM broadcast from April 1994 which was entered into evidence by the prosecution. Therein, Gaspard

[26] *Prosecutor v Nahimana* (Judgement and Sentence) ICTR-99-52-T, T Ch I (3 December 2003) ('*Nahimana* judgment and sentence' or '*Media* case') para 439.

[27] *Prosecutor v Bikindi* (Transcript) ICTR-01-72-T, T Ch III (Various dates) ('*Bikindi* transcript') 19 October 2006, 37.

[28] *Bikindi* transcript, 5 October 2007, 13.

[29] *Bikindi* transcript, 26 September 2006, 28.

[30] 'Signal' is the Schaferian terminology. Signals, Schafer writes, 'are foreground sounds and they are listened to consciously. In terms of the psychologist, they are figure rather than ground. Any sound can be listened to consciously, and so any sound can become a figure or signal, but for the purposes of our community-oriented study we will confine ourselves to mentioning some of those signals which *must* be listened to because they constitute acoustic warning devices: bells, whistles, horns and sirens'. It is worth pointing out, however, that despite Schafer's insistence that 'signals' are listened to consciously, each example he gives depends partly on its ability to trigger a startle response too. The line between conscious and unconscious, in other words, is sometimes very fine indeed. In this respect the difference between a siren and gunfire is perhaps smaller than Schafer would have us believe. Schafer (1977) 10.

[31] *Prosecutor v Karera* (Judgment and Sentence) ICTR-01-74-T, T Ch I (7 December 2007) ('*Karera* judgment') n 324.

Gahigi, the presenter in question, makes explicit the link between noise and his community of listeners. The association between the two, he claims, was often exploited by the Tutsi-associated *Inkotanyi* as a kind of acoustic trick: a merging of the signs and techniques of war. 'Now, when Inkotanyi arrive at a place, for them to be able to kill people who are at roadblocks, they shout and blow whistles. So, the citizens rush up, thinking that it is their fellows and then, they fire at them. So, be careful about people who come blowing whistles … be careful about that and know that soldiers are around'.[32] In Rwanda in 1994, evidently, noise and genocide were intimately related.

The ICTR's depiction of the Rwandan soundscape sits squarely within both a tradition and a continuum of familiar stories about noise then. The juridical consequences were as follows. First, the presentation of Rwanda's sonic environment during the genocide as noisy—buses full of *Interahamwe* militia 'blowing whistles and making lots of noise with clubs and firearms'[33]—helped both in evidentiary terms and rhetorically to establish a narrative of conflict. Noise registers in the *Bikindi* judgment as a technique, if not necessarily of direct physical harm, then certainly of intimidation, and as both sign and symptom of actual social dysfunction, the breakdown of civil order.

Second, this sonic narrative conforms to a parallel and similarly familiar technological discourse. The particular *kinds* of noise depicted at the Tribunal were all decidedly 'lo-tech': whistles blowing, clubs banging on the metal of car doors, gunshots fired into the air: the acoustic manifestation of a famously lo-tech conflict in which so-called 'small' arms and 'light' weapons rather than 'heavier' munitions such as planes, tanks, rockets, and bombs were central. Indeed, in the standard historical accounts, a large part of the horror of 1994 derives precisely from this technological aspect, revealed here at the level of sonics: the grotesque proximity, the brutal *lack* of mediation, between genocidaire and victim, Hutu and Tutsi, which this technological dimension implies.[34] It is as if war in the West

[32] Exhibit No P11(E), 'Transcript of RTLM Broadcast of 15 April 1994', *Prosecutor v Bikindi*, ICTR-01-72-0070 (2 June 1997), 7.

[33] *Bikindi* judgment, para 268.

[34] Verwimp, Des Forges, Goose and Smyth all refer to the munitions used in the Rwandan genocide as 'small arms' and 'light weapons'. See Philip Verwimp, 'Machetes and Firearms: The Organization of Massacres in Rwanda', *Journal of Peace Research* 43(1) (2006) 5; Stephen D Goose and Frank Smyth, 'Arming Genocide in Rwanda: The High Cost of Small Arms Transfers', *Foreign Affairs* 73(5) (1994) 86. Verwimp's study of data collected by IBUKU, an organization of the survivors of the genocide, in relation to Rwanda's Kibuye Prefecture revealed the following statistics. Of the nearly 85,000 total records, in 59,050 cases the cause of death was known. In more than 50 per cent of such cases, machetes were used, 16 per cent of the killings were attributed to clubs, 14.7 per cent to guns and rifles, only 1.8 per cent to grenades, and the rest to even lower tech means such as drowning, burying alive, stoning, burning, and starvation. This is not surprising. In her account of the genocide for Human Rights Watch, Alison Des Forges writes that businessmen close to President Habyarimana 'imported large numbers of machetes' in preparation for the genocide, 'enough to arm every third adult Hutu male', which is to say around 581,000. See Alison Des Forges, *Leave None to Tell the Story: Genocide in Rwanda* (Human Rights Watch, 1999) 9, 97. For an account of the specific involvement of the French government in arming Rwandans, see Mel McNulty, 'French Arms, War and Genocide in Rwanda', *Crime, Law and Social Change* 33(1–2) (2000) 105.

were somehow more civilized, and specifically by virtue of its technical 'sophistication': the clinical, anaesthetic distance of drone warfare and targeted aerial bombardment.[35] So the particular forms of noise being depicted in the judgment in the *Bikindi* case—whistles, clubs on metal, handguns—map well onto a story about the supposedly 'tribal' or even 'primitive' nature of the Rwandan conflict which we also see reflected in its discourse about radio.[36] The Tribunal's endorsement of the phrase 'Radio Machete' to describe RTLM in the *Media* case, for instance, its metaphorization of RTLM as 'drumbeat' of the genocide:[37] these are all too overt echoes of media theorist Marshall McLuhan's dubious claims about the association between radio and Africanness, both replete with 'tribal magic', as we will see.[38]

Third, and most importantly for an acoustic jurisprudence, noise is positioned by the Tribunal as both counterpoint and backdrop to Bikindi's songs and speech. It is in this original act of segregation that the Tribunal's peculiar doctrinal concerns begin to manifest themselves at the level of acoustics. Whereas in the law of nuisance, for instance, noise often appears as the object of juridical inquiry, here it is both the limit and other of responsibility in relation to sound.[39] Noise maps to genocide itself. It is the social problem from which individual, juridical responsibility must be distinguished. In doctrinal terms, noise is presented by the Tribunal as precisely the *opposite* of legally relevant 'expression', the *absence* of a 'direct' and clearly articulated 'idea' or 'opinion' for the purposes of the law of freedom of expression and the doctrine of incitement, as we saw in Chapters 3 and 5. It is not just the ungoverned therefore but, in doctrinal terms, also the ungovernable in sound: that part of the soundscape to which the Tribunal's jurisdiction did not extend. For the ICTR, noise begins where responsibility ends. It is the disorderly backdrop from which Bikindi's voice must emerge—direct, public, and meaningful—into the realm of criminal accountability.

[35] For a discussion of the (an)aesthetics of drone warfare and its specifically juridical dimensions, even as a 'prosthetics of law', see Joseph Pugliese, 'Prosthetics of Law and the Anomic Violence of Drones', *Griffith Law Review* 20(4) (2011) 931.

[36] US President Bill Clinton, for instance, referred to the conflict as the product of 'tribal resentments'. And one adviser to French President François Mitterand suggested that brutal slaughter was a usual practice among Africans and could not be easily eradicated. Des Forges (1999) 21.

[37] *Media* case, para 1031.

[38] Marshall McLuhan, *Understanding Media: The Extensions of Man* (2nd edn, New American Library, 1964) 261, 259.

[39] For a dense but brief historical account of the rise of noise as a legal problem, see Schwartz (2011) 653–72. For a specifically American perspective on early twentieth century efforts at noise abatement, and in particular the relation between law and engineering, see Emily Thompson, *The Soundscape of Modernity: Architectural Acoustics and the Culture of Listening in America, 1900–1933* (MIT Press, 2004) 115–68 (ch 4, 'Noise and Modern Culture, 1900–1933'). For a critical reading of legal approaches to noise and specifically the problems involved with focusing on volume, decibel levels, as its primary feature, see Hydaralli (2012). See also Lily E Hirsch, *Music in American Crime Prevention and Punishment* (University of Michigan Press, 2012) 29–49 ('"Sound for Sound": A New Approach to Punishment in Noise Abatement'); Karin Bijsterveld, *Mechanical Sound: Technology, Culture, and Public Problems of Noise in the Twentieth Century* (MIT Press, 2008).

Radio

By far the predominant means by which it did so was on the radio. It was on the radio that Bikindi was alleged to have 'participated in the campaign to defeat the enemy in the media'.[40] The privately owned RTLM had been 'created as a vehicle for anti-Tutsi propaganda', the prosecution alleged, 'with a media programming objective of sensitising and inciting the listening public to target and commit violent acts against Tutsi, extolling Hutu solidarity, and targeting the Tutsi as accomplices of the enemy'.[41] Bikindi was said to have collaborated with a number of high-ranking officials, including President Habyarimana, in founding it as such. Not only did RTLM feature his songs 'several times a day', 'usually during an early morning broadcast, at lunchtime and in the early evening',[42] Bikindi had conspicuously failed to exercise his right under Rwandan law to 'forbid or enjoin' their public broadcast.[43] In doing so he had 'acquiesced', the prosecution claimed, 'in the manner in which RTLM used his songs to promote death and destruction'.[44]

Those were the allegations. In its judgment, the Trial Chamber determined as follows. First, it was on the radio that Bikindi's songs had reached their maximum diffusion. The Chamber ruled that they had been played 'repeatedly on RTLM and Radio Rwanda in 1992, 1993 and the first half of 1994'. Moreover, *Nanga Abahutu/Akabyutso* and *Bene Sebahinzi/Intabaza* were played 'even more frequently during the genocide',[45] 'over and over', according to one witness, 'more than five times per day'.[46] Another claimed to have heard them 'continuously', 'all day long'.[47] Second, although RTLM had undoubtedly *become* a 'vehicle for anti-Tutsi propaganda' as early as the end of 1993, which is to say only a few months after it began broadcasting,[48] it was not clear it had been *created* for such a purpose.[49] Furthermore, there was no evidence that either Bikindi's involvement in launching the station 'with 49 other individuals' or his continued 'minor shareholding' in it gave him any control over programming.[50] When Bikindi was interviewed on RTLM in December 1993 and January 1994, for instance, he had supported President Habyarimana and 'vigorously criticised' Fuastin Twagiramungu, who had been designated Prime Minister of Rwanda by the Arusha Accords, but 'nothing in these interviews show(ed) that Bikindi had any kind of authority over the radio programming or over RTLM in general'.[51] The charges in relation to conspiracy to commit genocide, therefore, were not made out.[52] Finally, not only had the prosecution failed to prove that Bikindi had the right to prohibit the broadcasting of his songs under Rwandan legislation,[53] 'mere acquiescence' was not

[40] *Prosecutor v Bikindi* (Indictment) ICTR-01-72-I (4 July 2001) ('*Bikindi* indictment') para 9.
[41] *Bikindi* judgment, para 112. [42] *Bikindi* indictment, paras 9, 14.
[43] *Bikindi* judgment, para 116. [44] *Bikindi* transcript, 26 May 2008.
[45] *Bikindi* judgment, para 257. [46] *Bikindi* transcript, 4 October 2006, 15.
[47] *Bikindi* transcript, 2 October 2006, 36.
[48] RTLM began broadcasting in July 1993. See *Media* case, para 342.
[49] *Bikindi* judgment, para 122. [50] *Bikindi* judgment, paras 122, 404–7.
[51] *Bikindi* judgment, para 119. [52] *Bikindi* judgment, paras 404–7.
[53] *Bikindi* judgment, para 122.

sufficient to constitute criminal responsibility in international criminal law anyway. The prosecution would have needed to establish a *duty* to stop the broadcast of his songs, which it failed to do.[54] How was radio itself presented on the way to these findings? What kind of account did the Tribunal's juridical concerns enable or produce? Why? And with what consequences?

Scott Straus has argued that in the years since 1994 radio has become a 'symbol' of the Rwandan genocide in the international imaginary.[55] In his highly influential *Rwanda: Les médias du génocide*, Jean-Pierre Chrétien put it like this: 'Two tools, one very modern, the other less so, were used particularly widely during the genocide of the Tutsis in Rwanda: the radio and the machete, the first to give and receive orders, the second to execute them'.[56] 'Killers often carried a machete in one hand, and a transistor radio in the other', writes Samantha Power.[57] And for Linda Melvern RTLM was a 'propaganda weapon like no other', 'radio murder'.[58] Alison Des Forges, in her renowned account of the genocide for Human Rights Watch, variously metaphorized radio as the 'voice of extremism', the 'voice of the government', the 'voice of the campaign', and simply the 'voice of genocide'.[59] In a more recent collection, introduced and endorsed by none other than Kofi Annan, Allan Thompson called RTLM 'the voice of Hutu Power'.[60]

The approach we find throughout the *Bikindi* case is very similar. This was not a coincidence. Not only might we expect many of those involved in the case to have read and absorbed some of this literature, much of it was explicitly incorporated at the level of expertise. Excerpts from Chrétien's book were both admitted into evidence in the *Bikindi* case and cited on a number of occasions in the Chamber's judgment.[61] In fact, both Chrétien and Des Forges were key expert witnesses for the prosecution in the *Media* case in which two of RTLM's other more influential founders Ferdinand Nahimana and Jean-Busco Barayagwiza were prosecuted and eventually convicted of incitement to genocide,[62] and which bore a significant influence on the Tribunal's thinking in relation to Bikindi.[63] Radio was both a privileged feature of the Rwandan soundscape for the ICTR and heavily 'instrumentalized' by it, as we will see. The Tribunal consistently rendered radio as a tool or technique of *amplification*, a means of preaching hate more widely and more effectively than the natural, untechnologized voice would allow.

[54] *Bikindi* judgment, para 439.

[55] Scott Straus, 'What is the Relationship between Hate Radio and Violence? Rethinking Rwanda's "Radio Machete"', *Politics and Society* 35(4) (2007) 609, 610.

[56] Jean-Pierre Chrétien, *Rwanda: Les médias du génocide* (Karthala, 1999). Translation my own.

[57] Samantha Power, 'Bystanders to Genocide: Why the United States Let the Rwandan Genocide Happen', *The Atlantic* 288(2) (2001) 89.

[58] Linda Melvern, *A People Betrayed: The Role of the West in Rwanda's Genocide* (Zed Books, 2000) 71; Linda Melvern, 'Radio Murder', *Times Literary Supplement*, 9 September 2005, 25.

[59] Des Forges (1999) 58, 60, 190, 496.

[60] Allan Thompson (ed), *The Media and the Rwanda Genocide* (Pluto, 2007) 2.

[61] Exhibit No P72, 'Excerpts from Jean-Pierre Chrétien, *Rwanda: Les médias du génocide* (Karthala, 1999)', *Prosecutor v Bikindi*, ICTR-01-72; *Bikindi* judgment, paras 195, 249, 257.

[62] *Media* case, para 53. Alison Des Forges testified at the ICTR on eleven separate occasions.

[63] The *Media* case was cited constantly throughout the *Bikindi* judgment.

In the *Bikindi* judgment, as in each of the indictments,[64] RTLM was constantly referred to as a 'vehicle' for the 'dissemination' of anti-Tutsi propaganda.[65] 'The Chamber finds beyond reasonable doubt that RTLM was a vehicle for anti-Tutsi propaganda.'[66] 'Upon reading of the transcripts of RTLM broadcasts admitted into evidence', it wrote, 'RTLM clearly and effectively disseminated anti-Tutsi propaganda as early as the end of 1993'.[67] The role of radio here is clear. It is a method for the dispersal of incendiary political 'expression', and a particularly efficient one at that. The Chamber cited the following testimony, for instance, without either comment or critique. 'The Defence Expert testified that a radio broadcast throughout the entire territory would have a far more considerable impact than a public performance'.[68]

The same approach can be seen even more clearly in the *Media* case.[69] Again, radio is constantly figured there as a 'vehicle', 'used' to 'transmit', 'convey', 'spread', and 'disseminate' 'messages', 'ideology', and 'views': a technique, in other words, for the expression and distribution of intentional thought as manifested in the technologized voice.[70] To 'disseminate', after all, from the Latin *seminare*, to sow, means to scatter one's seed widely. The roots of the word 'broadcast' are similarly agricultural. It literally meant to cast broadly: to spread out or disperse.[71] But radio also featured extensively in the *Media* case as an 'object', a 'tool', and a 'weapon'. According to one witness whose evidence was endorsed by the Chamber, 'one would find little radios in offices, cafes, bars and other public gathering places, even in taxis'.[72] 'Radios and weapons' were 'the two key objects that would be found at roadblocks', the witness claimed.[73] According to another, 'almost everyone had a radio and listened to RTLM'.[74] Elsewhere, RTLM was described as 'the crucial propaganda tool',[75] a 'tool for killing',[76] the '*radio que tue*',[77] 'Radio Machete'.[78]

What made the radio *so* effective, *such* an ideal 'vehicle' for the purposes of 'disseminating' propaganda, even if RTLM had not originally been intended as such? In its judgment in the *Media* case, the Trial Chamber explained:

> The nature of radio transmission made RTLM particularly dangerous and harmful, as did the breadth of its reach. Unlike print media, radio is immediately present and active. The power of the human voice, heard by the Chamber when the broadcast tapes were played in Kinyarwanda, adds a quality and dimension beyond words to the message conveyed. In this setting, radio heightened the sense of fear, the sense of danger and the sense of urgency

[64] *Bikindi* indictment, para 10.
[65] *Bikindi* judgment, especially paras 115, 122.
[66] *Bikindi* judgment, para 122.
[67] *Bikindi* judgment, para 114.
[68] *Bikindi* judgment, para 258.
[69] *Media* case.
[70] See *Media* case, paras 428, 449, 455, 478, 487, 488, 509, 516, 574, 606, 668, 672, 754, 837, 957, 971, 1028.
[71] John Durham Peters, *Speaking into the Air: A History of the Idea of Communication* (University of Chicago Press, 1999) 206–14.
[72] *Media* case, para 343.
[73] *Media* case, para 343.
[74] *Media* case, para 342.
[75] *Media* case, para 457.
[76] *Media* case, para 538.
[77] *Media* case, para 457. The phrase literally translates as 'the radio that kills' but the translation offered in the Chamber's judgment is 'the killer radio station'.
[78] *Media* case, para 1031.

giving rise to the need for action by listeners. The denigration of Tutsi ethnicity was augmented by the visceral scorn coming out of the airwaves—the ridiculing laugh and the nasty sneer. These elements greatly amplified the impact of RTLM broadcasts.[79]

Two qualities made RTLM 'particularly dangerous and harmful' as far as the ICTR was concerned. First, the 'breadth' of its 'reach', the precise extent of which, interestingly, was never actually addressed by the Tribunal.[80] Second, the potency of its effects, which are glossed immediately as essential to radio's 'nature'. This natural potency derives, apparently, from the peculiar immediacy of the radio voice which, unlike the text-oriented 'print media', is imagined as being both particularly 'present and active'.[81]

The echoes of Sterne's 'audio-visual litany' will, I hope, be clear by this point. The depiction of radio naturalized at the ICTR conforms closely to ancient and deeply held theological and metaphysical attitudes or commitments, whereby vision maps to distance, disengagement, reason, and intellect, and sound is immersive, present, embodied, affective, even divine.[82] We have already seen these arrangements play out elsewhere in the book, especially in Chapters 5 and 6. Here, they have simply been technologized, translated into the field of radio.

Radio on this account is an extension of the speaking body in exactly the same way that the machete might be thought of as merely an extension of the arm or hand.[83] Both are figured as prosthetics: one acoustic, the other haptic. Where one improves the reach and power of the voice in the 'expression' of incendiary 'ideas' and 'opinions', the other does the same for the arm in the infliction of pain. Radio, thus, like some supercharged version of the voice, is rendered as intrinsically 'powerful' and 'visceral'. It 'heightens', 'augments', and, finally, 'amplifies the impact' of the 'messages' being broadcast.

Here, finally, is some recognition on the Tribunal's part of the voice's non-transparency. Yet, far from disrupting or exceeding the register of intention, far from undermining the sovereignty of the speaker in any way or engaging the 'unknowing body' as we saw in the accounts of Butler, Felman, Kristeva, and Barthes in Chapter 5, it simply reinforces it. This, in other words, is precisely the voice of authority we identified in Chapter 6, flush with the 'metaphysical

[79] *Media* case, para 1031.

[80] The prosecution did call a Rwandan radio technician to testify at trial. He claimed that RTLM had a 100-watt transmitter that could reach the whole of the capital Kigali and a few areas south and east of Kigali as well as a less powerful transmitter on Mount Muhe in western Rwanda that could reach some areas in that part of the country. Scott Straus notes that, 'if true, then RTLM would not have reached large segments of the country, including northern, northeastern, southern, and southwest area, where genocide occurred'. Radio Rwanda, by contrast, did have national reach. Straus (2007) 617. *Prosecutor v Nahimana* (Transcript) ICTR-99-52-T, T Ch I (Various dates) ('*Nahimana* transcript' or '*Media* case transcript') 4 July 2001.

[81] *Media* case, para 1031. In this instance, the text in question is *Kangura*, the Rwandan newspaper also under consideration in the *Media* case.

[82] Jonathan Sterne, *The Audible Past: Cultural Origins of Sound Reproduction* (Duke University Press, 2003) 15.

[83] McLuhan (1964).

charisma' of Horkheimer and Adorno's dictator.[84] In his award-winning account of the genocide *Shake Hands with the Devil*, General Roméo Dallaire, who led the UN's peace-keeping force to Rwanda between 1993 and 1994 and who also testified a number of times at the Tribunal,[85] famously wrote that in Rwanda 'radio was akin to the voice of God'.[86] There is very little in either the *Bikindi* or the *Media* case to suggest that the ICTR would disagree.

One suspects that a number of related racial and cultural prejudices may have been in play here too. In the *Bikindi* case the Chamber was happy to endorse witness BHH's testimony, for instance, that 'the African population, and the Rwandan population in particular, has the tendency to respect what is broadcast on government radio stations which stand as official sources. He added that people tend to think that what is broadcast on the national radio station has a legal force or some kind of authority'.[87] The sentiment is very similar to one expressed by renowned media theorist Marshall McLuhan, for whom radio's potency in totalitarian regimes was related directly to its supposed Africanness. Hitler's Germany 'danced entranced to the tribal drum of radio' he wrote in 1964's *Understanding Media*,[88] the clear implication being: if only Germany had been less aural, more literate, less African, more European.[89] For McLuhan:

> Radio affects most people intimately, person-to-person … That is the immediate aspect of radio. A private experience. The subliminal depths of radio are charged with the resonating echoes of tribal horns and antique drums. This is inherent in the very nature of the medium, with its power to turn the psyche and society into a single echo chamber.[90]

[84] Max Horkheimer and Theodor W Adorno, *Dialectic of Enlightenment: Philosophical Fragments*, ed Gunzelin Schmid Noerr, trans Edmund Jephcott (Stanford University Press, 2002) [trans of: *Gesammelte Schriften: Dialektik der Aufklärung und Schriften 1940–1950* (first published 1987)] 129. On the role of radio in Nazi Germany, its particular relations to the dictator's voice and especially the way in which music and other modes of 'entertainment' were integrated into programming schedules, see Horst J P Bergmeier and Rainer E Lotz, *Hitler's Airwaves: The Inside Story of Nazi Radio Broadcasting and Propaganda Swing* (Yale University Press, 1997); Brian Currid, *A National Acoustics: Music and Mass Publicity in Weimar and Nazi Germany* (University of Minnesota Press, 2006).

[85] *Prosecutor v Akayesu* (Judgement) ICTR-96-4-T, T Ch I (2 September 1998); *Prosecutor v Bagosora* (Judgement and Sentence) ICTR-98-41-T, T Ch I (18 December 2008); *Prosecutor v Bizimungu* (Judgement and Sentence) ICTR-99-50-T, T Ch II (30 September 2011).

[86] Roméo Dallaire, *Shake Hands with the Devil: The Failure of Humanity in Rwanda* (Random House, 2003) 272.

[87] *Bikindi* judgment, para 258. The citations are to *Bikindi* transcript: 25 October 2007, 26; 20 February 2007, 13.

[88] McLuhan (1964) 260.

[89] It is only barely implicit. Later in the same essay, McLuhan writes, 'Radio provided the first massive experience of electronic implosion, that reversal of the entire direction and meaning of literate Western civilization. For tribal peoples, for those whose entire social existence is an extension of family life, radio will continue to be a violent experience. Highly literate societies, that have long subordinated family life to individualist stress in business and politics, have managed to absorb and to neutralise the radio implosion without revolution. Not so, those communities that have had only brief or superficial experience of literacy. For them, radio is utterly explosive'. McLuhan (1964) 262.

[90] McLuhan (1964) 261.

Notice how similar McLuhan's language is here to that of the Tribunal above, and how in both cases the account of radio is presented as 'natural'. Consider too just how little agency is granted to the listeners in both accounts. In its presence and its intimacy, radio does things to you, whether you like it or not.[91] 'RTLM broadcasting was a drumbeat', the Chamber wrote in the *Media* case, 'calling on listeners to take action against the enemy and enemy accomplices'.[92] The association between rhythm and the compulsive African body is an old one. There is a long history, Simon Frith writes, 'of defining black culture, specifically African culture, as the body, the other of the bourgeois mind'. 'The primitive in music (rhythm), the primitive in social evolution (the medieval, the African), and the primitive in human development (the infantile) are thus reflections of each other'.[93] Similarly familiar is the elision between so-called 'oral traditions'—in the *Bikindi* case, the Rwandan tradition was repeatedly referred to in these terms[94]—and either critical or intellectual deficit. In her influential study *Oral Literature in Africa*, for instance, Ruth Finnegan writes that 'in the popular view [the concept of an *oral* literature] seems to convey on the one hand the idea of mystery, on the other that of crude and artistically undeveloped formulations'.[95] Indeed, the entire book can be read as an attempt to reconfigure the deep association between orality and the 'primitive', to revalorize oral traditions, in other words, for the Western reader. The ICTR's portrayal of the Rwandan radio listener is consistent with such stereotypes about both Rwandans and Africans more generally: that 'they obey orders blindly, that they are poorly educated and thus easily manipulated, and that they are immersed in a culture of prejudice'.[96] This time, the prejudice simply comes with a technological gloss, which also operates as an obfuscation.

So far we have identified two main features of the Tribunal's account of radio in the *Bikindi* case. First, a real consistency with the broader discourse in relation to the medium's role in the Rwandan genocide, inherited partly in the form of expert evidence. Second, the work of certain familiar attitudes regarding the relations between sight and sound, reason and unreason, the West and Africa, playing out this time at the level of technology. I now want to identify two further elements to the Tribunal's approach, both of which were the result of a specifically juridical orientation. On the one hand, a tendency towards *reification*. On the other, an entrenched *instrumentalism*.

In the work of Georg Lukács, 'reification' refers to the objectification of social relations, and particularly of commodity structures. As taken up by Jonathan

[91] This way of treating broadcast media is common in media law. For one classic example in relation to the regulation of public indecency, see the decision of the United States Supreme Court in *Federal Communications Commission v Pacifica Foundation*, 438 US 726 (1978).

[92] *Media* case, para 1031.

[93] Simon Frith, *Performing Rites: Evaluating Popular Music* (Oxford University Press, 1996) 127, 130.

[94] *Bikindi* transcript: 4 October 2006, 12; 12 February 2007, 7; 13 February 2007, 33, 42; 14 February 2007, 8; 16 February 2007, 6.

[95] Ruth Finnegan, *Oral Literature in Africa* (Clarendon Press, 1970) 1.

[96] Straus (2007) 617. *Media* case transcript, 4 July 2001.

Sterne, however, the term names the same process in relation to media. It refers to the tendency to mistake the historical conditions of a medium for its fundamental nature, to understand the complex constellation of technical and social practices embodied in a medium like radio or television as if they were somehow inevitable or intrinsic to the technology itself.[97] This is precisely the logic we find in relation to radio at the ICTR.

Technologically, analogue (as opposed to digital) radio depends on the bringing together of microphones, amplifiers, and loudspeakers as well as the ability to send and receive electroacoustic signals by way of electromagnetic radiation with minimal noise or interference. At the level of infrastructure, it requires the alignment of these technologies in a very particular way. A whole host of decisions need to be made and then carefully regulated and maintained in relation to how they are networked. If radio was predominantly centralized and uni-directional in Rwanda, therefore, which is to say truly a broadcast medium rather than modular and dialogical like the telephone, neither of these characteristics were inherent to the technologies themselves.[98] They had to be designed. Transmitters with a significant range had first to be funded and then built. In order to establish an audience, receivers needed to have been distributed and the network 'heavily promoted by UNESCO and other international aid agencies' as a method of modernization and 'development'.[99] Then there are the related questions of programming and listenership: the particular ways in which radio stations present themselves to the ear and are integrated into the lives of their listeners, none of which are either necessary or stable; the specific forms of attention and affect the medium both nurtures and produces; the way in which the audience is addressed and encouraged to interact; the specific modes of listening facilitated, whether individual or communal, concentrated or distracted.[100] All this nuance was simply elided at the crucial moments in the *Bikindi* case. Once radio had been reified as a 'tool', 'object', or 'vehicle' for the 'dissemination' of propaganda, it was presented by the Tribunal as ready and waiting to be put to inflammatory use: an instrument of genocide.

As critical media theorist Andrew Feenberg explains, 'instrumentalism' refers to the 'common sense idea that technologies are "tools" standing ready to serve the purposes of their users'.[101] Not only do technologies have an 'essence' on such an account, that essence, by definition, 'distinguishes it from the human (essence) that, as its efficient cause, makes and uses technology'.[102] This is why for Martin

[97] See Georg Lukács, *History and Class Consciousness: Studies in Marxist Dialects*, trans Rodney Livingstone (MIT Press, 1971) [trans of: *Geschichte und klassenbewusstsein* (first published 1968)] 83; Jonathan Sterne, 'Television under Construction: American Television and the Problem of Distribution, 1926–62', *Media, Culture and Society* 21(4) (1999) 503, 504.

[98] On the telephone's brief history as a broadcast medium, see Sterne (2003) 192–4.

[99] Christine L Kellow and H Leslie Steeves, 'The Role of Radio in the Rwandan Genocide', *Journal of Communication* 48(3) (1998) 107, 115.

[100] On the history and development of broadcast radio see Susan J Douglas, *Inventing American Broadcasting 1899–1922* (John Hopkins University Press, 1987); Susan Smulyan, *Selling Radio: The Commercialization of American Broadcasting 1920–1934* (Smithsonian Institution Press, 1994).

[101] Andrew Feenberg, *Critical Theory of Technology* (Oxford University Press, 1991) 5.

[102] Gordon Coonfield, 'Thinking Machinically, or, the Techno-Aesthetic of Jackie Chan: Toward a Deleuze-Guattarian Media Studies', *Critical Studies in Media Communication* 23(4) (2006) 285, 287.

Heidegger instrumental thinking is necessarily anthropological too.[103] Presupposed in the separateness of the (reified) tool is a theory of man capable of 'mastering' it, of wielding it at will.[104] This same anthropocentrism is also why for Félix Guattari the instrumentalist conception of technology tends to depict such mastery in terms of 'the extension and the projection of the living being'.[105] 'With every tool man is perfecting his own organs', wrote Sigmund Freud in *Civilization and its Discontents*.[106] Even if that perfection is sometimes to insidious ends.

But instrumental thinking is not just anthropological. It is thoroughly juridical too. As an entire media apparatus—which is to say a historically specific network of technologies, affects, people, and practices—radio is a social problem, and responsibility in relation to it is therefore necessarily diffuse. As a tool for the extension of the voice, by contrast, responsibility is individualized. Such individualization is at the very core of the project of international criminal law, where the attribution of responsibility actually *depends* on the subject's mastery of their tools. The responsible juridical subject could *never* simply be 'a component in the machine',[107] in Latour's language, a mere 'actant' in a network of objects, attitudes, ideas, and people.[108] In Chapter 3 we considered the Tribunal's approach to Bikindi's songs. We saw how by reducing the problem to one of hermeneutics and then by rendering the acoustic irrelevant to the task of interpretation, it was consistently deaf to their specifically musical qualities. Moreover, we saw how this was no mere accident on the Tribunal's part but rather a deafness of the law itself, enabled by the structure of the relevant doctrine in relation to 'freedom of expression' and further sedimented in practice by the kinds of experts employed and the terms of their employment. In Chapter 5, we observed a very similar dynamic at work in relation to speech. Like music, the voice was also presented as a means for the transmission and dispersal of 'ideas' and 'opinions'. We noticed how the voice did crucial work from a doctrinal perspective because, in its very transparency, its apparent proximity to the interiority of the speaking subject, it seemed to guarantee or secure Bikindi's intent. Moreover, we saw how, far from interrupting that logic, Bikindi's use of the loudspeaker on the road to Kayove that day, strengthened or improved it.

The Tribunal's instrumentalism in relation to radio was the product of the very same doctrinal concerns. As a 'tool' or 'vehicle', and specifically as a means of extending the voice, radio was presented by the ICTR as little more than a particularly effective

[103] Martin Heidegger, *The Question concerning Technology and Other Essays*, trans William Lovitt (Garland, 1977) [trans of: *Die technik und die kehre* (first published 1962)] 5.

[104] Heidegger (1977).

[105] Félix Guattari, *Chaosophy: Texts and Interviews 1972–1977*, ed Sylvère Lotringer, trans David L Sweet, Jarred Becker and Taylor Adkins (Semiotext(e), 2009) 92.

[106] Sigmund Freud, *The Standard Edition of the Complete Psychological Works of Sigmund Freud*, trans James Strachey (Hogarth Press, 1953–75) vol 21, 101 ('The Future of an Illusion, Civilization and Its Discontents and Other Works').

[107] Guattari (2009) 91.

[108] Bruno Latour, 'Where Are the Missing Masses? The Sociology of a Few Mundane Artifacts' in Wiebe E Bijker and John Law (eds), *Shaping Technology/Building Society: Studies in Sociotechnical Change* (MIT Press, 1992) 225.

loudspeaker.[109] It amplified the voice, even improved it, made it more authoritative, more compelling, more menacing. But it did nothing whatsoever to change the way legal responsibility attached. Just like the loudspeaker, radio simply added one more link in the *expressive chain*: between the interiority of the speaker, their will or intention, and the ears of the listening public. For the purposes of the doctrine of 'direct and public incitement to genocide', everything depended on the Tribunal's ability to maintain the continuity of this chain. The instrumentalization of radio was one thing that enabled it to do so.

We should be careful about the quality of our critique, therefore. Just as we saw in relation to the critique of voice in Chapter 5, although the sort of critical account of technology given above is crucial for an acoustic jurisprudence because it gives a sense of the complexity of audio-technology as a theoretical and juridical problem, it is less helpful when it comes to the specifically institutional registers of the task of adjudication. At the ICTR, the very same instrumentalism that, from a critical perspective, looks reductive, is clearly doing important work jurisprudentially. It followed directly from the institutional imperative to address *this* person's responsibility and no other's, on the one hand, and from the doctrinal structures to which it was beholden, on the other. If the ICTR's account of radio seems particularly thin, therefore, if it fails to address in some respects the fullness of radio as a sociological and technical problem, it may simply be that that is the price of *thinking radio juridically*. As we will now see, however, it may not have been in relation to radio that the consequences of the Tribunal's instrumentalism were at their greatest.

Audio Recording

When Bikindi's songs featured on RTLM and Radio Rwanda it was only ever in the form of recordings which the Chamber found had been made at a private studio in Kigali in early 1993 and then distributed on tape.[110] Two of the songs recorded, it said, had clearly been intended to 'disseminate pro-Hutu ideology and anti-Tutsi propaganda, and thus to encourage ethnic hatred'.[111] This fell short, however, of a specific intention to incite genocide, and it was not until the recordings were subsequently 'deployed' on the radio in 1994 that the provocative 'commentary' by radio announcers would lead to their re-branding for explicitly genocidal purposes.[112] 'A month into the genocide', the Chamber wrote, the 'interpretations' on RTLM were becoming increasingly 'inflammatory'.[113] On 17 May 1994, for

[109] Journalist Mary Kimani makes the link explicit when she writes that RTLM 'became the megaphone through which people were incited to mass murder'. Mary Kimani, 'RTLM: The Medium that Became a Tool for Mass Murder' in Allan Thompson (ed), *The Media and the Rwanda Genocide* (Pluto, 2007) 122.

[110] *Bikindi* judgment, para 121; *Bikindi* transcript: 31 October 2007, 31–2; 16 October 2007, 20.

[111] *Bikindi* judgment, para 254.

[112] *Bikindi* judgment, paras 261, 264.

[113] *Bikindi* judgment, para 239.

instance, the RTLM journalist Kantano Habimana had the following to say by way of introduction to *Bene Sebahinzi/Intabaza*:

> Now, let us allow Bikindi to predict the future of the *Inkotanyi* and to tell them the fact awaiting them once the sons of Sebahinzi unite and fight them … They are vanishing, gradually, as the bombs land on them, as they continue to be killed like rats … Bikindi will in a short while tell you what will happen in future [sic] … Please listen to Bikindi's advice to the *Inkotanyi*. He is warning them that they will all be wiped out, come what may, because all the sons of Sebahinzi are closely watching whatever has to do with the *Inkotanyi*, fighting them and hunting them down. That is what is happening now, and the *Inkotanyi* are on the verge of extinction.[114]

It was this sort of framing, the Chamber said, that manifested a truly genocidal intent. Recordings of Bikindi's songs were *used* for genocidal purposes, but that purpose was not Bikindi's. Because he had neither any 'control or influence over the programming of RTLM or Radio Rwanda' nor any positive duty in law to attempt to stop them from being broadcast, Bikindi could not be held responsible for any such use.[115]

Gregory Gordon has argued therefore that 'an implied "instrumentality" criterion' can be gleaned from the *Bikindi* judgment: that 'when recordings are involved, the recorded would-be inciter must be responsible for actual contemporaneous dissemination of the criminal speech (i.e., the playing of the recording) that is charged'.[116] Gordon is right in one respect. The Tribunal's logic here *was* 'instrumental'. It also involved the projection of a 'complex assemblage of human and tool, machines and meanings, codes and connections' onto a singular object, ready and waiting to be deployed at will.[117] This time, however, the object or tool in question was a tape recording as opposed to the radio. But Gordon goes too far in suggesting that the *Bikindi* case can be read as authority that the would-be inciter *must* be involved in the act of dissemination—of pressing play, as it were—for responsibility to ensue. There is nothing in the Chamber's judgment to suggest that if Bikindi's songs had been more overtly incendiary—if it had been possible to find in them a 'specific intention to incite genocide' in addition to the mere 'encouragement of ethnic hatred'—that the Chamber would in principle have required his involvement in their 'deployment' too. Composition and recording may well have been enough on their own. Nevertheless, audio-recording did present a problem for the Tribunal.

In R Murray Schafer's account, the electroacoustic transmission and reproduction of sound is referred to as 'schizophonia'.[118] The psychiatric and psychoanalytic connotations are quite deliberate. 'Related to schizophrenia', Schafer writes, the term was intended 'to convey the same sense of aberration and drama'.[119]

[114] *Bikindi* judgment, para 239; Exhibit No P3, 'Transcript of RTLM Broadcast of 17 May 1994', *Prosecutor v Bikindi*, ICTR-01-72-0207 (17 May 1994) 19–20, 22.

[115] *Bikindi* judgment, paras 262–3, 439.

[116] Gregory S Gordon, 'Music and Genocide: Harmonizing Coherence, Freedom and Nonviolence in Incitement Law', *Santa Clara Law Review* 50(3) (2010) 607, 622.

[117] Coonfield (2006) 288. [118] Schafer (1977) 88. [119] Schafer (1977) 91.

Schizophonia, from the Greek *schizo* meaning split and *phone* meaning voice, refers to the dislocation between an original sound and its electroacoustic reproduction louder, later, and elsewhere. It was precisely this split that caused the ICTR so much trouble. Whereas radio, in its apparent proximity to the loudspeaker and therefore to the natural voice, seemed to allow for the expressive chain between the present intention of the speaker/singer and the listener's ear to remain intact in the Tribunal's account, recording spectacularly interrupted it. In doing so, it enabled the intervention of another intentionality, another voice, and along with it another layer in the construction of any given recording's meaning and effects. As a result, it vastly complicated the hermeneutic project and therefore the task of judgment. The Tribunal never quite took this insight as far as it might have, however. It recognized that electroacoustic reproduction is never simply a matter of repetition, that it always also involves a difference, and that to reproduce is by its very nature to reframe: to change. But it failed to apply this same logic to the one moment where Bikindi himself *was* involved in the act of reproduction. For an acoustic jurisprudence, this failure is highly revealing.

When the Chamber wrote that there was 'no evidence that Bikindi played a role in the dissemination or deployment of his three songs in 1994', that was not entirely accurate.[120] Bikindi may not have played a decisive role in his songs' diffusion throughout the Rwandan radioscape, but there was at least one occasion in 1994 when he was undoubtedly involved in their 'broadcasting'. The Chamber even said as much in the very passage that would ultimately found his conviction. One last time then:

> Witness AKK testified that he saw Bikindi in June 1994, in a vehicle, as part of a convoy heading towards Kayove. AKK lived close to the road and saw buses full of *Interahamwe*, blowing whistles and making lots of noise with clubs and firearms. Bikindi was in a vehicle outfitted with a loudspeaker, over which songs were being broadcast with intermittent statements made by Bikindi. Witness AKK stated that Bikindi was not singing that day, as cassettes of his songs were being used. Witness AKK heard Bikindi say 'You sons of *Sebahinzi*, who are the majority, I am speaking to you, you know that the Tutsi are minority. Rise up and look everywhere possible and do not spare anybody'.[121]

When Witness AKJ, 'heard Bikindi ask over a loudspeaker "Have you killed the Tutsi here?" and whether they had killed the "snakes"', he also 'heard Bikindi's songs being played as the vehicles moved on'.[122]

What is this if not the very same sort of restaging which in the case of RTLM the Tribunal was happy to deem genocidal? If a journalist at RTLM was capable of 'deploying' Bikindi's songs for genocidal purposes by broadcasting them along with inflammatory commentary, why not the man himself? What I am arguing here is that *even if* the Chamber was right and Bikindi had not intended his songs to incite genocide at the time of their composition, it was entirely open to the Chamber, and moreover precisely by virtue of its own logic, to find that Bikindi's

120 *Bikindi* judgment, para 263.
121 *Bikindi* judgment, para 268.
122 *Bikindi* judgment, para 269.

own commentary—which in the Chamber's own analysis was intended to incite the killing of Tutsi—also constituted a reframing to genocidal ends. How else was Bikindi's audience meant to understand the performance of the songs in this context, backed by the noisy spectacle of an armed militia and punctuated by the rest of Bikindi's genocidal rhetoric? What purpose did the broadcasting of his songs play here if not to bolster the authority and effect of his statements? How could they fail to be coloured by the context of their performance, by all the shouts and gunfire and noise? How could they *not* be imbued with a renewed salience or gravitas?

I am not suggesting that the Chamber ought to have found Bikindi culpable in this respect. That the Tribunal failed even to *explore* this possibility, however, is highly revealing as far as an acoustic jurisprudence is concerned. Here was a man accused of inciting genocide with his songs and who was playing those very songs, moreover, at precisely the moment he spoke the words which would ultimately lead to his imprisonment. Yet somehow, this performance was deemed unworthy of consideration. It is as if, from an institutional perspective, the songs are totally besides the point here: as if, as far as the Tribunal is concerned, they have more in common with the noisy backdrop than with Bikindi's own utterances. When read alongside the ICTR's marginalization of music, in Chapter 3, and the singing voice, in Chapter 5, it is hard not to wonder if this wasn't always the case to some extent: if Bikindi's songs weren't *always* conceived by the Tribunal as being partly non-justiciable, *always* more noise than signal from a juridical perspective, *always* somehow secondary to the relative transparency of the word or text as expressive of the speaker's intentions for the purposes of the relevant doctrine. We could read the Tribunal's approach to audio-recording and reproduction, therefore—which admittedly displayed a certain sensitivity to the importance of context and framing in the production of a song's meaning and effect—as yet more evidence of an acute legal deafness when it came to Bikindi's songs and especially to the register of sound.

The account of the Rwandan soundscape produced by the Tribunal in the process of judgment both drew on familiar narratives, themes, prejudices, and traditions from outside an overtly juridical context and was the result of certain very specific juridical concerns, particularly at the level of doctrine. To begin with, the logic of incitement necessitated the segregation of the soundscape. On the one hand, the acoustic backdrop: noisy, social, and, most importantly, ungovernable, the limit of the Tribunal's jurisdiction in relation to sound. On the other hand, the acoustic foreground: Bikindi's songs and speech, both of which invariably distinguished themselves by means of technology: the radio, a loudspeaker, an audio recording. Radio, we saw, was in many respects the most important of these. It was radio, in the end, that gave Bikindi's songs their maximum diffusion both before and during the genocide and which, in doing so, worked to cement his popularity and fame. The Tribunal's representation of the radio was highly instrumental. It was not a network, but a tool, and specifically for the amplification of intentional human action; in this case, the vocalization of anti-Tutsi propaganda. Radio both flooded the Rwandan soundscape with such voices, for the Tribunal, and intensified their effects. Even though Bikindi's songs were in fact *deployed* to genocidal ends on Rwanda's airwaves, the fact that Bikindi was not himself involved in this deployment meant that he could not be deemed responsible to the extent that they were. Responsibility resolved instead to the journalists who, in the act of broadcasting and contextualization, also reframed them: were able to inject some of their own intentionality into the mix. Not so where Bikindi's own restaging was concerned. Just at the crucial moment, on the road to Kayove that day in June 1994, his songs receded once more into the background. As if, finally, the Tribunal was reluctant to find a musician culpable in law for the genocidal implications of his songs.

8

The ICTR as Soundscape

Home to the Waarusha people prior to German colonization at the end of the nineteenth century, Arusha is situated at the foot of Mount Meru and on the easternmost edge of the Great Rift Valley, roughly equidistant from two of East Africa's most popular travel destinations: the Kilimanjaro and Serengeti national parks. Today, along with Nairobi, it is one of the major hubs of tourism in the East African region. But it is a crucial legal and diplomatic centre too. On one side of town sits the African Court for Human and Peoples' Rights.[1] On the other, the Arusha International Conference Centre, which in addition to hosting a variety of international meetings year round,[2] has provided a home to the ICTR since November 1995,[3] and a headquarters for the East African Community since its re-establishment in mid-2000.[4] Much of this, moreover, is palpable at the level of acoustics, Arusha's very sound. The soundscape of the world, as Schafer argues, is not an 'indeterminate composition over which we have no control'.[5] We are its composers and performers.

The city centre in particular is constantly alive with an unmistakably cosmopolitan chatter.[6] Swahili, Maasai, Meru, Rwa, and a host of other languages local to

1 African Court on Human and Peoples' Rights, accessed 5 March 2015, <http://www.african-court.org/en/>.

2 Arusha International Conference Centre, accessed 5 March 2015, <http://www.aicc.co.tz/>.

3 First Annual Report of the International Criminal Tribunal for the Prosecution of Persons Responsible for Genocide and Other Serious Violations of International Humanitarian Law Committed in the Territory of Rwanda (24 September 1996) UN Doc A/51/399-S/1996/778, annex, 5.

4 East African Community, accessed 5 March 2015, <http://www.eac.int/index.php?option=com_content&view=article&id=44&Itemid=54>.

5 R Murray Schafer, *The Soundscape: Our Sonic Environment and the Tuning of the World* (Knopf, 1977) 5.

6 I am conscious here of a certain form of rhetoric which casts Africa's urban soundscape as 'noisy' in contrast to the ostensibly orderly sounds of the Western city. 'Mastery' over the soundscape, on this view, is understood as a marker of development and progress. Indeed, it is quite possible that just such a racist logic is implicit at some level in the practice of international justice in the practice of dislocating its institutions acoustically from the cities in which they are situated. I want to be clear, however, that this is not a view I endorse. My brief account of Arusha's soundscape is intended to be descriptive not critical. Nor is my intention to imply that Arusha's soundscape is anything other than highly ordered. The point is simply to situate the ICTR in its proper acoustic environment and to emphasize the fact that isolation from the immediate acoustic world is a condition of contemporary international justice mechanisms. This is not true, for instance, in many other juridical systems, notably in this context of Rwanda's *Gacaca* courts which frequently take place outdoors. Indeed, the Western tradition offers many ancient and contemporary examples of its own. For a discussion

the region intermingle with English and French predominantly, the languages of Africa's colonization, but also countless other global accents and tongues. Street vendors attracted to the region by the city's burgeoning commerce hawk fruit, newspapers, and safaris to anyone who will listen, as well as to many who would prefer not to. The low rumble of machinery and the high clang of metal upon metal signal the many new commercial building projects that are ongoing: hotels, particularly, but also office spaces. The drone of traffic is a constant. Wealth is inscribed directly here, at the level of mufflers and engine design. The luxury four-by-fours owned by rich locals and safari operators purr by quietly in violent contrast to the rumble and clatter of the many *daladalas* (mini-bus taxis) and *pikip-ikis* (motorbike taxis) that provide low-cost transport to everyone else. Drivers put their horns to extensive use, particularly after dark. With no street lighting to speak of and regular power cuts anyway, they announce, warn, and aggravate late into the night. Further away from the centre of town, as commercial and institutional life fades into the suburban sprawl, a different soundscape begins to emerge. Dogs, chickens, and the abundant red-winged starlings are all audible now. In the richer areas, so is the hum of generators. Music is everywhere. *Bongo Flava*—Tanzania's own particular fusion of American hip-hop and R&B with traditional Tanzanian styles such as *taarab* and *dansi*—emanates from bars and radios.[7] And then, on weekend mornings particularly, sacred music takes over,[8] echoing out from the numerous churches to be found here on the city's periphery. Praise songs are performed rapturously in close harmony, sometimes simply *a capella*, sometimes over tinny backing tracks on battered and blown out public address systems.

These are just some of the sounds that both accompany and produce the forms of daily life particular to contemporary Arusha. Anyone who has worked at the ICTR in recent years will be familiar with them. They are a few of the city's more obvious 'keynote sounds', its 'signals' and 'soundmarks'.[9] But as you enter the Conference Centre in which the Tribunal is housed, via the beep-beep-beeping of the x-ray equipment and the electronic gate as you pass through security, Arusha's acoustic particularity quickly begins to fade.

What kind of soundscape is produced inside these walls? How? Why? And with what consequences? We have already seen in Chapter 4 how the Tribunal's is fundamentally an oral soundscape, and how this heavily conditioned the way in which Bikindi's songs were heard there. In Chapter 6 we looked a little closer at the details

of many of these examples, see Linda Mulcahy, *Legal Architecture: Justice, Due Process and the Place of Law* (Routledge, 2011) ch 2. For an excellent treatment of the *Gacaca* system, see Phil Clark, *The Gacaca Courts, Post-Genocide Justice and Reconciliation in Rwanda: Justice without Lawyers* (Cambridge University Press, 2010).

[7] For a detailed account of the *taarab* and *dansi* styles as well as their role in 'performing' the Tanzanian nation, see Kelly M Askew, *Performing the Nation: Swahili Music and Cultural Politics in Tanzania* (University of Chicago Press, 2002). The 'bongo' in Bongo Flava is not a reference to the Cuban percussion instrument. It is a slang term for Dar Es Salaam, Tanzania's capital and the place where the genre originated.

[8] Bongo Flava often deals with religious themes in its lyrics. The strictness of the divide between sacred and secular music in Tanzania is not so pronounced as it is presently in many Western contexts.

[9] Schafer (1977) 9–10.

of courtroom orality, at when exactly the voice was called on by the Tribunal and to do what. This chapter widens the acoustic lens to take in the questions of architecture and technology, the gavel, simultaneous interpretation and the archive, and their role in shaping *the ICTR as soundscape*. The chapter begins, as we step through the thick walls of the Arusha Conference Centre, with the sounds of the Tribunal in general, and works from there through to those of the courtroom in particular. We will see how soundproofing has become a condition of international juridical practice and how the 'keynote sounds' at the ICTR speak of an institution which operates by means of a phenomenological dislocation from the particularities of time and place. We will notice how, at least in the international context, the courtroom has become increasingly compartmentalized acoustically such that the word 'courtroom' itself is practically misleading. With each room comprising six discreet spaces, headphones are now a condition of participation, an essential portal into the trial's acoustic world. So, next the chapter considers some of the implications of the wiring of the courtroom for sound: how the experience of listening through headphones produces an increasingly individuated, cellular, and bureaucratic listening practice, and how participants must learn to 'play' their microphones effectively in order to make themselves heard. I then turn briefly to the question of the gavel and to the judge's role in conducting the soundscape, before coming to the history and practice of 'simultaneous interpretation'. Simultaneous interpretation is both the child of international law—borne of specifically legal concerns in a specifically legal setting—and integral to its ongoing success. Not only was it responsible for having introduced many of the audio-technologies we find at the ICTR to the juridical context, but its consequences as far as the tempo, rhythm, and accent of judgment are concerned have been considerable. It is no exaggeration to say that simultaneous interpretation has been one of the single most important factors in shaping the soundscape of international justice today. Finally, the chapter arrives at the related questions of broadcasting and the archive, where the wiring of the courtroom for sound turns out to have had dramatic consequences for the nature and significance of the trial as audio-visual event.

Architectural Acoustics

The study of a soundscape always begins with the particular: a place, a time, a city, a building, an institution. This particular institution does as much as it can to separate itself acoustically from the particularity of its surrounds and to establish its sonic world as far as possible according to its own terms. This is the result of an architectural logic which—since 'noise' was first identified as a distinctive problem for modernity at the dawn of the industrial revolution—has increasingly made acoustics and the material conditions of sound-isolation one of its central concerns.[10] In 1931, editor of the *American Architect* Benjamin Betts expressed his

[10] Emily Thompson, *The Soundscape of Modernity: Architectural Acoustics and the Culture of Listening in America, 1900-1933* (MIT Press, 2004) ch 4, 115–57.

hopes for the then burgeoning 'business of sound control' in an article entitled 'Is This Our Next New Big Business?' 'Through its power', he wrote, 'outside noises can be shut out of offices and apartments'. 'The day is not far distant', he predicted, 'when prospective buyers and tenants of buildings will ask, "Is it soundproof?".'[11] Already in the early 1930s that day was at hand.[12] Today, the business of architectural acoustics is both deeply and globally entrenched. Soundproofing is one of the material conditions of international legal practice.

At the Arusha Conference Centre, thick concrete walls block all but the most obstinate traffic noise and the twittering of birds perched on windowsills. Linguistic variety diminishes as conversations converge upon French and English, the two official operational languages of the UN. The constant hum of strip-lighting, air-conditioning units, and computer fans provide the keynote sounds now, anchoring those who work at the Tribunal in a very particular kind of institutional space and mode of life. Even though these sounds may not always be heard consciously, even though one is able to learn *not* to listen to them, 'the fact that they are ubiquitously there', as Schafer argues, 'suggests the possibility of a deep and pervasive influence on our behaviour and moods'. The keynote sounds of a given place are important because they 'help to outline the character' of the men and women living among them.[13] In the ICTR's case, these sounds speak both of a financial situation considered appropriate to the workings of contemporary international justice mechanisms and a form of bureaucratic and technological efficiency which operates precisely by means of a dislocation from the immediate vicissitudes of time and place. Inside the walls of the Tribunal, Arusha's choking summer heat, its civic hubbub and even the waning light are of very little consequence.[14] Life and more importantly work, the day-to-day business of judgment, goes on regardless.[15]

From an acoustic perspective, the courtrooms themselves are undoubtedly the Tribunal's most carefully regulated spaces. This is true both in material terms, at the level of architecture and technology—soundproofing and wiring—and in social terms, at the level of behaviour—institutional *habitus*.[16] When I visited the ICTR in 2011, three so-called 'ultra-modern' courtrooms were still operational.[17] A fourth had been established temporarily by means of a grant provided by the Norwegian government in 1999 in order to help ease the Tribunal's increasing

[11] Benjamin F Betts, 'Is This Our Next New Big Business?' *American Architect* 140 (December 1931) 21.

[12] Thompson (2004) 175.

[13] Schafer (1977) 9.

[14] The Tribunal keeps relentlessly to the UN's timetable and calendar. Work starts at 8:30 am and continues to 5:00 pm or so all year round, except on Fridays when the day finishes at 12:00.

[15] For an account of the evolving relation between soundproofing and the quiet workspace in Victorian England and in particular on the sanctity of the bourgeois 'study', see John Picker, 'The Soundproof Study' in Jonathan Sterne (ed), *The Sound Studies Reader* (Routledge, 2012).

[16] Pierre Bourdieu, *The Logic of Practice*, trans Richard Nice (Stanford University Press, 1990) [trans of: *Le sens pratique* (first published 1980)] 52–65; Pierre Bourdieu and Loïc J D Wacquant, *An Invitation to Reflexive Sociology* (University of Chicago Press, 1992) 13–14, 120–40.

[17] This is the phrase used in a documentary produced by the Tribunal on its own history, procedure, mandate, and results: Bocar Sy, *Justice Today, Peace Tomorrow* (United Nations, *c*2002).

backlog of cases. But in 2011 it lay dormant. The active courtrooms, by contrast, were a hive of sound and industry. This much was clear even from the outside: from the brisk tip-tapping of footsteps along the concrete corridors, the discrete but urgent whispers at doorways, and the occasional throbbing of photocopiers in the hallway. A document, perhaps, was urgently needed in court.

Inside, it turns out that the word 'courtroom' is actually something of a misnomer. As we saw in Chapter 4, each one comprises six discrete and relatively well-soundproofed spaces, rather than a single open room. First, there is the central chamber where the defendant, judges, and lawyers sit along with various administrative personnel for the Registry and witnesses whenever they are called. This is a slim, low-ceilinged rectangular room walled with concrete on one side behind the judges' bench and bulletproof glass on the three others. The tables are lined with microphones and video-monitors and scattered with headphones, and the long wall opens onto the public 'gallery' which, unlike in many domestic courts in the West, is both physically and acoustically separated from the central judicial space. If one sits right up against the glass, it is just possible to make out the murmur of conversation on the other side. Otherwise it is necessary to 'tune in' via an infrared receiver and headphones which will have been handed to you by the security guard when you signed in and checked your bag and mobile phone. On one short wall, behind counsel for the prosecution, are the three interpretation booths: one for the English, one for the French, and one for the Kinyarwanda interpreters. Again, each booth is acoustically separate from the central space, but this time, as in the main chamber itself, they are equipped with microphones for the transmission as well as headphones for the reception of audio-signals. Finally, on the other short wall, behind counsel for the defence, is the audio-visual booth from where the sound- and videoscapes of the rest are monitored and controlled.

What does it sound like here, inside a 'courtroom' at an international tribunal like the ICTR? Clearly there is an extent to which the answer to that question depends on who you are, what your role in proceedings is, and to which rooms you therefore have access. The soundscape of the central chamber, for instance, is utterly different to that in the public gallery or any of the four booths. Sit in the gallery during a hearing with your eyes closed and your headphones by your side and you will be hard pushed to recognize your surroundings as legal at all. You will hear that familiar humming of the strip-lighting and air-conditioning unit, the slamming of a door off in the distance perhaps, the stirring of one of the journalists sitting along from you, and the faint and vaguely ghostly whisper of voices leaking from his and other observers' headphones. And that's about it. From the gallery, as from the interpretation and audio-visual booths, headphones are your exclusive portal into the juridical world you see before you through the glass. While that is obviously not the case in the central chamber itself, everyone there wears headphones nevertheless. Indeed, headphones are quite literally a condition of participation in a trial at the ICTR. As a result, acoustic experience there has become radically personalized. From the perspective of an acoustic jurisprudence, one of the most interesting aspects of the soundscape at the ICTR is not so much *what* it sounds like, but the technical means by which you are required to listen.

The obvious question, therefore, is this. What happens to the judicial soundscape when the courtroom is 'wired for sound'?[18]

Wired for Sound

There are four audio-channels to choose from on the little black infrared receivers attached to your headset: one corresponding to each of the three languages in which the trial is operating, and one, referred to as the 'floor channel', which allows you to hear whatever is being picked up by the microphones in the central chamber regardless of the language being spoken or, indeed, whether or not anything is being said at all.[19] Each and every person present at trial is not only able but actively required to organize their own listening experience. Headphones off or headphones on, volume up or down, English, French, or Kinyarwanda: cocooned in their 'Cartesian headsets', participants in the judicial soundscape must both occupy and arrange their own private acoustic worlds.[20]

What is interesting about the acoustic individuation at trial, however, is just how social it is. This is not the kind of headphone usage one sees on buses and trains. In such cases, the listening is specifically intended to produce a certain kind of isolation from the immediate social environment: a form of cloistered or reclusive listening if you like.[21] During a trial at the ICTR, although everyone present may be listening differently, they are nevertheless all listening together. Jonathan Sterne has captured the apparently paradoxical nature of this mode of listening nicely in his discussion of certain forms of the emergent 'headset culture' towards the end of the nineteenth century.[22] In Sterne's terms, the experience of listening to a trial at the ICTR is, 'highly individuated, standardized, yet also collectivized'.[23] Participants must listen 'alone together'.[24] Their isolation is collective.[25] What that means in practice is that listening at trial is frequently understood as a collaborative enterprise. Judges share tips with lawyers and, most frequently, with witnesses who are unaccustomed to the peculiar listening practices that participation in a trial at the ICTR requires.

[18] Paul G Greene and Thomas Porcello (eds), *Wired for Sound: Engineering and Technologies in Sonic Cultures* (Wesleyan University Press, 2004).

[19] The hardware is manufactured by a company called Danish Interpretation Systems. Product specifications for the IR 15 Infrared Receivers are available at: Danish Interpretation Systems, 'Infrared Digital Daylight Receivers' (Data Sheet No 4.05f, DIS), accessed 18 February 2015 <http://www.dis.su/pdf/IR15-xx_EN.pdf>.

[20] Sean Cubitt, *Digital Aesthetics* (Sage, 1998) 104.

[21] Michael Bull, *Sounding Out the City: Personal Stereos and the Management of Everyday Life* (Berg, 2000) 31. Bull's book also provides a general ethnography of contemporary personal stereo usage. See also Shuhei Hosokawa, 'The Walkman Effect' in Jonathan Sterne (ed), *The Sound Studies Reader* (Routledge, 2012).

[22] Jonathan Sterne, *The Audible Past: Cultural Origins of Sound Reproduction* (Duke University Press, 2003) 154.

[23] Sterne (2003) 165. [24] Sterne (2003) 163. [25] Sterne (2003) 161.

But the (collective) individuation of acoustic space at trial produces another important aesthetic effect too. 'Transmitted through air', Sean Cubitt explains, 'sound occupies and creates an environment'. This is the sound of the traditional 'cavernous court'[26]—London's historically high-ceilinged Royal Courts of Justice or the International Court of Justice's so-called Great Hall at the Peace Palace in the Hague[27]—where the resonance of the space, in collaboration with the scale of the architecture that is required to produce it, communicates its very pomp and seriousness: one might even be tempted to say its 'aura'.[28] In acoustic terms, the similarity to a Church or other sacred location is unmistakable. These are 'temples to justice'.[29] Speech, songs, and gavels resound and echo. Sound surrounds and envelopes you. Not only are the courtrooms at the ICTR constructed specifically to muffle sounds rather than to let them resonate, however, headphones produce a completely different kind of listening experience. 'Transmitted directly to the ear with whatever purity of reproduction, [acoustic] space is reduced to an optimal (and imaginary) point midway between the ears.'[30] The moment you put on headphones, architectural becomes punctual space. Experienced through headphones at the ICTR and via the audio-record at home, the courtroom sounds far more bureaucratic than sacred. It is less cavernous, more cellular.

If these are some of the general effects produced by the introduction of sound-reproduction technologies into the juridical environment, there are many specific ones too. Headsets and microphones are never very far from the forefront of peoples' minds. These are mediators which clearly do *not* 'vanish' in the act of mediation.[31] At the mundane level, participants are constantly fiddling with their headsets, switching between audio-channels and complaining about technical hitches. Episodes such as the following were common during the *Bikindi* case:

[26] Desmond Manderson, *Songs without Music: Aesthetic Dimensions of Law and Justice* (University of California Press, 2000) 42.

[27] On the Royal Courts of Justice and other examples from the nineteenth century 'heyday of court design' in the UK, see Mulcahy (2011) 112–38. On architecture at the Peace Palace, see 'Het Gebouw' ('The Building'), Vredespaleis, accessed 5 March 2015, <http://www.vredespaleis.nl/index.php?pid=57&page=The_building>.

[28] Walter Benjamin, *Illuminations*, trans Harry Zoh (Schocken Books, 1968) [trans of: *Illuminationen* (first published 1955)] 217 ('The Work of Art in the Age of Its Mechanical Reproduction').

[29] Mulcahy (2011) 118. [30] Cubitt (1998) 103.

[31] The phrase 'vanishing mediator' originally appears in Frederick Jameson's work, but has been picked up more recently in the work of Slavoj Žižek to refer to the fourth movement in Hegel's dialectic where, as Sterne puts it, 'the mediating term disappears, leaving its structure and effect but not its form'. Here, I use the term in the same sense intended by Sterne in relation to his cultural history of sound reproduction, to refer to the kind of 'pure' mediation imagined by a certain kind of media theory and which is most often deployed as a marketing device. This kind of approach likes to imagine a mediator between 'original' and 'copy' which would render itself completely transparent, as if it were not even there. This is a pipe dream. The mediator never vanishes, it simply affects the process of mediation differently. The crucial thing is to notice how. See Frederic Jameson, *Ideologies of Theory: Essays 1971–1986* (University of Minnesota, 1988) 3–34 ('The Vanishing Mediator; or, Max Weber as Storyteller'); Slavoj Žižek, *For They Know Not What They Do: Enjoyment as a Political Factor* (Verso, 1991) 179–88; Sterne (2003) particularly 218.

MADAM PRESIDENT: There is an—wait a minute, Mr Witness. There is an interference from the interpreter's booth. I don't know if the technicians can improve on that.

MR MORLEY: (*Microphones overlapping*) ... Your Honours, there is no interference in my headphones. I know not if there is a problem at the other end of the Court.

MADAM PRESIDENT: We have interference, and so has Defence, I see from Mr Ngeze nodding. So you are privileged.[32]

Indeed, for the first several months of Bikindi's trial, immediately following the recitation of appearances, Presiding Judge Weinberg de Roca would habitually check with Bikindi that he was able to follow correctly on his headphones before commencing substantive proceedings:

MADAM PRESIDENT: Thank you very much. Appearances for the Defence, please?

MR NDERITU: Thank you, Your Honour. Wilfred Nderitu, counsel for Mr Bikindi, together with Mr Jean de Dieu Momo, co-counsel for Mr Bikindi.

MADAM PRESIDENT: Thank you very much. Mr Bikindi, your headphones are fine? Can you follow the proceedings?[33]

In this example the headphones were functioning properly as it turned out, but Bikindi had forgotten to switch on his microphone.

Effective microphone usage is an ongoing struggle at the Tribunal, particularly—though not exclusively—where untutored witnesses are concerned.[34] It is not just that people forget to turn them on, and are therefore both inaudible and uninterpretable as a result. Participants need to learn to 'play' their microphones properly. Sometimes it is a question of efficiency: 'Mr Witness, don't switch your microphone off. Just leave it on. Then it is not a problem every time you have to answer.'[35] Sometimes proximity: 'Madam Witness, if you can please sit straight so that your mouth is nearer the microphone.'[36] And conversely 'Madam President, if the witness could be advised to sit back from the microphone. He is breathing into the microphone.'[37] Sometimes it is a matter of volume: 'Please make sure that you speak loudly enough that it comes through on the earphones, right, madam?'[38] Or again, 'Message to Madam President from the English booth. I do not believe she has her headphones on. Could the witness please be requested to speak clearly and loudly?'[39] And on another occasion the reverse, 'Mr Witness, please speak more softly because if you answer in a loud voice, we cannot hear the interpretation.'[40] The website of the International Association of Conference Interpreters (AIIC) says the following of what it calls 'microphone discipline':

[32] *Prosecutor v Bikindi* (Transcript) ICTR-01-72-T, T Ch III (Various dates) ('*Bikindi* transcript') 19 February 2007, 9–10. For other examples see, eg, *Bikindi* transcript: 27 September 2006, 2, 33; 3 October 2007, 13.

[33] *Bikindi* transcript, 22 September 2006, 1.

[34] Even several years into the trial, Presiding Judge Weinberg de Roca needed to be reminded to switch her microphone on: *Bikindi* transcript, 31 October 2007, 37.

[35] *Bikindi* transcript, 12 October 2006, 10.

[36] *Bikindi* transcript, 24 September 2007, 7.

[37] *Bikindi* transcript, 26 September 2006, 6.

[38] *Bikindi* transcript, 1 October 2007, 47.

[39] *Bikindi* transcript, 31 October 2007, 2.

[40] *Bikindi* transcript, 5 October 2007, 37.

'Microphones tend to amplify not only the interpreter's voice, but also all of the sounds in the booth around him/her (rustling papers, doors opening and closing, colleagues' coughs, pens scratching on paper). Consequently, strict discipline is recommended ... in order to spare the audience's ears.'[41] What these examples evidence is the obvious fact that sound-reproduction technologies do more than simply record and reproduce the sounds of the juridical environment. They change them. They alter how people at the ICTR act, speak, and, occasionally, sing.[42]

Mark Katz, in his study of the effects of technology on music-making practices in the twentieth century, has referred to this phenomenon as the 'phonograph effect': 'any observable manifestation', that is, 'of recording's influence'.[43] He gives the example of 'crooning', the 'soft, restrained vocal style popular from the 1920s to the 1950s, heard in the singing of Rudy Vallee, Bing Crosby, Perry Como, and Frank Sinatra'. Crooning, Katz argues, was made possible 'only with the microphone, because without amplification such singing would be expressively flat and nearly inaudible. Yet the technique achieved a remarkable effect. Crooning is akin to whispering, which under normal circumstances can be heard only when one is physically very close to the speaker; crooning thus provides a sense of intimacy between artist and audience, collapsing the technologically imposed distance that would seem to preclude such a relationship.'[44] The practice of contemporary international criminal justice, it turns out, is a lot like crooning. It too was made possible only with the microphone. Like Bing Crosby and Frank Sinatra before them, every lawyer, judge, and witness who wishes to participate in a trial at the ICTR must learn to use this instrument correctly. Sterne puts it like this. 'Machines [do] not simply "capture" sounds that already existed in the world', he says. As long as sound-reproduction technologies have existed, he says, people have always 'performed for the machines'.[45] In law, it falls to the judge to conduct this performance.

Conducting the Soundscape

Legal institutions have always been careful about how their soundscapes are arranged, policed, and conducted. The yellow signs which adorn the corridors outside the courtrooms at the ICTR are typical in this respect. 'SILENCE PLEASE!' they read, 'COURT IN SESSION': capitalized and with the exclamation mark. Red signs prohibit mobile phone usage both in the courtrooms themselves and

[41] 'Discipline au Micro', AIIC, accessed 6 March 2015, Available at: <http://web.archive.org/web/20120512190256/http:/aiic.net/glossary/default.cfm?ID=190> (snapshot dated 12 May 2012).

[42] On one occasion Bikindi stopped midway through a performance to complain that he was being put off by the interpretation he could hear on his headset: *Bikindi* transcript, 31 October 2007, 35.

[43] Mark Katz, *Capturing Sound: How Technology Has Changed Music* (University of California Press, 2010) 2.

[44] Katz (2010) 46.

[45] Sterne (2003) 235.

around them.[46] Relative quiet, it seems, is at once a condition and a sign of the proper administration of justice. Along with various symbolic and spatial aspects of a courtroom's architecture and design, it works to limit and determine both the modes of comportment and the 'enunciative modalities', to adopt the Foucaultian terminology, available at trial.[47] Above all, a quiet space suggests an attitude of respect and deference to whoever it is—whether priest, actor, conductor, or judge—that has presumably been authorized to breach the peace. This is why the gavel continues to be such an important object. Although at the ICTR it is used only infrequently, and even then mostly just to mark the adjournment of proceedings for the day, one can be found in every courtroom nevertheless.

There is a sense in which the gavel is an intensely practical device. Before it symbolizes anything, it has certain acoustical properties which make it well suited for disrupting noise and attracting attention. A sharp rap or two on the hardwood sounding-block is normally sufficient to pierce through any unwanted hubbub. Today, the gavel's significance is unquestionably more symbolic than practical. Or, to put it another way, its significance is practical precisely because it is symbolic. What it symbolizes is the judge's authority to determine who gets to speak, when, and in what ways. Apart from the 'illocutionary' force of the judicial word,[48] this is quite possibly the most significant power a judge yields at trial. It is not that it is necessarily crucial to the maintenance of orderly discourse. A court could, in principle, have an 'impartial' moderator of sorts, along the lines of the 'speaker' in the parliamentary system. But in practical and aesthetic terms the fact that it chooses not to is important. The very fact that control over juridical discourse *is* invested in the judge in this way both signals and regularly underlines the completeness of their authority at the level of performance: day in, day out, session after session, hearing after hearing.

The gavel, then, is the acoustic equivalent of the judges' robes, or the raising of their bench. It is a symbol of power, of the right to speak and determine who speaks, to decide who gets to hear what and when: an acoustic index, in other words, of the judge's authority to decide per se. Within the parameters of the material limits set by architecture and technology, the gavel invests control over the judicial soundscape exclusively in the office of the judge. Moreover, the fact that this control has been so successfully internalized by the legal institution that, in practice, judges rarely need to use their gavel at all, does not render it any less potent. Quite the opposite in fact. The gavel's silence only serves to make the judge's authority over the soundscape all the more complete.

[46] According to what has come to be an internationally accepted semiotics, yellow signifies a 'warning' whereas 'red' refers to a prohibition. Nametags on office doors at the Tribunal are mostly blue.

[47] See Peter Goodrich, *Languages of Law: From Logics of Memory to Nomadic Masks* (Weidenfeld and Nicolson, 1990) especially 188–93. See also Mulcahy (2011); Michel Foucault, *The Archaeology of Knowledge*, trans A M Sheridan Smith (Routledge, 1989) [trans of: *L'Archéologie du savoir* (first published 1969)] 50–6.

[48] See Chapter 6.

At the ICTR at least, judges are increasingly delegating their work in this respect to technology.[49] At trial, lawyers, judges, and witnesses regularly need to convey sensitive information without certain others present being able to hear. Prior to the wiring of the courtroom, the problem would most likely have been managed by whispering. And occasionally it still is.

MR GABAAKE: Mr Witness, listen; This gentleman works in my office, the one there. So whisper to him the address. He is part of the Prosecution, and then he will write it down, okay?

THE ENGLISH INTERPRETER: Madam President, could the microphones be switched off?[50]

But far more frequently the presiding judge will simply ask the person they do not want to hear a particular passage of conversation to remove their headphones so that the relevant legal officials may converse in a language which that person does not understand. Unable to hear the interpretation, they will have been rendered deaf for juridical purposes. 'Perhaps if the witness might remove his headphones, please. I'm raising this without the witness being able to hear it, so that my learned friend may make any observations and Your Honours may reflect on it.'[51] Rather than asking the interpreter not to translate what is being said, the task is delegated to the audio-technology itself. Moreover, this is a practice which is reproduced constantly. On the second day of Bikindi's trial alone, for example, I count no less than eight separate occasions on which witnesses were asked temporarily to remove their headphones.[52] It was not atypical in this respect. Now, this may admittedly not be an especially breath-taking advance for contemporary juridical practice. But what it does evidence is an institution which has learned to be sensitive to the particularities of its acoustic ecology, and is able to develop specialized listening practices and techniques in response. If the gavel symbolizes the authority of the judge over the soundscape, headphones are increasingly their tools for exercising it.

Simultaneous Interpretation

The child of international law

By this point it should be clear that the wiring of the courtrooms for sound accounts for many of the distinctive features of the judicial soundscape at the ICTR. I hope it is also clear that the reason they have been wired this way is to facilitate the system of so-called 'simultaneous interpretation', and that it is this system which makes dialogue across three languages at the Tribunal possible. It is time now to say a little more about simultaneous interpretation, its origins—which

[49] Sterne (2003) ch 1 ('Machines to Hear for Them').
[50] *Bikindi* transcript, 12 October 2006, 20.
[51] *Bikindi* transcript, 18 September 2006, 44.
[52] *Bikindi* transcript, 19 September 2006, 9, 14, 18, 19, 29, 36, 40, 41.

are steadfastly juridical—and its most important effects on the soundscape in the practice of international law.

The system of simultaneous interpretation employed by the ICTR today was crafted, according to Francesca Gaiba, 'by trial and error in an attic room of the Nuremberg Palace of Justice'.[53] This was in 1945, in preparation for the famous Nuremberg Trial at which twenty-four defendants (including Hermann Göring and Rudolf Hess) were tried for war crimes by the Allied powers in the immediate aftermath of World War II. Today, the trial is most often remembered for its historical and political dimensions, and for its influence on the then nascent norms of International Humanitarian, Criminal and Human Rights Law which would go on to be developed in a number of key treatises and conventions at the end of the 1940s.[54] But it was crucial for another reason too, particularly if one is looking at it from the perspective of an acoustic jurisprudence. Nuremberg was the first trial ever to be conducted multilingually, in several languages at the same time (namely English, French, Russian, and German). The multilingual trial has since become the standard mechanism of international justice, but in 1945 it was unheard of: a completely novel juridical form. The system that made it feasible, by means of a marriage between recent technological developments and an established but exceptionally difficult form of interpretative practice, is quite possibly *the* unsung hero of international justice, especially in technical or material terms. It is not just that without it 'the Nuremberg Trial would not have been possible'.[55] None of the Tribunals established to mete out international justice since then would have been possible either. At Nuremberg, the 'bizarre view of a courtroom full of people with earphones competed for media and public interest with the presence of Hermann Göring and Rudolf Hess'. One reporter even thought it 'looked like a telephone exchange.'[56] Today, by contrast, if you were to browse the websites of any major international organization, it wouldn't be very long before you stumbled across a photograph of some key figure wearing headphones. Since Nuremberg, headphones have become virtually symbolic of international order itself, the material signifier of a discursive field that is utterly reliant on the technics of simultaneous interpretation for its success.

In 1945 interpretation was nothing new. It had been around since Babel. It was only in the twentieth century, however, that it was professionalized following the abandonment of French as the *lingua franca* of European diplomacy at the Paris Peace Conference in 1920 and the subsequent founding of the first School for Interpretation in Geneva in 1941. The British insisted that English be recognized as an official diplomatic language, creating a permanent need for oral

[53] Francesca Gaiba, *The Origins of Simultaneous Interpretation: The Nuremberg Trial* (University of Ottawa Press, 1998) 11.

[54] George Ginsburgs and Vladimir N Kudriavtsev (eds), *The Nuremberg Trial and International Law* (Kluwer, 1990); Ellis Washington, *The Nuremberg Trials: Last Tragedy of the Holocaust* (University Press of America, 2008); Arnold Krammer, *War Crimes, Genocide, and the Law: A Guide to the Issues* (Praeger, 2010); Gerry Simpson, *Law, War and Crime: War Crimes Trials and the Reinvention of International Law* (Polity, 2007).

[55] Gaiba (1998) 20. [56] Gaiba (1998) 59.

interpretation from that point forward. At the numerous international conferences which followed World War I, two primary techniques were used. First and most commonly, so-called 'consecutive interpretation'. With this method, the interpreter takes notes during the delivery of a speech and the speaker stops either at the end of every sentence or every section, depending on what has been agreed, so that the interpreter can reformulate what they have heard in the target language by reading back from their notes. The second method is known as 'whispered interpretation'. Here the interpreter sits next to the person who does not understand the working language and whispers the translation into their ear whilst the speech is actually ongoing. The problem in the first case is that it makes proceedings excruciatingly slow. The problem in the second case is that it is intrusive, noisy, and only workable on a very small scale.[57] When it came to preparing for Nuremberg, therefore, the International Military Tribunal found itself in a bind. On the one hand, its enabling charter granted defendants the right to a fair trial, one requirement of which, according to Articles 16 and 25 of the Tribunal's Charter, was that proceedings be comprehensible to them in their native tongue, which in this case was German.[58] On the other hand, Articles 18 and 19 also sought to guarantee that the trial be carried out as quickly as practically possible. Defendants were granted the right to justice at a reasonable tempo.

'In order to reduce costs and time, and to keep the attention of the public and the media', the trial had not only to be 'just', but 'expeditious' too.[59] According to Article 18, the Tribunal would be confined 'strictly to an expeditious hearing of the cases raised by the charges' and was required to 'take strict measures to prevent any action which will cause reasonable delay'.[60] According to Article 19, it would not be bound by the 'technical rules of evidence' and should 'adopt and apply to the greatest possible extent expeditious and nontechnical procedure'.[61] Today, proceedings at the ICTR too must be both 'fair' and 'expeditious' too.[62] Consecutive interpretation may have worked well enough for long diplomatic speeches at large conferences, but the relatively quick-fire dialogue of legal discourse would be a different matter entirely. A system was needed that would maintain something of the 'spontaneity and rapidity' of legal questioning.[63] And because whispered

[57] The AIIC recommends that the method not be used 'when there are more than two listeners or when several interpreters need to work at the same time in the same room (since this could create too much noise and is as unpleasant for the interpreters as for the audience)': 'Conference Interpretation Modes', AIIC, accessed 5 March 2015, <http://aiic.net/page/1629/conference-interpretation-modes/lang/1>.

[58] Agreement for the Prosecution and Punishment of the Major War Criminals of the European Axis (signed and entered into force 8 August 1945) 82 UNTS 279, annex ('Charter of the International Military Tribunal') arts 16, 25.

[59] Gaiba (1998) 32.

[60] Charter of the International Military Tribunal, art 18.

[61] Charter of the International Military Tribunal, art 19.

[62] This requirement appears at art 19(1) of the ICTR Statute: 'The Trial Chambers shall ensure that a trial is fair and expeditious and that proceedings are conducted in accordance with the rules of procedure and evidence, with full respect for the rights of the accused with due regard for the protection of victims and witnesses.' See also, International Criminal Tribunal for Rwanda, 'Rules of Procedure and Evidence' (29 June 1995) UN Doc ITR/3/REV.1 ('Rules of Procedure and Evidence').

[63] Colonel Léon Dostert, the inventor of simultaneous interpretation, quoted by Gaiba (1998) 101.

interpretation was obviously unworkable on the requisite scale, the only available solutions were to conduct proceedings solely in German or to come up with a better system. Given that a German trial was both politically and practically unworkable—it would be impossible to find both judges and prosecutors from each of the four countries responsible for conducting the trial who were both competent enough legally and sufficiently fluent in German—clearly some less intrusive and more efficient method needed to be devised.

By the end of the war, the technology required for simultaneous interpretation—the system of microphones, headsets, and the ability to switch between several audio-channels—had been available for some time already in the form of IBM's Hushaphone system.[64] Prior to Nuremberg, however, it had only ever been used for a variant of the consecutive method known as 'simultaneous successive interpretation' where the interpretations were simultaneous with each other, but not with the original speech. According to Gaiba:

> At the League of Nations and the [International Labour Organization], for example, the various interpreters would take notes on the original speech, as for [normal] consecutive interpretation; after the end of the speech, one of the interpreters, usually the French interpreter, would take the stand and translate consecutively into his language. At the same time, the other interpreters, sitting in the booths and speaking into their microphones, gave their version of the speech in English, Spanish etc., reading from their notes. In this way, the translation was still consecutive and therefore fairly accurate, and the time required to translate into all languages greatly reduced, in comparison to the normal consecutive mode.[65]

For a trial, though, this system was still far too slow. And in the end, it was Eisenhower's old interpreter, Colonel Léon Dostert, who convinced the Tribunal that the Hushaphone system could be adapted for the purposes of 'spontaneous, immediate interpretation'.[66] According to this system, the interpreter would speak at the same time as they were listening, as with the whispering method, but because they were speaking into microphones rather than to a pair of listeners at close quarters, a single interpreter would suffice for each language such that only twelve interpreters would be needed in all[67] (see Figure 8.1).

When Colonel Dostert explained the system he was about to implement to the Tribunal's delegations from France, the Soviet Union, and Great Britain, however, the reaction apparently 'swung between simple concern and overt scepticism'. Evidently, 'it seemed to them a task beyond human capabilities to hear and speak

[64] Not to be confused with the Hush-A-Phone device, which went on to become the subject of a famous ruling in the United States telecommunications law. See *Hush-A-Phone v United States*, 238 F 2d 266 (DC Cir, 1956). IBM's Hushaphone was patented in 1926 and used for the first time in 1927 at the International Labour Conference in Geneva. See Gaiba (1998) 30–1.

[65] Gaiba (1998) 31.

[66] Gaiba (1998) 35, quoting E Peter Uiberall, one of the interpreters who worked on the trial, in a letter to the author.

[67] This system is known as the 'non-relay system'. The ICTR uses the 'relay system' instead, and therefore only requires three interpreters at a time. I explain this system at Figure 8.2.

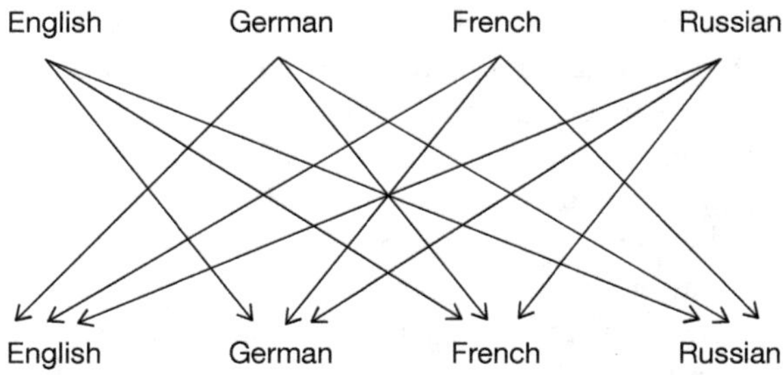

Figure 8.1 Simultaneous interpretation at Nuremberg
© James E K Parker.

at the same time in different languages'.[68] And it is certainly difficult. On top of an excellent knowledge of both relevant languages, it requires an exceptionally refined audile technique which in normal circumstances can take many years to acquire.[69] It is a skill that even the best interpreters are not always able to master. More than 200 highly qualified interpreters were tested prior to the Nuremberg trial before the Tribunal's translation division was able to obtain the thirty-six simultaneous interpreters it needed: that is, three teams of twelve.[70] In general, they succeeded admirably,[71] and particularly with so little time for preparation.[72] The trial lasted more than ten months and comprised some 216 days in court; a long time by any standards. Without simultaneous interpretation, however, it would undoubtedly have lasted much, much longer.[73] Indeed, according to Evelyn Moggio-Ortiz, the system worked so well that Göring is said to have complained that it had cut his lifespan by three-quarters.[74]

Though it is probably best known today as a commonplace at international meetings and conferences the world over, and particularly at the UN, simultaneous interpretation is indisputably the child of international law. It was conceived in a court, by a court, and for specifically legal reasons. First, the system arose

[68] Gaiba (1998) 37.

[69] The degree of concentration required for this kind of interpretation is so great that in principle interpreters at the ICTR are supposed to work in shifts of only thirty minutes at a time. In practice, this is not always possible.

[70] Gaiba (1998) 48.

[71] See Gaiba (1998) 95–131 (ch 3, 'Reliability and Impact of the Interpretation').

[72] While the interpreters at Nuremberg had just a few weeks, and in some cases a matter of days, to learn how to use the system effectively, the standard contemporary qualification takes a number of years to complete. See, eg, 'Faculty of Translation and Interpreting', University of Geneva, accessed 5 March 2015, <http://www.unige.ch/eti/enseignements_en.html>. On the training of interpreters at Nuremberg see also Gaiba (1998) 49.

[73] Gaiba (1998) 11.

[74] Evelyn Moggio-Ortiz, *The Interpreters: A Historical Perspective* (United Nations, 1995)—film produced on the occasion of the 50th anniversary of the United Nations; 'A Video Film on Conference Interpreters', AIIC, accessed 5 March 2015, <http://www.aiic.net/ViewPage.cfm/article1104.htm>; Evelyn Moggio-Ortiz, 'Multilingualism as a Path to Multilateralism: Interpreters Meet History', *UN Special*, No 678, (November 2008) <http://www.unspecial.org/UNS678/t21.html>.

partly as a simple matter of doctrine. As long as the issue of interpretation was framed in terms of economic and temporal efficiency, the need to innovate was not felt sufficiently strongly to warrant the difficult step of training large numbers of interpreters to listen and speak at the same time. By making the tempo of judicial proceedings a matter of right, however, the Charter of the International Military Tribunal provided a different kind of impetus entirely. And it was the combination of this juridical imperative with more material considerations that proved decisive in the end. Although the technology to implement the system had existed already for some twenty or so years, it was not until interpreters were confronted with the specifically judicial soundscape—the constant to-ing and fro-ing of legal discourse, complete with interruptions, objections, and asides: the 'breathtaking rhythm' of examination as Gaiba eloquently terms it—that the necessity of a completely novel interpretative method became clear.[75]

Judgment has a tempo and a rhythm

Now that simultaneous interpretation has become embedded in the practice of international law, what impact has it had on the way international legal discourse actually sounds? And, correlatively, on the way in which legal actors are required to listen? Today, proceedings at the ICTR still move almost painfully slowly. The word 'simultaneous', it turns out, is misleading to say the least. Interpreters, obviously, must understand a minimum of information before they can begin their translation. The lag between the original and interpreted version is called *décalage*. It varies between interpreters, but it can easily be as much as about seven or eight seconds. What this means in practice is that everyone is constantly waiting for the interpretation to filter through on their headphones before proceedings can move on. As a result, the kind of speech patterns that emerge are incredibly fragmented. Simultaneous interpretation, that is, radically changes the nature of legal eloquence. Inside a courtroom at the Tribunal, speech has its own very particular tempo and rhythm.

'Every thought must have weight, every word must be impressive', opined Cicero in *De Oratore*. 'To this must be joined a delivery that is varied, vehement, full of ardour and energy, full of real emotion.'[76] Well, not at the ICTR. Oratory at the ICTR sounds sluggish and fractured. It is slow and disjointed and, what's more, not at all easy to master. It requires an extraordinary amount of patience both on the part of the person speaking and the listener. Judges and interpreters are constantly putting the brakes on speakers who lapse into their preferred metre. The following was typical at Bikindi's trial:

MADAM PRESIDENT: Mr Witness, please give us a short answer and speak more slowly. It's very difficult for the interpreters when you speak so quickly. So speak slowly, make

[75] Gaiba (1998) 102.

[76] Marcus Tullius Cicero, *On the Ideal Orator*, trans James M May and Jakob Wisse (Oxford University Press, 2001) [trans of: *De Oratore* (first published 55 BCE)] Book II, 142, para 73.

pauses, and stop after giving a short answer so that Prosecution can tell you whether they want you to continue with what you are saying or want you to go in a different direction. Please answer the questions. Don't repeat what you want to say. But, first, listen to the question.

MS WRIGHT (assistant counsel for the prosecution): Thank you, Your Honours. That's helpful.[77]

In this example, Presiding Judge Weinberg de Roca actually performs the very rhythm and tempo of speech that she wants the witness to imitate. Her speech here is so fragmented, so broken up with pauses, that in any other context it would sound comedic. Although it probably took you only about fifteen or twenty seconds to read, at trial the short passage above lasted for over a minute.

It is not just inexperienced witnesses that require coaching. More experienced legal officials regularly forget themselves too.

MADAM PRESIDENT: Slow down, please.

MR NDERITU (counsel for the defence): I beg your pardon. Yes, I was saying that it is my belief that the Prosecution is in possession of the original passport. And the passport or, at least a copy of it has been used in the previous proceedings before this Tribunal. What we have quite clearly is the referencing by the OTP which is K0073632. I'm sure the Prosecutor would be in a position to assist us in this regard. Thank you.

MR EGBE (counsel for the prosecution): Your Honour, we do not have the passport of the Accused. And as a matter of fact, the Accused, himself, when he was interrogated by the Dutch police indicated, it is in the written statement, that he destroyed his passport. He lost his passport. It's documented. Now, what was provided were copies.

MADAM PRESIDENT: Slowly, please.

MR EGBE: What were provided were photocopies of some pages of that passport. And that was provided, photocopies.

MADAM PRESIDENT: Slow, please.[78]

Or consider the following example from 17 October 2007. Both the witness and the lawyer examining him speak English, but neither has been leaving sufficient pauses for the interpreters. Rather than simply mandating that they speak slower, however, Judge Weinberg de Roca's asks that they modify their listening practice too, their audile technique. In a neat juridical manifestation of what John Drever, in a different context, has termed 'periscopic listening', she suggests to counsel for the defence that he wear his headphones in such a way that he can listen to the witness with one ear and the French interpretation with the other.[79] That way, he will know precisely when the interpretation has finished and will be able to determine the rhythm and tempo of his examination accordingly.

[77] *Bikindi* transcript, 27 September 2006, 35.

[78] *Bikindi* transcript, 18 September 2006, 27–8.

[79] John Levack Drever, 'Ochlophonics Hong Kong: Everyday Sound Practices within the Crowd' (Paper presented at Music, Sound and the Reconfiguration of Public and Private Space, Cambridge, United Kingdom, 18–19 April 2008).

French booth:

- English (floor channel) ⟶ French

English booth:

- French (floor channel) ⟶ English
- French* (from Kiny. booth) ⟶ English

Kinyarwanda booth:

- English (floor channel) ⟶ Kinyarwanda
- French (floor channel) ⟶ Kinyarwanda
- Kinyarwanda (floor channel) ⟶ French* (which is then relayed into English in the English booth)

Figure 8.2 The relay system at the ICTR

MADAM PRESIDENT: Please, we need a pause between question and answer, and we need you to speak slower ... You're not giving the French reporters nor the interpreters an opportunity to catch up ... Please, pause both of—Mr O'Shea, Mr Witness, a pause. Mr O'Shea, I suggest you do what I'm doing, have one—have the headphone on French with one ear, then you can follow.

MR O'SHEA (counsel for the defence): Okay. Is that number two? All right. That's much better.[80]

If tempo was amongst the most common practical concerns during the *Bikindi* case, matters were not helped by the fact that, for reasons of efficiency, the Tribunal has elected to use the so-called 'relay system' rather than the method employed at Nuremberg. What this means in practice is that rather than the Kinyarwanda spoken in the trial chamber being translated directly into English, it always goes by way of French first. And obviously this increases the duration of the *décalage* between original and interpretation considerably: doubles it, in fact.

The system at the ICTR works like this. The interpreters in the French booth translate everything said in English on the floor channel into French. The interpreters in the English booth translate everything said on the floor channel in French directly into English and everything said in Kinyarwanda into English via French relay. The interpreters in the Kinyarwanda booth translate everything said on the floor channel in English and French into Kinyarwanda as well as everything said in Kinyarwanda on the floor channel into French, both for those who want to listen in French and for the English booth to re-interpret into English (see Figure 8.2).

By employing the relay system, the ICTR is able to get by with only three interpreters at any given moment. This is obviously a major improvement over the Nuremberg system at the level of resources even if it does produce an additional *ritardando* in

[80] *Bikindi* transcript, 17 October 2007, 12–13.

practice. But one thing is abundantly clear. As far as the tempo of international justice is concerned, simultaneous interpretation—and especially when practised according to the relay system—represents a compromise: a compromise which, since 1945, has now become settled at the level of international legal policy. The great achievement of simultaneous interpretation—and it is a great one—is to render international justice *lento ma non troppo*: slow, but not too slow. As David Maxwell-Fyfe, the British Prosecutor at Nuremberg put it at the time, the slow pace of examination was 'not a high price to pay for ... justice in four voices'.[81] At the ICTR we get it in three.

Judgment has an accent

So far we have been concerned with how simultaneous interpretation alters the character of legal eloquence prior to interpretation. Now I want to consider the sound of interpreted speech. Strictly speaking, interpreters at the ICTR are meant to reproduce the intonation, emphasis, pace, and tone of the speech they are interpreting.[82] This isn't an absolute rule. If a witness is crying as they testify, interpreters are not meant to mimic their distress: first, because it would be insensitive to do so and, second, because the distress will most likely be sufficiently evident visually in any case. Similarly, when Bikindi sang at trial, which he did on several occasions, interpreters were not expected to do likewise. When one particularly bold interpreter did attempt to sing his interpretation, this was regarded as an amusing anomaly rather than a breach of courtroom etiquette. Counsel for the defence joked: 'If you get acquitted, Mr Bikindi, there's a gentleman in the interpreter's booth who's worthy of review for his singing talent. I'll just inform you.'[83] Nevertheless, the basic operating principle at the ICTR is that interpreted speech should remain as faithful to the original as possible, in all its various semantic dimensions, prosodic as well as verbal. After all, as Mladen Dolar points out, 'intonation can turn the meaning of a sentence upside down; it can transform it into its opposite. A slight note of irony, and a serious meaning comes tumbling down; a note of distress, and the joke will backfire.'[84] If a lawyer or a witness employs a sarcastic tone of voice, that is supposed to be maintained. Likewise if they are angry or timid, calm or enthused. The first principle of the interpreter, to paraphrase Eric Prenowitz, is that they should 'never really be there'.[85] They should vanish, in

[81] Gaiba (1998) 102.

[82] According to one paper on the AIIC's website, 'ideally, interpreters should reproduce the same intonation as the speaker'. This is a position that was corroborated in my conversations with interpreters working at the ICTR during my visit in 2011. Chantal Besson et al, 'The Importance of Non-Verbal Communication in Professional Interpretation', AIIC, 19 January 2005 (updated 22 May 2012) <http://www.aiic.net/ViewPage.cfm/page1662.htm#51>.

[83] *Bikindi* transcript, 1 November 2007, 35.

[84] Mladen Dolar, *A Voice and Nothing More* (MIT Press, 2006) 21.

[85] This is an appropriation of Eric Prenowitz's turn of phrase in relation to his translation of Derrida's *Mal d'Archive: Une Impression Freudienne* into English. It applies equally well, I think, in the context of interpretation. See Jacques Derrida, *Archive Fever: A Freudian Impression*, trans Eric Prenowitz (University of Chicago Press, 1996) [trans of: *Mal d'archive: Une impression Freudienne* (originally presented as a lecture in London, 5 June 1994)] 105 ('Translator's Note').

other words, even in the very act of mediation. They should render themselves as transparent, as pure a conduit of the original speech as possible. In theory at least, this rule applies at the level of sound as well as words.

The question for an acoustic jurisprudence, therefore, is as follows. What are we to make of the fact that despite the very best efforts of the ICTR's Interpretation Unit, interpreted speech at the Tribunal sounds *nothing* like uninterpreted speech at all? That when you listen to the recordings of the *Bikindi* case you simply can't help but be aware that you are hearing an interpretation? It's not just that so much is clearly being 'lost in translation'. That is a real problem, but it is to be expected. Interpretation, as we have already seen, represents a kind of necessary compromise and its first principle, therefore, is more aspirational than realistic.[86] The really important point for an acoustic jurisprudence is that simultaneous interpretation fundamentally changes the sound of legal discourse and, with it, the way in which legal actors are required to listen.

To some extent, the fact of interpretation is so palpable acoustically because of the *décalage* already discussed. *Décalage* doesn't just fracture 'original' speech in the courtroom, it fractures interpreted speech too. Because interpreters are forced to pause so frequently mid-phrase, the emphasis of a sentence is constantly being forced onto the wrong word or syllable, altering its cadence and flow. Interpreted speech often sounds lopsided, its metre strange. More than this, however, it has a tendency to sound flat and expressionless. The introduction of simultaneous interpretation into the courtroom doesn't simply change the tempo and the rhythm of justice, it gives it a very particular accent too.

If it is possible in principle to discern and 'reproduce' many of the structural elements of prosodic expression, doing so in practice—across languages and cultures, under extreme time pressure and with the additional mediation of the relay system thrown in to boot—is a different matter entirely.[87] And as a result interpreted speech can sound strangely neutral, lifeless somehow, expressively bland. Occasionally it will even have a faintly irritating quality to it, a timbre and a pitch that grates. As the AIIC's website explains: 'The interpreter's voice is an essential working instrument. Interpreters must maintain good control over their voice, timbre, diction and articulation so that listening is pleasant and comfortable for the audience.'[88] Evidently, this is not always an easy task. Even where the interpreter is able to inject a degree of vigour into their speech, it invariably retains a certain mediated quality. You can tell acoustically that the sentiment comes second

[86] For treatments of court interpreting specifically, see Elena M de Jongh, *An Introduction to Court Interpreting: Theory & Practice* (University Press of America, 1992); Susan Berk-Seligson, *The Bilingual Courtroom: Court Interpreters in the Judicial Process* (University of Chicago Press, 1990); Nancy A Combs, *Fact-Finding without Facts: The Uncertain Evidentiary Foundations of International Criminal Convictions* (Cambridge University Press, 2010) especially ch 3. For general discussion of the problem of translation per se, see Lawrence Venuti (ed), *The Translation Studies Reader* (3rd edn, Routledge, 2012).

[87] See Chapter 5.

[88] 'Voix', AIIC, accessed 6 March 2015, Available at: <http://web.archive.org/web/20120512190117/http:/aiic.net/glossary/default.cfm?ID=286> (snapshot dated 12 May 2012).

hand. Often it is possible to detect surprise too. You can actually hear the shock in the interpreter's voice: not at the content of what they are interpreting, but at their having been able to interpret it at all. To be an interpreter, after all, is to live on the edge, in the moment, never quite sure what is coming next, but obliged to react instantly no matter what. Interpreted speech does not sound natural because it is not natural. It never comes naturally. It is always work.

The upshot of all this is that listening to interpreted speech is difficult. Simultaneous interpretation means that legal actors must learn not only to speak differently as we saw in the previous section, but to listen differently too. The listening practice required of participants in a trial at the ICTR simply involves an unusual degree of concentration. This is listening as a form of 'straining'.[89] In order to participate effectively in contemporary international justice mechanisms one must learn to listen past the blandness and the lengthy delays, force oneself to make sense of the stumbling cadence, to 'strain toward a possible meaning'.[90] And this straining, this listening practice, turns out to engage the eye as well as the ear.

Listening with your eyes

A soundscape is never purely acoustic. For French composer, critic, and pioneering sound-in-film scholar Michel Chion there is a fundamental interconnection between sight and sound: what Chion refers to as the 'audio-visual contract'.[91] 'We never see the same thing when we also hear', he argues, and nor do we 'hear the same thing when we see as well'.[92] It is this fact which accounts for the phenomenon of *synchresis* in film: 'the spontaneous and irresistible weld produced between a particular auditory phenomenon and visual phenomenon when they occur at the same time' and 'independently of any rational logic'.[93] In films, the socio-neuro-biological work of *synchresis* is what allows us to understand the sound of cornstarch being pressed as the crunch of footsteps in the snow, or the sound of a watermelon being crushed as a deadly blow to the head. Judicial practice at the ICTR might not be 'synchretic' exactly, but the intimacy of the connection between sight and sound is knowingly exploited by the Tribunal in order to maximize intelligibility. Interpreters, for example, insist on being able to see the people whose speech they are interpreting.

> Body language and gestures are an integral part of any discourse and need to be taken in by the interpreter in order to fully understand a speaker. The reaction of an audience, the expressions on participants' faces, the goings and comings in the room, are all part of the message the interpreter needs for his/her job. This is why the location of the booths is so

[89] Jean-Luc Nancy, *Listening*, trans Charlotte Mandell (Fordham University Press, 2007) [trans of: *À l'écoute* (first published 2002)] 6.

[90] Nancy (2007).

[91] Michel Chion, *Audio-Vision: Sound on Screen*, ed and trans Claudia Gorbman (Columbia University Press, 1994) [trans of: *L'Audio Vision: son et image au cinéma* (first published 1990)] pt 1.

[92] Chion (1994) xxvi.

[93] Chion (1994) 63.

important. They must be placed so that the interpreters, from their seats, can see the rostrum, the speakers, the screens and as much as possible of the room.[94]

Sure enough, this audio-visual logic is built right into the architecture of the courtrooms at the ICTR. And not only in respect of the interpreters, either. The courtrooms are designed in such a way that everyone can see each other, such that no one's audio-vision is obscured. On the rare occasion that the Tribunal permits testimony *in absentia* this is always by 'video-conference'.[95] The witness must be seen as well as heard.

One possible response to the Tribunal's reliance on the visual in this respect would be to call it evidence of law's complicity in the 'Platonic metaphysical project of conjoining knowledge and vision'.[96] For Piyel Haldar, for instance, 'oral evidence seems to be locked into a visual mode of estimating and examining testimony' such that 'what matters most is the visibility of the speaker'.[97] We believe witnesses' words *because* we see them. Maybe so. But at the ICTR, there is a distinctly non-metaphysical rationale at work too. The fact that listeners are able to see the person speaking is useful because it can help compensate for the interpreters' inability to convey vocally certain aspects of the original speech. The Tribunal understands that what we say with our voices, we often also inscribe on our bodies: in the grammar of the torso and the face. This mapping may not be perfect. Indeed, it can sometimes be genuinely misleading. But that is simply an argument in favour of greater audio-visual literacy, including the recognition of its necessary limitations, not a reason to avoid looking altogether. When the interpreters' voice nullifies the more expressive notes of a distraught witness' testimony, their shuddering body *does* affect the way we hear the corresponding interpretation. Our ability to see the testimony of a female witness *does* undo some of the violence of that testimony being rendered in the voice of a male interpreter and vice versa. When an interpreter renders both sides of a conversation in a single voice, our ability to see who is speaking *does* structure the way in which we hear and understand the dialogue. Just as we saw in Chapter 6 with the advent of the 'real time' transcript, sight is often put to work by the Tribunal expressly *in the service*

[94] AIIC, accessed 5 March 2013, <http://www.aiic.net/glossary/default.cfm?ID=36>. See also Chantal Besson, Daria Graf, Insa Hartung, Barbara Kropfhäusser, and Séverine Voisard, 'The Importance of Non-verbal Communication in Professional Interpretation' *AIIC*, 2004 <http://aiic.net/page/1662/the-importance-of-non-verbal-communication-in-professional-interpretation/lang/1#52>.

[95] Although the general rule is that witnesses should testify 'directly' as per r 90(A), r 71(D) allows for the provision of testimony 'by means of a video-conference' in exceptional circumstances. Teleconferencing is, however, permitted for the purpose of Status Conferences at r 65*bis*(C). See 'Rules of Procedure and Evidence', as amended on 8 June 1998.

[96] Piyel Haldar, 'Acoustic Justice' in Lionel Bently and Leo Flynn (eds), *Law and the Senses: Sensational Jurisprudence* (Pluto, 1996) 125. For further developments on this theme, see also Piyel Haldar, 'The Evidencer's Eye: Representations of Truth in the Laws of Evidence', *Law and Critique* 2(2) (1991) 171; Piyel Haldar, 'The Return of the Evidencer's Eye: Rhetoric and the Visual Technologies of Proof', *Griffith Law Review* 8(1) (1999) 86.

[97] Haldar (1996) 124.

of sound, not in order to ground or authorize it metaphysically, but simply in order to help make sense of it. We don't just look with our eyes, we listen with them too.

Broadcasting and the Archive

So far this chapter has treated the judicial soundscape as if it were bound by the walls of the courtroom and the duration of the trial as event. But the wiring of the courtroom for sound puts both those limits into question. This last section of the chapter considers some of the ways in which it is now possible to experience a trial such as Bikindi's 'acousmatically', entirely separated, that is, from the trial itself in terms of both time and space. These issues are particularly urgent for this book because it is only by virtue of recordings produced, edited, and curated by the Tribunal's Judicial Records and Archives Unit that much of the analysis both undertaken and advocated here was made possible.

Broadcast media

The main method available to the general public if they wished to access audio of proceedings at the ICTR was always by means of the traditional news media: the likes of the BBC, RFI, or CNN. News organizations such as these were able to access audio 'recordings' of ongoing trials at the ICTR in two ways. First, by sending a reporter to a hearing in person and having them make a recording directly from an infrared receiver so that it can then be incorporated into a radio or TV broadcast soon afterwards. Second, by 'tuning in' to the so-called ICTR by Satellite service which broadcasts 'live' audio-visual coverage of ongoing trials on an ongoing basis.[98] Of the two methods, the former was by far the most frequently used, the major news networks tending to tune in directly only for 'high impact' moments such as the delivery of a particularly significant judgment or the provision of high profile testimony such as that of Roméo Dallaire at the 'Military 1 Trial' in January 2004.[99]

With the Tribunal's last judgment delivered in December 2012, and with international interest having dwindled significantly even earlier, the ICTR's press room

[98] The coverage is transmitted with a five-minute delay to allow any sensitive information to be edited out in an emergency. Although the service is 'entirely free of charge' as the ICTR's website explains, the hardware required to actually receive the signal in the first place is very expensive, meaning that it is primarily large broadcasters that make use of it. 'ICTR by Satellite', International Criminal Tribunal for Rwanda, accessed 5 March 2015, Available at <http://207.150.203.251/tabid/67/default.aspx>.

[99] The 'Military 1 Trial' included Theoneste Bagosora, Gratien Kabiligi, Aloys Ntabakuze, and Anatole Nsengiyumva: *Prosecutor v Bagosora* (Judgement and Sentence) ICTR-98-41-T, T Ch I (18 December 2008). See 'General Romeo Dallaire Begins to Testify in Military Trial', *Hirondelle News Agency*, 19 January 2004, <http://www.hirondellenews.org/ictr-rwanda/343-trials-ended/military-i-trial/20169-en-en-general-romeo-dallaire-begins-to-testify-in-military-trial92209220>.

has been largely empty for some time, with one major exception.[100] Day in, day out, only the Hirondelle News Agency—the Rwandan arm of the Swiss-based and partially UN funded *Fondation Hirondelle* which specializes in the provision of media in conflict and post-conflict environments—persevered.[101] It is the only media organization which will have been present at the Tribunal throughout its duration. Operating in English, French, Kinyarwanda, and Swahili in text and audio only, today it is the primary source of up-to-date information and commentary on proceedings at the Tribunal both in Rwanda and the rest of the world. Government run Radio Rwanda, for instance, one of the stations directly implicated in the *Bikindi* case as we saw in Chapter 7, regularly includes excerpts from Hirondelle's weekly summary podcasts in its own broadcasts.[102] A re-tooling that is not without irony, moreover, considering the Tribunal's own statements about the inherent 'danger' of radio as a medium.[103] Here it is, twenty years after the genocide, projecting its own voice by the very same means throughout the Rwandan soundscape and beyond.

The audio-visual archive

As of the start of 2015, the Residual Mechanism is well into the process of compiling a complete audio and, as far as possible, audio-visual archive of proceedings conducted during the life of the ICTR, which it plans to make publicly available in redacted form.[104] Doing so will have required a huge amount of work at a tremendous expense. Every minute of every tape of every hearing has had to be digitized. Because in the early days of the Tribunal the video-recording equipment had not yet been installed, a number of trials are available in audio only. And because video equipment was never fitted at all in the Tribunal's fourth courtroom, no hearings held there, including significant portions of the *Bikindi* case (twenty-seven of the more than seventy days' worth of hearings), have yielded a video record. These audio tapes were all digitized manually using an analogue-to-digital tape deck. For the remaining audio-visual recordings, however, the Tribunal purchased and installed two robots which initially ran twenty-four hours a day, seven days a week, taking the analogue tapes, digitizing them as they played in real time, encoding

100 *Prosecutor v Ngirabatware* (Judgement and Sentence) ICTR-99-54-T, T Ch II (20 December 2012). 'Report on the Completion Strategy of the ICTR (as at 5 November 2012)' (14 November 2012) UN Doc S/2012/836 ('ICTR Completion Strategy Report, 14 November 2012') 4.

101 In addition to its branch at the ICTR in Arusha, since 1995 the *Fondation Hirondelle* has run media outlets, primarily radio, in Kosovo, East Timor, Nepal, the Central African Republic, Sierra Leone, Liberia, Sudan, and the Democratic Republic of Congo. Currently, it claims to reach an audience of 30 million. 'Our Media Outlets', Fondation Hirondelle, 31 January 2014, <http://www.hirondelle.org/index.php/en/our-media-outlets>.

102 'Weekly Summary', *Hirondelle News Agency*, accessed 5 March 2015, <http://www.hirondelle-news.org/weekly-summary>.

103 See Chapter 7.

104 'Report on the Completion Strategy of the International Criminal Tribunal for Rwanda (as at 5 November 2014)' (18 November 2013) UN Doc S/2014/829, 19; UNSC Progress Report (18 November 2013) UN Doc S/2013/679, annex I, paras 55–59.

them in multiple different file formats and then finally filing them electronically using a 'digital asset management system' called DIVA.[105] Both the hardware and the software involved in this process are absolutely cutting edge as far as current archival practice is concerned. The equipment was supplied by a company called Front Porch Digital which mostly works with large television networks, movie studios, museums, and major libraries, including, for instance, the American Broadcasting Company, the United States Holocaust Memorial Museum, and the Library of Congress.[106] Such was the weight of analogue material accrued by the Tribunal that, by the time they were finished, the robots had been running continuously for over a year.[107]

Once the audio and/or audio-visual 'masters' for a case had been digitized, the long process of redaction could begin. Whereas broadcasts from the Tribunal are left unmodified, the procedure for making a day's worth of archival recordings fit for public ears is lengthy and involved. First, a team of three 'audio-redactors' meets to discuss any potentially 'sensitive material' that may need to be removed from the recording of each of the English, French, and 'floor' channels respectively (the Kinyarwanda channel is not independently archived). Obviously, the redacted transcripts are a useful starting point in this respect, but as the manual developed collaboratively by members of the Judicial Records and Archives Unit during a pilot scheme run at the end of 2009 puts it, 'they are not to be used as a substitute for listening to the audio recordings'.[108] And the audio-redactors are therefore permitted to make further amendments as they see fit.[109]

Having carefully read the transcripts and debated them together as a group, each member then listens again to their respective audio file individually. This time, they are listening for both content and form: not just for the sort of 'sensitive information' necessary to safeguard the many protected witnesses' identities, but also for numerous other features which are removed in order to provide the tidiest, most user-friendly file possible. In the case of the English archive, for example, any words spoken in either French or Kinyarwanda which may have found their way onto the recording are to be removed, and vice versa.[110] Similarly for any instances of 'overlapping language',[111] or 'noise', which in this instance is understood in

[105] 'Solutions: Migrate, Manage, Market', Front Porch Digital, accessed 5 March 2015, <http://www.fpdigital.com/solutions>.

[106] For details on Front Porch Digital and some of the projects they have worked on, see: 'Case Studies: Migration', Front Porch Digital, accessed 5 March 2015, <http://www.fpdigital.com/case-studies/migration-case-studies>.

[107] As of November 2012, the ICTR and the ICTY had collectively digitized over 37,000 hours of audio-visual recordings: ICTR Completion Strategy Report, 14 November 2012.

[108] International Criminal Tribunal for Rwanda, *Redaction of the Audio-Visual Recordings of the UN ICTR: Methodology and Procedures Developed by the Judicial Records and Archives Unit, Court Management Section* (January 2011) ('*Audio-Visual Redaction Manual*') 8.

[109] *Audio-Visual Redaction Manual*, 13–14.

[110] *Audio-Visual Redaction Manual*, 15.

[111] *Audio-Visual Redaction Manual*, 16.

terms of audio quality.[112] Eventually, it is expected that the voices of protected witnesses will be distorted to the point of unrecognizability too.[113]

What is so interesting about this sort of practice for an acoustic jurisprudence is just how directly the nature of this work has required this particular branch of the Tribunal to confront the question of sound. The Judicial Records and Archives Unit is home to some of the most sophisticated listening practices in evidence at the Tribunal, as well as to the most explicitly prescribed. Its treatment of 'silence' is a particularly clear example in this respect.

There are three different shades of silence, apparently, which may occur in the Tribunal's audio files. Redactors need to be able to identify and appreciate the difference between each one. Silence is considered 'dead' if 'no background noise can be heard in the recording at all. It can occur, for instance, if the tape was recording in the deck while the audio was not on in the courtroom'.[114] Typically, a redactor will find 'dead' silence at the beginning and end of the file. But even if not, dead silences are easy to recognize visually in the software used for editing because 'there will be no variance in the waveform display and a flat line will be visible in the centre'.[115] This is a question of raw material fact, the simple presence or absence of recorded sound. Where a dead silence lasts for longer than half a second, it will be removed in the editing process and substituted with half a second's worth instead. Silence is considered to be 'noisy', on the other hand, if 'background noises (the shuffling of papers, atmospheric noise of the courtroom before trial starts, etc.) can be heard in the recording, but nothing is being said in the courtroom'.[116] Only noisy silences of longer than five seconds are to be marked for removal. This sort of silence is to be contrasted with the third and final category which comprises those deemed 'meaningful' and which, therefore, are not to be removed. As the *Audio-Visual Redaction Manual* explains:

> Identifying meaningful silence requires taking the context of the information into consideration. For example, if a witness pauses before answering a question, and it is evident that s/he is thinking about the answer, the silence is a meaningful part of the testimony, and should not be marked by the Redactor. Also, judges will occasionally mute their microphones so they can discuss an issue in private. While what they are saying is not a matter for the public records, the fact that they are having private discussions, and the duration of those private discussions, is a matter of interest, and should not be removed in the redaction process.[117]

Noise, as we saw in Chapter 7, is segregationist. In this case, the terms of that segregation are thoroughly juridical. The distinction between a silence that is 'noisy' and one that is 'meaningful' depends on quite a refined sense of legal oratory, one

[112] Occasionally, technical problems in the recording process can result in a poor quality recording. This can be evident, for instance, 'in mechanical hum or hiss, sound levels that are either too high or too low, or other foreign noises.' Any prominent examples of these are removed: *Audio-Visual Redaction Manual*, 15.

[113] *Audio-Visual Redaction Manual*, 15–16.

[114] *Audio-Visual Redaction Manual*, 14.

[115] *Audio-Visual Redaction Manual*, 14.

[116] *Audio-Visual Redaction Manual*, 14.

[117] *Audio-Visual Redaction Manual*, 14–15.

that is as sensitive to its rhythms and ellipses as its content. For archival purposes, both are equally in need of preservation.

After the three audio files have been 'marked up' by the redaction team, typically with a total of between one marker and 500, the audio files are passed first to a 'checker' and then, finally, to an 'editor', for both of whom the listening practice is different again. The 'checker' will not listen to a file all the way through. Their main function is to confirm that every 'sensitive information' marker has been applied correctly.[118] Once they have done so, the file can then be passed on to the 'editor' who is responsible for actually making the edits that have been marked. It is the editor, therefore, who removes any long periods of either 'dead' or 'noisy' silence, and it is the editor who replaces any 'sensitive information' with the short 'tone' which signals its removal to the listener.[119] Finally, it is also the editor who produces the uncompressed, 'preservation quality' 'redacted master file' (.wav) for archival purposes and the compressed 'redacted browsing file' (.mp3) which will eventually be made available to the public, enabling them to experience trials such as Bikindi's 'acousmatically'.[120]

Redefining the judicial soundscape

When Pierre Schaeffer resurrected the term 'acousmatic' in the 1960s, it was not with Pythagorean curtains or veils in mind, and certainly not judicial proceedings. Schaeffer was interested in the future of music and particularly in a form of compositional practice which, during the 1950s, had for the first time sought to employ recorded sounds as its primary source material rather than more traditional so-called 'live' instrumentation. The sounds Schaeffer was interested in were 'acousmatic' in the sense that, unlike an orchestra or a piano, their sources were neither visible nor spatially nor temporally present. One of Schaeffer's earliest works was entitled *Etude aux Chemins de Fer*, in English 'Study of Railroads', because it featured nothing but recordings he had made of trains—pulling into the station, blowing their whistles, and so on—which he would trigger in performance on the various phonographs laid out in front of him. For Schaeffer, a device such as the phonograph was acousmatic virtually by definition because it seemed to enable the removal of a sound from its 'original' context in order to recreate it at some other time and place.[121] As Sterne points out, however, we should be careful about taking the 'acousmatic definition of sound reproduction' too seriously, even if it has

[118] Checkers are also required to conduct 'random spot checks' of five other markers by way of quality control: *Audio-Visual Redaction Manual*, 27.

[119] *Audio-Visual Redaction Manual*, 29. Although the possibility of introducing a tone equal to the length of the excerpt removed was debated, it was decided that this would prove too distracting to listeners.

[120] For a discussion of the historical, political, and aesthetic dimensions of the mp3 and other audio formats, see Jonathan Sterne, *MP3: The Meaning of a Format* (Duke University Press, 2012).

[121] Chion (1994) 71.

become so entrenched as to pass for common sense.[122] And this is no less true in law than elsewhere.

Consider this notion of the 'reproduction', for instance. There is a sense in which it is simply a fallacy. What listeners heard when Schaeffer debuted his *Etude aux Chemins de Fer* in 1948 in Paris was not at all identical to the sounds produced by the trains themselves, just as what I hear when I listen to the 'recordings' of Bikindi's trial is significantly different to the experience of being present in court. It is not just that a huge amount of work has been done on them post-production, as we have seen: silences, noise, and 'overlapping language' removed. Even in the unadulterated recordings made for the purposes of broadcasting, the precise volume and timbre of the sounds of the courtroom, the 'perspective' of the recording in relation to acoustic space, the circumstances of the listener's own immediate sonic environment, the format of the recording, and the kind of device on which they are listening: all these things and more are different.

According to Sterne, the analytic response to the acoustic gap between 'original' and 'copy' has typically been in terms of what he calls the 'discourse of fidelity'. Thereby, the difference between the two is always figured as a loss: a loss, moreover, which the latest and greatest technology always promises to overcome. 'The idea that sound-reproduction technologies separated sounds from their sources turns out to have been an elaborate commercial and cultural project', Sterne claims.[123] Thus, even though a recording produced by Victor Records would sound laughably 'lo-fi' today, in 1908 the company was able to ask in one advertisement: 'You think you can tell the difference between hearing grand-opera artists sing and hearing their beautiful voices on the *Victor*. But can you?'[124] Very little has changed. Today, the company which manufactures a significant amount of the audio equipment at the ICTR trumpets its 'superior audio quality' on its website. 'The sound', it claims, 'comes out exactly as it goes in'.[125]

If the notion of the 'reproduction' is problematic then, so too is that of the 'original'. For Sterne, so-called 'original' sounds are as much a product of the recording medium as are their copies.[126] Or, to put it differently, the possibility of *re*-production transforms the very practice of production itself.[127] We have seen this idea already in this chapter in the form of the 'phonograph effect'. For musicians, as for practitioners at the ICTR, the performance is always *for* the medium to a certain degree. The singer sings, the lawyer speaks, the witness testifies *to* the microphone, *to* the media-technological network that will enable its later 'reproduction' and proliferation.[128] Where technologies of so-called sound reproduction are concerned, the 'original' itself is always already mediated. As we have seen throughout this chapter, legal actors are constantly modifying their behaviour

[122] Sterne (2003) 20. [123] Sterne (2003) 25. [124] Sterne (2003) 217.

[125] See Danish Interpretation Systems, 'Conference & Discussion System', accessed 5 March 2015, <http://www.dis.cc/sw26832.asp>; and Danish Interpretation Systems, 'DCS 6000 Digital Infrared Language Distribution System', accessed 5 March 2015, <http://www.dis-dk.com/graphics/dis/Brochures/DCS6000_DIGITAL_GB_LOWRES.pdf>.

[126] Sterne (2003) 219. [127] Sterne (2003) 220. [128] Sterne (2003) 226.

in order to accommodate the technologies that are supposedly 'recording' them. Practitioners have had to develop whole new performance techniques in order to produce 'originals' suitable for reproduction in the first place.[129]

There are two methods, therefore, by which the Tribunal has contrived to extend its acoustic reach out beyond the walls of the courtrooms in Arusha. First, by means of broadcasting and, second, by means of the audio and audio-visual archive. As the Judicial Records and Archives Unit puts it, both 'have an enormous outreach and educational potential'.[130] But it is important to be clear about what we are getting in both cases. Contrary to Schaeffer and his 'acousmatic definition' of sound recording, audio technologies do not offer us anything like unmediated access to the sound of the 'trial itself'. First, because the work of the 'phonograph effect' means that the 'trial itself' is always already mediated to begin with. Second, because there is a necessary non-equivalence between 'original' and 'reproduction' which no amount of technical refinement or rhetoric about so-called 'fidelity' can ever remedy. Third, because of the nature and extent of the work which goes on in relation to the audio-archive post-production.

Though we might plausibly identify a limited 'acousmatic effect' therefore in relation to proceedings at the ICTR, a sense in which it really is possible to hear a version of them many years after the trial is over, a more radical possibility presents itself. Audio technologies have become so deeply embedded into juridical practice, both at the ICTR and in relation to international justice mechanisms more generally, that the distinction between the 'trial itself' as a discrete media-spatio-temporal event and its 'reproduction'—later and elsewhere—has begun to break down. We should revise our original definition, therefore. The wiring of the courtroom for sound requires that we stop thinking of the judicial soundscape as being limited by the phenomenological range of those bodily present, the walls of the courtroom or the listening situation produced there.[131] We might think of the ability to broadcast and archive the trial in audio, in other words, not just as two new means of representing or 'recording' judicial proceedings, but as increasingly fundamental parts of the trial as media technology itself.

129 Sterne (2003) 25. 130 *Audio-Visual Redaction Manual*, 3.

131 Both Linda Mulcahy and Richard Mohr have made similar points about the 'dematerialization' of the trial. However, neither frames their argument in explicitly acoustic terms, and nor are they concerned with the question of the archive. In both cases they are more interested in the use of audio-visual broadcasting, on the one hand, and testimony via audio-video link, on the other. See Mulcahy (2011) ch 8; Richard Mohr, 'In between Power and Procedure: Where the Court Meets the Public Sphere' in Marit Paasche and Judy Radul (eds), *A Thousand Eyes: Media Technology, Law and Aesthetics* (Sternberg Press, 2011).

Conclusion

In the same building in which Bob Dylan recorded much of his seminal album *Blood on the Tracks*, there is a room within a room within a room.[1] The outermost of these is lined with foot-thick concrete, the inner two have double walls of insulated steel. The central cavity floats on I-beams and springs and is lined with fibreglass acoustic wedges more than three-feet thick. This is the anechoic chamber at Orfield Laboratories in southern Minnesota. With background noise levels at -9.4dBA, nine point four decibels below the normal range of human audition, it is officially the quietest place on earth.[2] If you were to spend any time in it, however, you would probably be surprised by what you heard. 'The total absence of sound outside your body makes you keenly aware of what's going on inside your body', journalist Patricia Kelly explains. Your heart pumps. Your lungs inflate and deflate. Your ears buzz. Your blood pulses. Your nervous system audibly fizzes. In an anechoic chamber, Kelly writes, 'you are one noisy organism'.[3] Following his own experience in a similar chamber at Harvard in 1952, American composer John Cage famously concluded that sound was simply a fact of life. 'Try as we may to make a silence', he wrote, 'we cannot'.[4]

The implications of this fact for legal thought and practice are significant. If life and law are necessarily lived in sound, the juridical community surely has a responsibility to pay attention. This book took root in my impression that recent scholarship has so far not been up to the task. Whereas there is a burgeoning literature on virtually every other dimension of law's institutional life and the practice of judgment—law's many and various relations with language, architecture, image, and screen, as well as its tools, technologies, and procedures—no sustained engagement yet exists in relation to sound. Where the acoustic is concerned, contemporary legal scholarship has been virtually silent. Sometimes the indifference in this respect has seemed almost wilful, as if at some point in recent history the linguistic

[1] Bob Dylan, *Blood on the Tracks* (Columbia Records, 1975).

[2] 'Quietest Place', Guinness World Records, accessed 6 March 2015, <http://www.guinnessworldrecords.com/world-records/3000/quietest-place>. Unofficially, the anechoic chamber at the University of Salford in Manchester is quieter, with a background noise level of -12.4dBA. See 'Anechoic Chamber', University of Salford, accessed 6 March 2015, <http://www.acoustics.salford.ac.uk/facilities/index.php?content=anechoic>.

[3] Patricia Kelly, 'The Quietest Room in the World', *Twin Cities Business*, 1 September 2008, <http://tcbmag.com/Industries/Technology/The-Quietest-Room-in-the-World-September-2008>.

[4] John Cage, *Silence: Lectures and Writings* (Marion Boyars, 1968) 8.

and visual life of law had simply surpassed or supplanted the acoustic as a major concern. But most of all the contemporary literature has been marked by a kind of innocence of sound, a failure to acknowledge that the acoustic dimensions of legal thought and practice might *ever* be worth considering (Chapter 1).

Such is our collective deafness where law is concerned that even when a person is accused of inciting genocide with his *songs*, it is possible for his trial to be conducted as if the sonority of those songs didn't matter: as if their musical and affective qualities, the way in which their sound, vocalization, and performance worked with and on their lyrics simply wasn't relevant to the task of adjudication (Chapters 3 and 5); and what's more for this remarkable fact to go wholly unnoticed in the subsequent commentary, both academic and otherwise. The poverty of the ICTR's imagination when it came to Bikindi's songs was both deep and pervasive. It was discernible from the earliest iterations of the indictment all the way through to the Trial Chamber's eventual judgment. It manifested itself everywhere from the rhetoric employed by both prosecution and defence, to the kinds of experts they called to testify, to the way in which the relevant international doctrine was understood and applied (Chapters 3 and 5). And although the ICTR was perfectly willing for Bikindi's songs to be performed at trial, its listening was often seriously attenuated. Right from the very start of proceedings, such performances were either exoticized as pleasant departures from the trial's ordinary soundscape or otherwise marginalized and contained: Bikindi's final 'statement' included (Chapter 4). Even the ICTR's depiction of radio—by its own account such a central feature of the Rwandan soundscape in 1994—was largely instrumental and crude (Chapter 7). And to the extent that Bikindi's voice mattered at all to the Tribunal, this was only ever in an extremely limited, though crucial way (Chapter 5). These are the most striking ways in which the Tribunal's approach to sound played out in the *Bikindi* case, where it bore most directly on the trial's outcome and legacy. And it is here, therefore, that I have been at my most critical in this book. If I have consistently refrained, however, from offering an alternative account of Bikindi's songs and their role in the genocide, that is partly a consequence of the Tribunal's deafness too. Despite the huge amount of time, energy, and resources invested in trying Bikindi, despite all the witnesses heard, all the evidence and documents filed, too many important questions remain unasked, let alone answered.

We can do much better. I know this because elsewhere at trial the ICTR was not so hard of hearing. Not only was the soundscape in the *Bikindi* case unusually rich, sometimes it was managed with real care and attention. The diverse ways in which the voice was called upon at the ICTR to perform the 'solemn declaration', to pronounce judgment and to produce a certain kind of written record, the variety of techniques the Tribunal used to manage protected witnesses and negotiate the complex dynamics between voice and text: all these examples suggest a definite institutional sensitivity to sound's role in the practice of judgment, even if that sensitivity was so clearly partial (Chapter 6). And when it came to the juridical use of architecture, audio-technology, broadcasting, and the archive, not only was the ICTR alert to matters of acoustics, in some respects it was genuinely innovative

(Chapter 8). If legal institutions are to deal better with cases like Bikindi's in the future, these are the seeds that must be nurtured.

To some extent it is simply a matter of consciousness raising. Legal scholars and practitioners must start tuning in to the diverse ways in which we *already* think and work with sound if we are to have any hope of doing so more responsibly. For Peter Szendy this kind of self-reflexivity is the first condition of any responsible listening practice.[5] Above all, for Szendy, one must learn to 'listen to oneself listening'.[6] To listen well is not therefore a matter of developing a singular, 'total or structural listening' capable of accounting for all sounds or all songs in all settings.[7] To listen well is to listen 'plastically', which is to say with one's ears open to the peculiarities of the context: first to notice how one is listening and then to be able to adjust that listening as the situation demands.[8] This is exactly what an acoustic jurisprudence requires. Since we are responsible for law's good conduct in so many different ways and for so many different reasons, what it means to listen well in law is always a matter of context. The dilemma of judgment is always a local one: always a matter of these facts, this institution, these laws. Plasticity and prudence are of a piece.

At its core, this book has argued for a fundamental shift in how we think about and relate to law's institutional life and the practice of judgment. We need to cultivate a new sensitivity to questions of sound and listening across legal thought and practice. Because legal institutions are so varied and because the issues they face are infinitely diverse—because, in short, an acoustic jurisprudence is as relevant to the law of property, immigration, or evidence as the law of genocide—it is neither possible nor desirable to offer a road-map in advance. There can be no complete theory of the law–sound relation. Nevertheless, I do think it is worth identifying a number of possible avenues of inquiry when it comes to further research.

First, we can read legal texts for what they reveal about *law's sonic imagination*. We can read them for what they suggest about a legal institution's musicology (Chapter 3), for how that institution understands the voice (Chapter 5), media, audio-technology, or a particular soundscape (Chapter 7), as well as for any consequences in each respect. In this book I was concerned mostly with the judgments, transcripts, and evidence produced in a single case by a single Tribunal, but there is no necessary reason for that limit. There are so many other cases in so many other institutions we could turn to: not just courts, but also legislatures and other law-making bodies, both official and non-official, sub- and supra-state. And of course we should think expansively across the huge range of contexts in which law and sound encounter each other. No doubt there will be other cases like Bikindi's, involving similar issues: music, song, radio, genocide, hate speech, incitement, freedom of expression. But we could equally look to areas where music and audio-technology, say, are regularly and self-consciously the object of legal regulation and inquiry: the law of copyright, trademarks, environmental protection,

[5] Peter Szendy, *Listen: A History of Our Ears* (Fordham University Press, 2008) 142.
[6] Szendy (2008) 142. [7] Szendy (2008) 128.
[8] On plastic listening, see Szendy (2008) 129–43.

venue licensing, public order, obscenity, and so on. Or, conversely, to issues that are less frequently remarked upon: from the problems of music torture and the increasing weaponization of sound in police and military contexts to the privacy concerns that arise now that your smart phone and TV are increasingly listening to you 24/7. In each instance it would be a matter of tracking, on the one hand, how these issues are made amenable to legal analysis—how sound is apprehended at the level of doctrine, rhetoric, or evidence—and, on the other hand, how things seem to play out differently in different contexts, why, and with what results.

Second, although the *judicial soundscape* will undoubtedly share certain common features from jurisdiction to jurisdiction and case to case, there will also be important differences. It is not just that some trials are more or less 'musical' than others, or that there is a whole range of ways in which songs and other aural evidence might be framed at trial for their listeners (Chapter 4). The ways in which courts make use of voice, text (Chapter 6), architecture, and audio-technology (Chapter 8) for the purposes of judgment are constantly in the process of change. Moreover, there are other legal soundscapes than the judicial. We could think equally, for instance, about how sound is made to operate at other moments in the course of legal practice: in the production of legislation (the *legislative soundscape*) or the negotiation and performance of contracts (the *contractual soundscape*), in police interviews or administrative hearings, and so on. Finally, we could consider the role and presence of law in soundscapes we do not tend to think of as being legal: at a musical festival, say, or a political rally, or in the comfort of one's home. Now the question would no longer be: how are legal institutions soundful? But rather: in what ways are sonic environments lawful? How is sound experienced through or in relation to law?

What does this book offer law? First and foremost an invitation to *think sonically*: to start paying attention to a dimension of legal thought and practice that is much more important than we tend to think. But the book has also suggested a provisional vocabulary and set of methods in the hope that they will be further refined and expanded in the future: not only a general concern for law's sonic imagination and the judicial soundscape as we have seen, but also for law's musicology and mediology, and for how these both feature and are produced at the level of doctrine, rhetoric, and evidence (Chapters 3, 5, and 7). This book has directed our ears towards law's keynote sounds, its sonic habitus and audile techniques, towards evidence of phonocentrism and the audio-visual litany, to the acousmatic, the phonograph effect, the audio-visual contract, and more besides (Chapters 4, 6, and 8).

An acoustic jurisprudence is necessarily eclectic. And if it borrows liberally from fields as diverse as musicology, philosophy, engineering, anthropology, linguistics, and history in terms of how it approaches sound, what then does it offer back? Most of all an invitation to *listen jurisprudentially*: to start attending to the peculiar dilemmas and techniques of legal judgment. On one level, this is simply a matter of insisting that law and legal institutions are a key part of the story to be told about sound in the contemporary moment. And moreover that it is possible to give a slightly thicker account in this respect than we usually get. But law also presents us with new faces to old problems. Certain issues familiar to musicology take on an importantly different shape in legal contexts, as we have seen. The problem of the ineffable, for instance, begins to look very different when it is paired with the urgency of legal judgment (Chapters 3 and 5). And the precise implications of the voice for how we conceive of the speaking subject—so important for the philosophers and critics—seem much less pressing from an institutional perspective, when the speaker is bound to be found guilty either way (Chapter 5). Jurisprudence is not musicology. Nor is it philosophy, or media studies, or sociology, or critique. So although an acoustic jurisprudence inevitably confronts questions familiar to those traditions, what it brings to them is an attention to the questions' specifically institutional registers, the ways in which they have been shaped by particular legal problems and techniques.

What is the purpose of an acoustic jurisprudence? To open scholars and practitioners' ears to the diverse ways in which law and sound are bound together, to hold institutions like the ICTR to account for how they think and work with sound, for the judgments they make, and to understand how law is both implicated in and to some extent productive of our sonic worlds. Walter Benjamin once observed that 'during long periods of history, the mode of human sense perception changes with humanity's entire mode of existence'.[9] Neither law nor sound is an exception to this rule. We would be well advised to pay attention.

[9] Walter Benjamin, *Illuminations*, trans Harry Zoh (Schocken Books, 1968) [trans of: *Illuminationen* (first published 1955)] 222 ('The Work of Art in the Age of its Mechanical Reproduction').

Bibliography

BOOKS AND ARTICLES

Abbate, Carolyn, 'Introduction' in Vladimir Jankélévitch, *Music and the Ineffable*, trans Carolyn Abbate (Princeton University Press, 2003) [trans of: *La musique et l'ineffable* (first published 1961)]

Abu Hamdan, Lawrence, 'Aural Contract: Forensic Listening and the Reorganisation of the Speaking-Subject', *Cesura//Acceso: Journal for Music, Politics and Poetics* 1 (2014) 200

Agbor, Avitus A, *Instigation to Crimes against Humanity: The Flawed Jurisprudence of the Trial and Appeal Chambers of the International Criminal Tribunal for Rwanda (ICTR)* (Brill, 2013)

Agnew, Vanessa, *Enlightenment Orpheus: The Power of Music in Other Worlds* (Oxford University Press, 2008)

Akhavan, Payam, 'Justice and Reconciliation in the Great Lakes Region of Africa: The Contribution of the International Criminal Tribunal for Rwanda', *Duke Journal of Comparative and International Law* 7(2) (1997) 325

Akhavan, Payam, *Reducing Genocide to Law: Definition, Meaning, and the Ultimate Crime* (Cambridge University Press, 2012)

Altmann, Jürgen, 'Acoustic Weapons—A Prospective Assessment', *Science & Global Security* 9(3) (2001) 165

Altmann, Jürgen, *Millimetre Waves, Lasers, Acoustics for Non-Lethal Weapons? Physics Analyses and Interferences* (Deutsche Stiftung Friedensforschung, 2008)

Alvarez, Jose E, 'Crimes of State/Crimes of Hate: Lessons from Rwanda', *Yale Journal of International Law* 24(2) (1999) 365

Anghie, Anthony, *Imperialism, Sovereignty and the Making of International Law* (Cambridge University Press, 2005)

Apollonius Rhodius, *The Argonautica*, trans Robert C Seaton (Harvard University Press, 1961)

Aristotle, *Nicomachean Ethics*, trans Martin Ostwald (Prentice Hall, 1962)

Aristotle, *The Art of Rhetoric*, trans H C Lawson-Tancred (Penguin, 1991)

Askew, Kelly M, *Performing the Nation: Swahili Music and Cultural Politics in Tanzania* (University of Chicago Press, 2002)

Atkinson, John Maxwell and Paul Drew, *Order in Court: The Organisation of Verbal Interaction in Judicial Settings* (Macmillan, 1979)

Attali, Jacques, *Noise: The Political Economy of Music*, trans Brian Massumi (University of Minnesota Press, 1985) [trans of: *Bruits: Essai sur l'économie politique de la musique* (first published 1977)]

Austern, Linda Phyllis and Inna Naroditskaya (eds), *The Music of the Sirens* (Indiana University Press, 2006)

Austin, John L, *How to Do Things with Words* (Harvard University Press, 1962)

Austin, Regina, 'Documentation, Documentary, and the Law: What Should Be Made of Victim Impact Videos?' *Cardozo Law Review* 31(4) (2010) 979

Balkin, Jack M, 'Deconstructive Practice and Legal Theory', *The Yale Law Journal* 96(4) (1987) 743

Balkin, Jack M, 'A Night in the Topics: The Reason of Legal Rhetoric and the Rhetoric of Legal Reason' in Peter Brooks and Paul Gewirtz (eds), *Law's Stories: Narrative and Rhetoric in the Law* (Yale University Press, 1996)

Balkin, Jack and Sanford Levinson, 'Interpreting Law and Music: Performance Notes on "The Banjo Serenader" and "The Lying Crowd of Jews"', *Cardozo Law Review* 20(5–6) (1999) 1513

Balsamo, Anne, *Designing Culture: The Technological Imagination at Work* (Duke University Press, 2011)

Banse, Rainer and Klaus Scherer, 'Acoustic Profiles in Vocal Emotion Expression', *Journal of Personality and Social Psychology* 70(3) (1996) 614

Barnett, Michael, *Eyewitness to a Genocide: The United Nations and Rwanda* (Cornell University Press, 2002)

Barsky, Robert, *Constructing a Productive Other: Discourse Theory and the Convention Refugee Hearing* (John Benjamins, 1990)

Barthes, Roland, *Image, Music, Text*, trans Stephen Heath (Fontana, 1977)

Barthes, Roland, *The Responsibility of Forms: Critical Essays on Music, Art, and Representation*, trans Richard Howard (Hill and Wang, 1985) [trans of: *L'obvie et l'obtus: Essais critiques III* (first published 1982)]

Barthes, Roland, *The Semiotic Challenge*, trans Richard Howard (University of California Press, 1994) [trans of: *L'aventure sémiologique* (first published 1985)]

Beigbeder, Yves, *International Criminal Tribunals: Justice and Politics* (Palgrave, 2011)

Belcher, Stephen, *Epic Traditions of Africa* (Indiana University Press, 1999)

Ben-Dor, Oren (ed), *Law and Art: Justice, Ethics and Aesthetics* (Routledge, 2011)

Benesch, Susan, 'Inciting Genocide, Pleading Free Speech', *World Policy Journal* 21(2) (2004) 62

Benesch, Susan, 'Vile Crime or Inalienable Right: Defining Incitement to Genocide', *Virginia Journal of International Law* 48(3) (2008) 485

Benjamin, Walter, *Illuminations*, trans Harry Zoh (Schocken Books, 1968) [trans of: *Illuminationen* (first published 1955)]

Bently, Lionel and Leo Flynn (eds), *Law and the Senses: Sensational Jurisprudence* (Pluto, 1996)

Bergmeier, Horst J P and Rainer E Lotz, *Hitler's Airwaves: The Inside Story of Nazi Radio Broadcasting and Propaganda Swing* (Yale University Press, 1997)

Berkeley, Bill, 'Sounds of Violence', *New Republic* 211(8–9) (1994) 18

Berk-Seligson, Susan, *The Bilingual Courtroom: Court Interpreters in the Judicial Process* (University of Chicago Press, 1990)

Besson, Samantha and John Tasioulas (eds), *The Philosophy of International Law* (Oxford University Press, 2010)

Betts, Benjamin F, 'Is This Our Next New Big Business?' *American Architect* 140 (December 1931) 21

Bijker, Wiebe E and John Law (eds), *Shaping Technology/Building Society: Studies in Sociotechnical Change* (MIT Press, 1992)

Bijsterveld, Karin, *Mechanical Sound: Technology, Culture, and Public Problems of Noise in the Twentieth Century* (MIT Press, 2008)

Bijsterveld, Karin, 'Acoustic Cocooning: How the Car Became a Place to Unwind', *The Senses and Society* 5(2) (2010) 189

Black, Christine F, *The Land Is the Source of the Law: A Dialogic Encounter with Indigenous Jurisprudence* (Routledge, 2011)

Boas, George, 'Ancient Testimony to Secret Doctrines', *The Philosophical Review* 62(1) (1953) 79

Bodin, John, *Colloquium of the Seven about Secrets of the Sublime*, trans Marion Leathers and Daniels Kuntz (Princeton University Press, 1975) [trans of: *Colloquium heptaplomeres de rerum sublimium arcanis abditis* (first published sixteenth century)]

Boethius, Anicius Manlius Severinus, *Fundamentals of Music*, ed Claude V Palisca, trans Calvin M Bower (Yale University Press, 1989) [trans of: *De institutione musica* (first published fifteenth century)]

Bourdieu, Pierre, *The Logic of Practice*, trans Richard Nice (Stanford University Press, 1990) [trans of: *Le sens pratique* (first published 1980)]

Bourdieu, Pierre and Loïc J D Wacquant, *An Invitation to Reflexive Sociology* (University of Chicago Press, 1992)

Bourgeois, René, *Banyarwanda et Burundi* (Institut Royal Colonial Belge, 1954)

Brandel, Rose, *The Music of Central Africa: An Ethnomusicological Study—Former French Equatorial Africa, the Former Belgian Congo, Ruanda-Urundi, Uganda, Tanganyika* (Martinus Nijhoff, 1973)

Briggs, Charles L, 'Metadiscursive Practices and Scholarly Authority in Folkloristics', *Journal of American Folklore* 106(422) (1993) 387

Brooks, Peter and Paul Gewirtz (eds), *Law's Stories: Narrative and Rhetoric in the Law* (Yale University Press, 1996)

Bruner II, Gordon C, 'Music, Mood, and Marketing', *Journal of Marketing* 54(4) (1990) 94

Bryant, Gregory A and Jean E Fox Tree, 'Recognizing Verbal Irony in Spontaneous Speech', *Metaphor and Symbol* 17(2) (2002) 99

Bryant, Gregory A and Jean E Fox Tree, 'Is There an Ironic Tone of Voice?' *Language and Speech* 48(3) (2005) 257

Bull, Michael, *Sounding Out the City: Personal Stereos and the Management of Everyday Life* (Berg, 2000)

Bull, Michael and Les Back, *The Auditory Culture Reader* (Berg, 2003)

Burdick, Alan, 'Now Hear This: Listening Back on a Century of Sound', *Harper's Magazine* 303(1804) (2001) 70

Burke, Edmund, *A Philosophical Enquiry into the Origins of Our Ideas of the Sublime and Beautiful*, ed Adam Philips (first published 1757, Oxford University Press, 1990)

Butler, Judith, *Excitable Speech: A Politics of the Performative* (Routledge, 1997)

Cage, John, *Silence: Lectures and Writings* (Marion Boyars, 1968)

Calvino, Ital, *Under the Jaguar Sun*, trans William Weaver (Yarcourt Brace, 1988)

Campbell, Don, *The Mozart Effect for Children: Awakening Your Child's Mind, Health and Creativity with Music* (Harper Collins, 2000)

Cape Jr, Robert W, 'Cicero and the Development of Prudential Practice at Rome' in Robert Hariman, *Prudence: Classical Virtue, Postmodern Practice* (Pennsylvania State University Press, 2003) 35–65

Carrington, John F, *Talking Drums of Africa* (Carey Kingsgate Press, 1949)

Cavarero, Adriana, *For More than One Voice: Toward a Philosophy of Vocal Expression*, trans Paul A Kottman (Stanford University Press, 2005) [trans of: *A piu voci: Per una filosofia dell'espressione vocale* (first published 2003)]

Chanan, Michael, *Musica Practica: The Social Practice of Western Music from Gregorian Chant to Postmodernism* (Verso, 1994)

Charland, Maurice, 'Lyotard's Postmodern Prudence' in Robert Hariman (ed) *Prudence: Classical Virtue, Postmodern Practice* (Pennsylvania State University Press, 2003)

Cheang, Henry S and Marc D Pell, 'The Sound of Sarcasm', *Speech Communication* 50(5) (2008) 366

Cheang, Henry S and Marc D Pell, 'Acoustic Markers of Sarcasm in Cantonese and English', *The Journal of the Acoustical Society of America* 126(3) (2009) 1394

Chion, Michel, *Audio-Vision: Sound on Screen*, ed and trans Claudio Gorbman (Columbia University Press, 1994) [trans of: *L'audio-vision: Son et image au cinema* (first published 1990)]

Chion, Michel, 'Let's Have Done with the Notion of "Noise"', trans James A Steintrager, *Differences* 22(2–3) (2011) 240

Chow, Rey and James A Steintrager, 'In Pursuit of the Object of Sound: An Introduction', *Differences* 22(2–3) (2011) 1

Chrétien, Jean-Pierre, *Rwanda: Les médias du génocide* (Karthala, 1999)

Cicero, Marcus Tullius, *On the Ideal Orator*, trans James M May and Jakob Wisse (Oxford University Press, 2001)

Cicero, Marcus Tullius, 'The Dream of Scipio' in *The Republic and the Laws*, trans Niall Rudd (Oxford University Press, 2009)

Cixous, Hélène and Mireille Calle-Gruber, *Rootprints: Memory and Life Writing*, trans Eric Prenowitz (Routledge, 1997) [trans of: *Photos de racine* (first published 1994)] 46

Clark, Phil, *The Gacaca Courts, Post-Genocide Justice and Reconciliation in Rwanda: Justice without Lawyers* (Cambridge University Press, 2010)

Clayton, Margin (ed), *Music, Words and Voice: A Reader* (Manchester University Press, 2008)

Cloonan, Martin and Bruce Johnson, 'Killing Me Softly with His Song: An Initial Investigation into the Use of Popular Music as a Tool of Oppression', *Popular Music* 21(1) (2002) 27

Combs, Nancy A, *Fact-Finding without Facts: The Uncertain Evidentiary Foundations of International Criminal Convictions* (Cambridge University Press, 2010)

Conaghan, Joanne, 'Reassessing the Feminist Theoretical Project in Law', *Journal of Law and Society* 27(3) (2000) 351

Condren, Conal, *Argument and Authority in Early Modern England: The Presupposition of Oaths and Office* (Cambridge University Press, 2006)

Conley, John M and William M O'Barr, *Rules versus Relationships: The Ethnography of Legal Discourse* (University of Chicago Press, 1990)

Conley, John M, William M O'Barr, and E Allan Lind, 'The Power of Language: Presentational Style in the Courtroom', *Duke Law Journal* 1978(6) (1979) 1375

Constable, Marianne, 'Genealogy and Jurisprudence: Nietzsche, Nihilism and the Social Scientification of Law', *Law and Social Inquiry* 19(3) (1994) 551

Constable, Marianne, *Just Silences: The Limits and Possibilities of Modern Law* (Princeton University Press, 2005)

Constable, Marianne, 'Our Word is Our Bond' in Austin Sarat (ed), *Speech and Silence in American Law* (Cambridge University Press, 2010) 18

Constable, Marianne, *Our Word is Our Bond: How Legal Speech Acts* (Stanford University Press, 2014)

Coonfield, Gordon, 'Thinking Machinically, or, the Techno-Aesthetic of Jackie Chan: Toward a Deleuze-Guattarian Media Studies', *Critical Studies in Media Communication* 23(4) (2006) 285

Corbin, Alain, *Village Bells: Sound and Meaning in the 19th Century French Countryside*, trans Martin Thom (Columbia University Press, 1998) [trans of: *Les cloches de la terre: Paysage sonore et culture sensible dans les campagnes au XIXe siècle* (first published 1998)]

Cornell, Drucilla, Michel Rosenfeld, and David Gray Carlson (eds), *Deconstruction and the Possibility of Justice* (Routledge, 1992)

Cotterrell, Roger, *The Sociology of Law: An Introduction* (2nd edn, Butterworths, 1992)

Cotterrell, Roger, 'Why Jurisprudence is not Legal Philosophy', *Jurisprudence* 5(1) (2014) 41

Cover, Robert, 'The Supreme Court, 1982 Term—Foreword: Nomos and Narrative', *Harvard Law Review* 97(1) (1983) 4

Cover, Robert, 'Violence and the Word', *The Yale Law Journal* 95(8) (1986) 1601

Cowie, Jefferson R and Lauren Boehm, 'Dead Man's Town: "Born in the USA", Social History and Working-Class Identity', *American Quarterly* 58(2) (2006) 353

Cox, Christoph, 'Beyond Representation and Signification: Toward a Sonic Materialism', *Journal of Visual Culture* 10(2) (2011) 145

Cox, Christoph and Daniel Warner (eds), *Audio Culture: Readings in Modern Music* (Continuum, 2004)

Craig, Dylan and Nomalanga Mkhize, 'Vocal Killers, Silent Killers: Popular Media, Genocide, and the Call for Benevolent Censorship in Rwanda' in Michael Drewett and Martin Cloonan (eds), *Popular Music Censorship in Africa* (Ashgate, 2006) 39–52

Crenshaw, Kimberlé, Neil Gotanda, Gary Peller, and Kendall Thomas (eds), *Critical Race Theory: The Key Writings that Formed the Movement* (New Press, 1995)

Cubitt, Sean, *Digital Aesthetics* (Sage, 1998)

Cullen, Jim, *Born in the USA: Bruce Springsteen and the American Tradition* (Wesleyan University Press, 1997)

Cunliffe, Emma, '(This is Not a) Story: Using Court Records to Explore Judicial Narratives in *R v Kathleen Folbigg*', *Australian Feminist Law Journal* 27 (December 2007) 71

Currid, Brian, *A National Acoustics: Music and Mass Publicity in Weimar and Nazi Germany* (University of Minnesota Press, 2006)

Cusick, Suzanne G, 'Music as Torture/Music as Weapon', *Transcultural Music Review* 10 (2006) <http://www.sibetrans.com/trans/a152/music-as-torture-music-as-weapon>

Cusick, Suzanne G, '"You Are in a Place That Is Out of the World ..." Music in the Detention Camps of the "Global War on Terror"', *Journal of the Society for American Music* 2(1) (2008) 1

Dahlberg, Lief, 'Emotional Tropes in the Courtroom: On Representation of Affect and Emotion in Legal Court Proceedings', *Law and Humanities* 3(2) (2009) 175

Dallaire, Roméo, *Shake Hands with the Devil: The Failure of Humanity in Rwanda* (Random House, 2003)

Dalton, Clare, 'An Essay in the Deconstruction of Contract Doctrine', *The Yale Law Journal* 94(5) (1985) 997

Darian-Smith, Eve (ed), *Ethnography and Law* (Ashgate, 2007)

Davies, Margaret, 'Pathfinding: The Way of the Law', *Oxford Literary Review* 14(1) (1992) 107

Davies, Margaret, *Asking the Law Question* (3rd edn, Thomson, 2008)

Davis, Kevin R, 'Kantian "Publicity" and Political Justice', *History of Philosophy Quarterly* 8(4) (1991) 409

Davis, Mike, *The Ecology of Fear: Los Angeles and the Imagination of Disaster* (Metropolitan Books, 1998)

de Jongh, Elena M, *An Introduction to Court Interpreting: Theory & Practice* (University Press of America, 1992)

de Saussure, Ferdinand, *Course in General Linguistics*, trans Roy Harris (Duckworth, 1998) [trans of: *Cours de linguistique générale* (first published 1916)]

de Saussure, Ferdinand, *Course in General Linguistics*, trans Roy Harris (first published 1986, Open Court Classics, 2006) [trans of: *Cours de linguistique générale* (first published 1916)]

Debray, Régis, 'The Three Ages of Looking', trans Eric Rauth, *Critical Inquiry* 21(3) (1995) 529

Deflem, Mathieu, *Sociology of Law: Visions of a Scholarly Tradition* (Cambridge University Press, 2008)

Demers, Joanne, *Steal This Music: How Intellectual Property Law Affects Musical Creativity* (University of Georgia Press, 2006)

Derrida, Jacques, *Speech and Phenomena and Other Essays on Husserl's Theory of Signs*, trans David B Allison (Northwestern University Press, 1973) [trans of: *La voix et le phénomène* (first published 1967)]

Derrida, Jacques, *Of Grammatology*, trans Gayatri Chakravorty Spivak (John Hopkins University Press, 1976) [trans of: *De la grammatologie* (first published 1967)]

Derrida, Jacques, 'The Law of Genre', trans. Avital Ronnel, *Critical Inquiry* 7(1) (1980) 55

Derrida, Jacques, *Dissemination*, trans Barbara Johnson (The Athlone Press, 1981) [trans of: *La dissémination* (first published 1972)]

Derrida, Jacques, *Margins of Philosophy*, trans Alan Bass (University of Chicago Press, 1982) [trans of: *Marges de la philosophie* (first published 1972)]

Derrida, Jacques, *Limited Inc*, trans Samuel Weber, Jeffrey Mehlman, and Alan Bass (Northwestern University Press, 1988)

Derrida, Jacques, *Of Spirit: Heidegger and the Question*, trans Geoffrey Bennington and Rachel Bowlby (University of Chicago Press, 1989) [trans of: *De l'esprit: Heidegger et la question* (first published 1987)]

Derrida, Jacques, 'Force of Law: The "Mystical Foundations of Authority"', trans Mary Quaintance [trans of: 'Force de loi: Le "fondement mystique de l'autorité"'] *Cardozo Law Review* 11(5–6) (1990) 920

Derrida, Jacques, *Archive Fever: A Freudian Impression*, trans Eric Prenowitz (University of Chicago Press, 1996) [trans of: *Mal d'archive: Une impression Freudienne* (originally presented as a lecture in London, 5 June 1994)]

Derrida, Jacques, *Of Grammatology*, trans Gayatri Chakravorty Spivak (Johns Hopkins University Press, 1998) [trans of: *De la grammatologie* (first published 1967)]

Des Forges, Alison, *Leave None to Tell the Story: Genocide in Rwanda* (Human Rights Watch, 1999)

Des Forges, Alison and Timothy Longman, 'Legal Responses to Genocide in Rwanda' in Eric Stover and Harvey M Weinstein (eds), *My Neighbor, My Enemy: Justice and Community in the Aftermath of Ethnic Cleansing* (Cambridge University Press, 2004) 49–68

Di Renzo, Anthony, 'His Master's Voice: Tiro and the Rise of the Roman Secretarial Class', *Journal of Technical Writing and Communication* 30(2) (2000) 155

Dick, Bernard F, 'The Artes Liberales as the Basis of the Humanities', *International Journal of the Humanities* 5(8) (2007) 111

Dittrich, Marie-Agnes, 'The Lieder of Schubert', trans Sven Hansell in James Parsons (ed), *The Cambridge Companion to the Lied* (Cambridge University Press, 2004)

Dolar, Mladen, *A Voice and Nothing More* (MIT Press, 2006)

Dorsett, Shaunnagh and Shaun McVeigh, 'Just So: The Law Which Governs Australia Is Australian Law', *Law and Critique* 13(3) (2002) 289

Dorsett, Shaunnagh and Shaun McVeigh, *Jurisdiction* (Routledge, 2012)

Douglas, Mary, *How Institutions Think* (Syracuse University Press, 1986)

Douglas, Susan J, *Inventing American Broadcasting 1899–1922* (Johns Hopkins University Press, 1987)

Douzinas, Costas, 'The Metaphysics of Jurisdiction' in Shaun McVeigh (ed), *Jurisprudence of Jurisdiction* (Routledge-Cavendish, 2007) 21–32

Douzinas, Costas and Adam Gearey, *Critical Jurisprudence: The Political Philosophy of Justice* (Hart, 2005)

Douzinas, Costas and Lynda Nead (eds), *Law and the Image: The Authority of Art and the Aesthetics of Law* (University of Chicago Press, 1999)

Douzinas, Costas and Ronnie Warrington with Shaun McVeigh, *Postmodern Jurisprudence: The Law of Text in the Texts of Law* (Routledge, 1991)

Drever, John Levack, 'Ochlophonics Hong Kong: Everyday Sound Practices within the Crowd' (Paper presented at Music, Sound and the Reconfiguration of Public and Private Space, Cambridge, United Kingdom, 18–19 April 2008)

Drewett, Michael and Martin Cloonan (eds), *Popular Music Censorship in Africa* (Ashgate, 2006)

Duff, Antony, 'Authority and Responsibility in International Criminal Law' in Samantha Besson and John Tasioulas (eds), *The Philosophy of International Law* (Oxford University Press, 2010) 589–604

Duncan, Michelle, 'The Operatic Scandal of the Singing Body: Voice, Presence, Performativity', *Cambridge Opera Journal* 16(3) (2004) 283

Dworkin, Ronald, *Law's Empire* (Harvard University Press, 1986)

Eco, Umberto, *A Theory of Semiotics* (Macmillan, 1977)

Edmond, Gary, Kristy Martire and Mehera San Roque, 'Unsound Law: Issues with ("Expert") Voice Comparison Evidence', *Melbourne University Law Review* 35(1) (2011) 52

Eliot, Thomas S, *The Use of Poetry and the Use of Criticism: Studies in the Relation of Criticism to Poetry in England* (Harvard University Press, 1986)

Ellul, Jacques, *The Technological Society*, trans John Wilkinson (Random House, 1964) [trans of: *La technique ou l'enjeu du siècle* (first published 1954)]

Erlmann, Veit, *Reason and Resonance: A History of Modern Aurality* (Zone Books, 2010)

Eshun, Kodwo, *More Brilliant than the Sun* (Quartet Books, 1998)

Evan, William M (ed), *The Sociology of Law: A Social-Structural Perspective* (Free Press, 1980)

Evans, David, 'Theatre of Deferral: The Image of the Law and the Architecture of the Inns of Court', *Law and Critique* 10(1) (1999) 1

Feenberg, Andrew, *Critical Theory of Technology* (Oxford University Press, 1991)

Feld, Steve and Donald Brenneis, 'Doing Anthropology in Sound', *American Ethnologist* 31(4) (2004) 462

Feldman, Morton, *Give My Regards to Eighth Street: Collected Writings of Morton Feldman*, ed Bernard H Friedman (Exact Change, 2000)

Fellerer, Karl G, 'Church Music and the Council of Trent', *The Musical Quarterly* 39(4) (1953) 576

Felman, Shoshana, *The Scandal of the Speaking Body: Don Juan with J L Austin, or Seduction in Two Languages* (Stanford University Press, 1983)

Finnegan, Ruth, *Oral Literature in Africa* (Clarendon Press, 1970)

Finnegan, Ruth, *The Oral and Beyond: Doing Things with Words in Africa* (University of Chicago Press, 2007)

Fisher, David, *My Bloody Valentine's Loveless: The Epitome of a Genre* (VDM Verlag, 2008)

Fitzpatrick, Peter and Alan Hunt (eds), *Critical Legal Studies* (Blackwell, 1987)

Foucault, Michel, *The Archaeology of Knowledge*, trans A M Sheridan Smith (Routledge, 1989) [trans of: *L'Archéologie du savoir* (first published 1969)]
Frank, Jerome, 'Words and Music: Some Remarks on Statutory Interpretation', *Columbia Law Review* 47(8) (1947) 1259
Frank, Jerome, 'Say It with Music', *Harvard Law Review* 61(6) (1948) 921
Fraser, Helen, Bruce Stevenson, and Tony Marks, 'Interpretation of a Crisis Call: The Persistence of Primed Perception of Speech', *The International Journal of Speech Language and the Law* 18(2) (2011) 261
Freud, Sigmund, *The Standard Edition of the Complete Psychological Works of Sigmund Freud*, trans James Strachey (Hogarth Press, 1953–1975) vol 21
Frith, Simon, *Sound Effects: Youth, Leisure, and the Politics of Rock 'n' Roll* (Pantheon Books, 1981)
Frith, Simon, *Music for Pleasure: Essays in the Sociology of Pop* (Routledge, 1988)
Frith, Simon, *Performing Rites: Evaluating Popular Music* (Oxford University Press, 1996)
Frith, Simon, and Lee Marshal, *Music and Copyright* (2nd edn, Routledge, 2004)
Furniss, Graham and Liz Gunner (eds), *Power, Marginality and African Oral Literature* (Cambridge University Press, 2008)
Gabel, Peter and Duncan Kennedy, 'Roll over Beethoven', *Stanford Law Review* 36(1) (1984) 1
Gaiba, Francesca, *The Origins of Simultaneous Interpretation: The Nuremberg Trial* (University of Ottawa Press, 1998)
Gaita, Raimond, *A Common Humanity: Thinking about Love and Truth and Justice* (Routledge, 2002)
Gansemans, Jos, *Les instruments de musique du Rwanda: Étude ethnomusicologique* (Leuven University Press, 1988)
Garofolo, Reebee (ed), *Rockin' the Boat: Mass Music and Mass Movements* (South End Press, 1992)
Gearey, Adam, 'Outlaw Blues: Law in the Songs of Bob Dylan', *Cardozo Law Review* 20(5–6) (1999) 1401
Geertz, Clifford, 'Thick Description: Toward an Interpretive Theory of Culture' in *The Interpretation of Cultures: Selected Essays* (Basic Books, 1973) 3–30
Geiselmann, Ralph E and Francis S Bellezza, 'Incidental Retention of Speaker's Voice', *Memory & Cognition* 5(6) (1977) 658
Getman, Julius G, 'Colloquy: Human Voice in Legal Discourse', *Texas Law Review* 66(3) (1988) 577
Gilbert, Martin, *Never Again: A History of the Holocaust* (Universe, 2000)
Gilbert, Shirli, *Music in the Holocaust: Confronting Life in the Nazi Ghettos and Camps* (Oxford University Press, 2005)
Ginsburgs, George and Vladimir N Kudriavtsev (eds), *The Nuremberg Trial and International Law* (Kluwer, 1990)
Gleick, James, *Information: A History, A Theory, A Flood* (Pantheon Books, 2011)
Goddar, Michael, Benjamin Halligan and Paul Hegarty (eds), *Reverberations: The Philosophy, Aesthetics and Politics of Noise* (Continuum, 2012)
Godwin, Joscelyn (ed), *The Harmony of the Spheres: A Sourcebook of the Pythagorean Tradition in Music* (Inner Traditions International, 1993)
Godwin, Joscelyn, *Harmonies of Heaven and Earth: The Spiritual Dimension of Music from Antiquity to the Avant-Garde* (Thames and Hudson, 1987)
Golan, Tal, 'Visual Images in the Courtroom: A Historical Perspective', *Parallax* 14(4) (2008) 77

Goodman, Steve, *Sonic Warfare: Sound, Affect and the Ecology of Fear* (MIT Press, 2010)
Goodrich, Peter, 'Law and Language: An Historical and Critical Introduction', *Journal of Law and Society* 11(2) (1984) 173
Goodrich, Peter, 'Rhetoric as Jurisprudence: An Introduction to the Politics of Legal Language', *Oxford Journal of Legal Studies* 4(1) (1984) 88
Goodrich, Peter, *Reading the Law: A Critical Introduction to Legal Method and Techniques* (Blackwell, 1986)
Goodrich, Peter, *Languages of Law: From Logics of Memory to Nomadic Masks* (Weidenfeld and Nicolson, 1990)
Goodrich, Peter, *Law in the Courts of Love: Literature and Other Minor Jurisprudences* (Routledge, 1996)
Goodrich, Peter, 'Operatic Hermeneutics: Harmony, Euphantasy, and Law in Rossini's *Semiramis*', *Cardozo Law Review* 20(5–6) (1999) 1649
Goodrich, Peter, 'Europe in America: Grammatology, Legal Studies, and the Politics of Transmission', *Columbia Law Review* 101(8) (2001) 2033
Goodrich, Peter, 'The Visial Line: On the Prehistory of Law and Film', *Parallax* 14(4) (2008) 55
Goodrich, Peter, 'Screening Law', *Law and Literature* 21(1) (2009) 1
Goose, Stephen D and Frank Smyth, 'Arming Genocide in Rwanda: The High Cost of Small Arms Transfers', *Foreign Affairs* 73(5) (1994) 86
Gordon, Gregory S, '"A War of Media, Words, Newspapers, and Radio Stations": The ICTR Media Trial Verdict and a New Chapter in the International Law of Hate Speech', *Virginia Journal of International Law* 45(1) (2004) 139
Gordon, Gregory S, 'Music and Genocide: Harmonizing Coherence, Freedom and Nonviolence in Incitement Law', *Santa Clara Law Review* 50(3) (2010) 607
Gourevitch, Philip, *We Wish to Inform You That Tomorrow We Will Be Killed with Our Families: Stories from Rwanda* (Picador, 1998)
Gozza, Paolo, 'Number to Sound' in Philippe Vendrix (ed), *Music and the Renaissance: Renaissance, Reformation and Counter-Reformation* (Ashgate, 2011)
Gray, Michael, *The Art of Bob Dylan* (Hamlyn, 1981)
Green, Lucy, *Music on Deaf Ears: Musical Meaning, Ideology, Education* (Manchester University Press, 1988)
Greene, Paul G and Thomas Porcello (eds), *Wired for Sound: Engineering and Technologies in Sonic Cultures* (Wesleyan University Press, 2004)
Greenfield, Steve, Guy Osborn, and Peter Robson (eds), *Film and the Law: The Cinema of Justice* (2nd edn, Hart, 2010)
Griffiths, John, 'What is Legal Pluralism?', *Journal of Legal Pluralism and Unofficial Law* 24(1) (1986) 1
Grout, Donald J and Claude V Palisca, *A History of Western Music* (5th edn, Sony Music, 1996)
Guattari, Félix, *Chaosophy: Texts and Interviews 1972–1977*, ed Sylvère Lotringer, trans David L Sweet, Jarred Becker and Taylor Adkins (Semiotext(e), 2009)
Habermas, Jürgen, *The Structural Transformation of the Public Sphere: An Inquiry into a Category of Bourgeois Society*, trans Thomas Burger with Frederick Lawrence (Polity Press, 1992) [trans of: *Strukturwandel der Öffentlichkeit: Untersuchungen zu einer Kategorie der bürgerlichen Gesellschaft* (first published 1962)]
Haldar, Piyel, 'The Evidencer's Eye: Representations of Truth in the Laws of Evidence', *Law and Critique* 2(2) (1991) 171
Haldar, Piyel, 'In and Out of Court: On Topographies of Law and the Architecture of Court Buildings (a Study of the Supreme Court of the State of Israel)', *International Journal for the Semiotics of Law* 7(2) (1994) 185

Haldar, Piyel, 'Acoustic Justice' in Lionel Bently and Leo Flynn (eds), *Law and the Senses: Sensational Jurisprudence* (Pluto, 1996)

Haldar, Piyel, 'The Function of the Ornament in Quintilian, Alberti, and Court Architecture' in Costas Douzinas and Lynda Nead (eds), *Law and the Image: The Authority of Art and the Aesthetics of Law* (University of Chicago Press, 1999) 117–36

Haldar, Piyel, 'The Return of the Evidencer's Eye: Rhetoric and the Visual Technologies of Proof', *Griffith Law Review* 8(1) (1999) 86

Hall, Timothy S, 'The Score As Contract: Private Law and the Historically Informed Performance Movement', *Cardozo Law Review* 20(5–6) (1999) 1589

Hariman, Robert, 'Prudence/Performance', *Rhetoric Society Quarterly* 21(2) (1991) 26

Hariman, Robert, *Prudence: Classical Virtue, Postmodern Practice* (Pennsylvania State University Press, 2003)

Hariman, Robert and Francis A Beer, 'What Would be Prudent? Forms of Reasoning in World Politics', *Rhetoric & Public Affairs* 1(3) (1998) 299

Hart, H L A, *The Concept of Law* (2nd edn, Oxford University Press, 1994)

Heidegger, Martin, *The Question concerning Technology and Other Essays*, trans William Lovitt (Garland, 1977) [trans of: *Die technik und die kehre* (first published 1962)]

Herzog, George, 'Drum Signalling in a West African Tribe' in Margin Clayton (ed), *Music, Words and Voice: A Reader* (Manchester University Press, 2008) 56–61

Hibbitts, Bernard J, '"Coming to Our Senses": Communication and Legal Expression in Performance Cultures', *Emory Law Journal* 41(4) (1992) 873

Hilmes, Michele, 'In Focus: Sound Studies—Foregrounding Sound: New (and Old) Directions in Sound Studies', *Cinema Journal* 48(1) (2008) 115

Hirsch, Lily E, *Music in American Crime Prevention and Punishment* (University of Michigan Press, 2012)

Hofmeyr, Isabel, 'The Letter and the Law: The Politics of Orality and Literacy in the Chiefdoms of the Northern Transvaal' in Graham Furniss and Liz Gunner (eds), *Power, Marginality and African Oral Literature* (Cambridge University Press, 2008) 35–47

Homer, *The Odyssey*, trans Walter Shewring (Oxford University Press, 1980)

Honeycutt, Lee, 'Literacy and the Writing Voice: The Intersection of Culture and Technology in Dictation', *Journal of Business and Technical Communication* 18(3) (2004) 294

Hooper, Giles, *The Discourse of Musicology* (Ashgate, 2006)

Horace, *The Poetic Art: A Translation of Horace's "Ars Poetica"*, trans Charles H Sisson (Carcanet Press, 1975)

Horkheimer, Max and Theodor W Adorno, *Dialectic of Enlightenment: Philosophical Fragments*, ed Gunzelin Schmid Noerr, trans Edmund Jephcott (Stanford University Press, 2002) [trans of: *Gesammelte Schriften: Dialektik der Aufklärung und Schriften 1940–1950* (first published 1987)]

Hosokawa, Shuhei, 'The Walkman Effect' in Jonathan Sterne (ed), *The Sound Studies Reader* (Routledge, 2012) 104–16

Howland, Todd and William Calathes, 'The UN's International Criminal Tribunal: Is it Justice or Jingoism for Rwanda? A Call for Transformation', *Virginia Journal of International Law* 39(1) (1998) 135

Hydaralli, Saeed, 'What Is Noise? An Inquiry Into Its Formal Properties' in Michael Goddar, Benjamin Halligan and Paul Hegarty (eds), *Reverberations: The Philosophy, Aesthetics and Politics of Noise* (Continuum, 2012) 219–32

Iamblichus, *On the Pythagorean Life*, trans Gillian Clark (Liverpool University Press, 1989)

Irvine, Thomas, 'Musical Performance, Natural Law and Interpretation' in Oren Ben-Dor (ed), *Law and Art: Justice, Ethics and Aesthetics* (Routledge, 2011)

Jackson, Bernard S, *Semiotics and Legal Theory* (Routledge & Kegan Paul, 1985)

Jackson Knight, William F, *St Augustine's De Musica: A Synopsis* (Hyperion Press, 1979)

Jacobson, Arthur J, 'Origins of the Game Theory of Law and the Limits of Harmony in Plato's Law', *Cardozo Law Review* 20(5–6) (1999) 1335

James, Jamie, *The Music of the Spheres: Music, Science, and the Natural Order of the Universe* (Abacus, 1993)

Jameson, Frederic, *Ideologies of Theory: Essays 1971–1986* (University of Minnesota Press, 1988)

Jankélévitch, Vladimir, *Music and the Ineffable*, trans Carolyn Abbate (Princeton University Press, 2003) [trans of: *La Musique et l'ineffable* (first published 1961)]

Jasanoff, Sheila (ed), *States of Knowledge: The Co-Production of Science and the Social Order* (Routledge, 2004)

Jasanoff, Sheila, 'Future Imperfect: Science, Technology and the Imaginations of Modernity' in Sheila Jasanoff and Sang-Hyn Kim (eds), *Dreamscapes of Modernity Sociotechnical Imaginaries and the Fabrication of Power* (University of Chicago Press, 2015)

Jay, Martin, *Downcast Eyes: The Denigration of Vision in Twentieth-Century French Thought* (University of California Press, 1993)

Johnston, Moira and Dewitt Jones, 'Queen Charlotte Islands, Homeland of the Haida', *National Geographic* 172(1) (1987) 102

Jones, Simon C and Thomas G Schumacher, 'Muzak: On Functional Music and Power', *Critical Studies in Mass Communication* 9(2) (1992) 156

Kagame, Alexis, *La poésie dynastique au Rwanda* (IRSAC, 1951)

Kant, Immanuel, *On History*, ed Lewis White Beck, trans Lewis White Beck, Robert E Anchor and Emil L Fackenheim (Bobbs-Merrill, 1963)

Kasirer, Nicholas (ed), *Étudier et enseigner le droit: Hier, aujourd'hui et demain—Études offertes à Jacques Vanderlinden* (Éditions Yvon Blais, 2006)

Katz, Mark, *Capturing Sound: How Technology Has Changed Music* (University of California Press, 2010)

Keeling, Kara and Joshua Kun, 'Introduction: Listening to American Studies', *American Quarterly* 63(3) (2011) 445

Keith, Kirsten M F, 'Justice at the International Criminal Tribunal for Rwanda: Are Criticisms Just?', *Law in Context* 27(1) (2009) 78

Kelley, Donald R, *The Human Measure: Social Thought in the Western Legal Tradition* (Harvard University Press, 1990)

Kellow, Christine L and H Leslie Steeves, 'The Role of Radio in the Rwandan Genocide', *Journal of Communication* 48(3) (1998) 107

Kelly, Jack, *Gunpowder: Alchemy, Bombards, and Pyrotechnics: The History of the Explosive That Changed the World* (Basic Books, 2005)

Kelman, Mark, *A Guide to Critical Legal Studies* (Harvard University Press, 1987)

Kelsen, Hans, *Pure Theory of Law*, trans Max Knight (University of California Press, 1967) [trans of: *Reine rechtslehre* (first published 1934)]

Kepler, Johannes, *The Harmony of the World*, trans E J Aiton, Alistair M Duncan, and Judith V Field (American Philosophical Society, 1997) [trans of: *De harmonices mundi* (first published 1619)]

Kerman, Joseph, *Contemplating Music: Challenges to Musicology* (Harvard University Press, 1985)

Kerruish, Valerie, *Jurisprudence as Ideology* (Routledge, 1992)

Kevelson, Roberta, *The Law as a System of Signs* (Plenum Press, 1988)

Khan, Naveeda, 'The Acoustics of Muslim Striving: Loudspeaker Use in Ritual Practice in Pakistan', *Comparative Studies in Society and History* 53(3) (2011) 571

Kim, Hyun-Ah, 'Erasmus on Sacred Music', *Reformation and Renaissance Review* 8(3) (2006) 277

Kimani, Mary, 'RTLM: The Medium that Became a Tool for Mass Murder' in Alan Thompson (ed), *The Media and the Rwanda Genocide* (Pluto, 2007) 110–24

Kim-Cohen, Seth, *In the Blink of an Ear: Toward a Non-Cochlear Sonic Art* (Continuum, 2009)

Koch, Grace, *We Have the Song, So We Have the Land: Song and Ceremony as Proof of Ownership in Aboriginal and Torres Strait Islander Land Claims*, AIATSIS Discussion Paper 33 (July 2013)

Koenigsberger, Helmut Georg, 'Music and Religion in Early Modern European History' in Philippe Vendrix (ed), *Music and the Renaissance: Renaissance, Reformation and Counter-Reformation* (Ashgate, 2011)

Kottman, Paul A, 'Introduction' in Adriana Cavarero, *For More than One Voice: Toward a Philosophy of Vocal Expression*, trans Paul A Kottman (Stanford University Press, 2005) [trans of: *A piu voci: Per una filosofia dell'espressione vocale* (first published 2003)] vii–xxv

Krammer, Arnold, *War Crimes, Genocide, and the Law: A Guide to the Issues* (Praeger, 2010)

Kreiman, Jody and Diana Sidtis, *Foundations of Voice Studies: An Interdisciplinary Approach to Voice Production and Perception* (Wiley-Blackwell, 2011)

Kristeva, Julia, *Revolutions in Poetic Language*, trans. Margaret Waller (Columbia University Press, 1984) [trans of: *La révolution du langage poétique* (first published 1974)]

Kurzon, Dennis, '*Peters Edition v Batt*: The Intertextuality of Silence', *International Journal for the Semiotics of Law* 20(4) (2007) 285

La Mort, Justin, 'The Soundtrack of Genocide: Using Incitement to Genocide in the Bikindi Trial to Protect Free Speech and Uphold the Promise of Never Again', *Interdisciplinary Journal of Human Rights Law* 4(1) (2010) 43

LaBelle, Brandon, 'Pump Up the Bass: Rhythm, Cars, and Auditory Scaffolding', *The Senses and Society* 3(2) (2008) 187

Lacey, Nicola, *Unspeakable Subjects: Feminist Essays in Legal and Social Theory* (Hart, 1998)

Lahav, Pnina, 'Theater in the Courtroom: The Chicago Conspiracy Trial', *Law and Literature* 16(3) (2004) 381

Lastra, James, 'Fidelity versus Intelligibility' in Jonathan Sterne (ed), *The Sound Studies Reader* (Routledge, 2012) 248–53

Latour, Bruno, 'Mixing Humans and Nonhumans Together: The Sociology of a Door-Closer', *Social Problems* 35(3) (1988) 298

Latour, Bruno, 'Where Are the Missing Masses? The Sociology of a Few Mundane Artifacts' in Wiebe E Bijker and John Law (eds), *Shaping Technology/Building Society: Studies in Sociotechnical Change* (MIT Press, 1992) 151–80

Latour, Bruno, *We Have Never Been Modern*, trans Cathy Porter (Harvard University Press, 1993) [trans of: *Nous n'avons jamais été modernes: Essai d'anthropologie symétrique* (first published 1991)]

Latour, Bruno, *Pandora's Hope: Essays on the Reality of Science Studies* (Harvard University Press, 1999)

Latour, Bruno, *The Making of Law: An Ethnography of the Conseil D'État*, trans Marina Brilman and Alain Pottage (Polity, 2010) [trans of: *La fabrique du droit* (grist published 2002)]

Latour, Bruno and Steve Woolgar, *Laboratory Life: The Social Construction of Scientific Facts* (Princeton University Press, 1986)

Lawlor, Leonard, *Derrida and Husserl: The Basic Problem of Phenomenology* (Indiana University Press, 2002)

Le Huray, Peter, *Music and the Reformation in England* (Cambridge University Press, 1978)
Leaver, Robin A, *Luther's Liturgical Music: Principles and Implications* (Wm B Eerdmans, 2007)
Leman, Peter, 'Singing the Law: Okot p'Bitek's Legal Imagination and the Poetics of Traditional Justice', *Research in African Literatures* 40(3) (2009) 109
Lerdahl, Fred and Ray Jackendoff, *A Generative Theory of Tonal Music* (MIT Press, 1983)
Levi, Ron and Mariana Valverde, 'Studying Law by Association: Bruno Latour Goes to the Conseil d'État', *Law and Social Inquiry* 33(3) (2008) 805
Levitin, Daniel, *This Is Your Brain on Music: Understanding a Human Obsession* (Atlantic, 2006)
Lippman, Edward A, *Musical Thought in Ancient Greece* (Columbia University Press, 1964)
Longman, Timothy, Phuong Pham, and Harvey M Weinstein, 'Connecting Justice to Human Experience: Attitudes Towards Accountability and Reconciliation in Rwanda' in Eric Stover and Harvey M Weinstein (eds), *My Neighbor, My Enemy: Justice and Community in the Aftermath of Ethnic Cleansing* (Cambridge University Press, 2004) 206–25
Lorenz, Aaron R S, *Lyrics and the Law: The Constitution of Law in Music* (Vandeplas, 2007)
Lukács, Georg, *History and Class Consciousness: Studies in Marxist Dialects*, trans Rodney Livingstone (MIT Press, 1971) [trans of: *Geschichte und klassenbewusstsein* (first published 1968)]
Macdonald, Roderick A, 'Critical Legal Pluralism as a Construction of Normativity and the Emergence of Law' in Andrée Lajoie et al (eds), *Théories et émergence du droit: Pluralisme, surdétermination et effectivité* (Éditions Thémis, 1998) 9–24
Macdonald, Roderick A, 'Here, There … and Everywhere: Theorizing Legal Pluralism; Theorizing Jacques Vanderlinden' in Nicholas Kasirer (ed), *Étudier et enseigner le droit: Hier, aujourd'hui et demain—Études offertes à Jacques Vanderlinden* (Éditions Yvon Blais, 2006) 381–413
Macdonald, Roderick A, 'Custom Made: For a Non-Chirographic Critical Legal Pluralism', *Canadian Journal of Law and Society* 26(2) (2011) 301
Macdonald, Roderick A and David Sandomierski, 'Against Nomopolies', *Northern Ireland Legal Quarterly* 57(4) (2006) 610
MacKinnon, Catherine, *Towards a Feminist Theory of the State* (Harvard University Press, 1989)
MacNeil, William P, *Novel Judgments: Legal Theory as Fiction* (Routledge, 2012)
Manderson, Desmond, '*Et Lex Perpetua*: Dying Declarations & Mozart's Requiem', *Cardozo Law Review* 20(5–6) (1999) 1621
Manderson, Desmond, *Songs without Music: Aesthetic Dimensions of Law and Justice* (University of California Press, 2000)
Manderson, Desmond, 'Apocryphal Jurisprudence', *Australian Journal of Legal Philosophy* 26 (2001) 27
Manderson, Desmond, 'Governor Arthur's Proclamation: Images of the Rule of Law' in Oren Ben Dor (ed), *Law and Art: Justice, Ethics and Aesthetics* (Routledge, 2011)
Manderson, Desmond, 'Trust Us Justice: *24*, Popular Culture and the Law' in Austin Sarat (ed), *Imagining Legality: Where Law Meets Popular Culture* (University of Alabama Press, 2011)
Manderson, Desmond, *Kangaroo Courts and the Rule of Law: The Legacy of Modernism* (Routledge, 2012)
Manderson, Desmond, 'Making a Point and Making a Noise: A Punk Prayer', *Law, Culture and the Humanities* (June 2013) 0(0) 1–13, doi: 10.1177/1743872113490664

Manderson, Desmond, 'Towards Law and Music', *Law and Critique* 25(3) (2014) 311
Manderson, Desmond and David Caudill, 'Modes of Law: Music and Legal Theory—An Interdisciplinary Workshop Introduction', *Cardozo Law Review* 20(5-6) (1999) 1325
Marcus, Greil, *Invisible Republic: Bob Dylan's Basement Tapes* (Picador, 1997)
Marcus, Greil, *Mystery Train: Images of America in Rock'n'Roll Music* (5th rev edn, Plume, 2008)
Marcus, Greil, *Bob Dylan by Greil Marcus: Writings 1968–2010* (Public Affairs, 2010)
Marett, Allan, *Songs, Dreamings, and Ghosts: The Wangga of North Australia* (Wesleyan University Press, 2005)
Margetts, Katharina and Nicole Janisiewicz, 'Current Developments at the Ad Hoc International Criminal Tribunals', *Journal of International Criminal Justice* 7(2) (2009) 397
Mauss, Marcel, *Sociology and Psychology: Essays*, trans Ben Brewster (Routledge and K Paul, 1979) [trans of: Parts III, IV, V, and VI of *Sociologie et anthropologie* (first published 1950)]
May, Larry, *Crimes Against Humanity: A Normative Account* (Cambridge University Press, 2005)
May, James M and Jakob Wisse, 'Introduction' in Marcus Tullius Cicero, *On the Ideal Orator*, trans James M May and Jakob Wisse (Oxford University Press, 2001) 3–43
Mbonimana, Gamaaliel, *La musique Rwandaise traditionelle* (Unpublished, 1971)
McCoy, Jason, 'Making Violence Ordinary: Radio, Music and the Rwandan Genocide', *African Music Journal* 8(3) (2009) 85
McCoy, Jason, 'Mbwirabumva ("I Speak to Those Who Understand"): Three Songs by Simon Bikindi and the War and Genocide in Rwanda' (PhD dissertation, Florida State University, 2013)
McDermott, Judy, 'If It's to Be Heard But Not Listened to, Then It Must Be Muzak', *Smithsonian* 20(10) (1990) 70
McLuhan, Marshall, *Understanding Media: The Extensions of Man* (2nd edn, New American Library, 1964)
McMillan, Nesam, '"Our" Shame: International Responsibility for the Rwandan Genocide', *Australian Feminist Law Journal* 28 (June 2008) 3
McNulty, Mel, 'French Arms, War and Genocide in Rwanda', *Crime, Law and Social Change* 33(1–2) (2000) 105
McVeigh, Shaun (ed), *Jurisprudence of Jurisdiction* (Routledge-Cavendish, 2007)
Melvern, Linda, *A People Betrayed: The Role of the West in Rwanda's Genocide* (Zed Books, 2000)
Melvern, Linda, 'Radio Murder', *Times Literary Supplement*, 9 September 2005, 25
Merry, Sally Engle, 'Legal Pluralism', *Law and Society Review* 22(5) (1988) 869
Mertz, Elizabeth, *The Language of Law School: Learning to 'Think Like a Lawyer'* (Oxford University Press, 2007)
Mills, C Wright, *The Sociological Imagination* (Oxford University Press, 1959)
Minar Jr, Edwin L, 'Pythagorean Communism', *Transactions and Proceedings of the American Philological Association* 75 (1944) 34
Mnookin, Jennifer L, 'The Image of Truth: Photographic Evidence and the Power of Analogy', *Yale Journal of Law & the Humanities* 10(1) (1998) 1
Mohr, Richard, 'In Between Power and Procedure: Where the Court Meets the Public Sphere' in Marit Paasche and Judy Radul (eds), *A Thousand Eyes: Media Technology, Law and Aesthetics* (Sternberg Press, 2011) 99–114
Monson, Craig A, 'The Council of Trent Revisited', *Journal of the American Musicological Society* 55(1) (2002) 1

Moran, Leslie J, *The Homosexual(ity) of Law* (Routledge, 1996)
Moran, Leslie J, Emma Sandon, Elena Loizidou, and Ian Christie (eds), *Law's Moving Image* (Cavendish, 2004)
Morrill, Hanna, 'Challenging Impunity? The Failure of the International Criminal Tribunal for Rwanda to Prosecute Paul Kagame', *Brooklyn Journal of International Law* 37(2) (2012) 683
Morris, Virginia and Michael P Scharf, *The International Criminal Tribunal for Rwanda* (Transnational Publishers, 1998) (2 vols)
Møse, Erik, 'Main Achievements of the ICTR', *Journal of International Criminal Justice* 3(4) (2005) 920
Mulcahy, Linda, *Legal Architecture: Justice, Due Process and the Place of Law* (Routledge, 2011)
Munson, Benjamin and Molly Babel, 'Loose Lips and Silver Tongues, or, Projecting Sexual Orientation through Speech', *Language and Linguistics Compass* 1(5) (2007) 416
Mussawir, Edward, 'The Cinematics of Jurisprudence: Scenes of *Law's Moving Image*', *Law and Literature* 17(1) (2005) 131
Mussawir, Edward, 'The Activity of Judgment: Deleuze, Jurisdiction and the Procedural Genre of Jurisprudence', *Law, Culture and the Humanities* 7(3) (2011) 463
Mussawir, Edward, *Jurisdiction in Deleuze: The Expression and Representation of Law* (Routledge, 2011)
Nancy, Jean-Luc, *Listening*, trans Charlotte Mandell (Fordham University Press, 2007) [trans of: *À L'écoute* (first published 2002)]
Negri, Stefania, 'The Principle of "Equality of Arms" and the Evolving Law of International Criminal Procedure', *International Criminal Law Review* 5(4) (2005) 513
Nkulikiyinka, Jean Baptiste, *Introduction à la danse Rwandaise traditionnelle* (Musée Royal de l'Afrique Centrale, 2002)
Ong, Walter J, *Presence of the Word: Some Prolegomena for Cultural and Religious History* (Yale University Press, 1967)
Ong, Walter J, 'African Talking Drums and Oral Noetics', *New Literary History* 8(3) (1977) 411
Ong, Walter J, *Orality and Literacy: The Technologizing of the World* (Routledge, 2002)
Ovid, *The Metamorphoses*, trans David R Slavitt (Johns Hopkins University Press, 1994)
Oxford English Dictionary (2nd edn, Oxford University Press, 1989)
p'Bitek, Okot, *Song of Lawino and Song of Ocol* (Heinemann, 1984)
p'Bitek, Okot, *Artist, the Ruler: Essays on Art, Culture and Values* (Heinemann, 1986)
Paasche, Marit and Judy Radul (eds), *A Thousand Eyes: Media Technology, Law and Aesthetics* (Sternberg Press, 2011)
Park, Joseph Sung-Yul and Mary Bucholtz, 'Public Transcripts: Entextualization and Linguistic Representation in Institutional Contexts', *Text and Talk* 29(5) (2009) 481
Parker, James, 'Spirited Away: Asylum Law and the Institutional Violence of Legal Discourse', *Law Text Culture* 11 (2007) 231
Parsons, James (ed), *The Cambridge Companion to the Lied* (Cambridge University Press, 2004)
Peller, Gary, 'The Metaphysics of American Law', *California Law Review* 73(4) (1985) 1151
Peters, John Durham, *Speaking into the Air: A History of the Idea of Communication* (University of Chicago Press, 1999)
Picker, John, 'The Soundproof Study' in Jonathan Sterne (ed), *The Sound Studies Reader* (Routledge, 2012) 141–51
Pieslak, Jonathan, *Sound Targets: American Soldiers and Music in the Iraq War* (Indiana University Press, 2009)

Pinch, Trevor and Karin Bijsterveld, 'Sound Studies: New Technologies and Music', *Social Studies of Science* 34(5) (2004) 635

Pinch, Trevor and Karin Bijsterveld, *The Oxford Handbook of Sound Studies* (Oxford University Press, 2011)

Pindar, *The Complete Odes*, ed Stephen Instone, trans Anthony Verity (Oxford University Press, 2007)

Piška, Nick, 'Review: Edward Mussawir, Jurisdiction in Deleuze, the Expression and Representation of Law', *The Modern Law Review* 76(1) (2013) 184

Pitman, Isaac, *A History of Shorthand* (I Pitman & Sons, 1891)

Plato, *The Republic*, trans Richard W Sterling and William C Scott (Norton, 1985)

Plato, *The Laws*, trans Benjamin Jowett (Prometheus, 2000)

Plato, *Timaeus*, trans Donald J Zeyl (Hackett, 2000)

Pottage, Alain, 'Law Machines: Scale Models, Forensic Materiality and the Making of Modern Patent Law', *Social Studies of Science* 41(5) (2011) 621

Pottage, Alain, 'The Materiality of What?' *Journal of Law and Society* 39(1) (2012) 167

Power, Samantha, 'Bystanders to Genocide: Why the United States Let the Rwandan Genocide Happen', *The Atlantic* 288(2) (2001) 89

Prunier, Gérard, *The Rwanda Crisis: History of a Genocide* (Columbia University Press, 1995)

Pugliese, Joseph, 'Prosthetics of Law and the Anomic Violence of Drones', *Griffith Law Review* 20(4) (2011) 931

Purandare, Amruta and Diane Litman, 'Humor: Prosody Analysis and Automatic Recognition for F*R*I*E*N*D*S*' (Paper presented at Conference on Empirical Methods in Natural Language Processing, Sydney, Australia, 22 July 2006)

Puttenham, George, *The Arte of English Poesie*, ed Gladys Doidge Willcock and Alice Walker (first published 1589, Cambridge University Press, 1939)

Quintilian, Marcus Fabius, *The Institutio Oratoria of Quintilian*, trans H E Butler (Harvard University Press, 1922) [trans of: *Institutio oratoria* (first published cad 95)]

Radano, Ronald M, 'Interpreting Muzak: Speculations on the Musical Experience in Everyday Life', *American Music* 7(4) (1989) 448

Raffield, Paul, 'Bodies of Law: The Divine Architect, Common Law and the Ancient Constitution', *International Journal for the Semiotics of Law* 13(3) (2000) 333

Ramshaw, Sara, 'Deconstructin(g) Jazz Improvisation: Derrida and the Law of the Singular Event', *Critical Studies in Improvisation* 2(1) (2006) 1 <http://www.criticalimprov.com/article/view/81/188>

Ramshaw, Sara, *Justice as Improvisation: The Law of the Extempore* (Routledge, 2013)

Raz, Joseph, *The Concept of a Legal System: An Introduction to the Theory of Legal System* (Clarendon, 1980)

Reese, Gustave, *Music in the Renaissance* (rev edn, W W Norton, 1959)

Reynolds, Simon, *The Sex Revolts: Gender, Rebellion and Rock'n'Roll* (Harvard University Press, 1995)

Reynolds, Simon, *Generation Ecstasy: Into the World of Techno and Rave Culture* (Routledge, 1999)

Reyntjens, Filip, 'Rwanda, Ten Years On: From Genocide to Dictatorship', *African Affairs* 103(411) (2004) 177

Reyntjens, Filip, 'Constructing the Truth, Dealing with Dissent, Domesticating the World: Governance in Post-genocide Rwanda', *African Affairs* 110(438) (2011) 1

Riles, Annelise, 'Infinity within the Brackets', *American Ethnologist* 25(3) (1998) 378

Riles, Annelise, "Models and Documents: Artefacts of International Legal Knowledge', *International and Comparative Law Quarterly* 48(4) (1999) 805

Riles, Annelise, *The Network Inside Out* (University of Michigan Press, 2000)
Riles, Annelise (ed), *Documents: Artifacts of Modern Knowledge* (University of Michigan Press, 2006)
Rouget, Gilbert, *Music and Trance: A Theory of the Relations between Music and Possession*, trans Brunhilde Beibuyck (University of Chicago Press, 1985) [trans of: *La musique et la transe: Esquisse d'une théorie générale des relations de la musique et de la posse* (first published 1980)]
Ruebsaat, Norbert, 'Speaking with Diane Brown: An Investigation of Testimony Presented Before His Honour, Mr Justice Harry McKay in the Supreme Court of BC, November 6th 1985, in the Matter of *Western Forest Products Ltd v Richardson and Others*' (MA thesis, Simon Fraser University, 1987)
Russolo, Luigi, *The Art of Noises: Futurist Manifesto*, trans Barclay Brown (Pendragon, 1986) [trans of: *L'arte dei dumori* (first published 1913)]
Ruwet, Nicolas, 'Musicology and Linguistics', *International Social Science Journal* 19(1) (1967) 79
Ryngaert, Cedric, 'State Cooperation with the ICTR', *International Criminal Law Review* 13(1) (2013) 125
Sarat, Austin and Thomas R Kearns (eds), *The Rhetoric of Law* (University of Michigan Press, 1994)
Sarat, Austin, 'Rhetoric and Remembrance: Trials, Transcription, and the Politics of Critical Reading', *Legal Studies Forum* 23(4) (1999) 355
Sarat, Austin (ed), *Law and Society Reconsidered* (Emerald, 2008)
Sarat, Austin (ed), *Speech and Silence in American Law* (Cambridge University Press, 2010)
Sarat, Austin (ed), *Imagining Legality: Where Law Meets Popular Culture* (University of Alabama Press, 2011)
Sarat, Austin, Lawrence Douglas, and Martha Merrill Umphrey (eds), *Law on the Screen* (Stanford University Press, 2005)
Schabas, William A, *The UN International Criminal Tribunals: The Former Yugoslavia, Rwanda and Sierra Leone* (Cambridge University Press, 2006)
Schaeffer, Pierre, *Traité des objets musicaux* (Seuil, 1967)
Schafer, R Murray, *The Book of Noise* (Prize Milburn, 1968)
Schafer, R Murray, *The New Soundscape* (Berandol Music, 1971)
Schafer, R Murray (ed), *The Music of the Environment* (Universal Edition, 1973)
Schafer, R Murray, 'The Vancouver Soundscape' in R Murray Schafer (ed), *The Music of the Environment* (Universal Edition, 1973)
Schafer, R Murray, *The Soundscape: Our Sonic Environment and the Tuning of the World* (Knopf, 1977)
Scharf, Michael P, 'Chaos in the Courtroom: Controlling Disruptive Defendants and Contumacious Counsel in War Crimes Trials', *Case Western Reserve Journal of International Law* 39(1–2) (2006–7) 155
Schedel, Margaret and Andrew V Uroskie, 'Writing about Audiovisual Culture', *Journal of Visual Culture* 10(2) (2011) 137
Scheffer, Thomas, 'Materialities of Legal Proceedings', *International Journal for the Semiotics of Law* 17(4) (2004) 365
Scherer, Klaus R, 'Personality Markers in Speech' in Klaus R Scherer and Howard Giles (eds), *Social Markers in Speech* (Cambridge University Press, 1979)
Scherer, Klaus R and Howard Giles (eds), *Social Markers in Speech* (Cambridge University Press, 1979)

Schlag, Pierre, '"Le Hors de Texte, C'est Moi": The Politics of Form and the Domestication of Deconstruction', *Cardozo Law Review* 11(4) (1990) 1631

Schlag, Pierre, 'Normative and Nowhere to Go', *Stanford Law Review* 43(1) (1990) 167

Schlag, Pierre, 'Normativity and the Politics of Form', *University of Pennsylvania Law Review* 139(4) (1991) 801

Schlag, Pierre, 'The Aesthetics of American Law', *Harvard Law Review* 115(4) (2002) 1047

Schlag, Pierre, 'A Brief Survey of Deconstruction', *Cardozo Law Review* 27(2) (2005) 741

Schwartz, Hillel, *Making Noise: From Babel to the Big Bang & Beyond* (Zone Books, 2011)

Seeger, Anthony, 'Ethnomusicology and Music Law', *Ethnomusicology* 36(3) (1992) 345

Senzel, Howard T, 'Looseleafing the Flow: An Anecdotal History of One Technology for Updating', *The American Journal of Legal History* 44(2) (2000) 115

Serres, Michel, *Genesis*, trans Geneviève James and James Nielson (University of Michigan Press, 1995) [trans of: *Genèse* (first published 1982)]

Sherwin, Richard, *When Law Goes Pop: The Vanishing Line between Law and Popular Culture* (University of Chicago Press, 2000)

Sherwin, Richard (ed), *Popular Culture and Law* (Ashgate, 2006)

Sherwin, Richard, *Visualizing Law in the Age of the Digital Baroque: Arabesques and Entanglements* (Routledge, 2011)

Sherwin, Richard and Ann Wagner (eds), *Law, Culture and Visual Studies* (Springer, 2013)

Sherwin, Richard, Neal Feigenson, and Christina Spiesel, 'What Is Visual Knowledge, and What Is It Good For?' *Visual Anthropology* 20(2–3) (2007) 143

Silbey, Jessica, 'Judges as Film Critics: New Approaches to Filmic Evidence', *University of Michigan Journal of Law Reform* 37(2) (2004) 493

Silbey, Jessica, 'Cross-Examining Film', *University of Maryland Law Journal of Race, Religion, Gender and Class* 8(1–2) (2008) 101

Simpson, Gerry, *Law, War and Crime: War Crimes Trials and the Reinvention of International Law* (Polity, 2007)

Simpson, John A and Edmund S C Weiner (eds), *Oxford English Dictionary* (2nd edn, Oxford University Press, 1989)

Small, Christopher, *Musicking: The Meanings of Performing and Listening* (University Press of New England, 1988)

Smith, Dorothy E, *Texts, Facts, and Femininity: Exploring the Relations of Ruling* (Routledge, 1990)

Smith, Dorothy E (ed), *Institutional Ethnography as Practice* (Rowman & Littlefield, 2006)

Smith, Merritt Roe and Leo Marx (eds), *Does Technology Drive History? The Dilemma of Technological Determinism* (MIT Press, 1994)

Smulyan, Susan, *Selling Radio: The Commercialization of American Broadcasting 1920–1934* (Smithsonian Institution Press, 1994)

Snyder, Robert H, '"Disillusioned Words like Bullets Bark": Incitement to Genocide, Music, and the Trial of Simon Bikindi', *Georgia Journal of International and Comparative Law* 35(3) (2007) 645

Solan, Lawrence M and Peter M Tiersma, 'Hearing Voices: Speaker Identification in Court', *Hastings Law Journal* 54(2) (2003) 373

Stadler, Gustavus, 'Introduction: Breaking Sound Barriers', *Social Text* 28(1) (2010) 1

Steintrager, James A, 'Speaking of Noise: From Murderous Loudness to the Crackle of Silk', *Differences* 22(2–3) (2011) 249

Sterne, Jonathan, 'Sounds like the Mall of America: Programmed Music and the Architectonics of Commercial Space', *Ethnomusicology* 41(1) (1997) 22

Sterne, Jonathan, 'Television under Construction: American Television and the Problem of Distribution, 1926–62', *Media, Culture and Society* 21(4) (1999) 503

Sterne, Jonathan, *The Audible Past: Cultural Origins of Sound Reproduction* (Duke University Press, 2003)

Sterne, Jonathan, *MP3: The Meaning of a Format* (Duke University Press, 2012)

Sterne, Jonathan (ed), *The Sound Studies Reader* (Routledge, 2012)

Stiegler, Bernard, *Technics and Time, 1: The Fault of Epimetheus*, trans Richard Beardsworth and George Collins (Stanford University Press, 1998) [trans of: *La technique et le temps, 1: La faute d'Epiméthée* (first published 1994)]

Stockfelt, Ola, 'Adequate Modes of Listening' in Christoph Cox and Daniel Warner (eds), *Audio Culture: Readings in Modern Music* (Continuum, 2004) 88–93

Straus, Scott, *The Order of Genocide* (Cornell University Press, 2006)

Straus, Scott, 'What Is the Relationship between Hate Radio and Violence? Rethinking Rwanda's "Radio Machete"', *Politics and Society* 35(4) (2007) 609

Street, John, Seth Hague and Heather Savigny, 'Playing to the Crowd: The Role of Music and Musicians in Political Participation', *The British Journal of Politics and International Relations* 10(2) (2008) 269

Sugarman, David, 'Legal Theory, the Common Law Mind and the Making of the Textbook Tradition' in William Twining (ed), *Legal Theory and the Common Law* (Blackwell, 1986) 26–62

Supiot, Alain, *Homo Juridicus: On the Anthropological Function of Law*, trans Saskia Brown (Verso, 2007) [trans of: *Homo juridicus: Essai sur la fonction anthropologique du droit* (first published 2005)]

Surkis, Judith, 'When Was the Linguistic Turn? A Genealogy', *The American Historical Review* 117(3) (2012) 700

Szendy, Peter, *Listen: A History of Our Ears* (Fordham University Press, 2008)

Taylor, Natalie and Jacqueline Joudo, 'The Impact of Pre-Recorded Video and Closed Circuit Television Testimony by Adult Sexual Assault Complainants on Jury Decision-Making: An Experimental Study' (Research and Public Policy Series No 68, Australian Institute of Criminology, 2005)

Tchakhotine, Sergei, *Mob Rape Prompted by Political Propaganda* (Editions Gallimard, 1952)

Temple-Raston, Dina, 'Journalism and Genocide', *Columbia Journalism Review* 41(3) (2002) 18

The Holy Bible (King James version)

Thompson, Allan (ed), *The Media and the Rwanda Genocide* (Pluto, 2007)

Thompson, Emily, *The Soundscape of Modernity: Architectural Acoustics and the Culture of Listening in America, 1900–1933* (MIT Press, 2004)

Tompkins, Dave, *How to Wreck a Nice Beach: The Vocoder from World War II to Hip-Hop* (Melville House, 2010)

Tuitt, Patricia, 'Legal Practice and Modes of Dying: Bruno Latour, Technology and the Critical Legal Instance', *Law and Critique* 16(1) (2005) 113

Twining, William (ed), *Legal Theory and the Common Law* (Blackwell, 1986)

Unger, Roberto, *The Critical Legal Studies Movement* (Harvard University Press, 1986)

Valverde, Mariana, 'Authorizing the Production of Urban Moral Order: Appellate Courts and their Knowledge Games', *Law and Society Review* 39(2) (2005) 419

Vansina, Jan, *Oral Tradition as History* (University of Wisconsin Press, 1985)

Vansina, Jan, *Antecedents to Modern Rwanda: The Nyiginya Kingdom* (University of Wisconsin Press, 2004)

Vendrix, Philippe (ed), *Music and the Renaissance: Renaissance, Reformation and Counter-Reformation* (Ashgate, 2011)
Venuti, Lawrence (ed), *The Translation Studies Reader* (3rd edn, Routledge, 2012)
Verwimp, Philip, 'Machetes and Firearms: The Organization of Massacres in Rwanda', *Journal of Peace Research* 43(1) (2006) 5
Vickers, Brian, 'Figures of Rhetoric/Figures of Music?' *Rhetorica* 2(1) (1984) 1
Vismann, Cornelia, *Files: Law and Media Technology*, trans Geoffrey Winthrop-Young (Stanford University Press, 2008) [trans of: *Akten: Medientechnik und recht* (first published 2000)]
Vismann, Cornelia, 'Flashback and Eyewitness', *Parallax* 14(4) (2008) 90
Vismann, Cornelia, 'Image and Law: A Troubled Relationship', *Parallax* 14(4) (2008) 1
Vismann, Cornelia, 'Three Versions of a Defendant's Final Statement to the Court', *Law and Literature* 23(3) (2011) 297
Walter, Bettyruth, *The Jury Summation as Speech Genre: An Ethnographic Study of What It Means to Those Who Use It* (John Benjamins, 1988)
Washington, Ellis, *The Nuremberg Trials: Last Tragedy of the Holocaust* (University Press of America, 2008)
Watson, Irene, 'Indigenous Peoples' Law-Ways: Survival against the Colonial State', *Australian Feminist Law Journal* 8 (March 1997) 39
Weber, Max, *The Rational and Social Foundations of Music*, ed and trans Don Martindale, Johannes Riedel and Gertrude Neuwirth (Southern Illinois University Press, 1977) [trans of: *Die rationalen und soziologischen grundlagen der musik* (first published 1921)]
Weintraub, Andrew and Bell Yung (eds), *Music and Cultural Rights* (University of Illinois Press, 2009)
Weisbrod, Carol, 'Fusion Folk: A Comment on Law and Music', *Cardozo Law Review* 20(5–6) (1999) 1439
Wembou, Djiena, 'The International Criminal Tribunal for Rwanda: Its Role in the African Context', *International Review of the Red Cross* 37(321) (1997) 685
West, Robin, 'Jurisprudence as Narrative: An Aesthetic Analysis of Modern Legal Theory', *New York University Law Review* 60(2) (1985) 145
Wetlaufer, Gerald B, 'Rhetoric and Its Denial in Legal Discourse', *Virginia Law Review* 76(8) (1990) 1545
White, James Boyd, *The Legal Imagination* (University of Chicago Press, 1973)
White, James Boyd, 'Law as Rhetoric, Rhetoric as Law: The Arts of Cultural and Communal Life', *The University of Chicago Law Review* 52(3) (1985) 684
White, James Boyd, *Heracles' Bow: Essays on the Rhetoric and Poetics of the Law* (University of Wisconsin Press, 1985)
White, James Boyd, *Justice as Translation: An Essay in Cultural and Legal Criticism* (University of Chicago Press, 1990)
Williams, Alastair, *Constructing Musicology* (Ashgate, 2001)
Willis, Jonathan, *Church Music and Protestantism in Post-Reformation England* (Ashgate, 2010)
Young, Alison, 'The Waste Land of the Law, the Wordless Song of the Rape Victim', *Melbourne University Law Review* 22(2) (1998) 442
Žižek, Slavoj, *For They Know Not What They Do: Enjoyment as a Political Factor* (Verso, 1991)

CASES

Afri-Forum v Malema 2011 (6) SA 240 (EqC)

Bikindi v The Prosecutor (Judgement) ICTR-01-72-A, Appeals Chamber (18 March 2010)

Federal Communications Commission v Pacifica Foundation, 438 US 726 (1978)

Hush-A-Phone v United States, 238 F 2d 266 (DC Cir, 1956)

Military and Paramilitary Activities in and against Nicaragua (Nicaragua v United States of America) (Jurisdiction and Admissibility) [1984] ICJ Rep 392

Prosecutor v Akayesu (Judgement) ICTR-96-4-T, T Ch I (2 September 1998)

Prosecutor v Bagosora (Judgement and Sentence) ICTR-98-41-T, T Ch I (18 December 2008)

Prosecutor v Bikindi (Judgement) ICTR-01-72-T, T Ch III (2 December 2008)

Prosecutor v Bizimungu (Judgement and Sentence) ICTR-99-50-T, T Ch II (30 September 2011)

Prosecutor v Kambana (Judgement and Sentence) ICTR-97-23-S, T Ch I (4 September 1998)

Prosecutor v Karera (Judgement and Sentence) ICTR-01-74-T, T Ch I (7 December 2007)

Prosecutor v Kayishema (Judgement) ICTR-95-1-T, T Ch II (21 May 1999)

Prosecutor v Nahimana (Judgement and Sentence) ICTR-99-52-T, T Ch I (3 December 2003)

Prosecutor v Ngirabatware (Judgement and Sentence) ICTR-99-54-T, T Ch II (20 December 2012)

NON-ICTR CASE MATERIALS

Mariya Vladimirovna Alekhina and Others v Russia, Application No 38004/12 (European Court of Human Rights, 19 June 2012)

Prosecutor v Yvonne Basebya (Summary of the Verdict of the District Court of the Hague, Unofficial Translation) LJN BZ4292 (1 March 2013) <http://www.asser.nl/upload/documents/20130328T104222-Unofficial%20english%20translation%20Decision%20Rechtbank%20den%20Haag%2001-03-2013.pdf>

ICTR MATERIALS

'Disclosure of Curriculum Vitae's [sic] of Expert Witnesses', *Prosecutor v Bikindi,* ICTR-01-72-0149 (11 July 2006)

'Request of Whereabouts of 3 Scripts of Mr A Waday', *Prosecutor v Bikindi,* ICTR-01-72-0026 (29 May 2002)

'Takeover of Mr Simon Bikindi', *Prosecutor v Bikindi,* ICTR-01-72-0016 (27 March 2002)

'Very Urgent Defence Motion Objecting to the Presentation of Experts Report by Jean de Dieu Karangwa Alone and Requesting the Compulsion of Gamaliel Mbonimana to Give Evidence', *Prosecutor v Bikindi,* ICTR-01-72-0208/1 (9 February 2007)

'Warrant of Arrest and Orders for Transfer and Detention and for Search and Seizure', *Prosecutor v Bikindi,* ICTR-01-72-0039 (5 July 2001)

Exhibit No D117(F), 'Defence Expert Report of Dr Eugène Shimamungu', *Prosecutor v Bikindi,* ICTR-01-72-0265 (3 October 2007)

Exhibit No P11(E), 'Transcript of RTLM Broadcast of 15 April 1994', *Prosecutor v Bikindi,* ICTR-01-72-0070 (2 June 1997)

Exhibit No P3, 'Transcript of RTLM Broadcast of 17 May 1994', *Prosecutor v Bikindi,* ICTR-01-72-0207 (17 May 1994)

Exhibit No P72, 'Excerpts from Jean-Pierre Chrétien, *Rwanda: Les Médias du Génocide* (Karthala, 1999)', *Prosecutor v Bikindi*, ICTR-01-72
Exhibit No P73(E), 'Prosecution Joint Expert Report of Gamaliel Mbonimana and Jean de Dieu Karangwa: "Thematic Analysis of the Songs"', *Prosecutor v Bikindi*, ICTR-01-72-0152 (13 September 2006)
International Criminal Tribunal for Rwanda, *Code of Professional Conduct for Defence Counsel* (entry into force 4 June 1998)
International Criminal Tribunal for Rwanda, *Directive for the Registry of the ICTR* (entry into force 8 June 1998)
International Criminal Tribunal for Rwanda, *Manual for English Court Reporting* (as at January 2011)
International Criminal Tribunal for Rwanda, *Redaction of the Audio-Visual Recordings of the UN ICTR: Methodology and Procedures Developed by the Judicial Records and Archives Unit, Court Management Section* (January 2011)
International Criminal Tribunal for Rwanda, 'Rules of Procedure and Evidence' (29 June 1995) UN Doc ITR/3/REV.1
Bikindi v The Prosecutor (Audio-Visual Record of the Appeals Hearing) ICTR-01-72-A, Appeals Chamber (30 September 2009)
Bikindi v The Prosecutor (Case Minutes) ICTR-01-72-A, Appeals Chamber (30 September 2009)
Bikindi v The Prosecutor (Transcript) ICTR-01-72-A, Appeals Chamber (Various dates)
Prosecutor v Bikindi (Amended Indictment) ICTR-01-72-I (22 October 2003)
Prosecutor v Bikindi (Audio Record of Proceedings) ICTR-01-72-T, T Ch III (Various dates)
Prosecutor v Bikindi (Audio-Visual Record of Proceedings) ICTR-01-72-T, T Ch III (Various dates)
Prosecutor v Bikindi (Case Minutes) ICTR-01-72-T, T Ch III (13 February 2007)
Prosecutor v Bikindi (Decision Authorizing the Site Visit in Rwanda) ICTR-01-72-R4 (12 March 2008)
Prosecutor v Bikindi (Indictment) ICTR-01-72-I (4 July 2001)
Prosecutor v Bikindi (Second Amended Indictment) ICTR-01-72-I (15 June 2005)
Prosecutor v Bikindi (Summary of Judgement and Sentence) ICTR-01-72-T (2 December 2008)
Prosecutor v Bikindi (Transcript) (French) ICTR-01-72-T, T Ch III (Various dates)
Prosecutor v Bikindi (Transcript) ICTR-01-72-T, T Ch III (Various dates)
Prosecutor v Nahimana (Transcript) ICTR-99-52-T, T Ch I (Various dates)

TREATIES

African Charter on Human and Peoples' Rights (entered into force 21 October 1986) 1520 UNTS 217
Agreement for the Prosecution and Punishment of the Major War Criminals of the European Axis (signed and entered into force 8 August 1945) 82 UNTS 279 annex ('Charter of the International Military Tribunal')
American Convention on Human Rights (entered into force 18 July 1978) 1144 UNTS 123
Declaration on the Elimination of All Forms of Racial Discrimination (20 November 1963) UNGA Res 1904
European Convention for the Protection of Human Rights and Fundamental Freedoms (opened for signature 4 November 1950, entered into force 3 September 1953) 213 UNTS 222

International Covenant on Civil and Political Rights (adopted 16 December 1966, entered into force 23 March 1976) 999 UNTS 171
Universal Declaration of Human Rights (adopted 10 December 1948) UNGA Res 217A (III)

UNITED NATIONS DOCUMENTS

'First Annual Report of the International Criminal Tribunal for the Prosecution of Persons Responsible for Genocide and Other Serious Violations of International Humanitarian Law Committed in the Territory of Rwanda' (24 September 1996) UN Doc A/51/399-S/1996/778, annex
'Report of the Independent Inquiry into the Actions of the United Nations during the 1994 Genocide in Rwanda' (16 December 1999) UN Doc S/1999/1257
'Report on the Completion Strategy of the International Criminal Tribunal for Rwanda (as at 5 November 2012)' (14 November 2012) UN Doc S/2012/836
'Report on the Completion Strategy of the International Criminal Tribunal for Rwanda (as at 5 November 2014)' (18 November 2013) UN Doc S/2014/829
'Secretary-General's Bulletin: International Criminal Tribunals—Information Sensitivity, Classification, Handling and Access' (20 July 2012) UN Doc ST/SGB/2012/3
Statement of Rwanda (6 October 1994) UN Doc A/49/PV.21
Statement of Rwanda (8 November 1994) UN Doc S/PV.3453
Statute of the International Tribunal for Rwanda, UNSC Res 955 (8 November 1994) UN Doc S/RES/955, annex
UNHCR, 'General Comment No 13: Article 14 (Administration of Justice) (1984)' (27 May 2008) UN Doc HRI/GEN/1/Rev.9 (Vol. I)
UNHCR, 'General Comment No 32: Article 14—Right to Equality before Courts and Tribunals and to a Fair Trial' (23 August 2007) UN Doc CCPR/C/GC/32
UNSC Progress Report (18 November 2013) UN Doc S/2013/679, annex I
UNSC Progress Report (15 May 2014) UN Doc S/2014/343
UNSC Res 808 (22 February 1993) UN Doc S/RES/808
UNSC Res 977 (22 February 1995) UN Doc S/RES/977
UNSC Res 1165 (30 April 1998) UN Doc S/RES/1165
UNSC Res 1966 (22 December 2010) UN Doc S/RES/1966

MUSIC

Bikindi, Simon, *Twasezereye (Ingoma Ya Cyami)* (1986)
Bikindi, Simon, *Bene Sebahinzi/Intabaza* (1993)
Bikindi, Simon, *Nanga Abahutu/Akabyutso* (1993)
Dylan, Bob, *Blood on the Tracks* (Columbia Records, 1975)
Handel, George Frideric, *Ode for St Cecilia's Day* (1739)
Hindemith, Paul, *Die Harmonie der Welt* (1957)
Springsteen, Bruce, *Born in the USA* (Columbia Records, 1984)
The Beatles, *She Loves You* (Parlophone, 1963)

FILM

Moggio-Ortiz, Evelyn, *The Interpreters: A Historical Perspective* (United Nations, 1995)
Sy, Bocar, *Justice Today, Peace Tomorrow* (United Nations, c2002)

ONLINE SOURCES

'20 Years Challenging Impunity' (video commemorating the twentieth anniversary of the Tribunal's establishment), International Criminal Tribunal for Rwanda, accessed 29 January 2015, <http://www.unictr.org/>

'A Video Film on Conference Interpreters', AIIC, accessed 5 March 2015, <http://www.aiic.net/ViewPage.cfm/article1104.htm>

'Anechoic Chamber', University of Salford, accessed 6 March 2015, <http://www.acoustics.salford.ac.uk/facilities/index.php?content=anechoic>

'Case CATalyst', Stenograph, accessed 28 February 2015, <http://www.stenograph.com/V3MiniSplash.aspx?id=V3Soft>

'Case Studies: Migration', Front Porch Digital, accessed 5 March 2015, <http://www.fpdigital.com/case-studies/migration-case-studies>

'China Sentences Two Tibetan Singers to Prison for Song Content', Voice Project, 2 December 2014, <http://voiceproject.org/post_news/tibetan-singer-sentenced-4-year-prison-term-songs/>

'City of Pittsburgh Settles G-20 Lawsuits', American Civil Liberties Union (ACLU), 14 November 2012, <http://www.aclupa.org/news/2012/11/14/city-pittsburgh-settles-g-20-lawsuits>

'Conference Interpretation Modes', AIIC, accessed 5 March 2015, <http://aiic.net/page/1629/conference-interpretation-modes/lang/1>

'Discipline au Micro', AIIC, accessed 6 March 2015. Available at: <http://web.archive.org/web/20120512190256/http:/aiic.net/glossary/default.cfm?ID=190> (snapshot dated 12 May 2012)

'Faculty of Translation and Interpreting', University of Geneva, accessed 5 March 2015, <http://www.unige.ch/eti/enseignements_en.html>

'General Romeo Dallaire Begins to Testify in Military Trial', *Hirondelle News Agency*, 19 January 2004, <http://www.hirondellenews.org/ictr-rwanda/343-trials-ended/military-i-trial/20169-en-en-general-romeo-dallaire-begins-to-testify-in-military-trial92209220>

'Het Gebouw' ('The Building'), Vredespaleis, accessed 5 March 2015, <http://www.vredespaleis.nl/index.php?pid=57&page=The_building>

'I Beat Pirates with a Hose and Sonic Cannon', *BBC News*, 17 May 2007, <http://news.bbc.co.uk/2/hi/uk_news/6664677.stm>

'ICTR by Satellite', International Criminal Tribunal for Rwanda, accessed 5 March 2015. Available at <http://207.150.203.251/tabid/67/default.aspx>

'Kenya Musicians Charged with Hate Speech', *BBC News*, 4 July 2012, <http://www.bbc.co.uk/news/world-africa-18712858>

'More ICTR Convicts Transferred to Mali and Benin to Serve Their Sentences', United Nations International Criminal Tribunal for Rwanda, 3 July 2012, <http://www.unictr.org/en/news/more-ictr-convicts-transferred-mali-and-benin-serve-their-sentences>

'Our Media Outlets', Fondation Hirondelle, 31 January 2014, <http://www.hirondelle.org/index.php/en/our-media-outlets>

'Press Aghast at Pussy Riot Verdict', *BBC News*, 18 August 2012, <http://www.bbc.co.uk/news/world-europe-19307077>

'Pussy Riot Members Jailed for Two Years for Hooliganism', *BBC News*, 17 August 2012, <http://www.bbc.co.uk/news/world-europe-19297373>

'Pussy Riot: Russia Frees Jailed Punk Band Members', *BBC News*, 23 December 2013, <http://www.bbc.com/news/world-europe-25490067>

'Putin Deems Fair Pussy Riot Sentence', *Interfax*, 8 October 2012, <http://www.interfax-religion.com/?act=news&div=9971>

'Quietest Place', Guinness World Records, accessed 6 March 2015, <http://www.guinnessworldrecords.com/world-records/3000/quietest-place>

'Rwanda/Netherlands—Hague Court Extends Yvonne Basebya's Detention', *Hirondelle New Agency*, 18 November 2011, <http://www.hirondellenews.org/ictr-rwanda/rwanda-other-countries/25772-en-en-181111-rwandanetherlands-hague-court-extends-yvonne-basebyas-detention-1482314823>

'Rwandan "Sang as She Urged on Killers", Hague Court Hears', *The Australian*, 23 October 2012, <http://www.theaustralian.com.au/news/world/rwandan-sang-as-she-urged-on-killers-hague-court-hears/story-e6frg6so-1226501079367>

'Singer Sentenced to 15 Years for Incitement', Freemuse, accessed 11 February 2015, <http://www.freemuse.org/sw31145.asp>

'Solutions: Migrate, Manage, Market', Front Porch Digital, accessed 5 March 2015, <http://www.fpdigital.com/solutions>

'Testimony of Arlo Guthrie', University of Missouri Kansas City (The Chicago Seven Trial: Excerpts from the Trial Transcript), accessed 18 February 2015, <http://law2.umkc.edu/faculty/projects/ftrials/Chicago7/Guthrie.html>

'Testimony of Philip David Ochs', University of Missouri Kansas City (The Chicago Seven Trial: Excerpts from the Trial Transcript), accessed 18 February 2015, <http://law2.umkc.edu/faculty/projects/ftrials/Chicago7/ochs.html>

'The Court Management Section', International Criminal Tribunal for Rwanda, accessed 28 February 2015, <http://207.150.203.251/tabid/108/default.aspx>

'Voix', AIIC, accessed 6 March 2015. Available at: <http://web.archive.org/web/20120512190117/http:/aiic.net/glossary/default.cfm?ID=286> . (snapshot dated 12 May 2012)

'Weekly Summary', *Hirondelle News Agency*, accessed 5 March 2015, <http://www.hirondellenews.org/weekly-summary>

African Court on Human and Peoples' Rights, accessed 5 March 2015, <http://www.african-court.org/en/>

Agence France-Press, 'China Jails Tibetan Singer Over Political Lyrics', *The Guardian*, 1 December 2014, <http://www.theguardian.com/world/2014/dec/01/china-jails-tibetan-singer-kalsang-yarphel-political-lyrics>

Arusha International Conference Centre, accessed 5 March 2015, <http://www.aicc.co.tz/>

Besson, Chantal, et al, 'The Importance of Non-Verbal Communication in Professional Interpretation', AIIC, 19 January 2005 (updated 22 May 2012) <http://www.aiic.net/ViewPage.cfm/page1662.htm#51>

Bigg, Claire and Natalya Dzhanpoladova, 'Who Owns the Pussy Riot Brand?' *The Atlantic*, 3 November 2012, <http://www.theatlantic.com/international/archive/2012/11/who-owns-the-pussy-riot-brand/264486/>

Bouwknegt, Thijs, 'Rwandan Genocide Singer Sentenced to Jail: The Drumbeats of Mass Slaughter', *Radio Netherlands Worldwide*, 2 December 2008 (copy on file with author)

Danish Interpretation Systems, 'Conference & Discussion System', accessed 5 March 2015, <http://www.dis.cc/sw26832.asp>

Danish Interpretation Systems, 'Conference Headphones' (Datasheet No 2.06c, DIS), accessed 18 February 2015, <http://www.prase.it/files/PDF/DH%209001+DH%20800x+DH%206005-2.06c.pdf>

Danish Interpretation Systems, 'DCS 6000 Digital Infrared Language Distribution System', accessed 5 March 2015, <http://www.dis-dk.com/graphics/dis/Brochures/DCS6000_DIGITAL_GB_LOWRES.pdf>

Danish Interpretation Systems, 'Infrared Digital Daylight Receivers' (Data Sheet No 4.05f, DIS), accessed 18 February 2015, <http://www.dis.su/pdf/IR15-xx_EN.pdf>

East African Community, accessed 5 March 2015, <http://www.eac.int/index.php?option=com_content&view=article&id=44&Itemid=54>

Hay Newman, Lily, 'This is the Sound Cannon Used Against Protestors in Ferguson', *Slate*, 14 August 2014, <http://www.slate.com/blogs/future_tense/2014/08/14/lrad_long_range_acoustic_device_sound_cannons_were_used_for_crowd_control.html>

International Criminal Tribunal for Rwanda, 'About ICTR', accessed 10 February 2015, <http://207.150.203.251/AboutICTR/GeneralInformation/tabid/101/Default.aspx>

International Criminal Tribunal for Rwanda, 'The ICTR in Brief', accessed 10 February 2015, <http://www.unictr.org/en/tribunal>

International Justice Desk, 'Three Kenyan Musicians on Ethnic Hate Speech Charges', *Radio Netherlands Worldwide*, 5 July 2012 (copy on file with author)

International Justice Tribune, 'Dutch Genocide Case Takes Shape', *Radio Netherlands Worldwide*, 18 November 2011 (copy on file with author)

Kelly, Patricia, 'The Quietest Room in the World', *Twin Cities Business*, 1 September 2008, <http://tcbmag.com/Industries/Technology/The-Quietest-Room-in-the-World-September-2008>

LRAD Corporation, accessed 7 March 2015, <http://www.lradx.com/site/>

McGreal, Chris, 'Palestinians Hit by Sonic Boom Air Raids', *The Guardian*, 3 November 2005, <http://www.theguardian.com/world/2005/nov/03/israel>

McNeil Jr, Donald G, 'Killer Songs', *The New York Times*, 17 March 2002, <http://www.nytimes.com/2002/03/17/magazine/killer-songs.html?src=pm>

Moggio-Ortiz, Evelyn, 'Multilingualism as a Path to Multilateralism: Interpreters Meet History', *UN Special*, No 678, (November 2008) <http://www.unspecial.org/UNS678/t21.html>

Moynihan, Colin, 'Concerns Raised Over Shrill Device New York Police Used During Garner Protests', *The New York Times*, 12 December 2014, <http://www.nytimes.com/2014/12/13/nyregion/lawyers-raise-concerns-over-shrill-device-used-by-police-during-garner-protests.html?_r=0>

NCRA: Setting the Standard for Capturing the Record, accessed 28 February 2015, <http://www.ncra.org/>

Oxford English Dictionary (3rd edn, Oxford University Press, December 2009) <http://www.oed.com>

Quaoar, '"Voice of God" Weapon Being Used in Iraq', Daily Kos blog, 23 December 2007, <http://www.dailykos.com/story/2007/12/23/425814/--Voice-of-God-weapon-being-used-in-Iraq>

Rumens, Carol, 'Pussy Riot's Punk Prayer Is Pure Protest Poetry', *The Guardian*, 20 August 2012, <http://www.guardian.co.uk/books/2012/aug/20/pussy-riot-punk-prayer-lyrics>

Tayler, Jeffrey, 'What Pussy Riot's "Punk Prayer" Really Said', *The Atlantic*, 8 November 2012, <http://www.theatlantic.com/international/archive/2012/11/what-pussy-riots-punk-prayer-really-said/264562/>

Thomas, Gavin, 'Sonic Device Deployed in London during Olympics', *BBC News*, 12 May 2012, <http://www.bbc.com/news/uk-england-london-18042528>

UN ICTR Judicial Database <http://trim.unictr.org/>

'Vehicle Mounted Solutions: Saving Lives through Communication', LRAD Corporation, (last modified 27 January 2011) <http://www.lradx.com/contact/support/downloads/>

Watercutter, Angela, 'Pussy Riot Appeals Convictions for "Hooliganism" to European Human Rights Court', *Wired*, 7 February 2013, <http://www.wired.com/underwire/2013/02/pussy-riot-human-rights-appeal/>

Index

Page numbers in *italics* refer to illustrations/diagrams. *n* = footnote.

The manufacturer's authorised representative in the EU for product safety is Oxford University Press España S.A. of el Parque Empresarial San Fernando de Henares, Avenida de Castilla, 2 – 28830 Madrid (www.oup.es/en or product.safety@oup.com). OUP España S.A. also acts as importer into Spain of products made by the manufacturer.

www.ingramcontent.com/pod-product-compliance
Lightning Source LLC
LaVergne TN
LVHW011819200926
848484LV00005B/1247
9780198735809